PULPHOPE

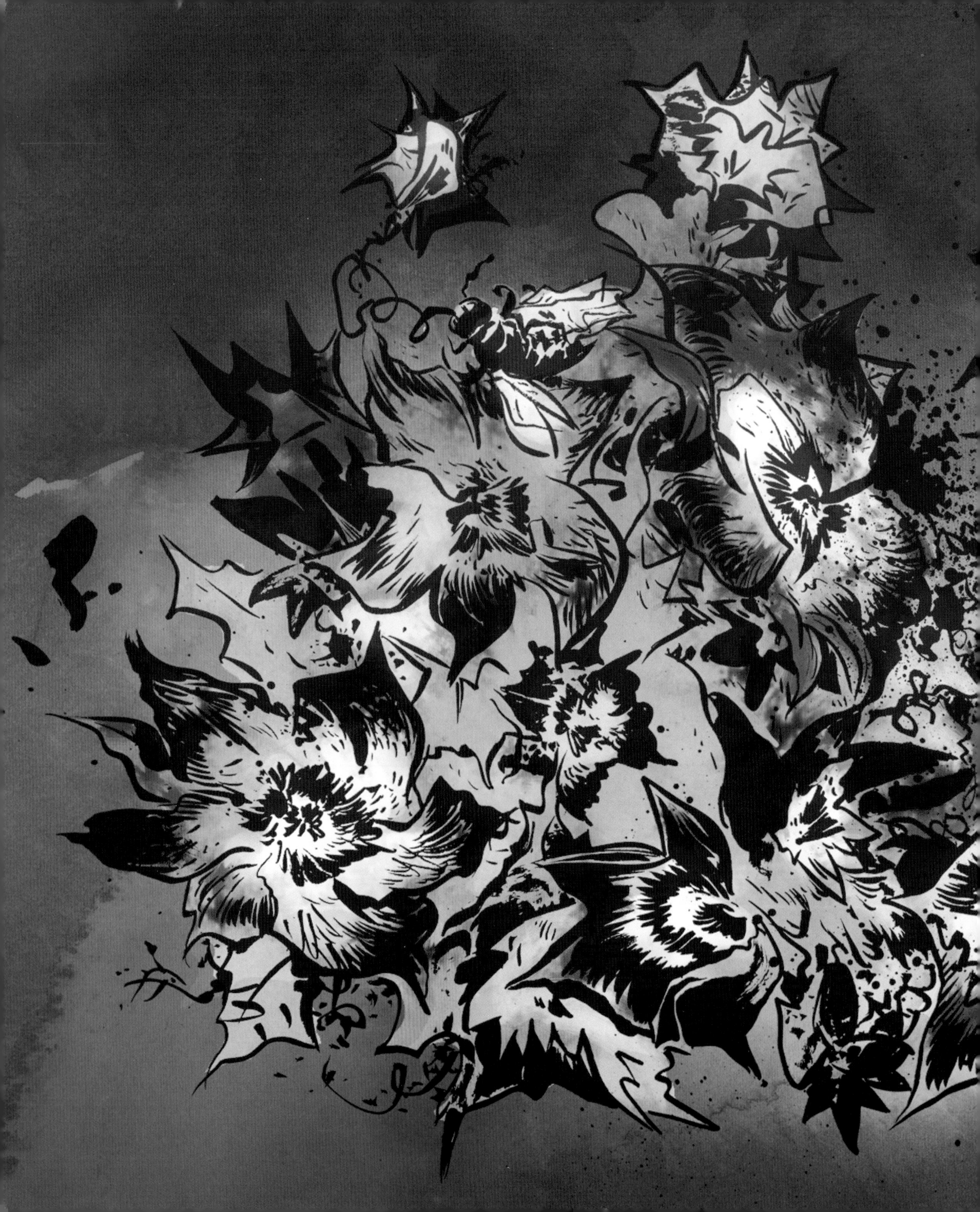

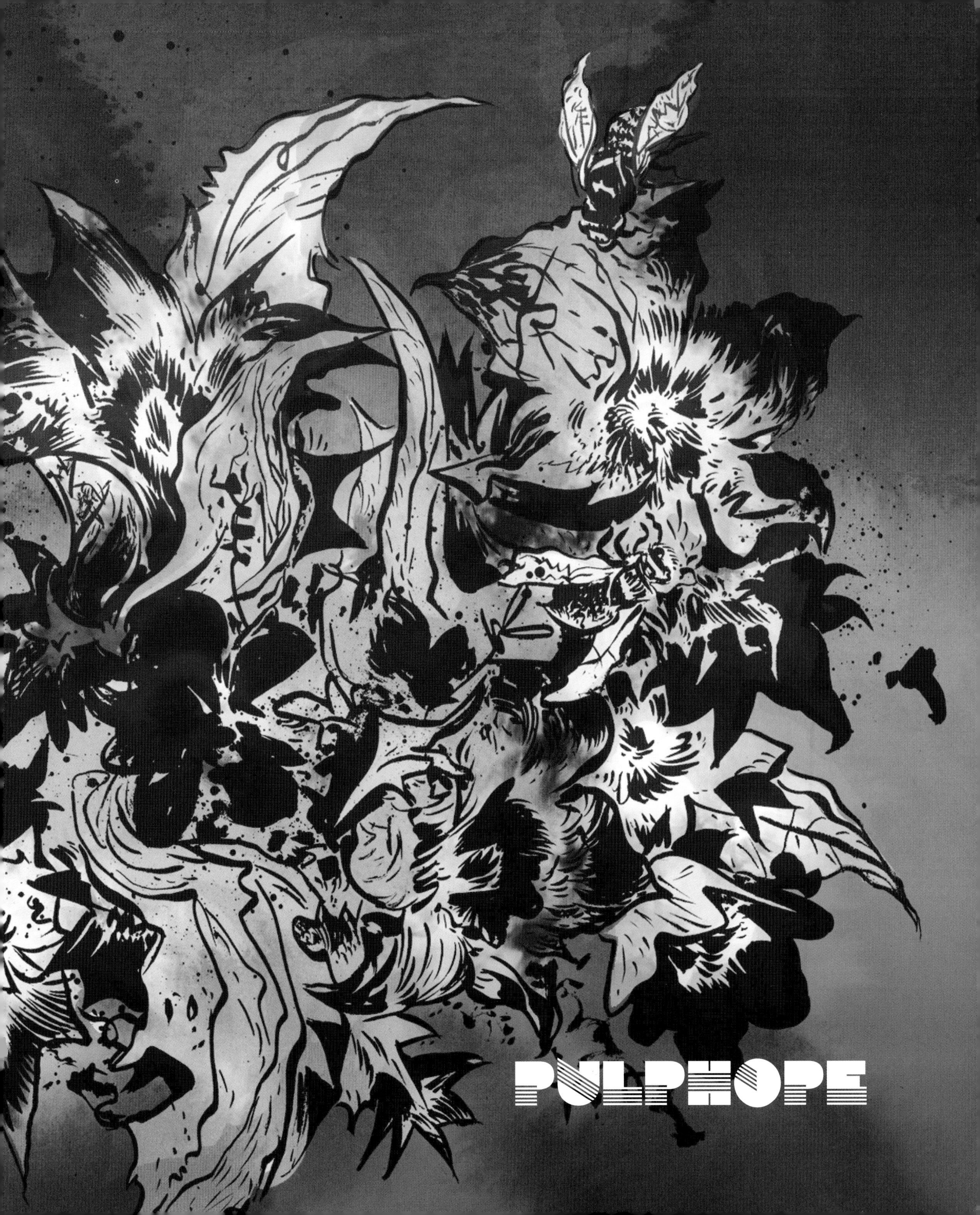
PULPHOPE

PULPHOPE: The Art of Paul Pope
Published by AdHouse Books.

Design and AdHouse logo are ©
copyright 2007 AdHouse Books.
Content is © copyright 2007 Paul
Pope, unless otherwise noted.

ISBN 0-9770304-2-3
ISBN 978-0-9770304-3-9
10 9 8 7 6 5 4 3 2 1

Design: Pitzer+Pope

AdHouse Books
1224 Greycourt Ave.
Richmond, VA 23227-4042
www.adhousebooks.com

First Printing, June 2007

Printed in Singapore

Table of Contents:

Acknowledgements: To Jonas Hjertberg and
Andrew Johnstone, who pushed me to do this.
To Doug Jaeger, Matt Spangler, Ben Neighbors,
Adrian "Air Conditioner" Clifford, Joshua Davis,
Yuko Shimizu, Istvan Banyai, James Jean, Dustin
Harbin, Mark Borg, and Calvin Reid...all of whom
are the "without whoms..."

To Tod Jatris, Stephen Daldry, Scott Rudin, James
Queen, Peter Birkemoe, and Leslie Converse.

To Aliya, Scott, Harvest, Luana, and Erika.
To Cass and Frank and Bob.

And finally, to Pitzer, for the firepower.

Fonts: Glypha for text, Sinaloa for essay headlines,
Vienna Black for title pages.

Proofreading: Lisa Pitzer

Photo Credits: frontcover flap HM King, page 35
Aliya Naumoff, pages 180-181 Chris Rubino, Paul
Pope and Luther Davis, page 217 Scott Mou

PULPHOPE
The Art of Paul Pope
DEBUJOS:
PAUL POPE

AdHouse Books
Richmond, VA

ET IN

ARCADI

EGO

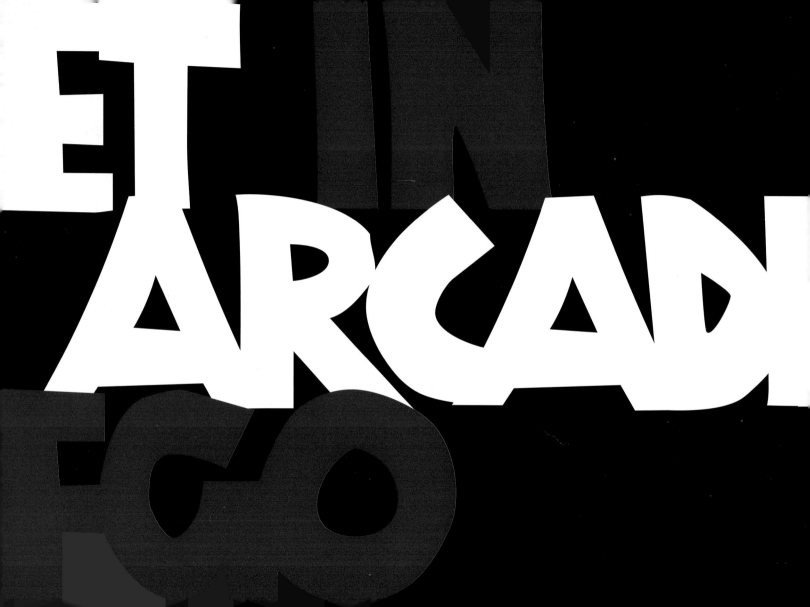

GOOD LUCK

A

A PICTURE IS A SUM OF DESTRUCTIONS

"In the old days pictures went forward towards completion by stages. Everyday brought something new. A picture used to be a sum of additions. In my case a picture is a sum of destructions. I do a picture — then I destroy it. In the end, though, nothing is lost: the red I took away one place turns up somewhere else.

It would be very interesting to preserve photographically, not the stages, but the metamorphoses of a picture. Possibly one might then discover the path followed by the brain in materializing a dream. But there is one very odd thing — to notice that basically a picture doesn't change, that the first "vision" remains almost intact, in spite of appearances. I often ponder on a light and a dark when I have put them into a picture; I try hard to break them up by interpolating a color that will create a different effect. When the work is photographed, I note that what I put in to correct my first vision has disappeared, and that, after all, the photographic image corresponds with my first vision before the transformation I insisted on."

— Picasso to Christian Zervos, 1935

A sum of destructions. Even from beyond the grave, this prolific painter-sculptor-printmaker telegraphs to us the startling, singular image of artist-as-destroyer. Every cheerful demolitionist, loving his job, knows this — in order to create you must first create space. You must remove what was there before. You must demolish it — destroy the blankness of the white canvas or the white page as the demolitionist flattens the old building or carpark or bridge. You must consume the arctic blankness with your colors and lines and forms as the cheerful demolitionist consumes his with dynamite, nitro, and implosion-physics. You must swallow the thing with work in order to build something new. Some destructions lead to new buildings, some only to more destruction. Picasso's destructions led to Cubism.

One must destroy in order to create. This is a poetic notion and perhaps not properly a philosophy. We mustn't forget Picasso was an arch-prankster as well as a Spaniard, so it is possible he was pulling the leg of the world. I think he meant what he was saying and the idea suggests to me what I take to be an elemental truth — life exists by eating other life. Life itself is an ignited consumption, a violence, a continuing energy exchange, sometimes conscious, sometimes unconscious, beginning with birth and ending in death, consumption, and destruction. It is a cheerful fatalism and nothing new. Man is born unto trouble as the sparks fly upward.

This is the key to "Comics Destroyer".

For a working cartoonist to call himself a "destroyer" of comics, when what he primarily does is create comics, it must be understood to be a form of the Greek double negative. It is to say, "I do not not create". It is a kind of playful linguistic trick, my own Spanish prank, reiterated through the visual metaphor of the cartoonist as a soulless, mechanical machine-man — the "Popemek". This image itself is intended to be humorous — since technically a machine cannot create anything, it can only perform a task it was designed to accomplish. The Popemek is the agent of the Comics Destroyer.

When I first started thinking along these lines, I was doing nothing but eating, sleeping, and making comics. I felt like a machine of comics. I remember one time going to my back door, looking out over the greened trees and realizing that not only was it the middle of the night, it was also the middle of the summer. It was pouring down rain in that languid summer way and as I sat on the stoop and drank it all in, it occurred to me the last time I noticed the weather it was snowing. I wondered if perhaps the artist, the art-machine, is only capable of doing what it was created to do. A sewing machine sews, a jack-hammer jack-hammers, a cartoonist cartoons. I was so absorbed in the act of making stories with words and pictures I missed months at a time.

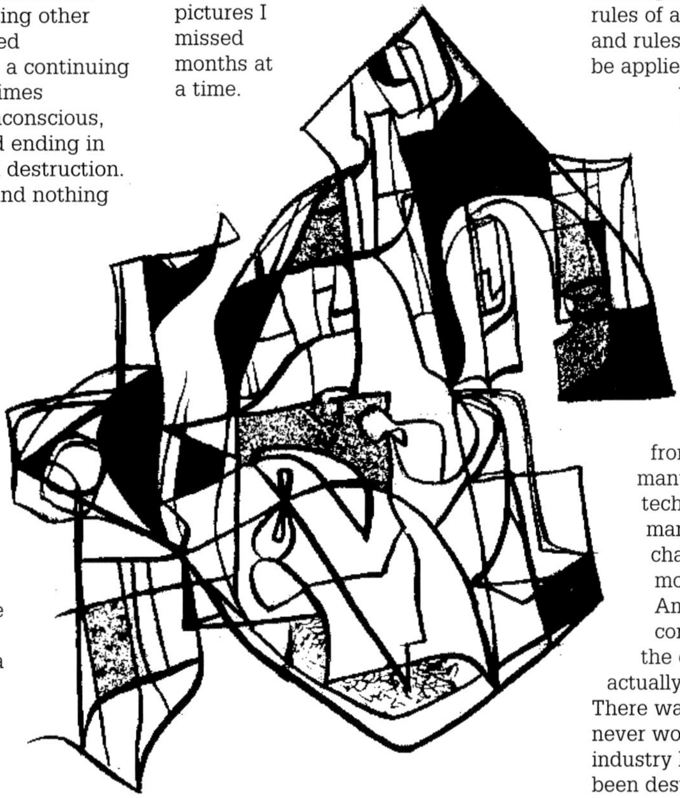

The "Comics Destroyer" became a kind of personal symbol, a self-assigned mandala, magic, a new-name. It was secret initiate's knowledge, it was amusing, and it helped push a tired brush through many long lonely nights.

"In order to save comics, I had to destroy it." It is agitprop, of course, and like all agitprop, it is shallow, misleading, and blunt, intended to confuse and alarm the uninitiated and reward those who know. It is a way of saying both "I embrace change", and "Comics must change if they're to survive." As indeed I do, and indeed they must — continually and evermore. Comics is a fertile seedbed of image, story, and myth, with rich plots, hybrid strains, and long-legged furroughs. Our proud medium shakes ideas off its vines like ripened fruit.

I take it as a moral imperative to question all traditions and presumed rules of the comics medium. As an artist, I will cleave to the traditions which point to real, true, and vital rules of art. I will borrow traditions and rules of other media if they can be applied successfully to comics. I will discard (i.e. "destroy") all local, static, inflated, and worn-out edicts which serve only to keep the medium of comics in stasis — rules which may've worked at one time and in one place, but no longer do.

This intolerance of the shop-worn and trite applies even to my own standards and rules, as it did when returning from Japan, having learned so many new traditions and techniques from manga, so many new ideas which challenged or broke even the most basic presumptions of American and European comics, I realized at the end of the day the only comics I was actually destroying was my own. There was a time when I thought I'd never work in film or the fashion industry but that presumption has been destroyed, too.

In the end is this Destroyer's affirmation: Comics, like all other arts, is elastic, open-ended and expansive. The medium has the power to contain and express all human thought, all feeling and experience, from the most sacred to the most profane, to heaven and hell and back again. There is absolutely nothing you can't express through the medium of comics. Nothing is beyond its scope. As long as there are artists-of-comics who wish to create, and ideas they wish to express, this one true and unchanging rule remains indestructible.

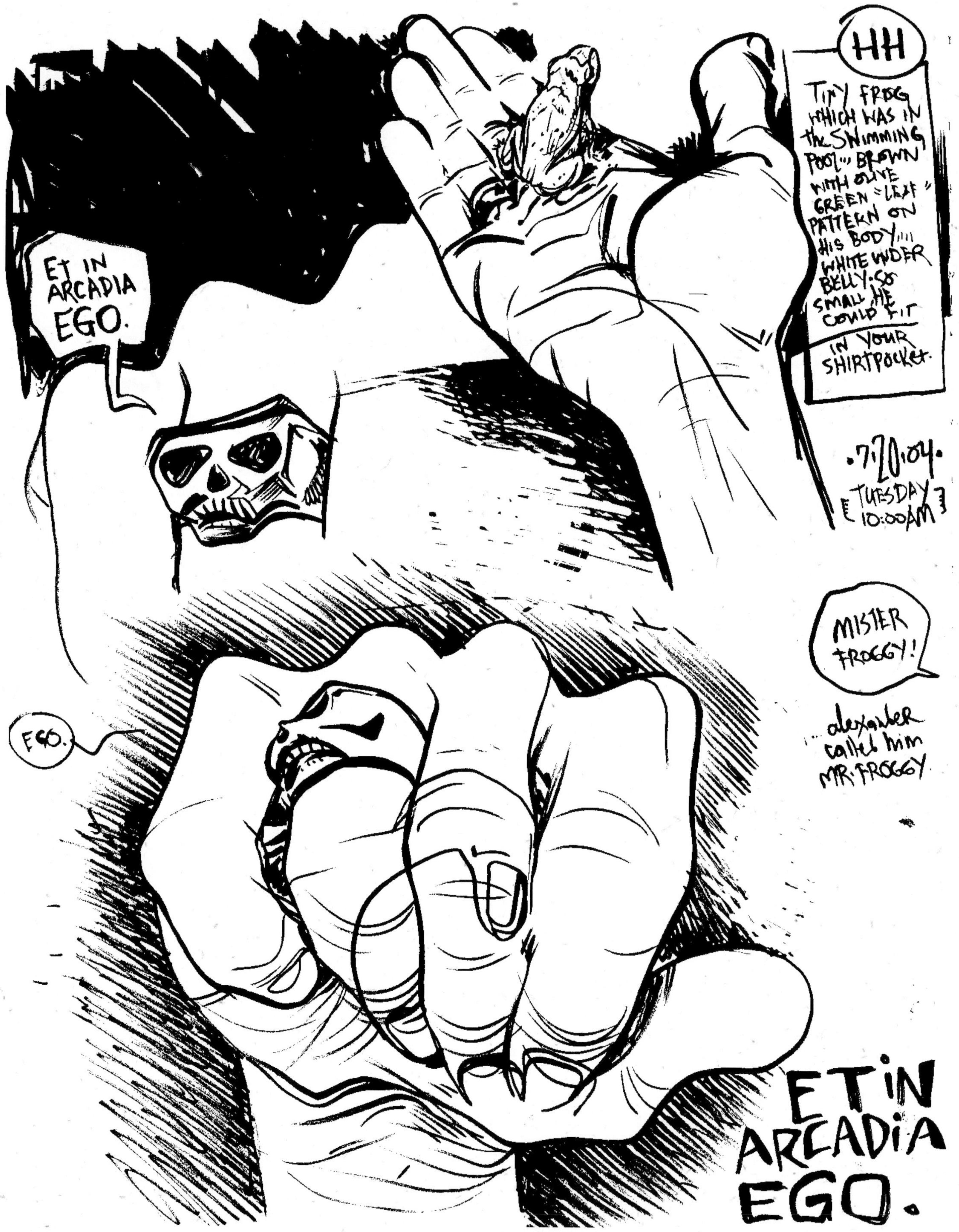
HH
TINY FROG WHICH WAS IN the SWIMMING POOL... BROWN WITH OLIVE GREEN "LEAF" PATTERN ON HIS BODY.... WHITE UNDER BELLY. SO SMALL HE COULD FIT IN YOUR SHIRTPOCKET.
ET IN ARCADIA EGO.
•7•20•04•
TUESDAY 10:00AM
MISTER FROGGY!
...alexander called him MR. FROGGY
EGO.
ET IN ARCADIA EGO.

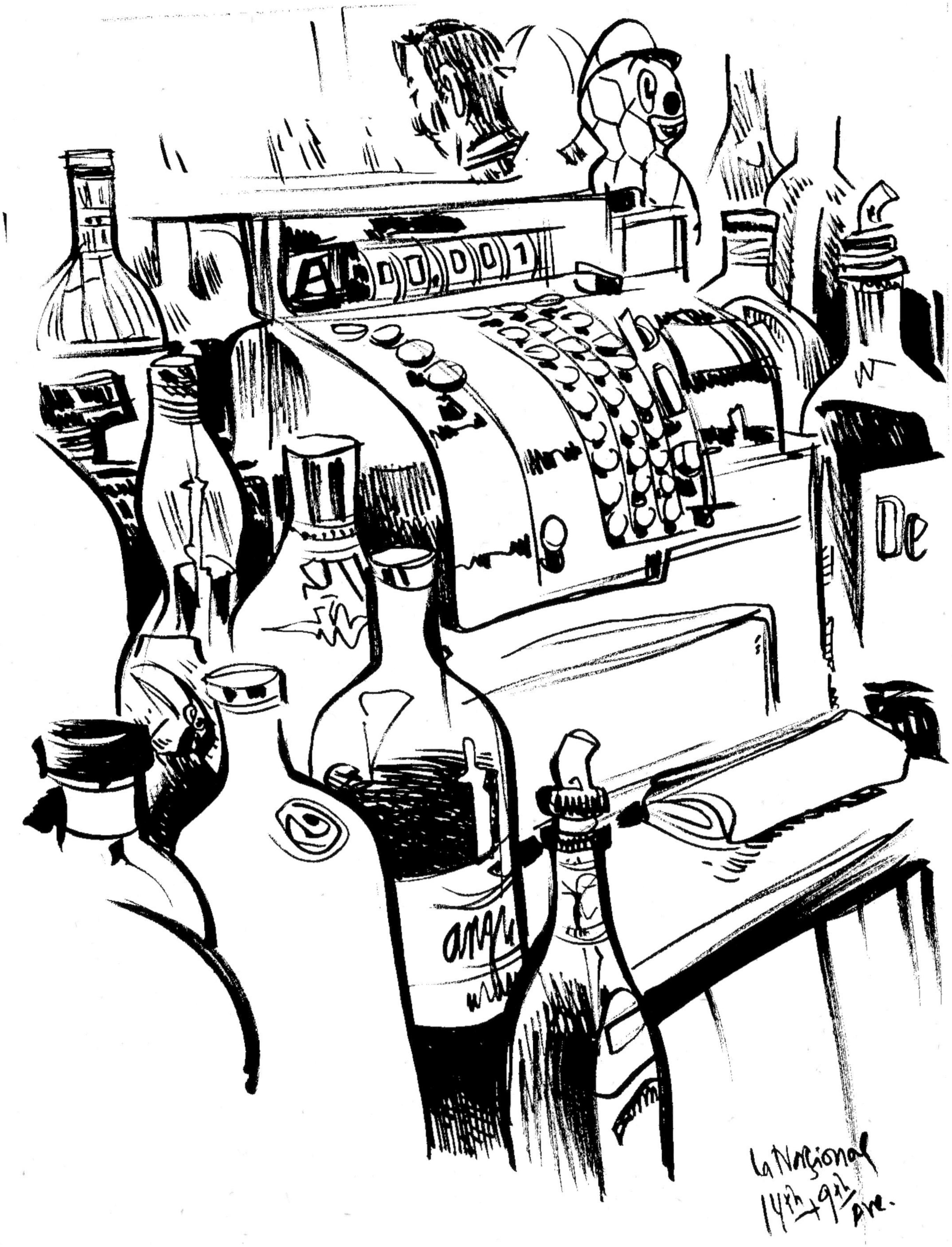
La Nacional
14th + 9th Ave.

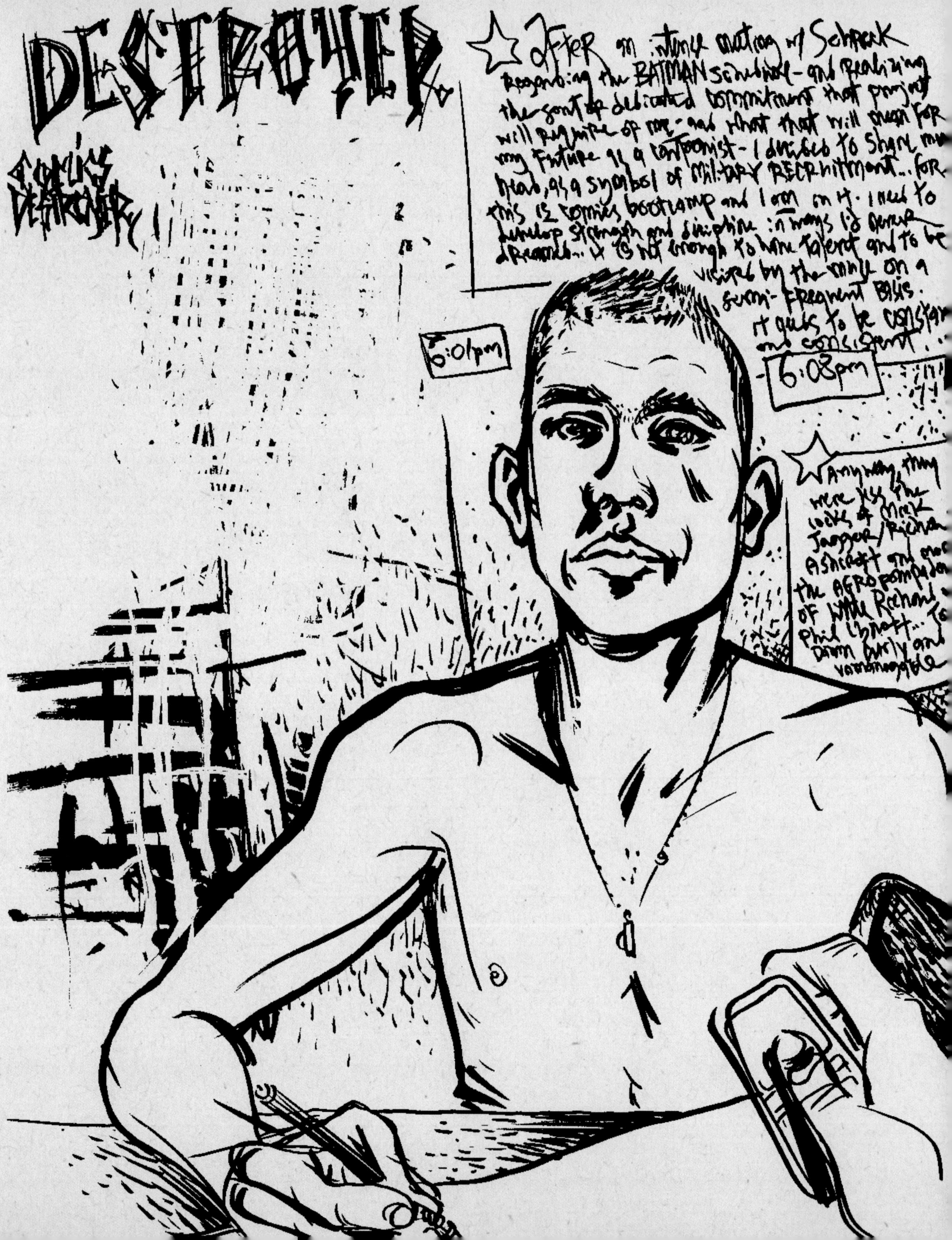
DESTROYER
COMICS DESTROYER
6:01pm
After an intense meeting w/ Schreck regarding the BATMAN schedule – and realizing the sort of dedicated commitment that project will require of me – and what that will mean for my future as a cartoonist – I decided to shave my head, as a symbol of military recruitment.. for this is comics bootcamp and I am on it. I need to develop strength and discipline in ways I'd never dreamed.. it is not enough to have talent and to be visited by the muse on a semi-frequent basis. it gets to be constan and consistent.
6:08pm
Anyway, they were just the locks of Mick Jagger/Richa Ashcroft and the AFRO pompadou of Little Richard / Phil Lynott.. To damn curly and unmanageable

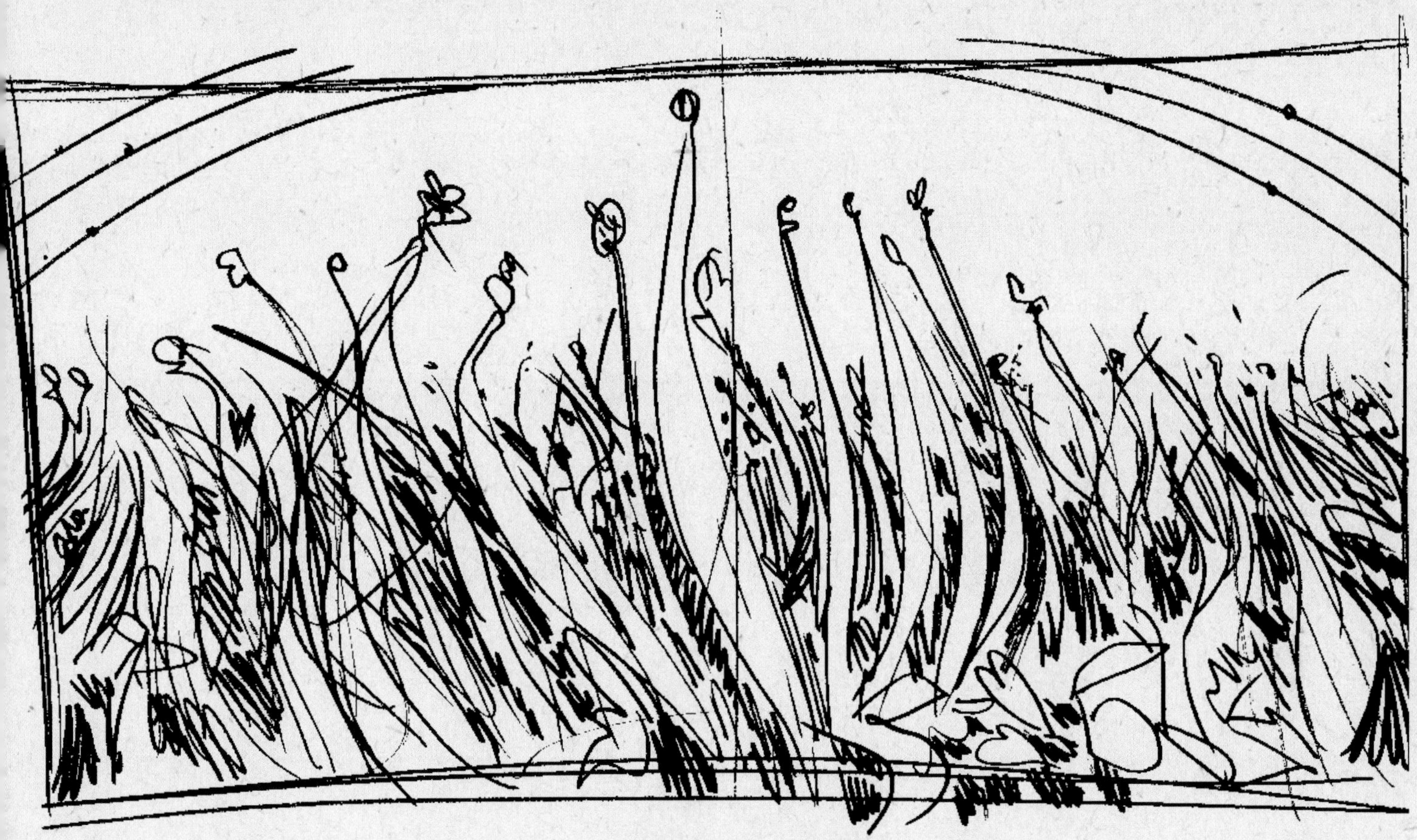

"OCEANS" A SEA OF STRANGE FLOWERS
SWARMING WITH FLIES, SUNSET
"ZODIAC/CIRCLES" ABOVE

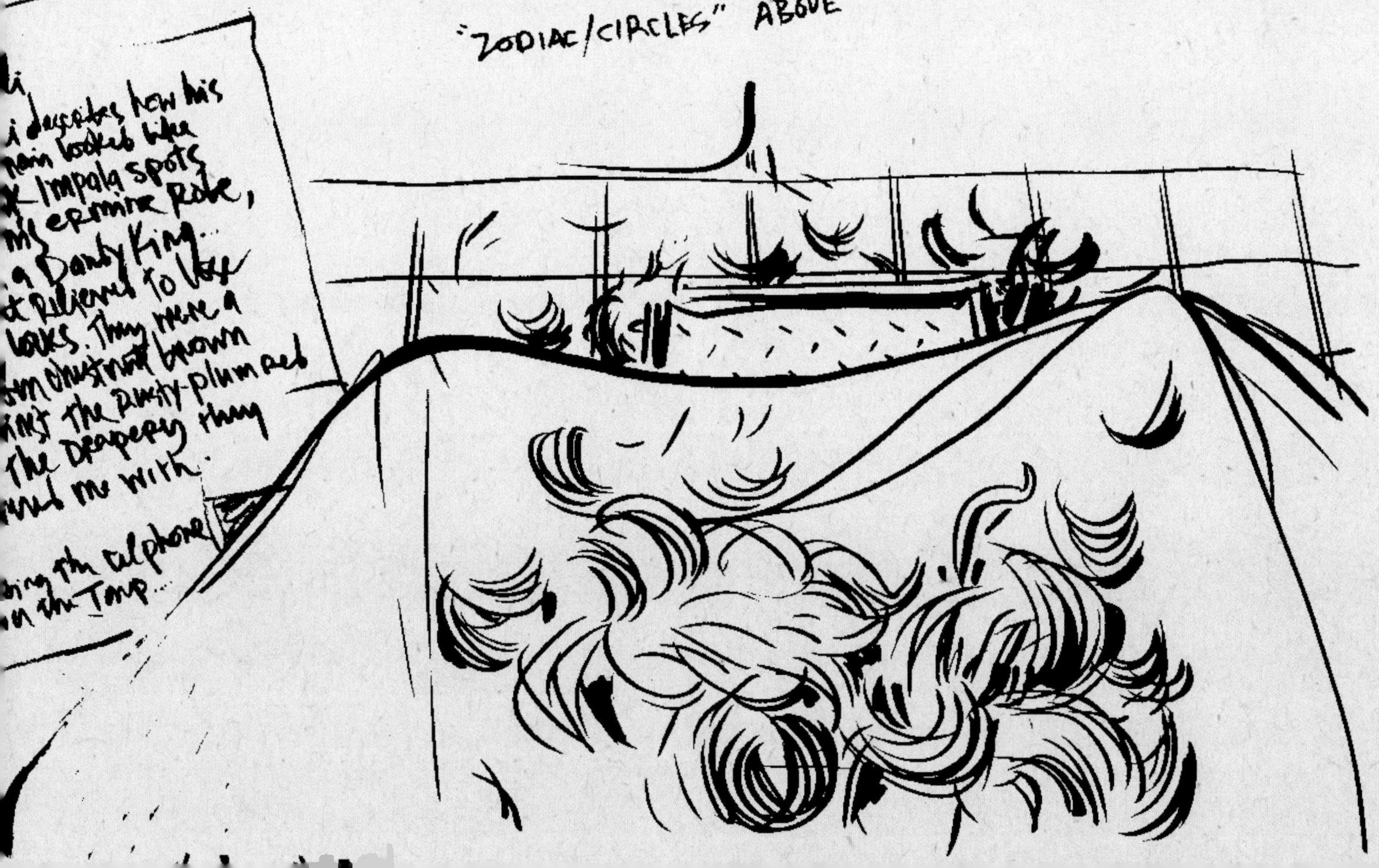
li
i describes how his
hair looked like
x Impala spots
n's ermine Robe,
a Dandy King...
t Relieved to lose
locks. They were a
om chestnut brown
inst the Dusty-plum red
The Drapery they
und me with.
ing the cellphone
on the Tarp...

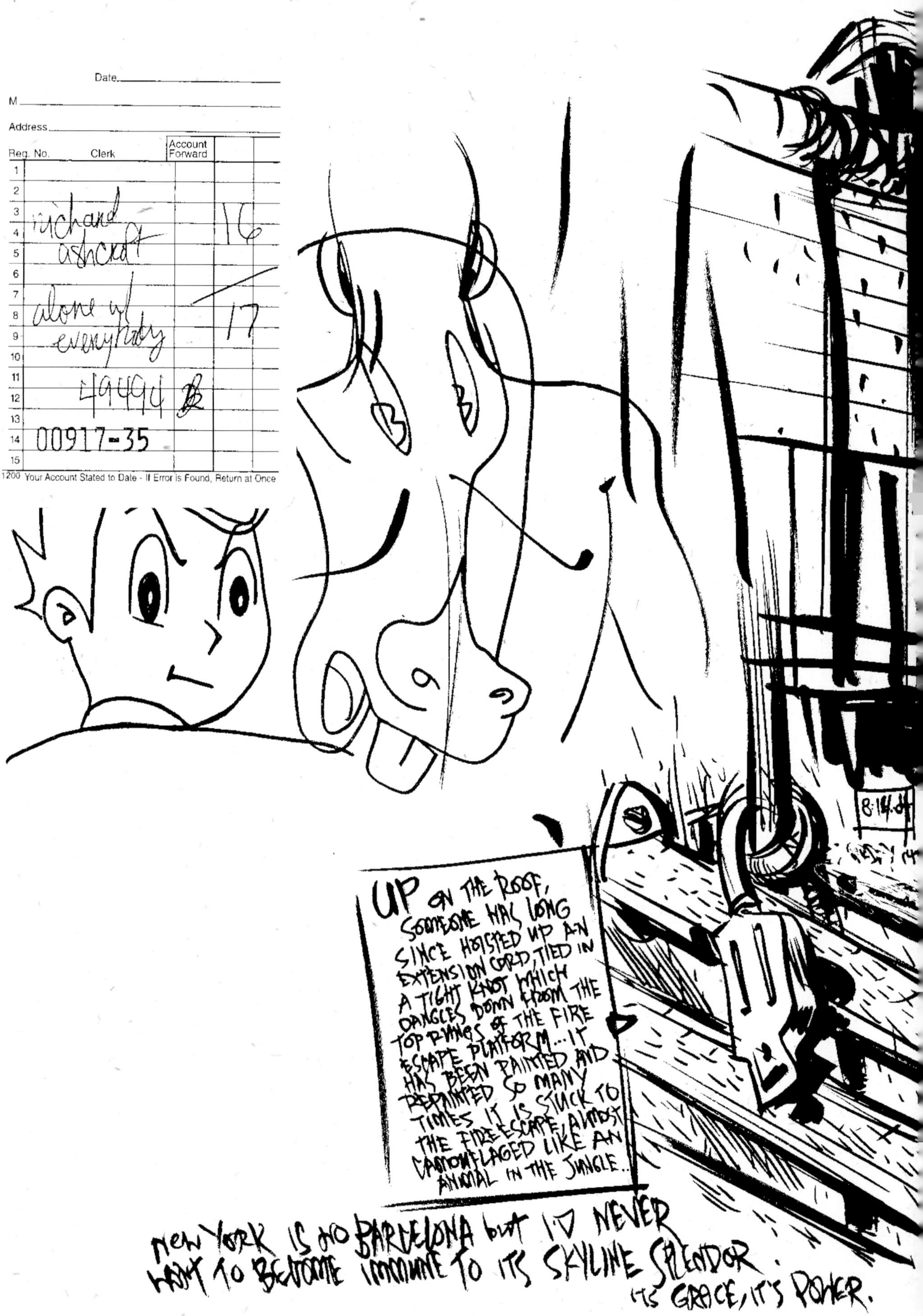
Date
M
Address
Reg. No.
Clerk
Account Forward
richard ashcroft
16
alone w/ everybody
17
49494
00917-35
1200 Your Account Stated to Date - If Error is Found, Return at Once
UP ON THE ROOF, SOMEONE HAS LONG SINCE HOISTED UP AN EXTENSION CORD, TIED IN A TIGHT KNOT WHICH DANGLES DOWN FROM THE TOP RUNGS OF THE FIRE ESCAPE PLATFORM... IT HAS BEEN PAINTED AND REPAINTED SO MANY TIMES IT IS STUCK TO THE FIRE ESCAPE, ALMOST CAMOUFLAGED LIKE AN ANIMAL IN THE JUNGLE..
NEW YORK IS NO BARCELONA BUT I'D NEVER WANT TO BECOME IMMUNE TO ITS SKYLINE SPLENDOR.
ITS GRACE, IT'S POWER.

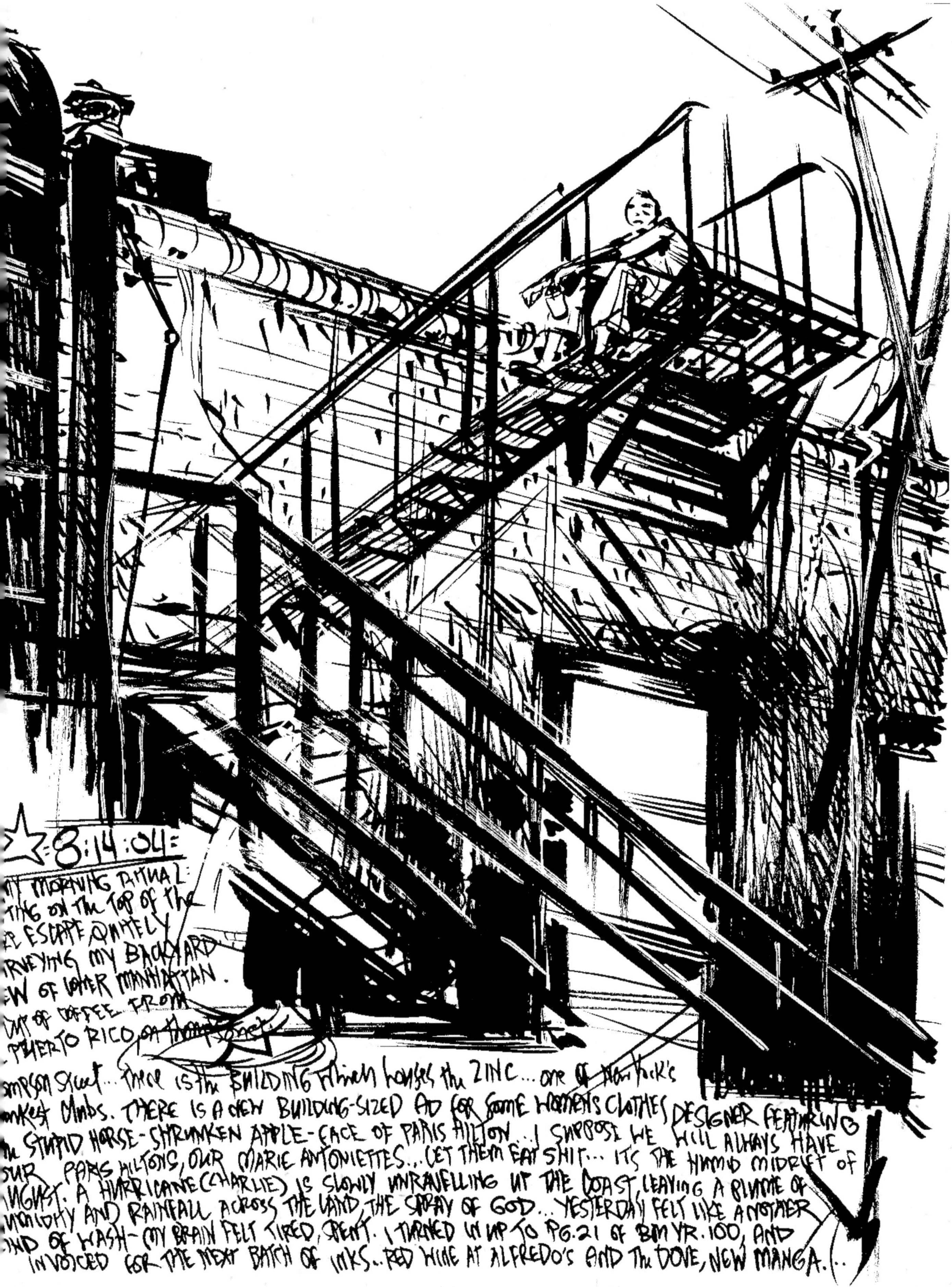

☆ 8:14:04

MY MORNING RITUAL: [S]ITTING ON THE TOP OF THE [FI]RE ESCAPE QUIETLY [SU]RVEYING MY BACKYARD [VI]EW OF LOWER MANHATTAN. [C]UP OF COFFEE FROM PUERTO RICO, on ~~Thompson~~ Street

[Th]ompson Street... There is the BUILDING which houses the ZINC... one of ~~New York's~~ [fu]nkest clubs. THERE IS A NEW BUILDING-SIZED AD FOR SOME WOMEN'S CLOTHES DESIGNER FEATURING [th]e STUPID HORSE-SHRUNKEN APPLE-FACE OF PARIS HILTON... I SUPPOSE WE WILL ALWAYS HAVE OUR PARIS HILTONS, OUR MARIE ANTONIETTES... LET THEM EAT SHIT... IT'S THE HUMID MIDRIFT OF [A]UGUST. A HURRICANE (CHARLIE) IS SLOWLY UNRAVELLING UP THE COAST, LEAVING A PLUME OF [H]UMIDITY AND RAINFALL ACROSS THE LAND, THE SPRAY OF GOD... YESTERDAY FELT LIKE ANOTHER [K]IND OF WASH— MY BRAIN FELT TIRED, SPENT. I TURNED IN UP TO PG.21 OF BM YR.100, AND INVOICED FOR THE NEXT BATCH OF INKS.. RED WINE AT ALFREDO'S AND THE DOVE, NEW MANGA. (...

IN REHEARSAL TO A VISION

"Midway along the journey of our life I woke to find myself in a dark wood, for I had wandered off from the straight path. How hard it is to tell what it was like, this world of wilderness, savage and stubborn ... but if I am to show the good that came of it I must talk about things other than the good."

With these words Dante opens his *Inferno*. He sets as the date for the beginning of his epic the night before Good Friday in the year 1300. Dante, having been born in 1265, would've been 35 at this time. In his day, in his Italy, in his Middle Ages, 35 was considered to be the middle. 35 was the number set perfectly between the 70 years allotted us according to the Bible. It was the time between the flush of apple-red youth and the creaking grim-gray of seniority. At 35, lost in a dark wood, the deeply devout Dante begins his descent into hell on a personal spiritual journey,

the ancient poet Virgil his guide. Dante warns in his opening preamble he must talk about things other than the good if he is going to show the good of it, and he does. From there we get hundreds of pages of terrifying mystical visions of how the damned live in hell, written out with curiously descriptive and animated care. You can find yourself and all the people you know in Dante's damned — the slothful, the prideful, the lazy, the gluttonous. He had a hell of an imagination, Dante. Makes you think he actually went there for himself. I suppose in his mind he did.

Meanwhile in the 20th century, some 600 years later and 1000 miles northwest, the Noble Prize-winning Irish poet and playwright W.B. Yeats addresses the question of life's middle in his own epic, *A Vision*. Yeats was a kind of Pre-Raphaelite mystic who had a lifelong preoccupation with hidden

knowledge and the occult. He famously edited the works of William Blake, making that poet available to new generations. He was friends with Ezra Pound and other luminaries of the so-called Lost Generation, and he had a profound effect on many of the greatest artists of the 20th century. Yeats claimed that much of *A Vision* was dictated to him from the spirits of dead mystics through the medium of his wife, the psychic George Hyde Lees. Whether we're to believe that or not, we do know one of the primary sources for *A Vision* to be a 16th century Alchemical text called *Speculum Hominum et Angelorum*, or, *Mirror of Man and the Angels*. This was an obscure text featuring a lengthy hermetic rumination on the cycle of human life corresponding to the cycles of the the sun and the moon. Yeats, taking a cue from the dead mystics, considered the point of middle age — that point set perfectly between life-

and-death, between youth and infirmary — to be best symbolized by the sight of the moon visible during daylight hours. In turn, this symbol corresponds to the middle of the month, when sometimes the simultaneous vision of a hot, reddening sun on the set and a pale white moon on the rise can be seen. Maybe this would be 4 or 5 o'clock in the afternoon, the hour when you feel the onset of night buried within the day. The hour when shadows grow longer and colors richer, yet the day is still everywhere around, brightly omnipresent, omnipotent.

I happened to observe this vision for myself the other day, walking up Mercer Street through SoHo. There it was, the bright white moon, hanging low and full and pockmarked, deadset in the middle of a cold January afternoon sky. It looked like nothing less than a huge, cracked fluorescent dinner plate laid out on a milky, dark blue cloth. Even in the daylight it was casting a slight, subtle glow from its eastern trajectory. I hurried home and took the six flights to the top of my building two steps at a time. Sunsets are so quick, so capricious, so disdainful. So easy to miss. Even here. But from the edge of the rooftop I had a perfect view of the sun and the moon, hanging about equally low in the sky. If I turned my head to the right, looking west out over Houston Street, I could see the sun dipping down, glowing in its red nuclear descent. To the east, above Broadway and the East Village, there it was, the bright pale moon on the rise. According to Joseph Campbell, when you find yourself at this moment, reflecting on this vision, "...your body and your consciousness are at their prime. And you are in a position to ask yourself, Who or what am I? Am I the consciousness or am I the vehicle of the consciousness? Am I this body which is the vehicle of light...or am I the light?" I am not a mystic, although I found myself sharing *A Vision* with a dead one, and it made me think of these things, standing there on that roof.

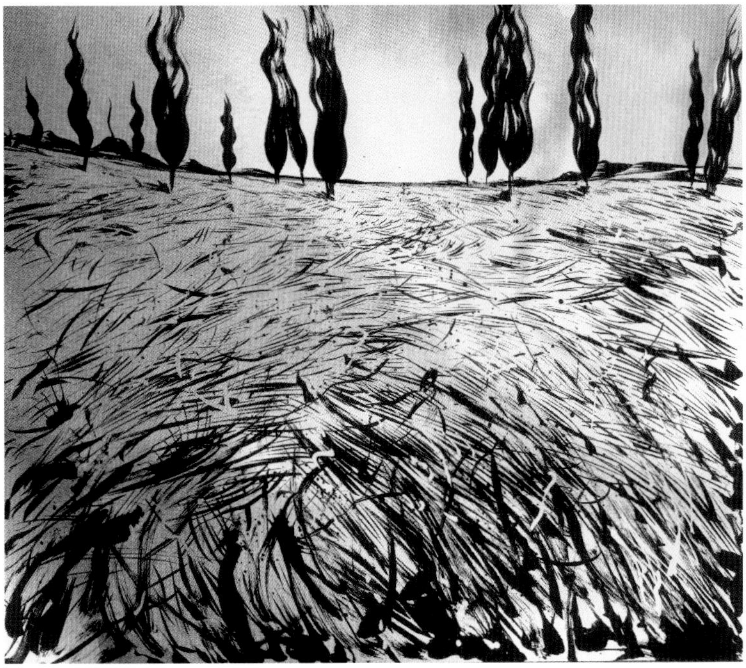

What are the important dates? I could think of a few. At 13 you are a teenager, at 18 you can vote and get drafted. At 21 you are legally an adult. And then there is 33. I never understood why 33 was supposed to mean anything. When I reached the age of 33, everyone asked me if it somehow resonated within me, if I had experienced any change in my psyche, something brought on by having achieved this hallowed number. 33 was the year Christ died and was resurrected, the year Jarvis Cocker — who is not Jesus although they have the same initials — decides to stay in and get the dishes done. 33 was the year of Alexander's death on the plains of Anatolia, dying under a battlefield tent, leaving behind his surgeons, his horse, and rows of wailing attendants. To Euclid and the early geometricians, preoccupied as they were with the symbolic significance of numbers even beyond our ability to add, subtract, and multiply them, 33 is a double-powered number. They considered three to be the most stable of numbers and the triangle (the isosoeles at any rate) the most stable of forms. Perhaps we could assume this numerical miracle is topped only by the number 333, a triad, a set of three of the most stable number. But no one lives to the age of 333.

As I approached the number 33, it meant nothing to me and I wondered at how and why it didn't. I was disappointed in myself. 33 was supposed to be important. Everyone said so and I supposed it should somehow, too. Eventually it would and did. 33 turned out to be a year of deep personal, very painful, very transformational change. Coincidentally, it was also the year I began work on Batman Year 100. 27 was always the age I had considered — the year of Morrison's death. Morrison was our Blake, our mystic wildman. He died at 27 under what I regard as depressingly mundane circumstances, in a bathtub in Paris, unceremoniously sliding off the edge in his bearded and gut-spread way into the realm of heroes and legends. Jim Morrison is not to be thought of as a regular human being anymore; he exists now as do Bruce Lee, Hemmingway, Che Guevara, Johnny Cash, and all too soon, Muhammad Ali. These are no longer men of flesh and blood. These men have become larger than life, existing now as spiritual avatars — as physical embodiments of principles shared and dreamed by millions and millions of people everywhere. MLK is another, larger one. It seems to me Morrison had no symbol of the middle, he had only the end. He was doomed to a young death, a hero's death. He was doomed by his own hand. He was not destined to reach 33. He was not destined for 35. But I am. As I write this, I am 35. I have lived as many years as Morrison has been dead.

For most of my life I have operated within the belief that I was destined to die young. The human animal is so fragile, so vulnerable, so prone to awkward accident and tragic circumstance. It is absurd, afterall, I adolescently reasoned, to expect to live to be old. It was beyond absurd, it was unthinkable. This early death-head of teenagehood was gradually codified into a belief system through the existentialism of Camus, which fit like an old jacket smelling of mothballs. It had a stiff collar and the sleeves were a little too short. Maybe it wasn't much to look at but it fit well enough and it kept me warm on cold nights when the batteries wore out. The Existentialism of Camus joyfully, or least clear-headedly, embraces the eventuality of death, with something like a positive attitude. At least it is a philosophy of action, and this is a better alternative to suicide. To my teenage head, at least there was some comfort in that.

I later found a way to romanticize this through a breezy reading of Lord Byron and Percy Shelley, and later Rimbaud. The purple prose of the Gothic; look at us hunchbacks up in our belfry with a dog-eared copy of *A Season In Hell*. Through the Byronic outlook, the morbid necessity of dying before your time becomes a virtue. The lone man on the mountain top, shouting into the unknowing and unknowable void, his haircut falling in perfect curls, his moustache manicured, his flowery white blouse opened attractively to the raging wind. Sturm und Drang! How appealing it all was. A blueprint for rock stars. Kick out the jams, motherfucker! Absenthe! Gun-running! This stuff is tailor-made for adolescents.

Morrison was a hero of adolescence, of abandon, and died as Byron or Rimbaud would've scripted him to die. He spoke of youthful life and of dying in big, loud syllables. In his

throat a monster of life raged to escape. He worked a howl like an animal and somehow something in it remained articulate, big blue, sexual, menacing and alive. We will never know what he would've thought or felt had he lived into the full maturity of manhood, had he walked through that door. Like Alexander and James Dean, and in some ways Rimbaud, he died in the bloom of youth. He took his eyes off the road and his hands left the wheel. He had no time to consider the road which led him there, or the one which could carry him on. Only the one which would carry him out. And I think that is a shame. I wish he was still here.

If you happen to live long enough to live with the realization that the future is uncertain and the end is always near, you will eventually live longer than you ever expected. Ultimately, this is what happened to me at 33. I had outlived every age I had expected to reach. 33 was much farther into my own future than I dared hope for, between The Bomb and the guns and the car wrecks and the accidental electrocutions. One day during 33 it suddenly occurred to me that I had successfully survived a youth due largely to what might be called an unconscious mindset of cheerful fatalism. Further, it occurred to me this morbid mind-set was very likely a reasonable and even emotionally healthy defense mechanism for a sensitive, creative child. But, eventually, if you manage to outlive all those years of adolescent turbulence, you realize that it is also a mind-set which cannot persist. It is the one that carried you to the doors of adulthood, but there it stops. Stubborn, adolescent, short-sighted and proud, this vision can't take you a step further. It is the philosophy of the passenger, not the pilot. And I still marvel at how this Teutonic grimness isn't self-evident to everyone. If you operate under the assumption that you will not live to see 30, and then you do, and even outstrip it by a few years, your very first premise is knocked out from under you and your philosophy topples like a tower of matchsticks. Something needs to change, because the road that led to here is not the road that will lead you out.

Midway through the journey of my life I find myself looking for a path through a dark wood. I am 35 and I am in rehearsal to a vision. I can honestly say that today I feel even more of the world's sickness than I did half a lifetime ago. There is certain evidence of it everywhere you look. It drips off the walls like sweat. The worst of it is that even though you made it this far into life and you know you can no longer rely on that bolstering adolescent defense, you are no more guaranteed the next day than you were when you were a child.

When I need my own mirror of men and angels, I too turn to hear the voices of the dead. Without even having faith in mystics, I too turn to take my cue from dead mystics. When I need voices, I turn to Emerson and Thoreau. Their Transcendentalism rings a bit hollow to me (I am no Platonist), but their words still ring clear and true. I turn to the dour civics of Confucius and the clear-eyed cynicism of Machiavelli. The life-embrace of Epicurus. I turn to the dreamtime of Jung and the pastorality of Tolkein. And to others. These poets and philosophers are the whispering dead I hear, pointing the way to the road which leads out of this inferno. These are the dead on the roof with me, these are my Virgils. They point their parchment fingers toward the arc of the heavens, helping make sense of a meaningless rising moon and a mute and dumb setting sun.

PP

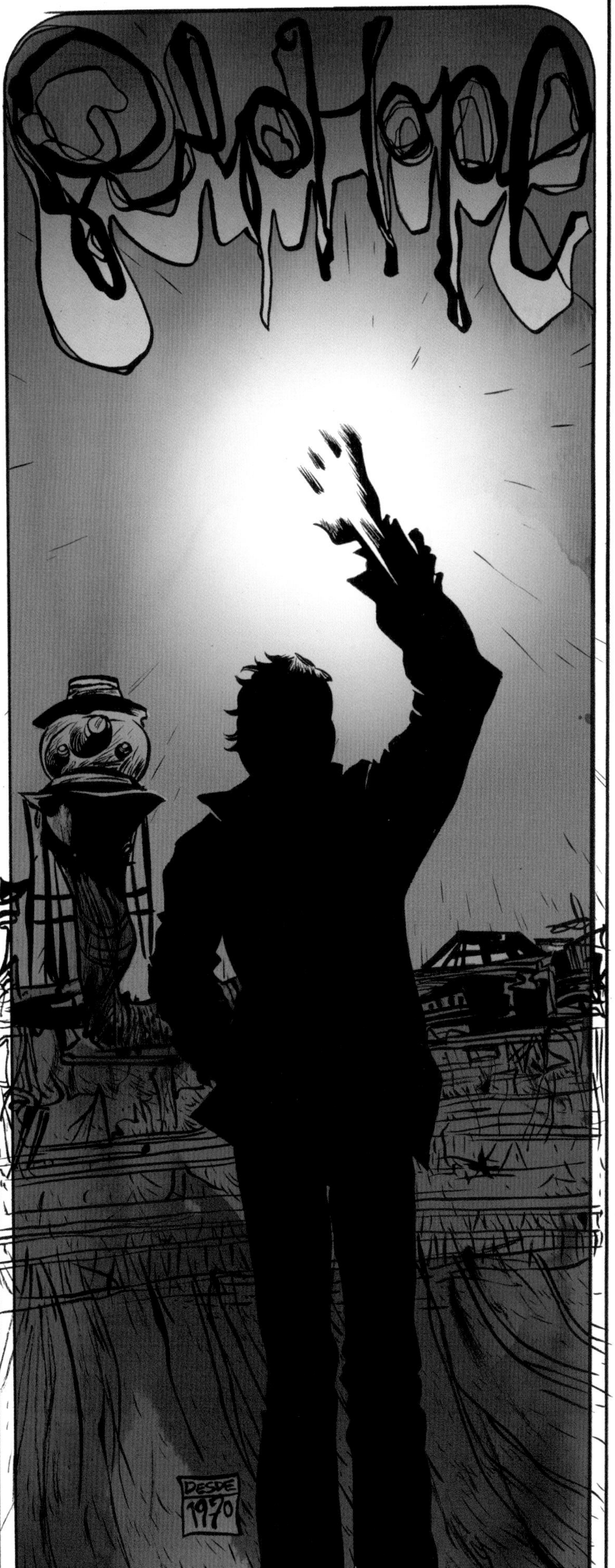
DESDE 1970

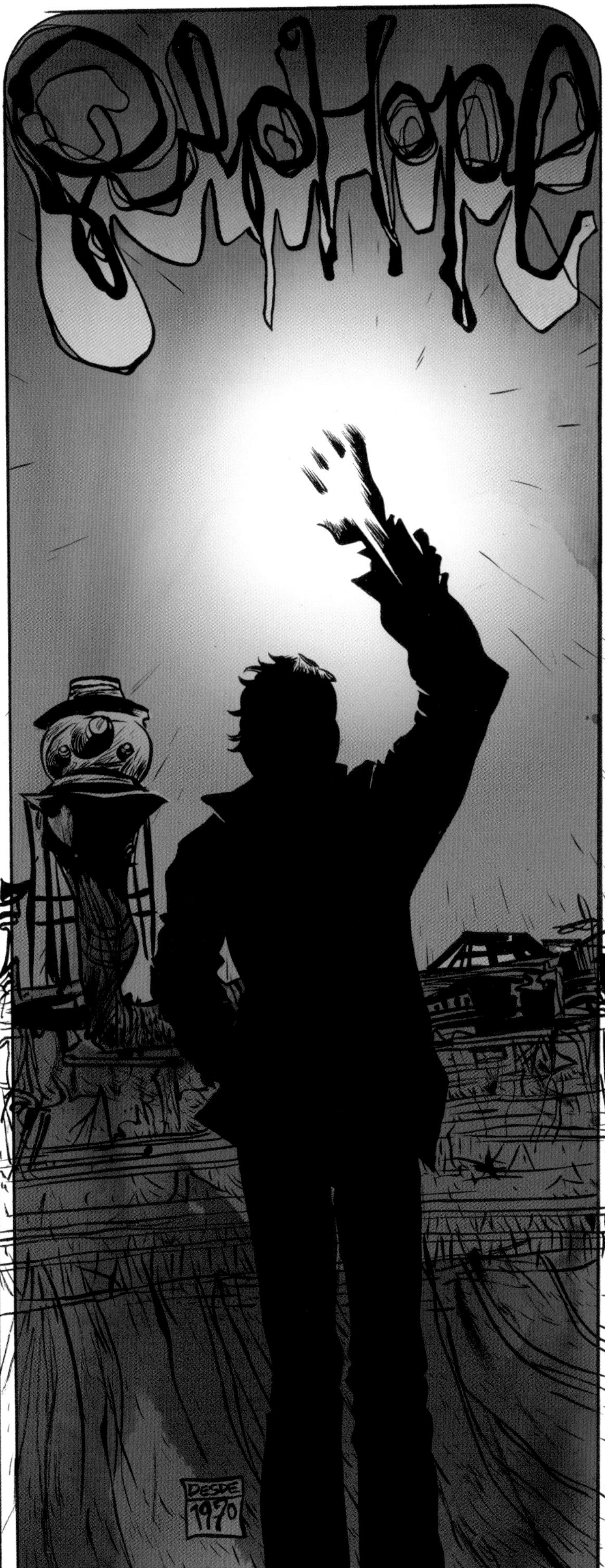
DESDE 1970

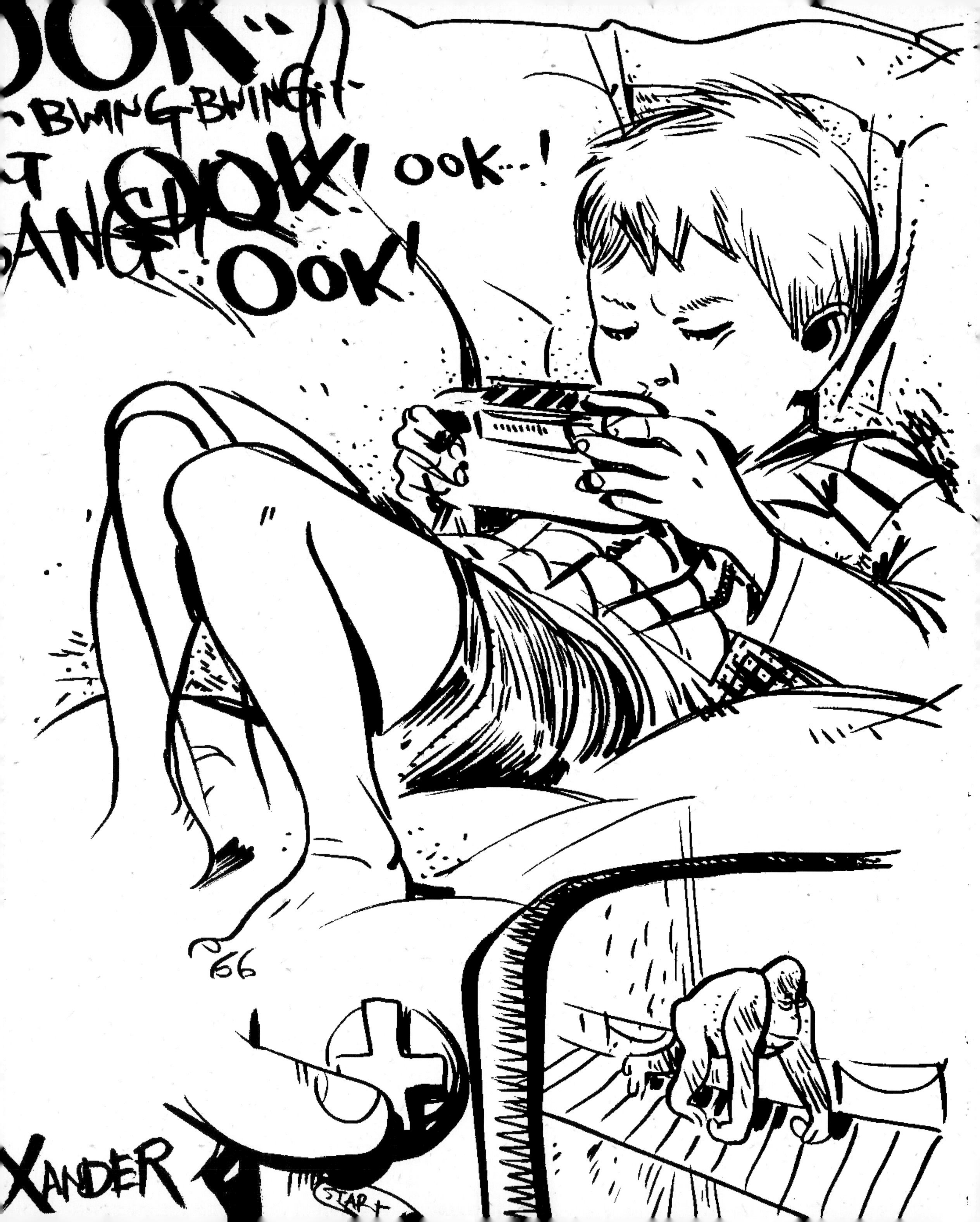
OOK
BWING BWING
OOK! OOK...!
OOK!
'06
XANDER
START

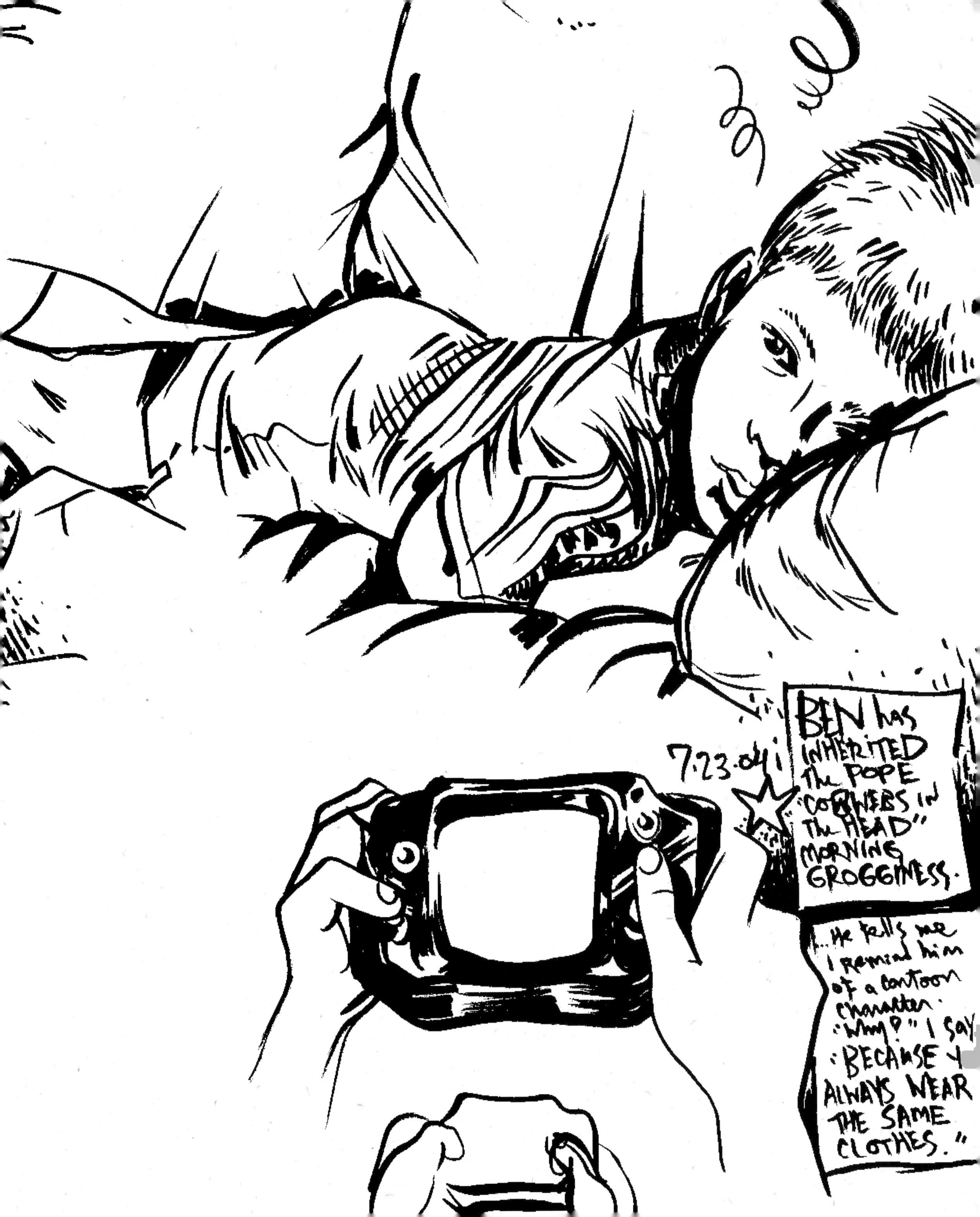
7.23.04
BEN has INHERITED The POPE "COBWEBS IN The HEAD" MORNING GROGGINESS.
...He tells me I remind him of a cartoon character. "Why?" I say. "BECAUSE Y ALWAYS WEAR THE SAME CLOTHES."

MEAN-WHILE:
UNCA' PAUL... Y'KNOW WHAT?
...YOU KINDA REMIND ME OF A CARTOON CHARACTER.
OH?
WHY'S THAT?
CUZ...
...YOU'RE ALWAYS WEARING THE SAME CLOTHES.
TRUE STORY.

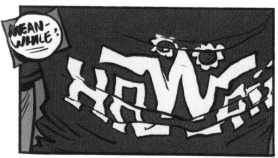

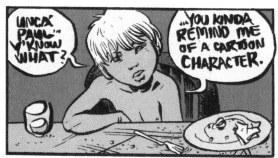

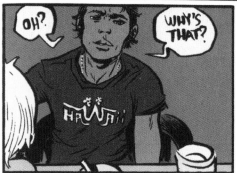

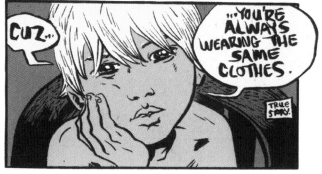

PALM READING

When I was a little over half-way finished with *Batman Year 100*, I was in Spain. This would've been August 2005. While visiting my friends at Norma publishing, I picked up two copies of a beautiful book called *Periplo Immaginario*, a massive retrospective of drawings and paintings by Hugo Pratt, published by Lizard Edizioni. This huge book serves as a multi-lingual catalogue for a travelling exhibition of Pratt's work, and it goes well beyond the familiar, iconic images of the sea-wandering *Corto Maltese* series. One copy of this book alone is as heavy as a slate floor tile, carrying two was like carrying two pancaked bowling balls on your back. The book is a bottomless well, a magic mirror, page after page of Pratt's lush sketches and watercolors, many of which I'd never seen before. Many images stretch back to a period in the 1950s and '60s in which Pratt created a number of stories and paintings using the world of American Indians — and more widely, the entire scope of 17th and 18th Century American history — as subject matter. Long before going on to dream up *Corto Maltese*, Pratt wrote and drew a number of stories with names such as *Fort Wheeling,* and *Sgt. Kirk,* stories set along the early American frontier. This setting was one he would return to again and again, as in the 80s, in the pages of a strangle little book called *Jesuit Joe,* a violent

and primal story set in the Canadian north during the days when the French trapped beaver in Ontario and Quebec, and trade was done with the Indians all the way down into the Ohio River valley. Jesuit Joe is a classic anti-hero, sometimes helping people, sometimes not, a Canadian native wearing stolen Royal Mounted gear. In one scene, Joe shoots a bird for being too happy. These are stark, existential musing on the human condition boiled down into words and pictures, a far cry from other idealized cowboys vs. Indians adventures. Pratt made another skirmish into this same wild territory in a book called *Indian Summer,* drawn by the great Italian cartoonist Milo Manara, a sort of free-form variation on Hawthorne's *Scarlet Letter.*

Something about Pratt's stories really speaks to me. Sometimes the art looks rushed and the characters speak in impossible soliloquies, but there is something really mysterious and convincing about them. The world of Pratt's Indians looks very much like the world I lived in growing up in northern Ohio, all snowy banks and black birds, rows of cattails and corn and spindly trees covered with a dusting of red and orange Autumn maple leaves. Growing up there, perfectly independent of the mind-achingly dull and inevitable suburban sprawl,

the John Deere rider lawnmowers and the rabbit antenna-fuzzy images of David Brinkley, the history and traditions of the place bled into your unconscious like an indelible folkloric ink. It was something to take pride in, and history seemed very much alive and real there, not just a lot of words in a book by James Fennimore Cooper. It meant there was more to the land than just the telephone wires and the truckstops; there was more than just the fast food windows and the three channels on the TV, plus the radio and PBS. It practically reverberated up from out of the ground. The Shawnee general Tecumseh's last stand was there (The Battle of Fallen Timbers, 1794), and so too the ancient astronomical Serpent Mound. After nearly two hundred years, the walled garrison of Fort Meigs still stands above a rocky outcropping along the southern bank of the Maumee River, all testaments to the lives and times that had come before. It meant people were there long before any of the people I came from were there — strange, old, silent and distant people with names like Hess and Gonyer and Wolfe and Pope, who had themselves come from the Black Forest region of Germany and northern Quebec and Geneva and southern Ireland. And as for that side which ends abruptly back with that fateful knock on the door and that proverbial baby on the doorstep in the mid-1800s, maybe it's better we don't know where those ones came from, maybe it's what they wanted for all the rest of us, it's the only rationale for why that happened that I can imagine.

So I grew up in that place, in Ohio. It's a question everyone asks, Where are you from? I am from Ohio. People ask it everywhere, even in New York. Everyone is curious to know where everyone else is from. I think it is rather more telling to find out when a person is from. *When are you from?* I am from that Ohio in the 1970s. It is a place which doesn't exist anymore.

That same Mediterranean summer I was in Spain I was also in Ohio. The *Batman Year 100* deadlines were kicking my ass and I really needed a break, a chance to step outside myself, an escape. My brain felt like oatmeal, my body like a sack of twigs. My cousin Julia was getting married and I missed the place I had come from and I wanted to see my mom. I found myself stepping from a plane into a dingy urinal in Michigan, southbound from Detroit. I looked at myself in the mirror and I couldn't recognize the person I saw. It was me, but it wasn't. It was a person in a black button-up silk shirt and a two piece black velvet suit, in hand-made Italian crocodile skin shoes, with a ten dollar quarter-inch brushcut, wearing a gaudy silver skull ring on my right hand and a big belt buckle on my waist. It was all so ridiculous, so incongruous, so clownish that it made no sense.

I got a truckstop coffee and somebody asked me where I was from. Well, I live in New York, I said. It was saying something without saying much of anything. Hours earlier I awoke listening to the screeching breaks of a big rusty garbage truck just outside the window. I was lying on a couch in a friend's living room in South Williamsburg, Brooklyn, my bags all packed and ready, that much closer to the airport. As I dialed a car service and looked outside, I saw jagged, angular sights, I saw grey-blue shapes shot through with bright white shards. Rattling car engines spluttered morning exhaust under dirty black rubber wheels on the way to JFK. The only sound was an

amorphous, cacophonous chorus of car horns puncturing the 8am air with machine-gunnish staccatos. Out on the streets, everything was lined with black bags of trash, half torn-open, half-rifled, broken glass and chicken bones and wet cardboard scraps lining the gutters. This is the place where I live. I am from this New York, now.

At my mom's that same night, as the sun set, I sat in her backyard, rocked in a plastic chair and just listened. There was nothing but the smooth near-silence of the leaves, the gentle punctuations of twilling night animals far off in their trees. Buzzing insects and the wind, like sand tipping in a giant scale, like what it might sound like from inside a giant hourglass. It sounded like endless voices breathing out the word "shush", "shusssh"... And there were stars, billions of them. I'd sat through nights like this so many times before over so many years and never noticed it. How could it be I never noticed?

Restless, I walked into town and suddenly realized how much it had changed. I'd slinked through the place so many times before looking neither left nor right. This time I let it all sink in. This time I noticed. I sat in an Italian restaurant which didn't exist last time I was there and had a good meal at the bar, something which would've been impossible before. I struck up a conversation with the owner and we talked a while and he pulled out a bottle of good 25 year old port and we drank some as he told me about his plans to open a dance club in the old Opera house he'd just bought. He wanted to show it to me, but I already knew the place. It was a place we used to think was haunted and we'd invent stories about it to scare each other. Outside, the shiny new cars rolled by like slow sharks with blue neon underlights blinking, hiphop booming from the powerful Kenwood or Bose sound systems inside. Young blondes walked by with trendy haircuts and jeans, cel phones hooked under their ears, locked in the talk about this or that. It was a Friday night. I looked down at the hand which held the port and wondered, when did I become a person who would enjoy a

glass of port? When did I become someone with a shaved head and a velvet suit? When did I become someone strangers would want to talk to?

I used to be an outsider on the inside, and it was lonely and hard. It'd helped define me. Now I am an outsider on the outside and I'm being invited back in. When did all this happen? Where did that place when I came from go?

I walked back to my mom's puzzled, opened the copy of *Periplo Immaginario* which I had brought with me, and studied the pictures.

That day I had found Pratt's book, I sat on the sands of the Mediterranean and drank red wine and looked at the lines on the palm of my drawing hand. I wondered —without really wanting to know — which of the lines was my fate line. According to the legend of Corto Maltese, he had a gypsy read his palm, only to discover he had no fate line at all. Alarmed, Corto (whose name means "cut" in Italian or "short"in Spanish) slashes a line into his palm using his dead father's shaving razor. He then runs away from home and takes up a life at sea, like his father before him, and wanders the world without ever really finding a home. Strangely, this significant, formative event in the life of Corto Maltese — the slicing of the palm — is one Pratt never actually depicted in the stories. Neither did Pratt show us the eventual death of Corto Maltese. It is hinted Corto dies early on in the Spanish Civil War, so we know he never grows old. Maybe for Pratt to commit those fateful lines to paper would be for him to find he'd cut his own line too short. Cause of death — the end of a life-sustaining dream. He chose to leave it wide open.

Like Kurosawa's wandering ronin and Leone's cowboy drifters, Pratt's alter ego's fate is to float suspended in a self-contained sea of fiction-time, immune to the limits of the rest of us, beyond the reaches of age and change and doubt and death.

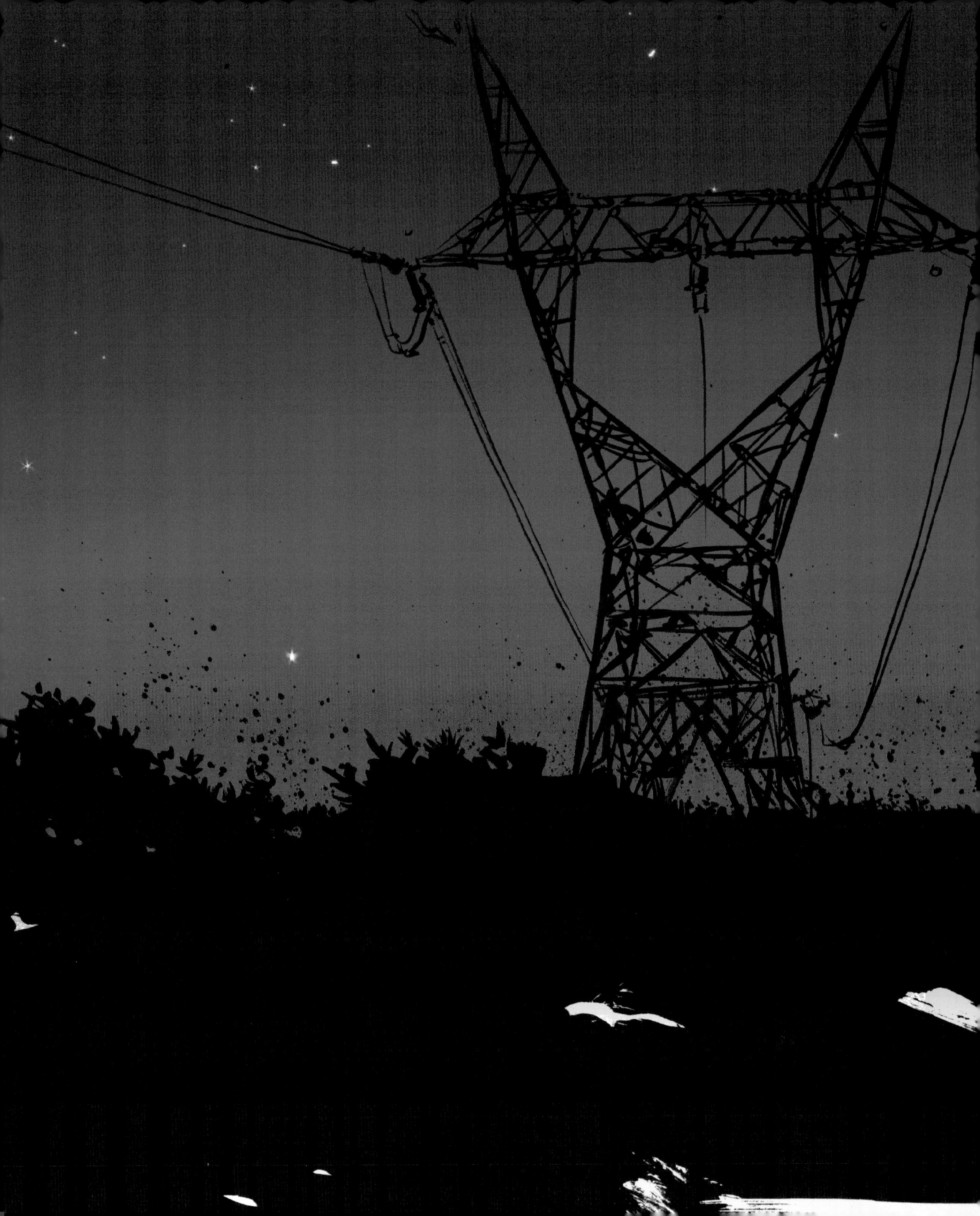

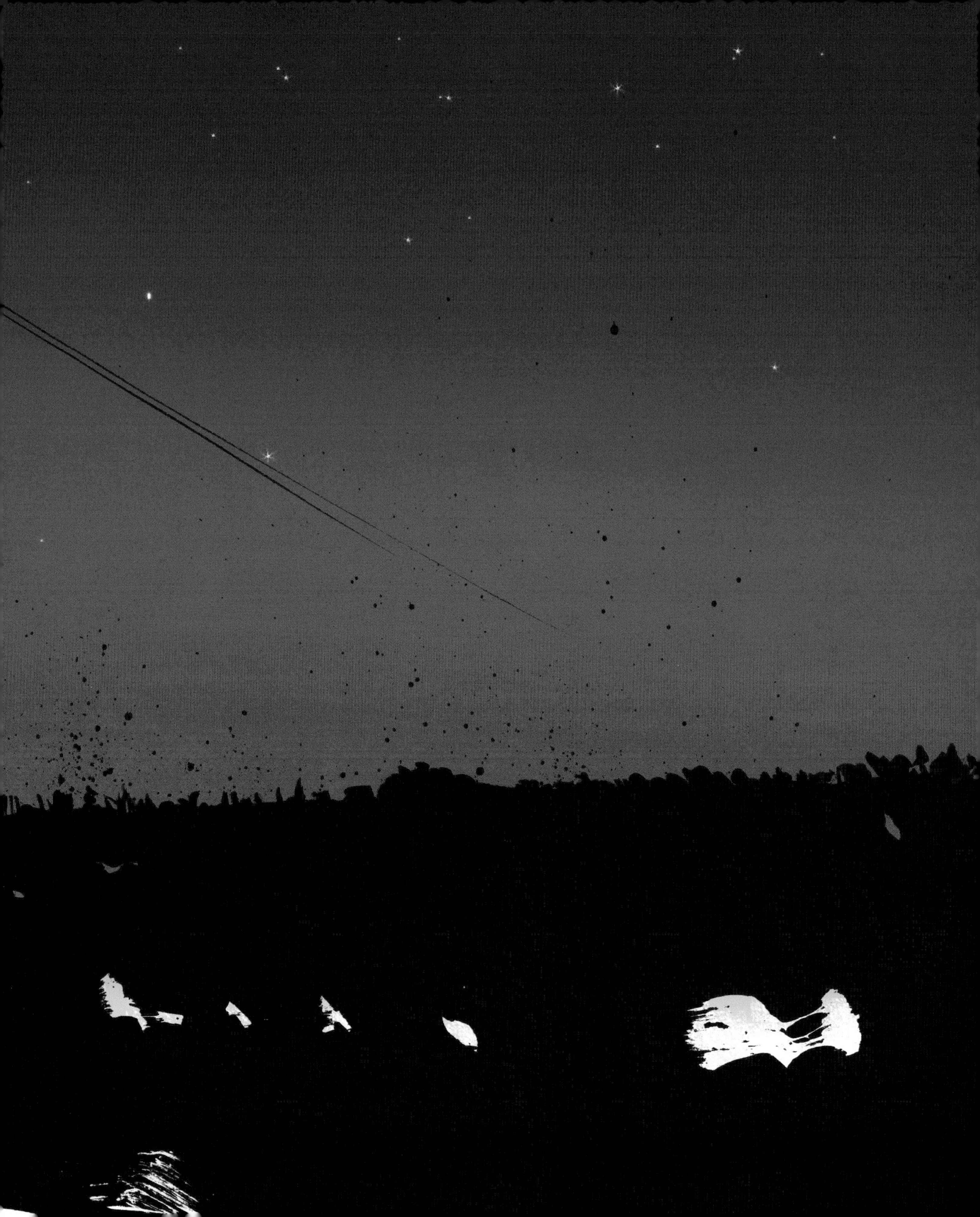

IN THE STUDIO

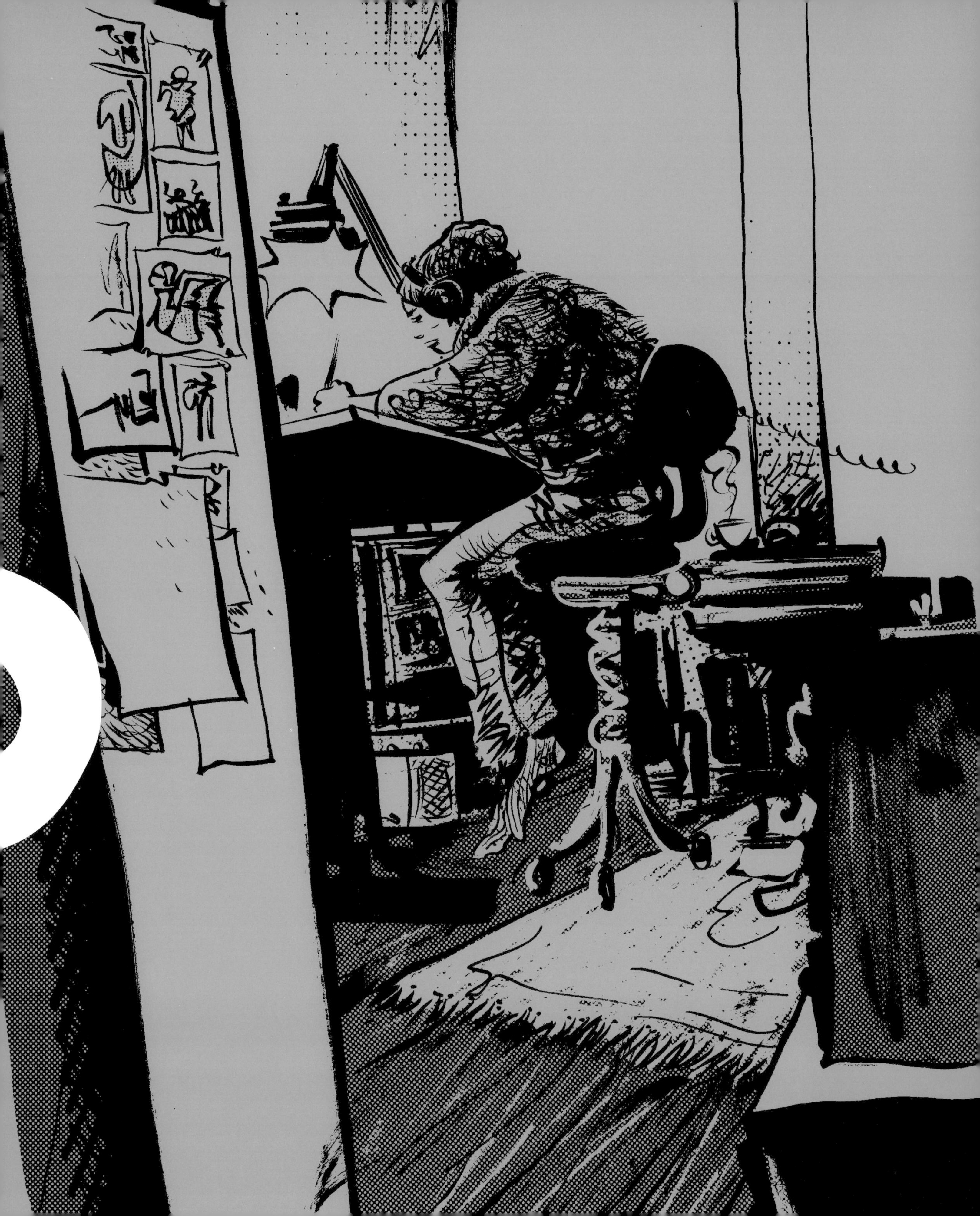

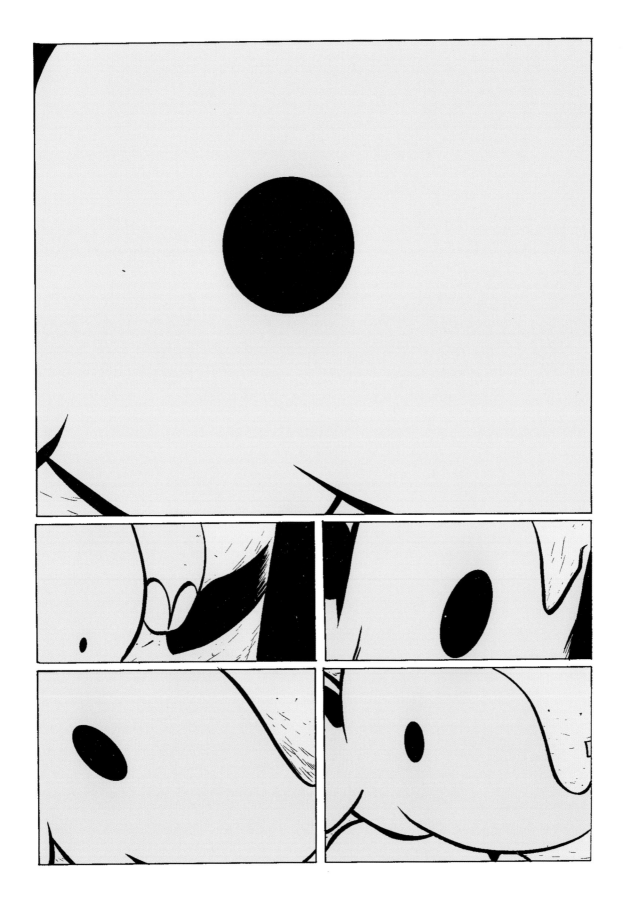

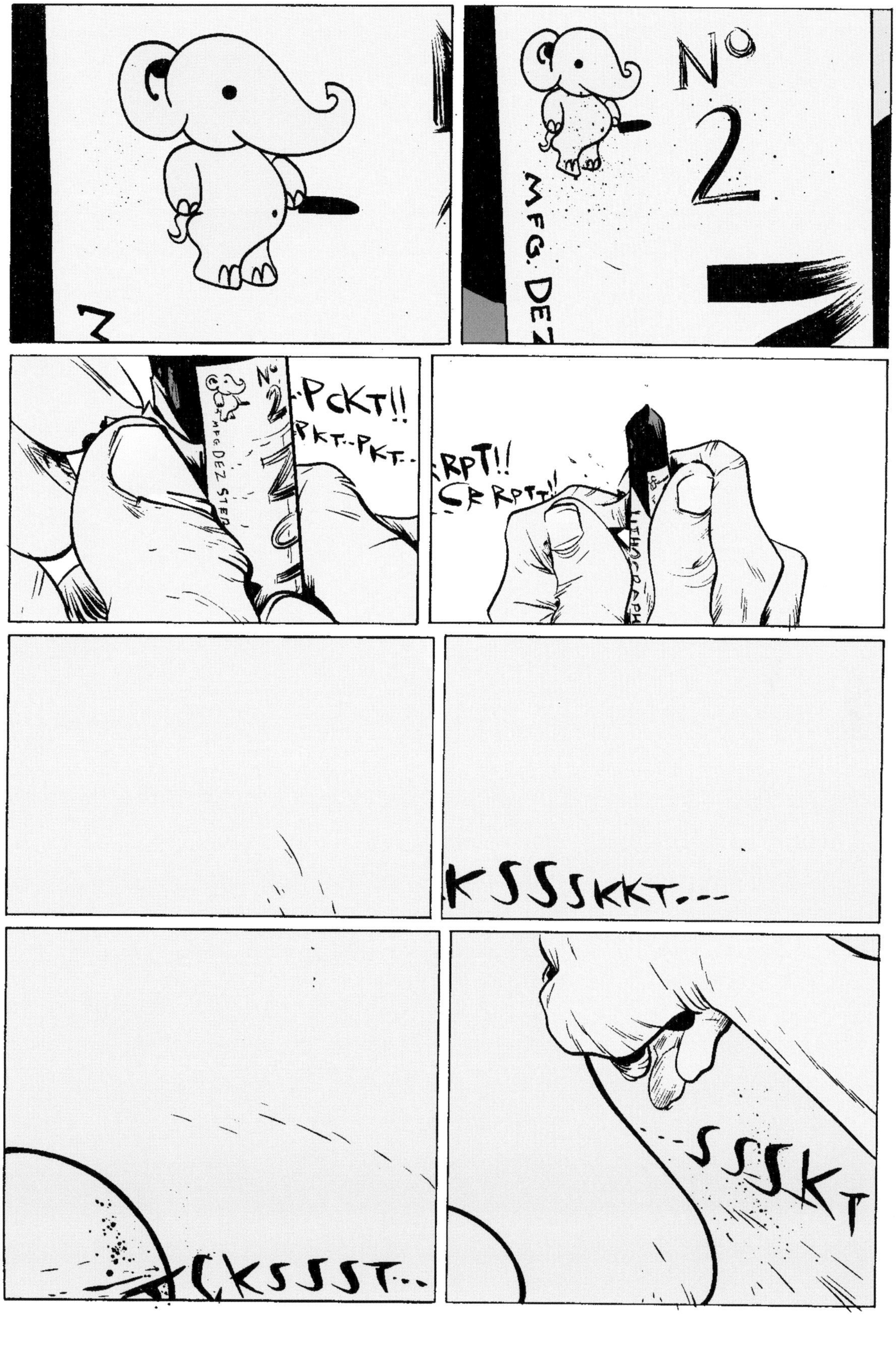

Nº 2
MFG. DEZ
..PCKT!!
PKT..PKT..
RPT!!
CRRPT!!
KSSSKKT...
CKSSSST..
SSSKT

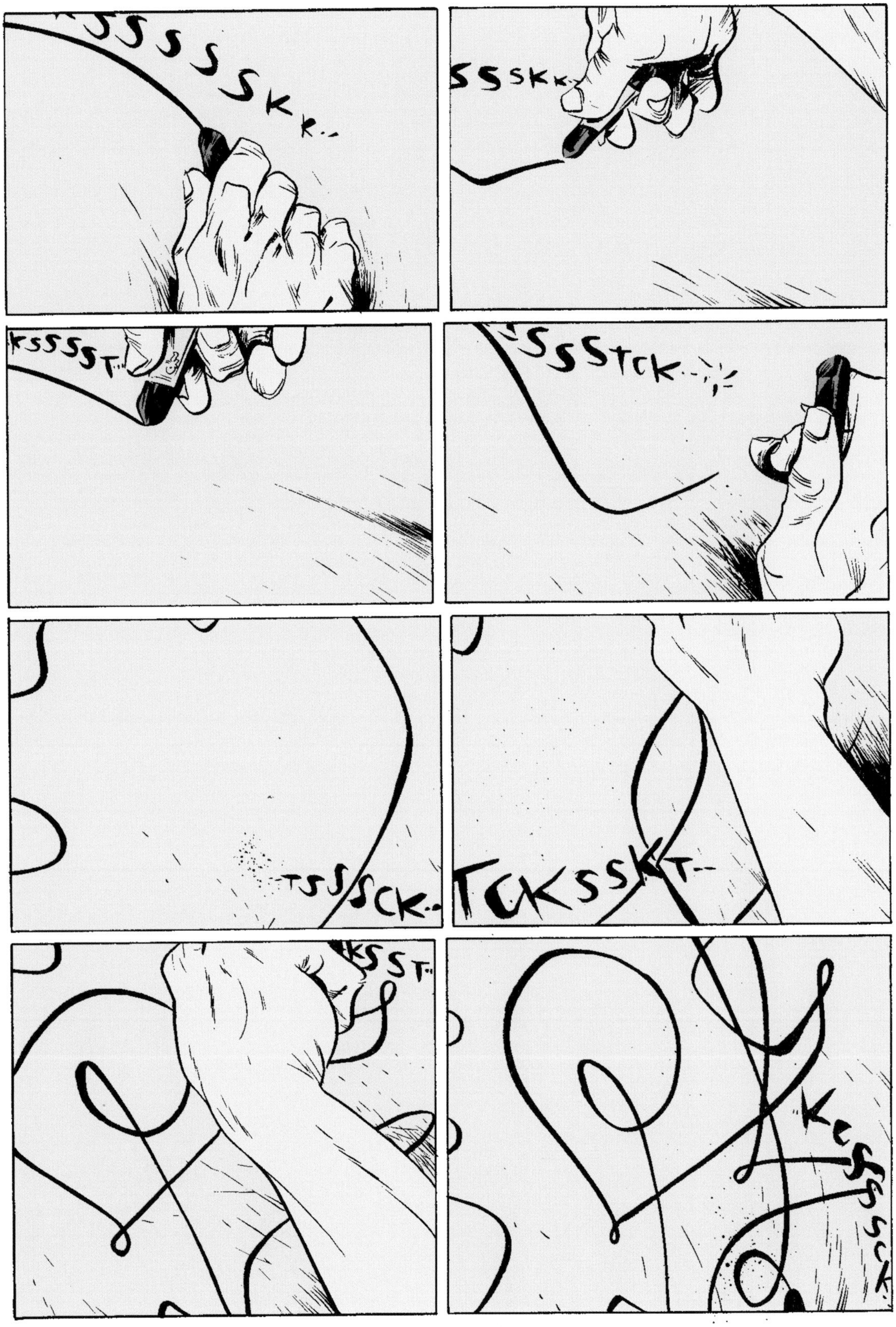
SSSSSSKK..
SSSKK..
KSSSST..
SSSTCK..
TSSSCK..
TCKSSKT..
KSST..
KSSSSCK.

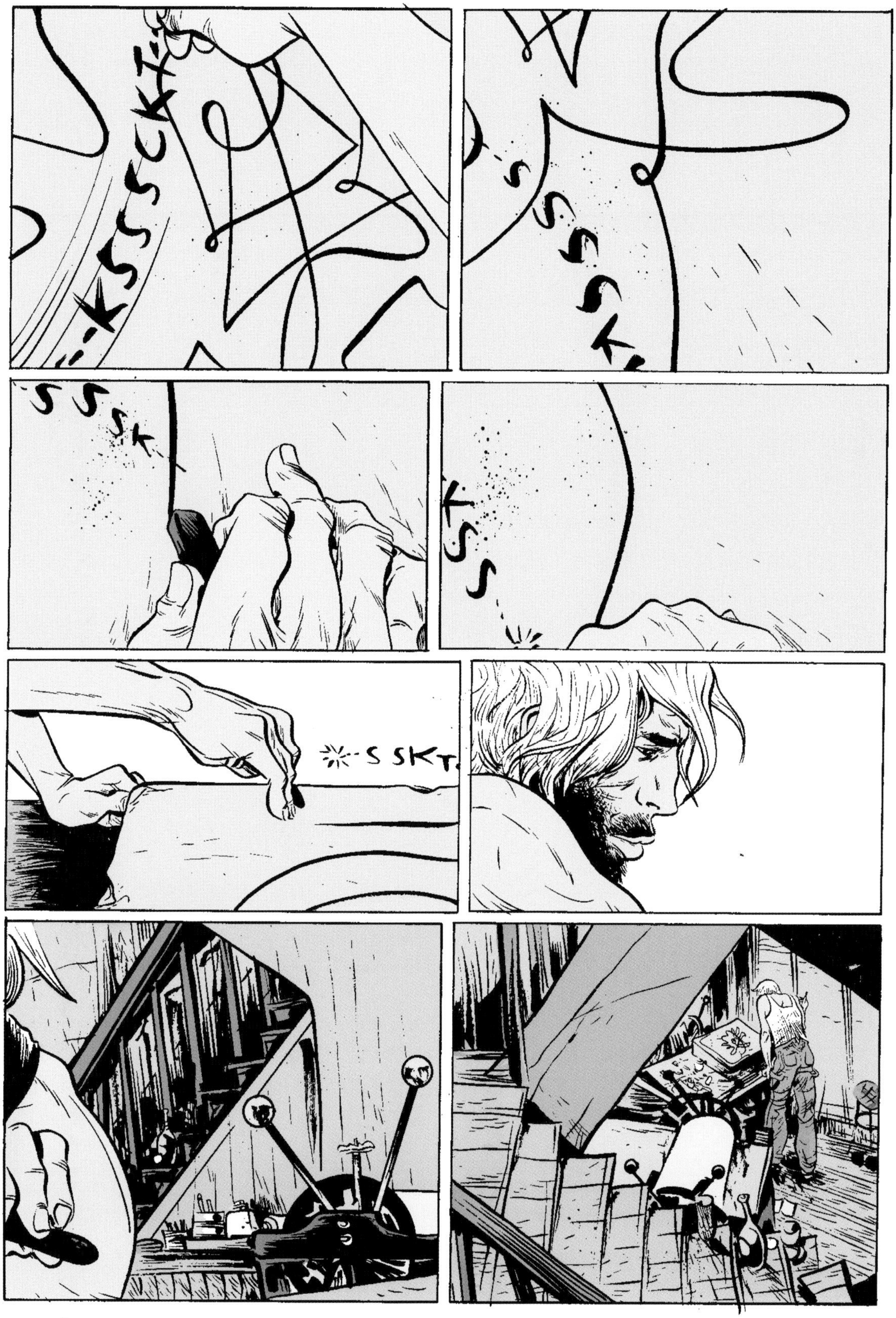
KSSSCKT
SSSK
S SKT

WHAT TO DO WHEN IT GOES AWAY AND HOW TO GET IT BACK

There are different ways to work. I find the best is to do nothing but make comics for up to three days straight, breaking only to eat and sleep. If it's more than three days, the work's usually no good, or worse, even bad. Work three days, take off a day. That's ideal — that's like a sensory deprivation tank in reverse. I like to wake up and get right into it, no distractions — no radio, no television, no phone calls, no internet, no door buzzers, no clock, nothing. No interface at all except the eye, the hand, the drawing tool

and the paper, maybe some music. Although I tend to do the serious work at night when it is quiet and you have fewer distractions, I find I get my best, most fertile ideas first thing in the morning, when my head is still swimming in the abstract shapes of dreams. The ideas then come like vague, half-heard voices, fuzzy and pliant, wanting for form and definition. I prefer to wake up and make coffee, sit at the drawing table, and begin writing or drawing, having a fresh, sleep-wrapped head and a smooth, clean slate for a brain.

This isn't possible on mornings when you wake up, having gone out the night before, drinking, laughing, talking, carousing, arguing, bullshitting. Mornings like that you wake up groggy and disturbed, reviewing the events, even if they are completely uninteresting, even if they are annoying. Mornings like that, I think pacing is a good idea. Pace, drink coffee, and let the thoughts unravel like a script for a film written on a scroll of toilet paper, image after image, scene after scene, line after line, until they're all thought of and used up. Once you've used them all up, you can start thinking your own thoughts again.

This three day stretch has always been my preferred method of working, and it is a method which has worked well for years and years. However, I must admit I haven't had three days of unbroken work time for longer than I can remember. I've had to build a trapdoor for the muse so she can come and go quickly. The luxury of the locked door is something I've had to leave behind. I accept this condition now as necessary, but not necessarily as permanent. I'm not comfortable with it. To live in Manhattan is to sometimes by default be forced to take a sabbatical from your own peace of mind. Now there is only a thin membrane between the inner spirit and the world outside. Now the world is pressing in and it seems like I am constantly looking at the clock, counting down the hours until the next meeting, returning emails, trudging something from UPS or Fed Ex up and down the stairs, tripping over boxes, doing online research for this or that, hearing the couple next door fighting or some delivery guy slide another neon green menu under my door for someplace I'll never go. Sometimes late at night I'm struck with the uncontrollable urge to pull back the drapes to check the fire escape to see if there is anyone standing outside waiting to come in. There's never anybody there, it's the residue of the day.

When I started making comics, I was always working in what I called the Hugo Pratt method, patiently working on a series of pictures in sequential order, starting with panel one, page one, and going panel by panel until the thing was done. This

tedious method needed refinement, and it gradually evolved into an assembly line procedure during the making of the original *THB* series, where I'd pencil, letter, ink and finish 16 pages at a time, using tape to hang up two rows of eight pages of comics side by side. Lined up in long rows, the pages stretch from about sternum level to just within arm's reach, each in various stages of completion. Working within an assembly line such as this is the most effective method for producing

comics I know of, and I credit it with how I could manage to finish seventy or eighty completely print ready pages a month, which was necessary sometimes while working for Kodansha (not that it was easy or particularly fun — or that the results looked that good). With this assembly line approach, I can comfortably finish about 30 pages a month on a project like *THB* or *Battling Boy*, and up to 45 if I am diligent. For some reason, by contrast, the work on *Batman Year 100* was very tedious and slow, although I used the same method. Something about that

project was like wading through a swamp — or scaling a sheer wall of granite. What should've taken about 8 months took two and a half years. I could manage to produce only about fifteen pages a month if I was lucky.

My interest level for a series of given images fluctuates throughout a work period, and I find it easier to work on many pages — and as many as three different projects — at once. That way of working is like skipping rope. It is somehow better to be able to jump from one project and set of creative concerns to another at will — it lets you have some sweet with the sour. Sweet for me are things like the pretty girls, the robots and super-meks, organic forms like trees or fruit, animals — anything curvy and expressive. The sour would definitely be things like cars and crowd scenes, cutlery, wooden ships and wagons, watches and computer keyboards and some types of architecture. It's a little more complicated to jump from different types of work — from, say, comics to designing patterns for camouflage prints for the lining of a jacket. The different types of brainwork required for both comics and design are almost moving at different speeds or frequencies, and not so easy to combine together within a given period. It sometimes seems half of the actual job of comics and design is just sitting there, thinking. Inking with a brush is by far the most fun part of the job, but it is also usually the last part and often the shortest. "Wait long and act fast, like the tiger," is an old Tibetan expression which I always think of when I think about inking.

The places where I've lived and worked are all pretty much the same — spartan cells with white walls and hopefully good lighting, facing away from the street, designed to facilitate the successions of looming deadlines. Eventually these rooms become deadline veterans, and for all their battles get covered in layers of books and boxes and eraser shavings and junk, and their floors get covered in shoes and dirty clothes. Stacks of reference materials as tall as your kneecap sit in precarious piles to the left and the right and behind the drawing table. To the right there are always scraps of cardboard and old xeroxes, hundreds of sheets of wadded up, discarded paper covered with a growing film of eraser rubbings burying the green plastic stencils used for making circles and ellipses. There are music discs and old cassette tapes stacked in rows like flat sonic vehicles, piles of DVD-Rs and CD-Rs for burning files. On the walls surrounding the drawing table, there are lots of little drawings and reference photos, tacked up alongside postcards and photocopies and whatever else I might need to look at, to keep me inspired or help me get done something needing to be done.

Deadlines are now the only time I get three days of uninterrupted time to work, and it is usually a frantic and stomach-turning blur. You simply can't only work when you feel inspired, that's the first thing you learn on deadline. You can't always rely on the caffeine or the juice in the iPod. You can't afford to only work when you feel "it".

"It" is that precious quality which lets you make artwork which is better than good and sometimes "it" allows for work which is truly inspired. I learned early on, you can't rely on "it" to get you out of a mess. It is capricious and wispy, disappearing for periods at a time, sometimes only half returning, or returning for only half as long as you need it. It's also a problem to have to work without "it." That is a killer. Too much of that kind of thing will sink you into a strange kind of self-loathing, hard to describe, but which makes it hard to face yourself in the mirror. And sometimes it just inexplicably goes away. But you can get "it" to come and stay with you when you have great discipline and work hard without distractions. That

is why I've always liked working for three days straight, and why I built the trapdoor for "it" so it can come and go quickly when I lost the three-day luxury. I find if you keep on working until "it" comes back, "it" always does eventually. It eventually gets curious and wants to see what you've been doing while it was away. When I'm feeling most discouraged, and begin thinking I've lost it, I recognize this as simply the lowest ebb of the process of making art and ride it out. Looking back on Kirby's work, or Toth's, they seemed to almost always have had "it," even in their obvious mistakes and their sloppy work. I get mad at myself, then, for the vain luxury of complaint. Deadlines, bah. You have no excuse, I say, or something in me says. You live in a part of the world where you can do just about anything you want. Not everything but anything. No one is firing mortar shells at your block. There are no attack dogs chewing at you, no mustard gases perforating your lungs. No one is poaching you for your tusks. Your eyes work, your head works, you've got no excuse, muse or no muse. So I try brewing coffee, then change the music on the CD player or look at some comics. Nothing helps. So I leave my place. I don't do the laundry, stuffed into the crevasses of the closet, I don't do my dishes, stacked in their sullen sinkside station. I don't shower or shave. I don't pay the bills, in their dizzying stack on the rickety table. I don't call my grandma who misses me and wishes I'd call more often. Instead, then, as I do now, when the the deadline stress is too great, I wait until I'm hungry, then, go eat Indian food. A good fish curry with garlic paratha, no butter. Aloo Matar, and Raita. Mint chutney over some Lamb Vindaloo or a sizzling Tandoori platter. And some good red wine, preferably in what Hemmingway called "a clean, well-lit place", where you can hear some good music and sit alone, pull out your problem and look at it again from a different point of view. And maybe more coffee, no dessert.

This ritual is intended to brace you for the hard time ahead, and let you celebrate it, too. After all, the deadlines are part of this lifestyle, take it or leave it, nothing to be

scared of. And if you sometimes take a week off, or maybe even two, and you do absolutely nothing, you're only really stealing it from some other week yet to come, and regardless, every third or fourth week seems to be this sleepless, fitful, awful deadline time, this stretch of fifteen hour a day acceleration. And there's nothing to do but learn to love this, even after the romance wears off. You must love this stress and learn how to burn with it, not to be burnt by it, otherwise it is a miserable servitude without much recompense. This is your choice, this is your garden. Now cultivate it.

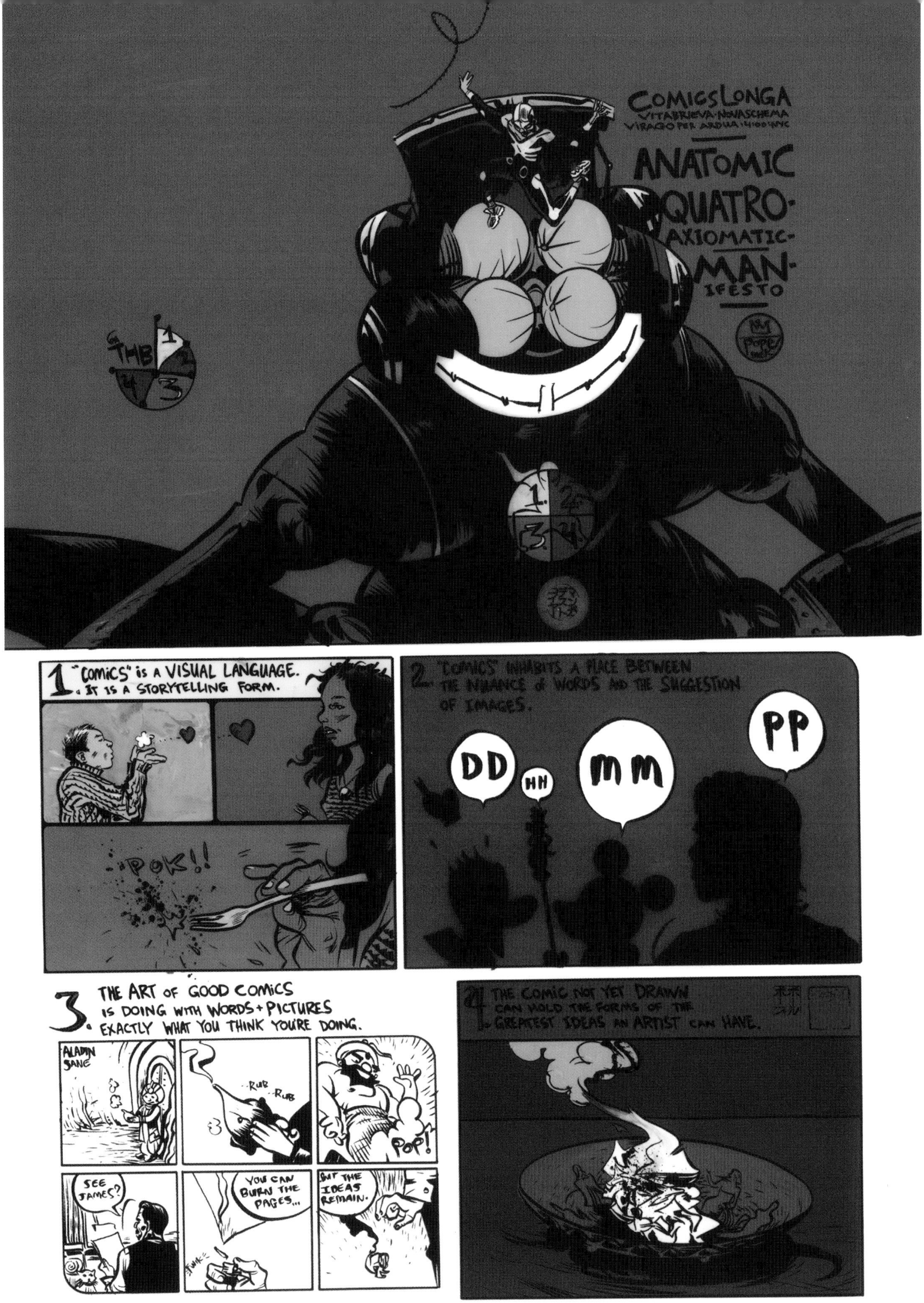
COMICS LONGA
VITA BREVA · NOVA SCHEMA
VIRAGO PER ARDUA · 4:00 · NYC
ANATOMIC
QUATRO-
AXIOMATIC-
MAN-
IFESTO
THB
1
2
3
4
1. "COMICS" IS A VISUAL LANGUAGE.
IT IS A STORYTELLING FORM.
POK!!
2. "COMICS" INHABITS A PLACE BETWEEN
THE NUANCE of WORDS AND THE SUGGESTION
OF IMAGES.
DD
HH
mm
PP
3. THE ART of GOOD COMICS
IS DOING WITH WORDS + PICTURES
EXACTLY WHAT YOU THINK YOU'RE DOING.
ALADIN SANE
RUB RUB
POP!
SEE JAMES?
YOU CAN BURN THE PAGES...
BUT THE IDEAS REMAIN.
4. THE COMIC NOT YET DRAWN
CAN HOLD THE FORMS OF THE
GREATEST IDEAS AN ARTIST CAN HAVE.

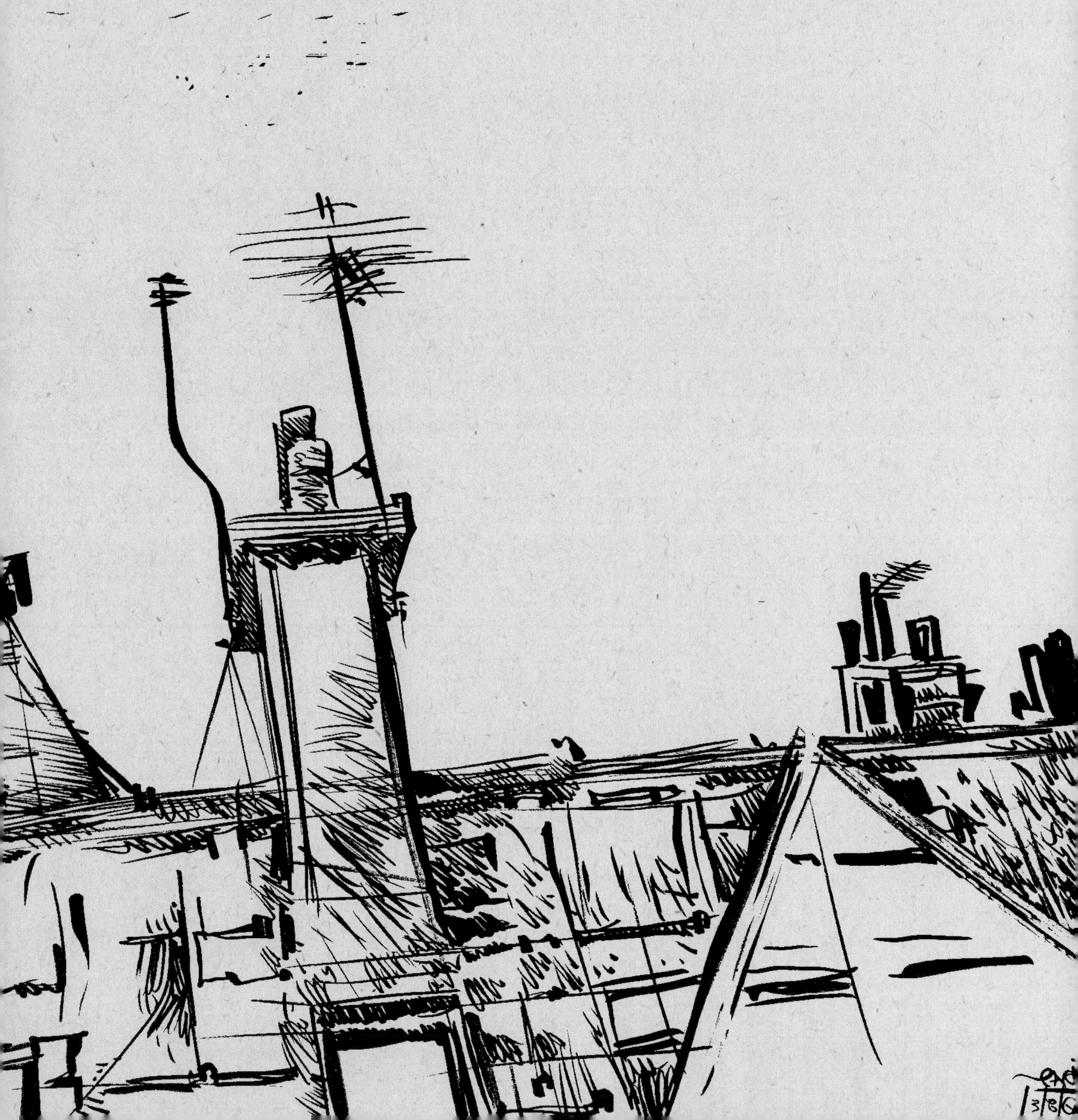

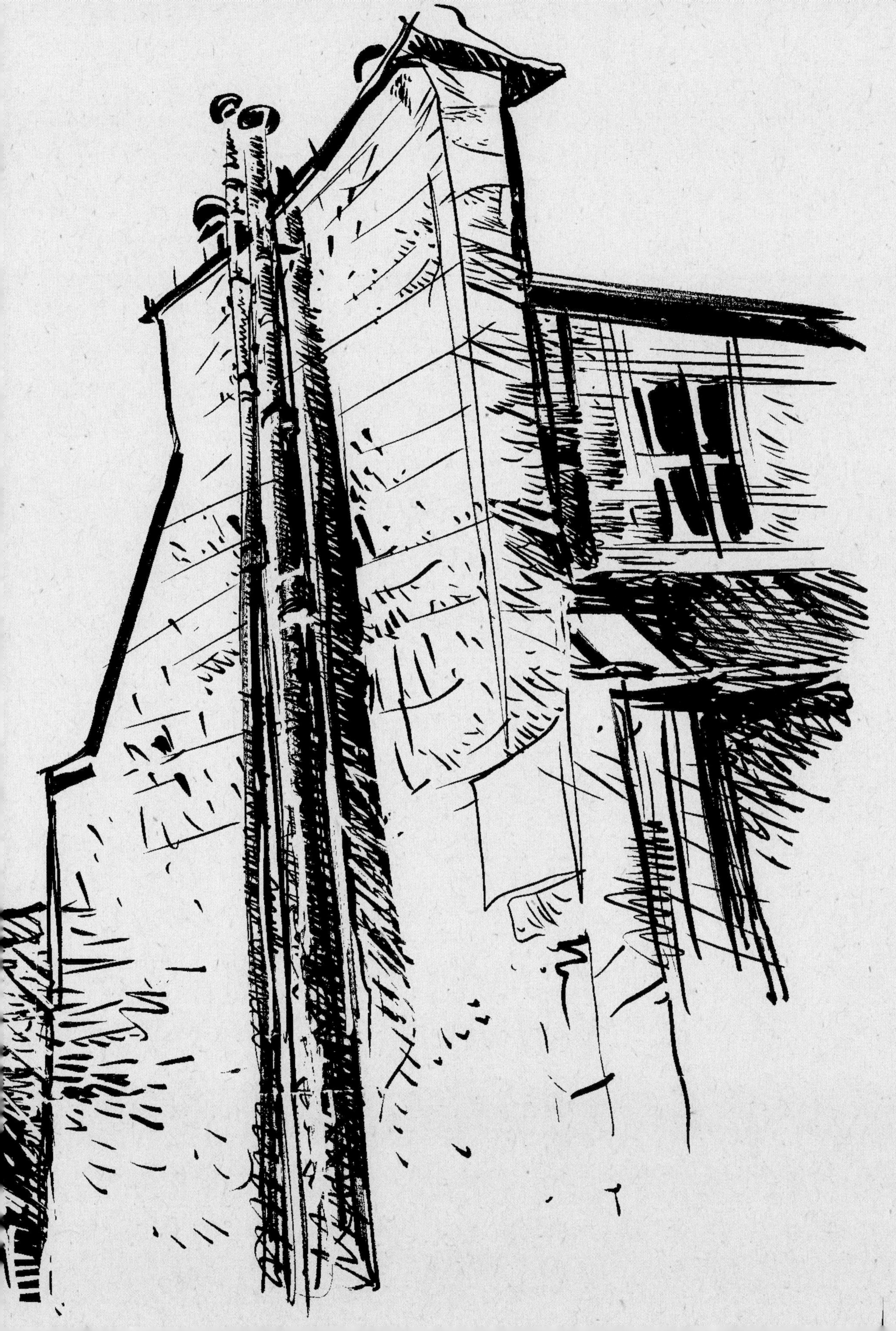

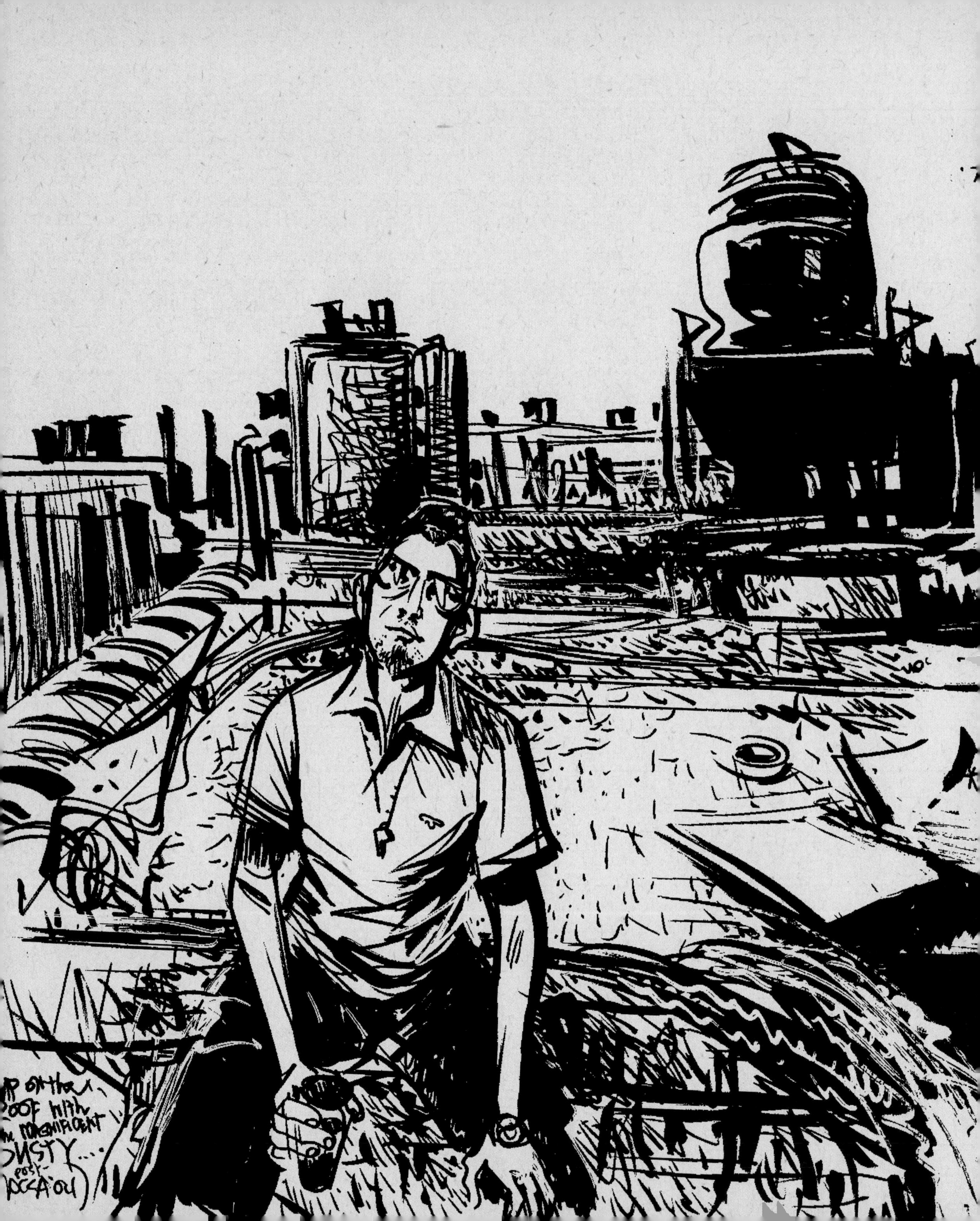
P on the
OOF with
MAGNIFICENT
USTY....
post-
CCA '04

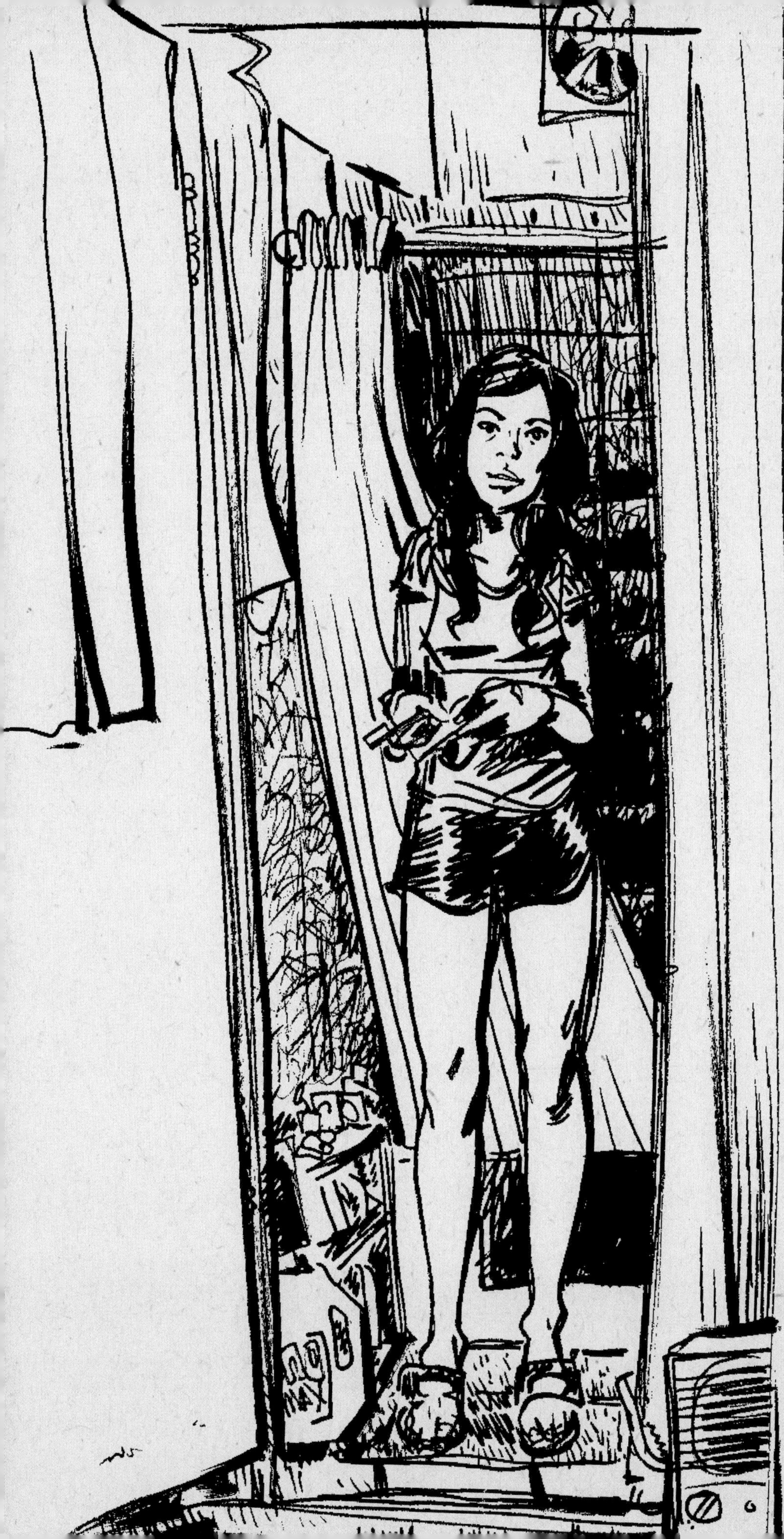

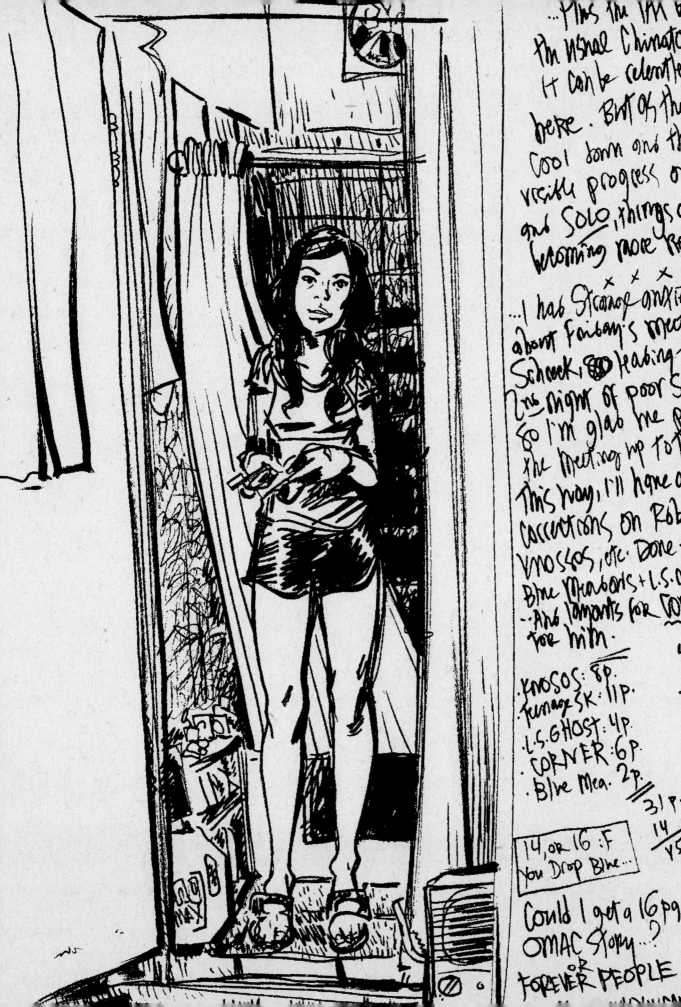

...Plus the 1M out w/ the usual Chinatown woes: It can be relentless down here. But as the days cool down and there is visible progress on THB and SOLO, things are becoming more relaxed.

× × ×

...I had strange anxiety dreams about Friday's meeting w/ Schreck, leading to a 2nd night of poor sleep, so I'm glad he pushed the meeting up to Thursday. This way, I'll have all the corrections on Robin, Knossos, etc. Done -- plus Blue Meadows + L.S.M Ghost --And layouts for Corner for him.

- Knosos: 8p.
- Teenage SK: 11p.
- L.S. GHOST: 4p.
- CORNER: 6p.
- Blue Mea. 2p.

31p.

45
31
14

31
14
45p.

14, or 16: If You Drop Blue...

Could I get a 16 pg. OMAC Story...? or FOREVER PEOPLE

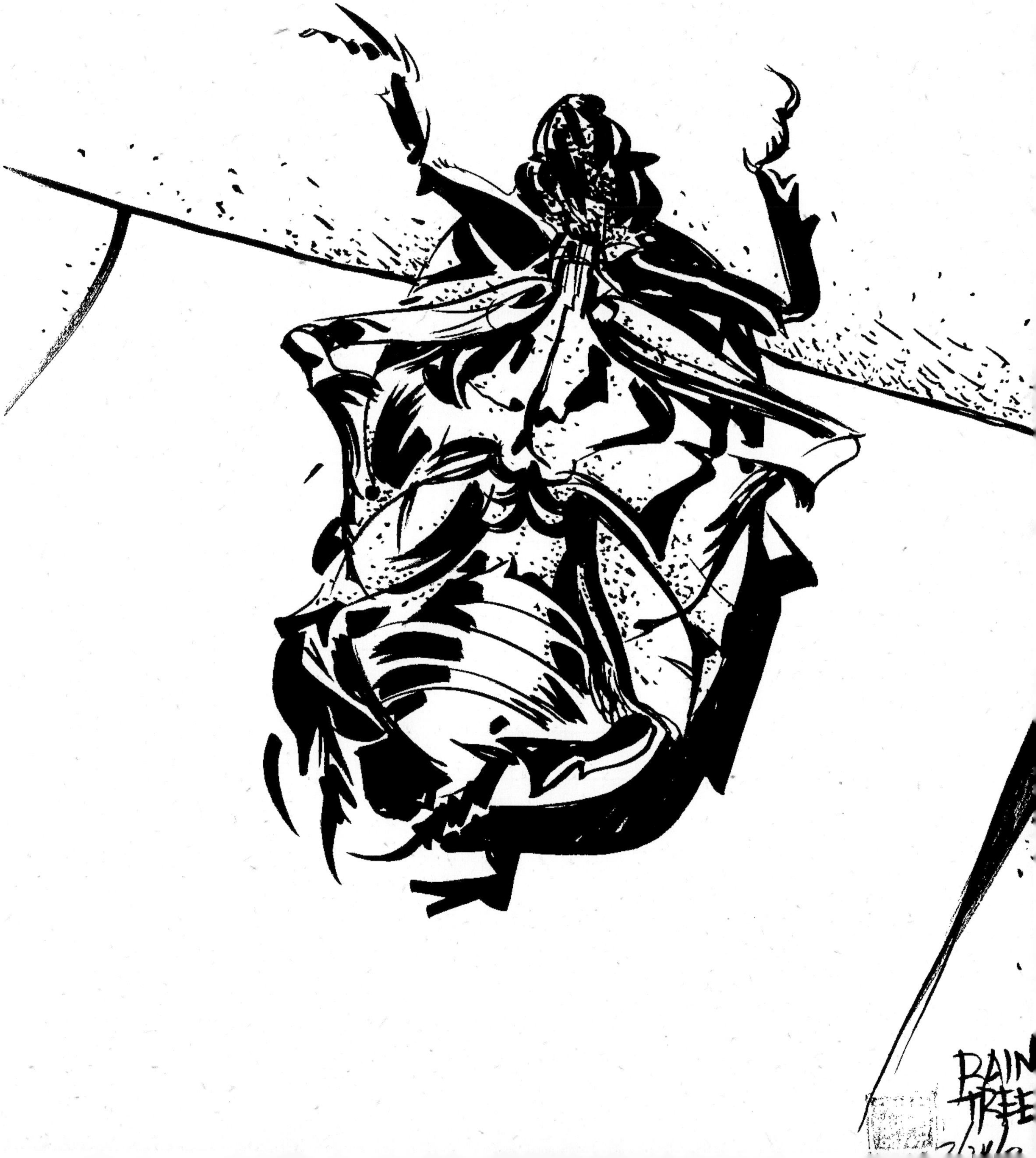
RAIN
TREE

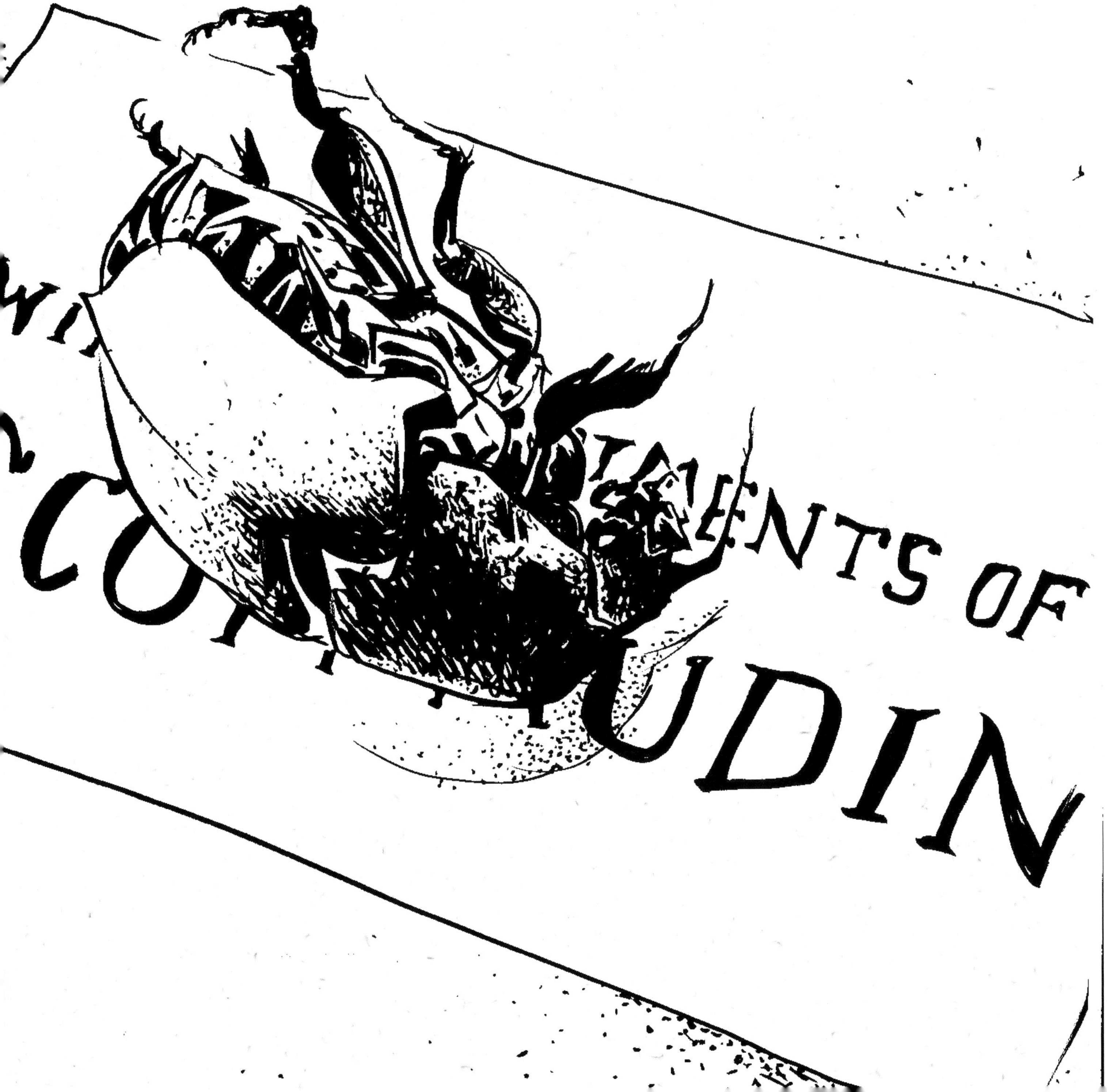
ENTS OF
UDIN

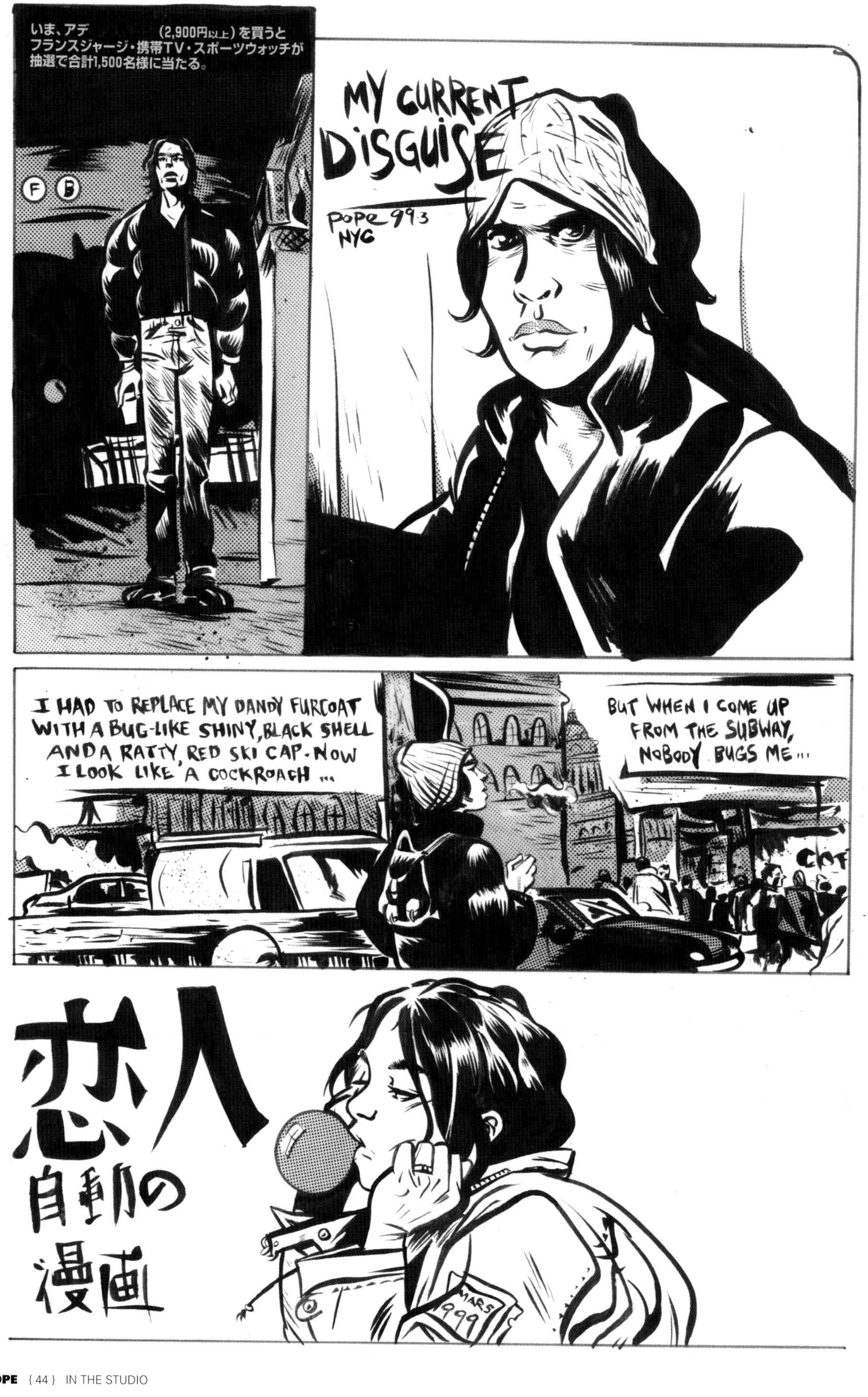

いま、アデ (2,900円以上) を買うと
フランスジャージ・携帯TV・スポーツウォッチが
抽選で合計1,500名様に当たる。
MY CURRENT DISGUISE
POPE 99.3 NYC
I HAD TO REPLACE MY DANDY FURCOAT WITH A BUG-LIKE SHINY, BLACK SHELL AND A RATTY, RED SKI CAP- NOW I LOOK LIKE A COCKROACH ...
BUT WHEN I COME UP FROM THE SUBWAY, NOBODY BUGS ME...
恋人
自動の
漫画
MARS 1999

The Girl who said "NO"

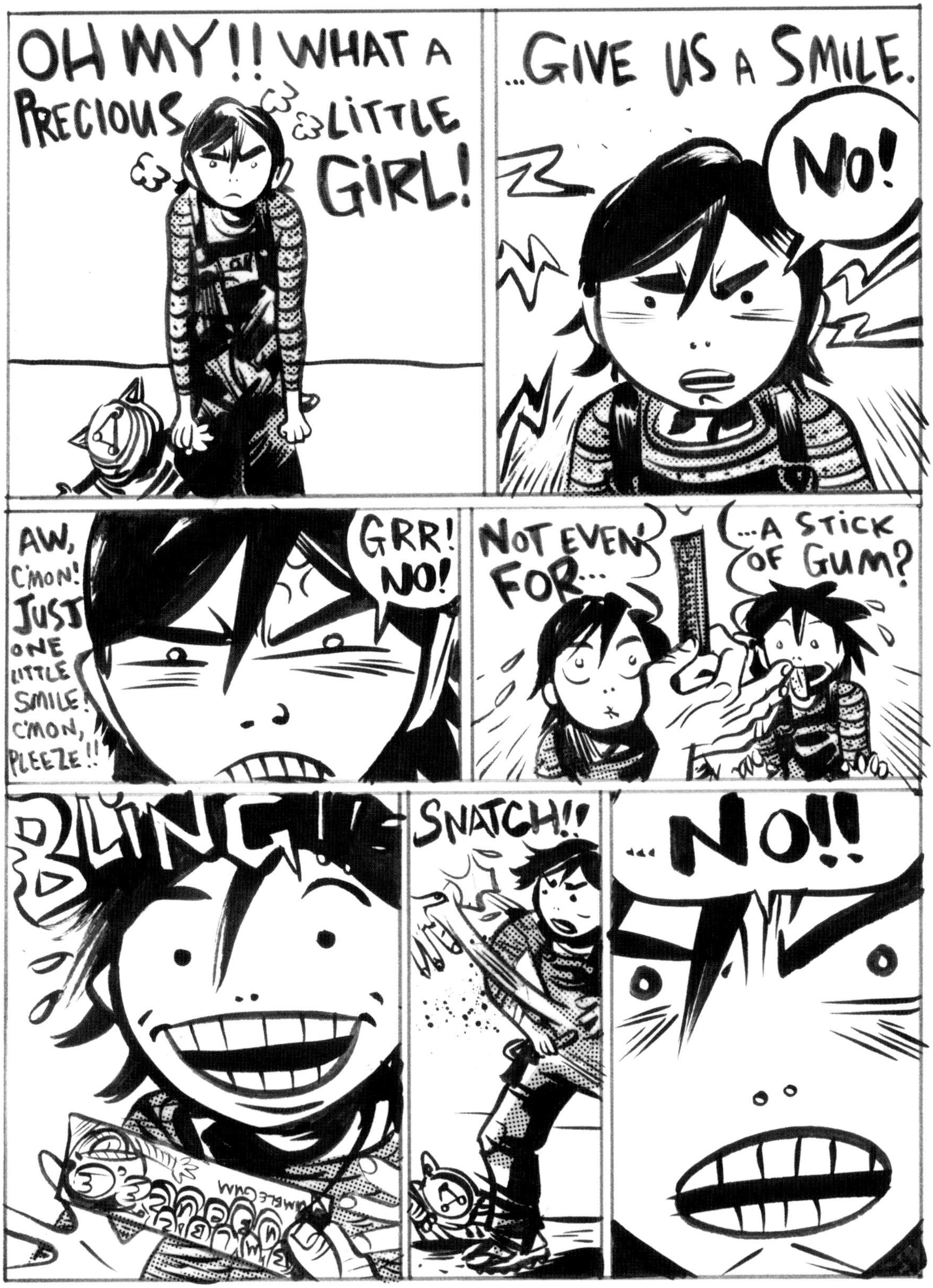
OH MY!! WHAT A PRECIOUS LITTLE GIRL!
...GIVE US A SMILE.
NO!
AW, C'MON! JUST ONE LITTLE SMILE! C'MON, PLEEZE!!
GRR! NO!
NOT EVEN FOR...
...A STICK OF GUM?
BLING!!
SNATCH!!
...NO!!

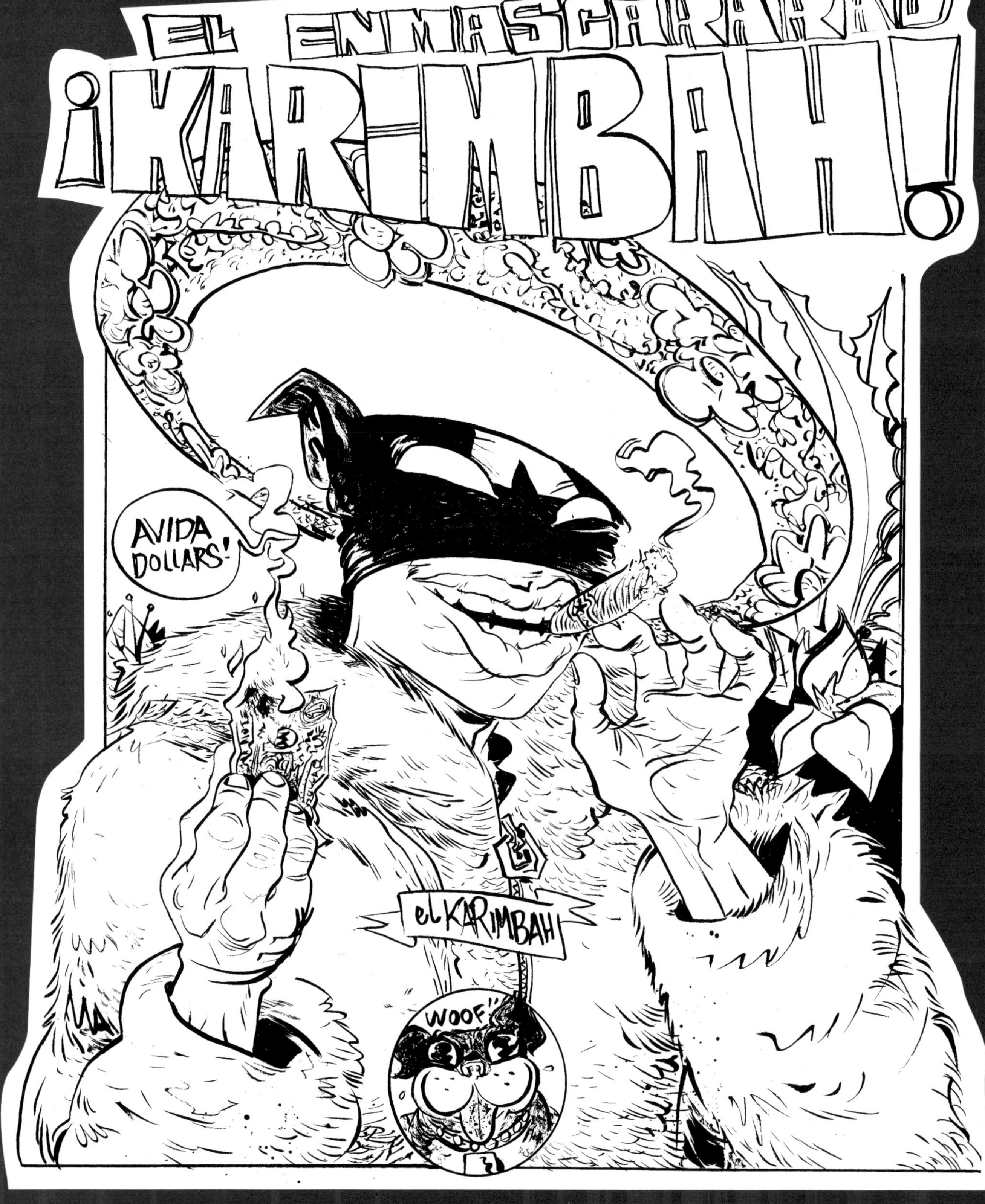
EL ENMASCARADO
¡KARIMBAH!
AVIDA DOLLARS!
el KARIMBAH
WOOF!!

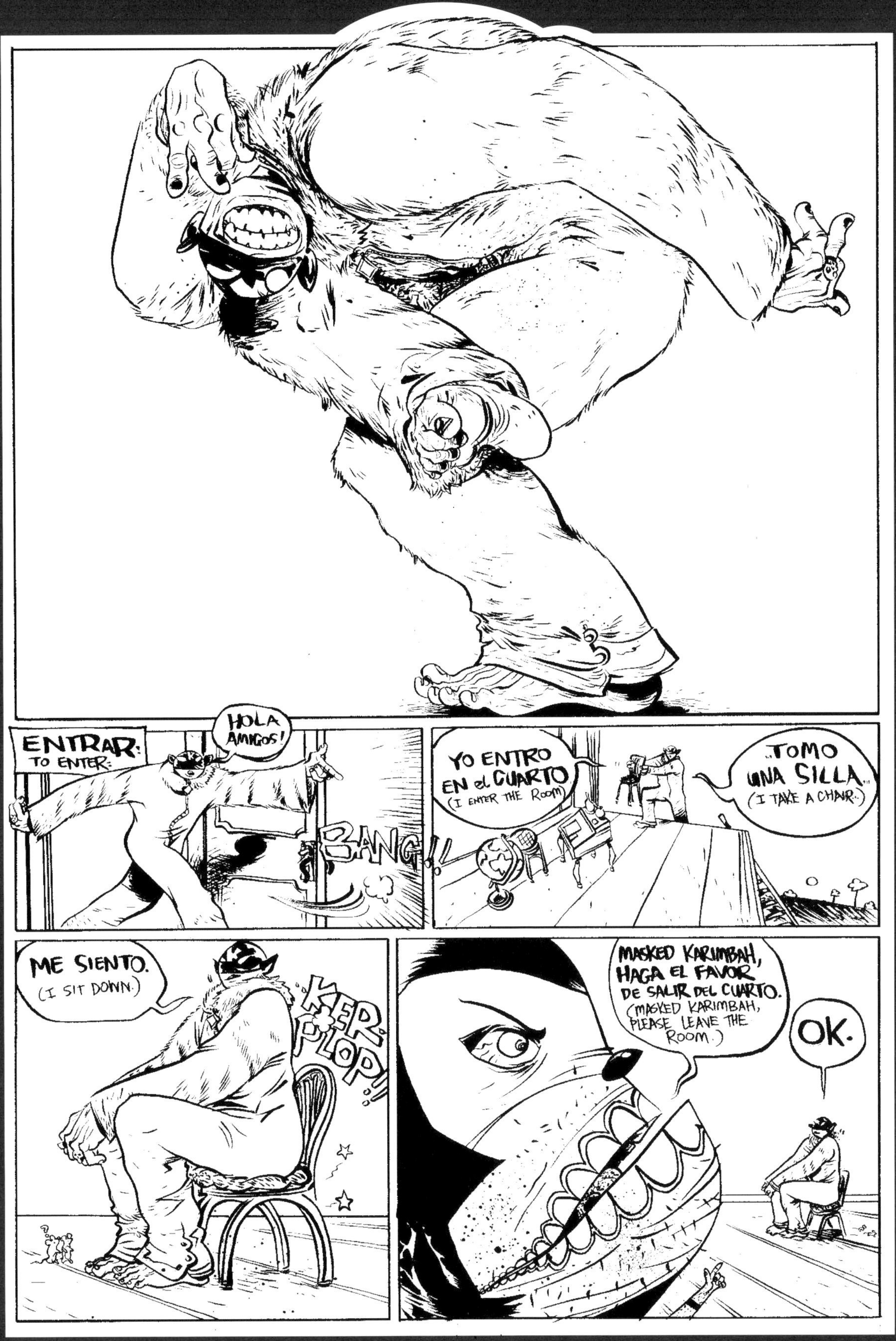
ENTRAR:
TO ENTER:
HOLA AMIGOS!
BANG!!
YO ENTRO EN el CUARTO (I ENTER THE ROOM)
..TOMO UNA SILLA.. (I TAKE A CHAIR..)
ME SIENTO. (I SIT DOWN.)
KER-PLOP!!
MASKED KARIMBAH, HAGA EL FAVOR DE SALIR DEL CUARTO. (MASKED KARIMBAH, PLEASE LEAVE THE ROOM.)
OK.

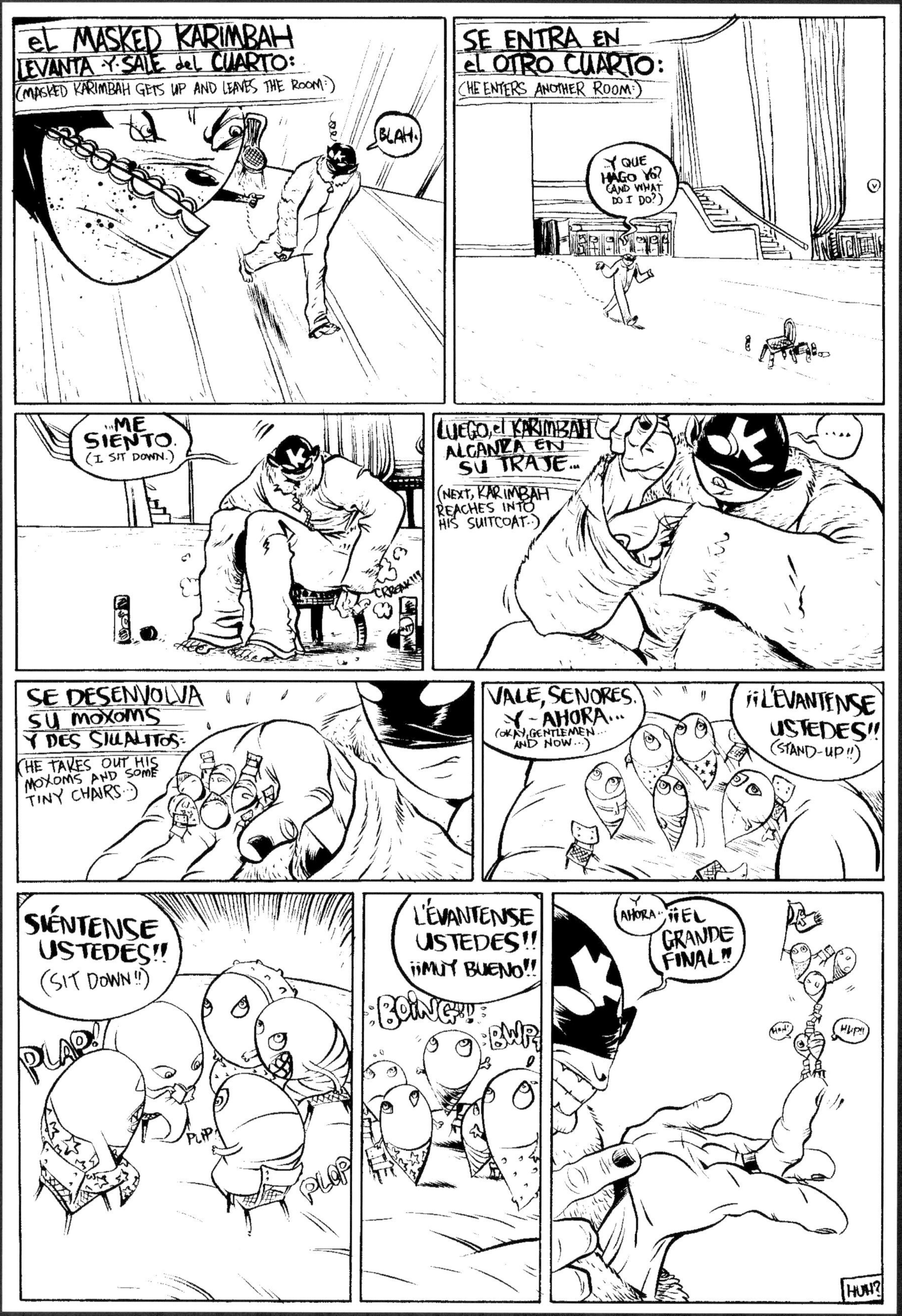
eL MASKED KARIMBAH LEVANTA ·Y· SALE deL CUARTO:
(MASKED KARIMBAH GETS UP AND LEAVES THE ROOM:)
BLAH.
SE ENTRA EN eL OTRO CUARTO:
(HE ENTERS ANOTHER ROOM:)
..Y QUE HAGO YO? (AND WHAT DO I DO?)
...ME SIENTO. (I SIT DOWN.)
CREAK!!!
LUEGO, el KARIMBAH ALCANZA EN SU TRAJE...
(NEXT, KARIMBAH REACHES INTO HIS SUITCOAT.)
...
SE DESENVOLVA SU MOXOMS Y DES SILLALITOS:
(HE TAKES OUT HIS MOXOMS AND SOME TINY CHAIRS..)
VALE, SENORES. ·Y· AHORA... (OKAY, GENTLEMEN... AND NOW...)
¡¡L'EVANTENSE USTEDES!! (STAND-UP!!)
SIÉNTENSE USTEDES!! (SIT DOWN!!)
PLAP!
PLIP
PLOP
L'EVANTENSE USTEDES!! ¡¡MUY BUENO!!
BOING!!
BWP
Y AHORA..
¡¡EL GRANDE FINAL!!
HUP!
HUP!!
HUH?

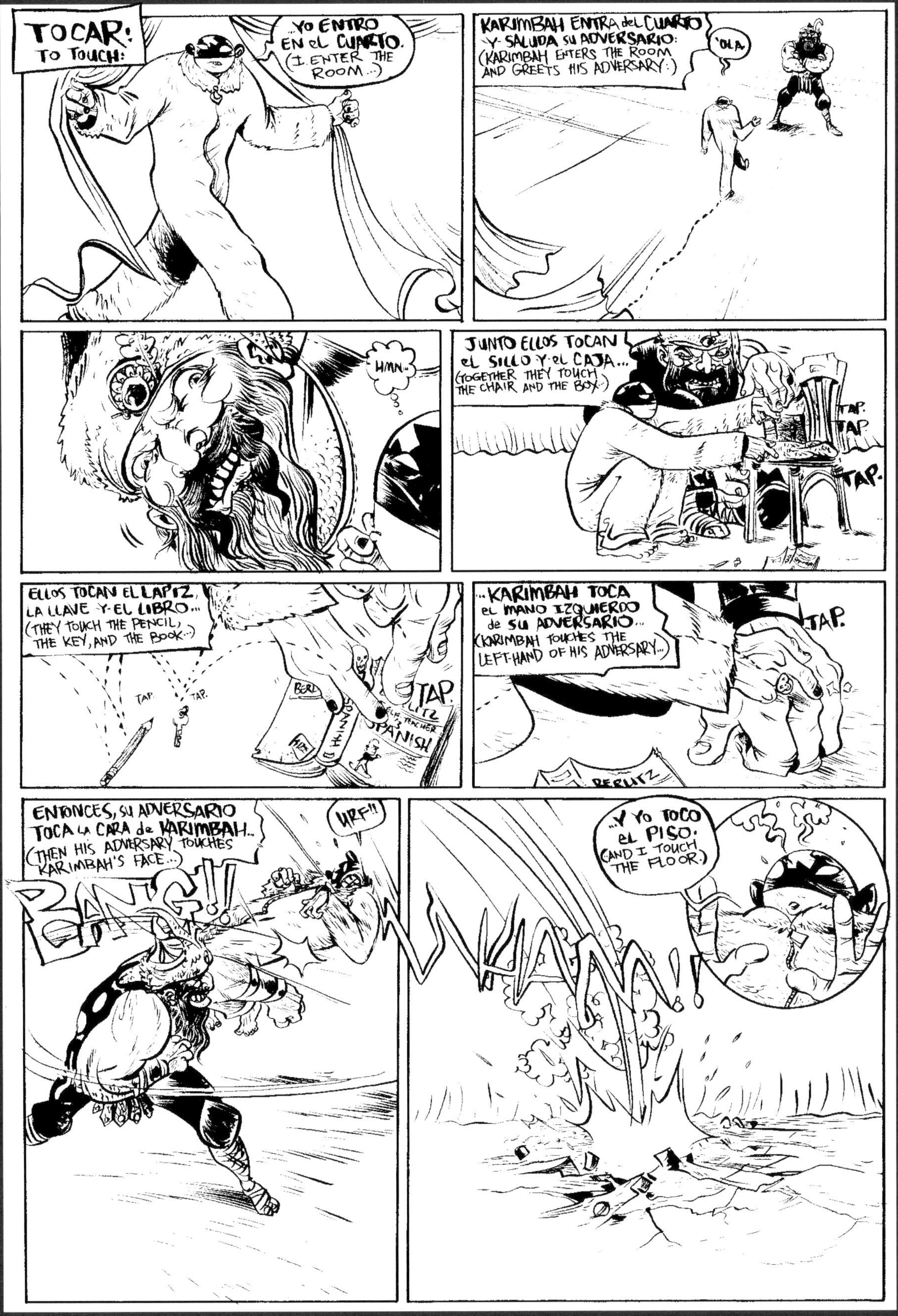
TOCAR: TO TOUCH:
...YO ENTRO EN el CUARTO. (I ENTER THE ROOM...)
KARIMBAH ENTRA del CUARTO Y SALUDA SU ADVERSARIO: (KARIMBAH ENTERS THE ROOM AND GREETS HIS ADVERSARY:)
'OLA.
HMN..
JUNTO ELLOS TOCAN el SILLO Y el CAJA... (TOGETHER THEY TOUCH THE CHAIR AND THE BOX...)
TAP.
TAP.
TAP.
ELLOS TOCAN EL LAPIZ, LA LLAVE Y EL LIBRO... (THEY TOUCH THE PENCIL, THE KEY, AND THE BOOK...)
TAP.
TAP.
TAP.
...KARIMBAH TOCA el MANO IZQUIERDO de SU ADVERSARIO... (KARIMBAH TOUCHES THE LEFT-HAND OF HIS ADVERSARY...)
TAP.
ENTONCES, SU ADVERSARIO TOCA LA CARA de KARIMBAH... (THEN HIS ADVERSARY TOUCHES KARIMBAH'S FACE...)
URF!!
BANG!!
WHAM!
...Y YO TOCO el PISO. (AND I TOUCH THE FLOOR.)

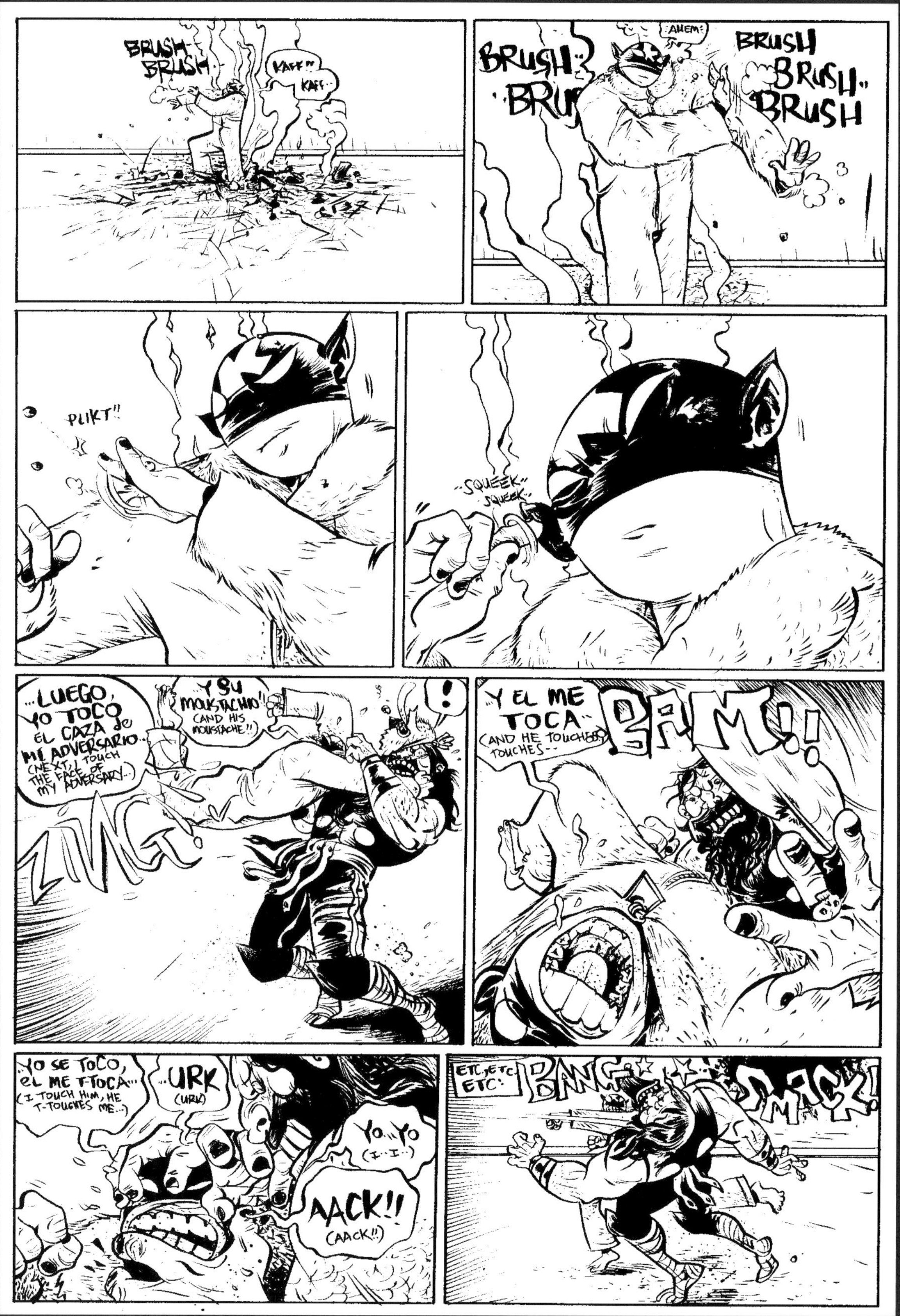
BRUSH BRUSH
KAFF!! KAFF
BRUSH BRUSH
AHEM
BRUSH BRUSH BRUSH
PLIKT!!
SQUEEK!! SQUEEK
...LUEGO, YO TOCO EL CAZA de MI ADVERSARIO... (NEXT, I TOUCH THE FACE OF MY ADVERSARY...)
Y SU MOUSTACHIO!! (AND HIS MOUSTACHE!!)
!
ZING!
Y EL ME TOCA (AND HE TOUCHES TOUCHES...)
BAM!!
YO SE TOCO, el ME T-TOCA... (I TOUCH HIM, HE T-TOUCHES ME...)
...URK (URK)
YO...YO (I...I...)
AACK!! (AACK!!)
ETC, ETC, ETC.
BANG!
SMACK!

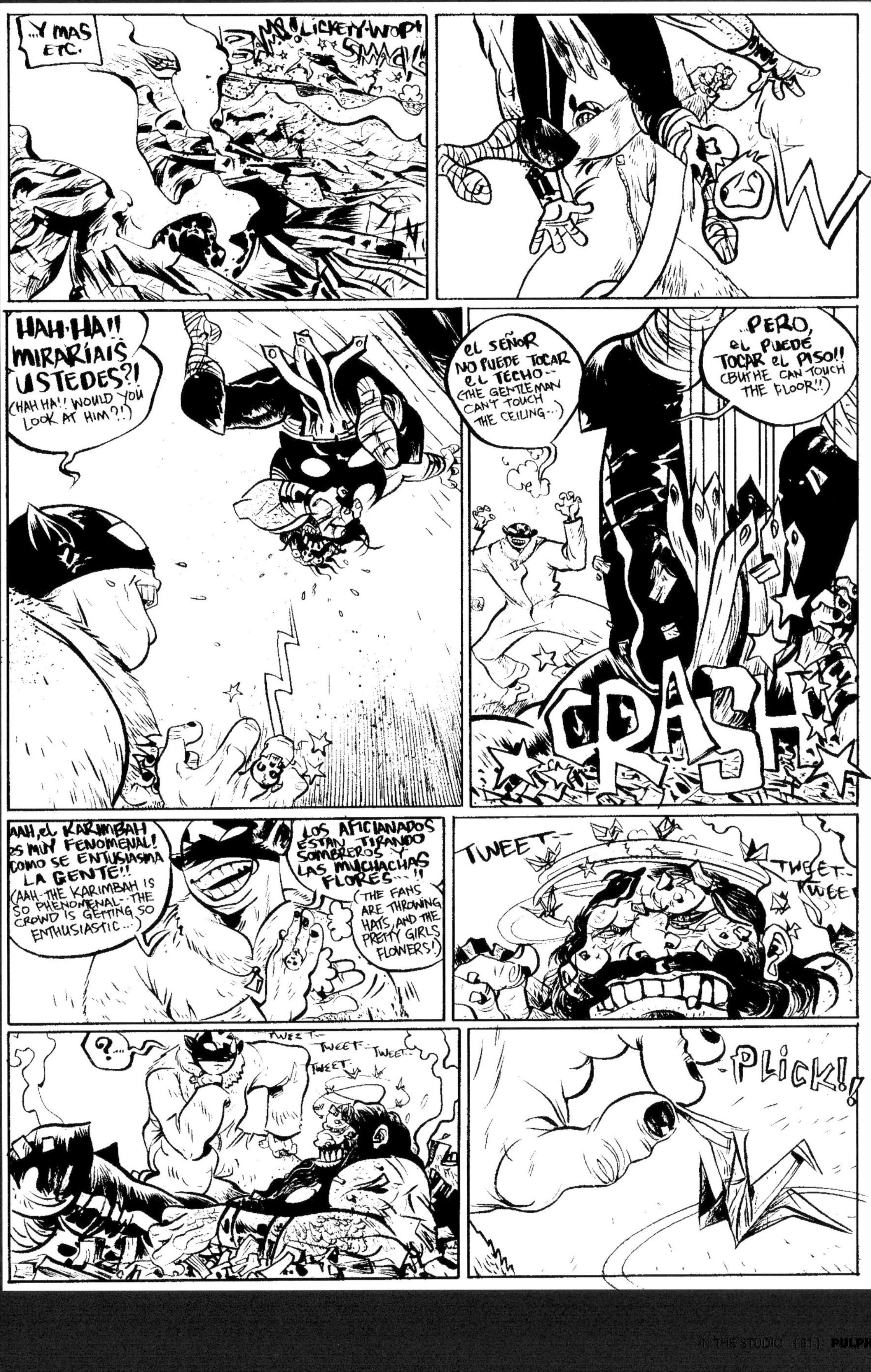
...Y MAS ETC.
LICKETY-WOP!
SMACK!
POW
HAH-HA!! MIRARÍAIS USTEDES?!
(HAH HA!! WOULD YOU LOOK AT HIM?!)
el SEÑOR NO PUEDE TOCAR el TECHO...
(THE GENTLEMAN CAN'T TOUCH THE CEILING...)
...PERO, el PUEDE TOCAR el PISO!!
(BUT HE CAN TOUCH THE FLOOR!!)
CRASH
AAH, el KARIMBAH es MUY FENOMENAL! COMO SE ENTUSIASMA LA GENTE!!
(AAH-THE KARIMBAH IS SO PHENOMENAL-THE CROWD IS GETTING SO ENTHUSIASTIC...)
LOS AFICIANADOS ESTAN TIRANDO SOMBREROS Y LAS MUCHACHAS FLORES...!!
(THE FANS ARE THROWING HATS, AND THE PRETTY GIRLS FLOWERS!)
TWEET-
TWEET-
TWEE
?...
TWEET-
TWEET-
TWEET-
TWEET-
PLICK!!

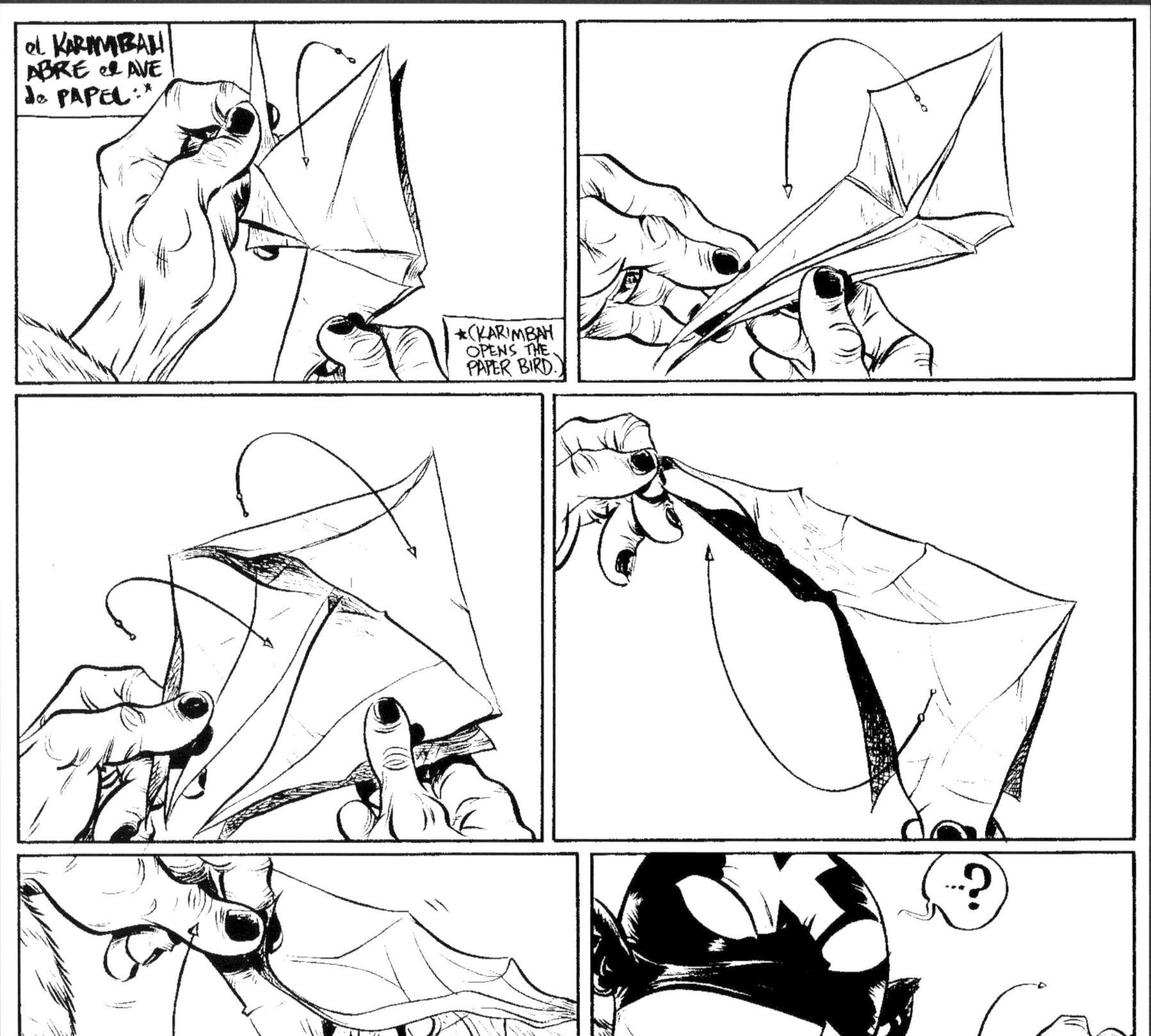
el KARIMBAH ABRE el AVE de PAPEL:*
*(KARIMBAH OPENS THE PAPER BIRD.)
...?
...KARIBAH, HAGA el FAVOR de SALIR del CUARTO. (...KARIMBAH, PLEASE LEAVE THE ROOM...)

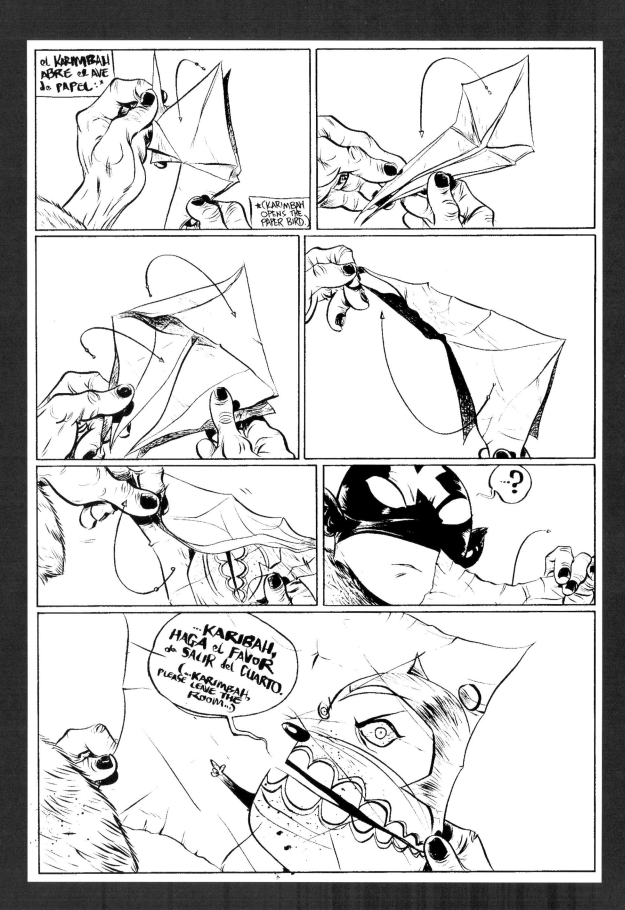

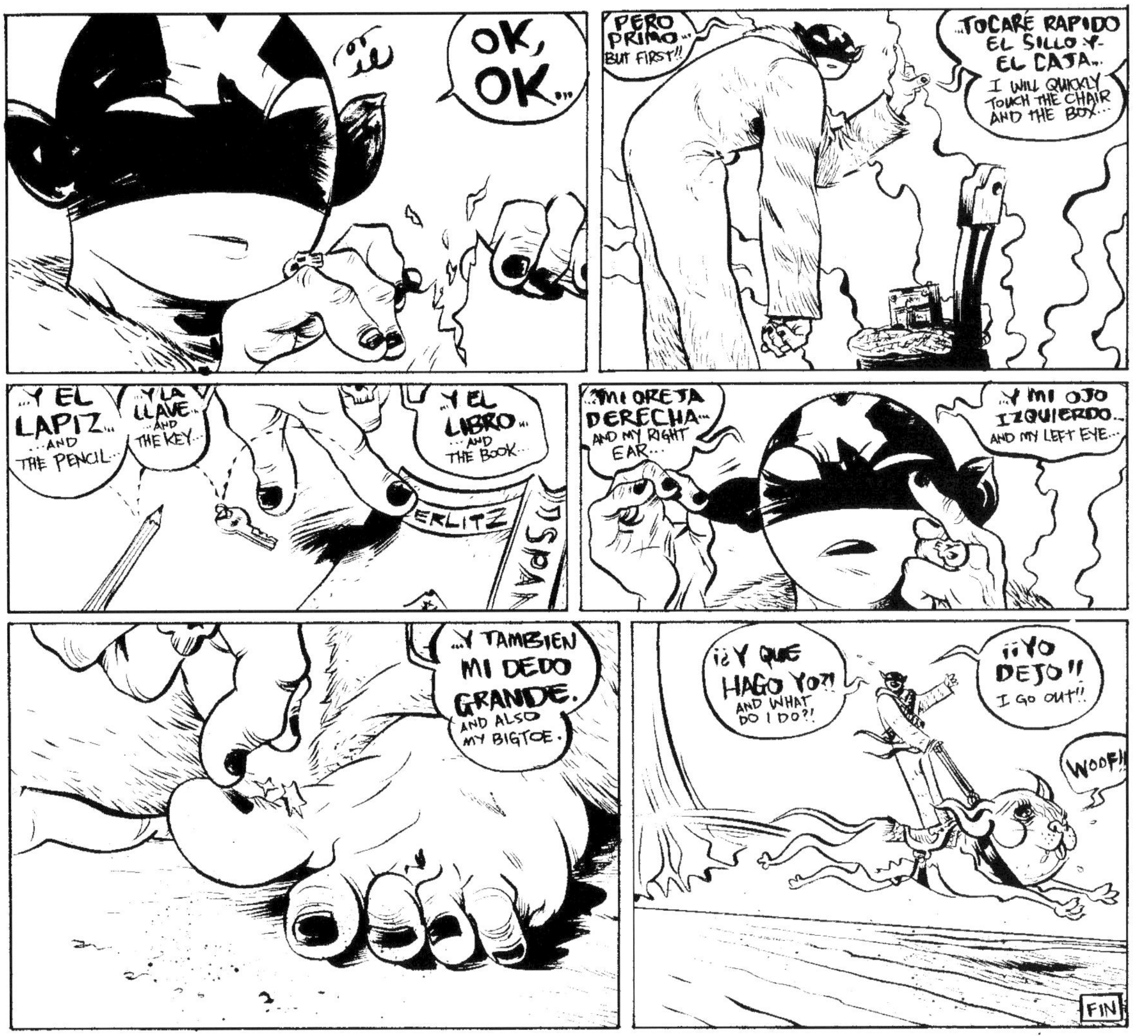
OK, OK...
PERO PRIMO... BUT FIRST!!
...TOCARÉ RAPIDO EL SILLO Y EL CAJA... I WILL QUICKLY TOUCH THE CHAIR AND THE BOX...
...Y EL LAPIZ... ...AND THE PENCIL...
...Y LA LLAVE... ...AND THE KEY...
...Y EL LIBRO... ...AND THE BOOK...
...MI OREJA DERECHA... AND MY RIGHT EAR...
...Y MI OJO IZQUIERDO... AND MY LEFT EYE...
...Y TAMBIEN MI DEDO GRANDE. AND ALSO MY BIGTOE.
¡¿Y QUE HAGO YO?! AND WHAT DO I DO?!
¡¡YO DEJO!! I GO OUT!!
WOOF!!
FIN

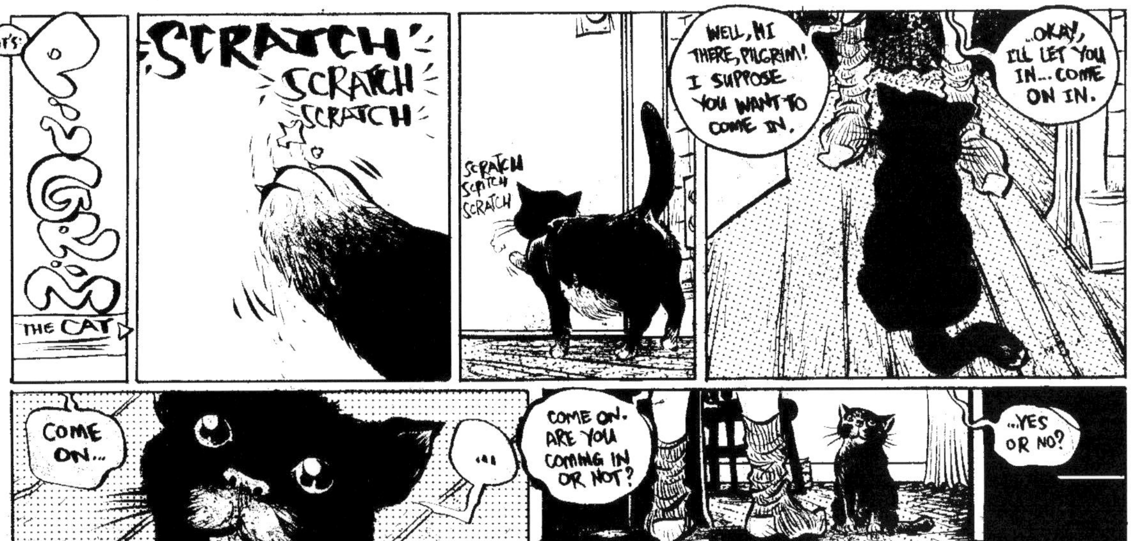
It's PILGRIM THE CAT
SCRATCH SCRATCH SCRATCH
SCRATCH SCRATCH SCRATCH
WELL, HI THERE, PILGRIM! I SUPPOSE YOU WANT TO COME IN.
...OKAY, I'LL LET YOU IN... COME ON IN.
COME ON...
...
COME ON. ARE YOU COMING IN OR NOT?
...YES OR NO?
...ETC, ETC.

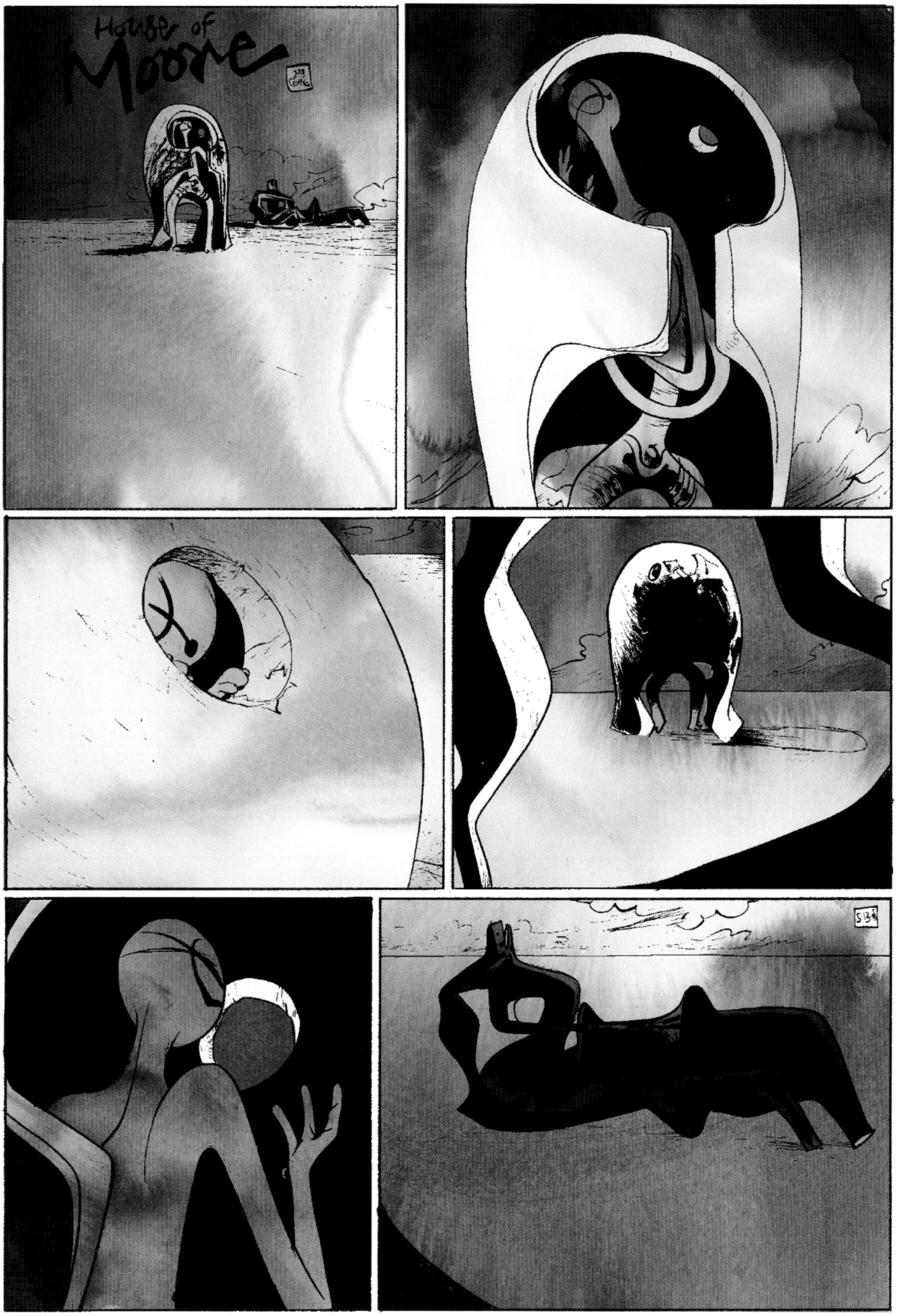
House of Moore

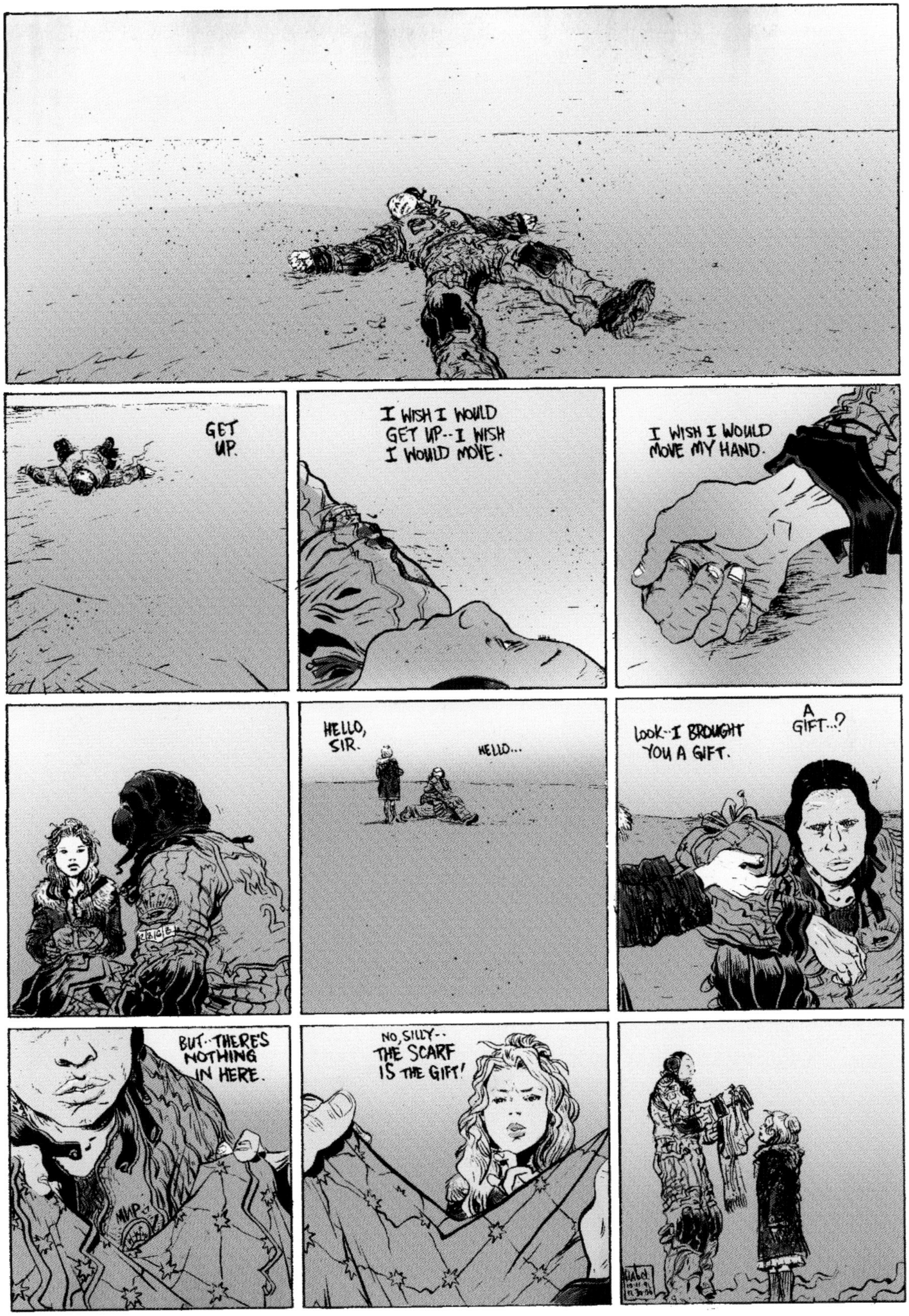
GET UP.
I WISH I WOULD GET UP-- I WISH I WOULD MOVE.
I WISH I WOULD MOVE MY HAND.
HELLO, SIR.
HELLO...
LOOK-- I BROUGHT YOU A GIFT.
A GIFT...?
BUT-- THERE'S NOTHING IN HERE.
NO, SILLY-- THE SCARF IS THE GIFT!

STOP GO

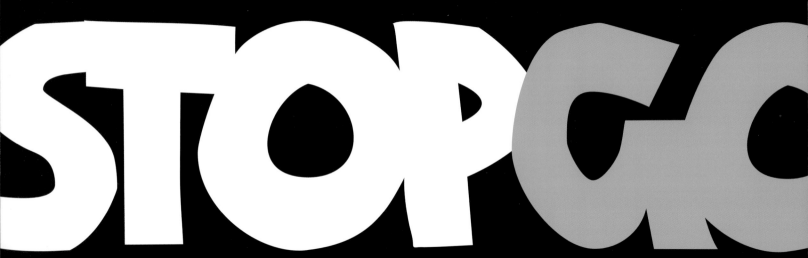

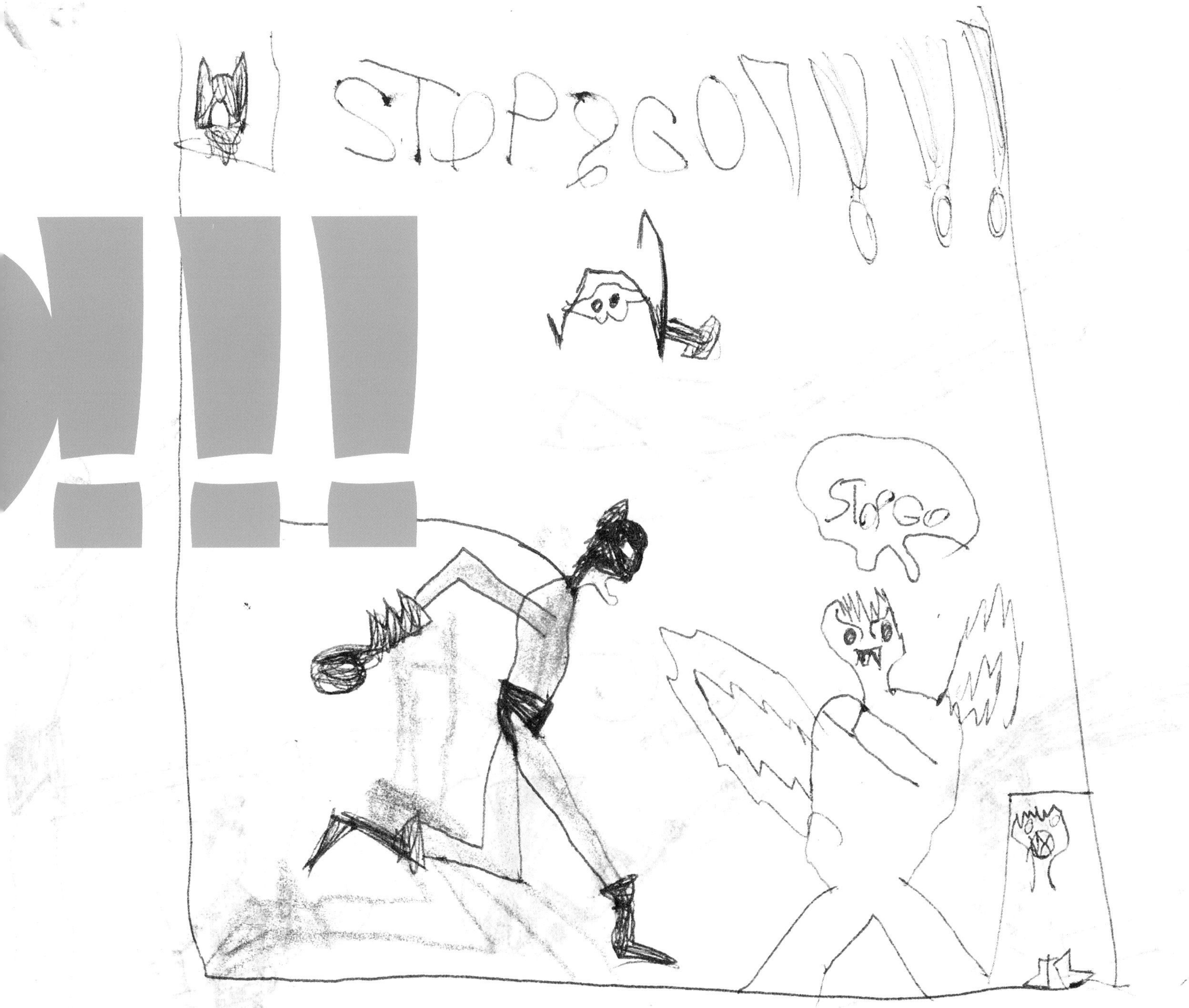
STOPGO!!!
STOPGO

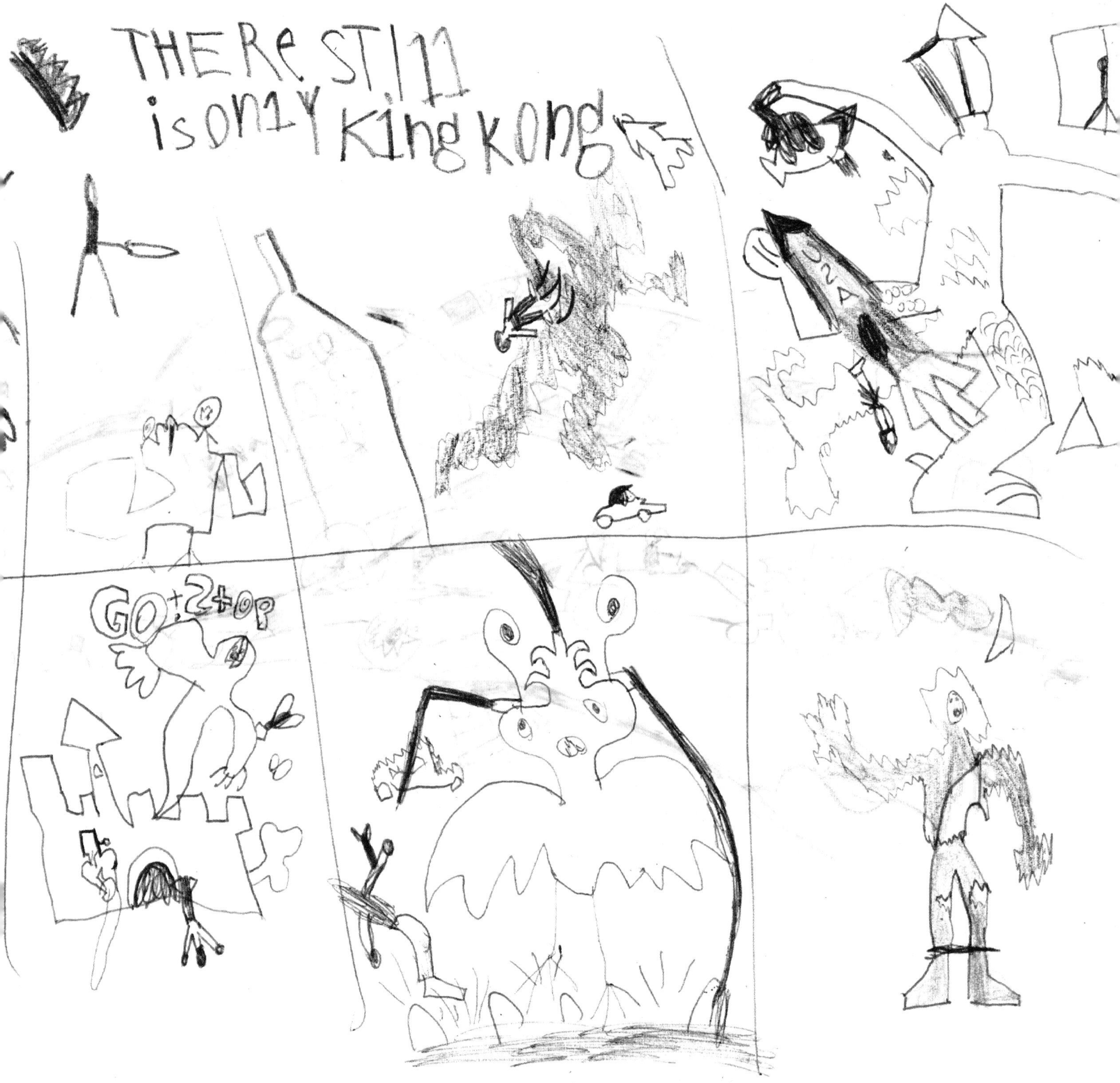
THERe STIll
is On1Y King Kong

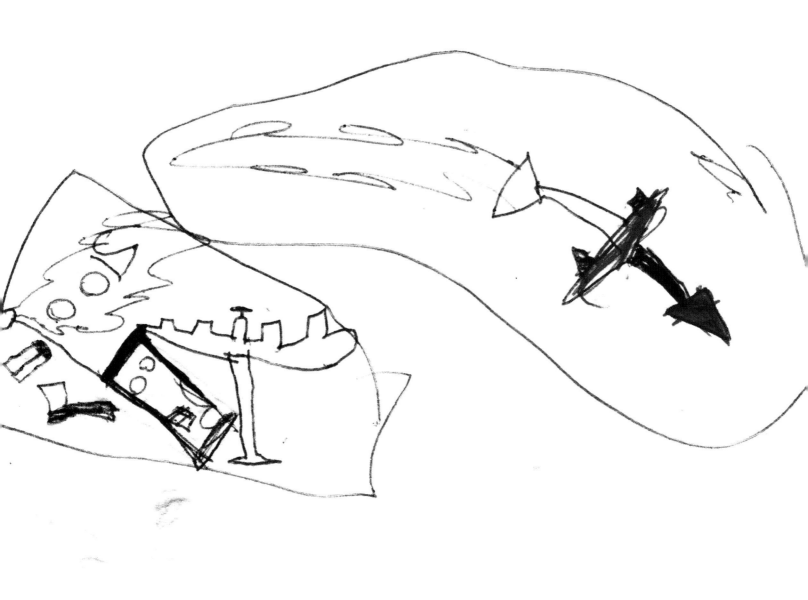

KID ART

Not long ago I stumbled across a stack of pictures I drew when I was four or five, which had been stashed away somewhere on a shelf in my studio and promptly forgotten. I'm lucky in that my mom and grandmother kept piles of my drawings, tucked into deep black envelopes with silver metal clips, just waiting for the day. I had gotten them back a few years ago as a Christmas present, and it was a shock to see these misplaced things return. To say I'd forgotten having drawn them would be an understatement — it is one of those things which, without the sort of documentary evidence a drawing is, you'd never have remembered. I do remember drawing as a child — I've been drawing since before I can remember — but with one exception, I have no specific memories of drawing from before about five years old or so. It was as if the repetition of events hadn't quite yet gelled into memory. Nevertheless, there was the proof — dozens upon dozens of pages covered in wobbily, frenetic lines, pictures drawn with pencils and crayons and some with one of those old ball point pens with four ink cartridges inside — red, black, blue, and green. They seemed like mute and distant heiroglyphs from a little person who is no longer here, who is unable to speak in any other way. But just what was it he's trying to say?

Rudolf Arnheim argues in his book *Visual Thinking* that one primary reason children draw is that they are slowly, methodically trying to define for themselves the very shape of reality through the tools of picture-making. Before we had writing, we had drawing, going all the way back to the caves of Lascaux. "All thought is visual," he continues. "My...work has taught me that artistic activity is a form of reasoning, in which perceiving and thinking are indivisibly intertwined...a person who paints, writes, composes, dances thinks with his senses". Through their rough attempts on a page, children are trying to map out the important visual attributes through which the things of the world can be identified. Elsewhere, Arnheim points out that another primary reason children draw is simply to enjoy the feeling of muscles flexing, watching their hands magically invent brightly colored shapes on pieces of paper. In truth, drawings of this sort are not drawings of anything at all, they're more accurately kinetic streaks contained on a page, graphic snapshots cataloguing incidental motion. Some of my kid drawings seem to be of this type. Others are more clearly attempts at crudely recognizable monsters, robots, and superheroes, sometimes arranged along with simple logo-like word groupings (STOP&GO!!!). These drawings are like miniaturized one-note operas, sweeping epics of good versus evil compressed upon a tiny matchbox stage. Still others resemble obsessive, spartan landscapes, blank vistas defined by a single rough mark torn across a snowy sheet, white wells of infinite space sliced in two by one wiry line. Across these wobbling wastelands, endless arrangements of melting machines and strange, oblong buildings bob up and down over the thumbtack horizons like marching armies of immediate expression. There are some which are apparently drawings I'd started and abruptly quit, probably out of boredom or distraction. Others are baffling things, hard to compare to anything else.

One drawing in particular interested

me more than the others, and I found myself thinking about it if I ever woke up in the middle of the night. It was a drawing of a blue rhombic shape containing a series of fairly uniform circles, hatchet-like rectangles, and explosively jagged zig-zags. It resembled nothing less than a cubist composition. Being that I drew it and it is my own original idea, afterall, (although very different from anything I would or could think of drawing now), I occurred to me I might be able to reclaim the process behind the drawing if I carefully traced it and a few others like it on a lightbox, then redrew them again as I would a page of comics, following the implicit path of the hand which made the original drawings. As I drew, I could feel my hand moving in different, older ways as I reworked the trail of lines on the page, following the thoughts behind the pictures. As I did so, I could sense how the earlier artist's hand moved, how his muscles would've controlled the drawing tool (curiously lurching up and to the right, the opposite of how my drawing hand moves now). I could tell which lines had been put down fast and which were more laboriously considered. Gradually, I began to remember the place where I drew as a kid, how it smelled, what the lighting was like. I remembered the room I slept in, with its knocking radiator and that lovely old vacuum tube radio which got gently warmer the longer you left it on, its dim yellow dial face glowing in the dark. I remembered the Heckle and Jeckle patch on my dirty blue jeans, the stiff blue bedspread, the carpet and the cupboard with the strange coconut-head my grandparents must've gotten on some long-distant vacation, and the pewter cup where I kept my pencils. I could see that boy there, sitting at his desk, drawing as I was drawing, listening to music, incessantly twirling a pen cap with the fingers of his right hand.

In the middle of the curious rhombic composition was another form which looked at first like a diagram for an office garage viewed simultaneously from above and from the side, as if scribbled by an inebriated architect on a messy cocktail napkin. It also looked a bit like a shoebox which had been skin-grafted to the side of an airplane, complete with a tail and jet engines on the wings. A longer teardrop shape pouring out and down to the right revealed another airplane facing the opposite direction. This plane was coated with an aggressive red and black patina. From these clues, I could tell this could only be a drawing of an air battle over Germany during World War Two.

The old folks my sister and I lived with talked about World War Two a lot. We'd sit and listen to them relive those old days. Over countless dinners, we'd hear the stories of all the colorful people from their youth. They were living, breathing characters to us, all these nurses and soldiers and farmers and the others too young to go. We heard their fractured stories in disjointed episodes, like old time radio serials, randomly, and out of order. There was the one, who, half starving in the middle of a Berlin winter, had turned over a cardboard box only to find a frozen dead man hidden underneath. There was the one with the large tattoo of a half-naked hula girl inked into his forearm. She could shimmy back and forth when he flexed his ropecoil Popeye muscles. There was the one about the one who wasn't there, who had been killed in a head on collision in Yuma, Arizona, and the other one who wasn't there, and the other one who died of diabetes at thirteen. Some were told by a man named Luther, who had been a pilot, and so was both a character in the stories, as well as the narrator. I was fascinated by the stories of the "burp guns" he encountered over German battlefields, huge cannons which the Nazis used to shoot improvised shells made of metal junk and shrapnel when they ran out of proper ammo. Luther the narrator said one time Luther the character had a huge metal bolt shoot right through the bottom of his plane, up between his legs, clearing the top of his cockpit without touching him. This sounded a lot like other larger-than-life scenes in a comic book I'd looked at called *Enemy Ace*, hidden in a stash belonging to my uncle. If I was careful crawling up the wooden ladder, my grandparents would let me sit up there and leaf through those old comics, kept in a box in the attic. These were all classic, yellowed Silver Age comics, and as with the stories of the old folks, I could wander through the various old episodes of *Magnus Robot Fighter, Captain America, Sgt. Rock, Donald Duck,* and *Batman,* randomly and out of order, and try to piece together the missing parts.

Tracing that drawing of mine while playing out these memories, I realized the thing I at first took to be a cubistic composition was in fact an early attempt at a comics page by a person too young to realize comics were not a bunch of pictures piled one on top of the other. However, it made sense to try to translate Luther's stories in that fashion, and it was a natural way for me to respond to my environment — his "burp gun" sounded like something which belonged in a Sgt. Rock comic (the story even came with its own sound effect), and both were elements of the actual world I lived in, no less real than anything else. Plus I simply enjoyed drawing, it all fit. What at first looked abstract was actually quite concrete, evidence of a young mind slowly, methodically trying to define the shapes of reality through the use of pictures. The page "There is sti11 on1y K1ng Kong" also comes across like some kind of comic, or perhaps a cover to a comic. This time the picture is broken down into a more cartoony 6 panel grid. Within this picture we find a series of six separate, smaller pictures. In these, we see a line-up of what I imagine must have been at the time my favorite monsters, including Godzilla (center, top), Jack the Ripper (top left), and a ghost in the lower left corner rising out of a haunted castle with the now familiar refrain, "Go+Stop".

The title refers less to the fact that I liked King Kong the best as it does to the fact that, although I could more or less draw them all, his was probably the only name I could spell.

PP

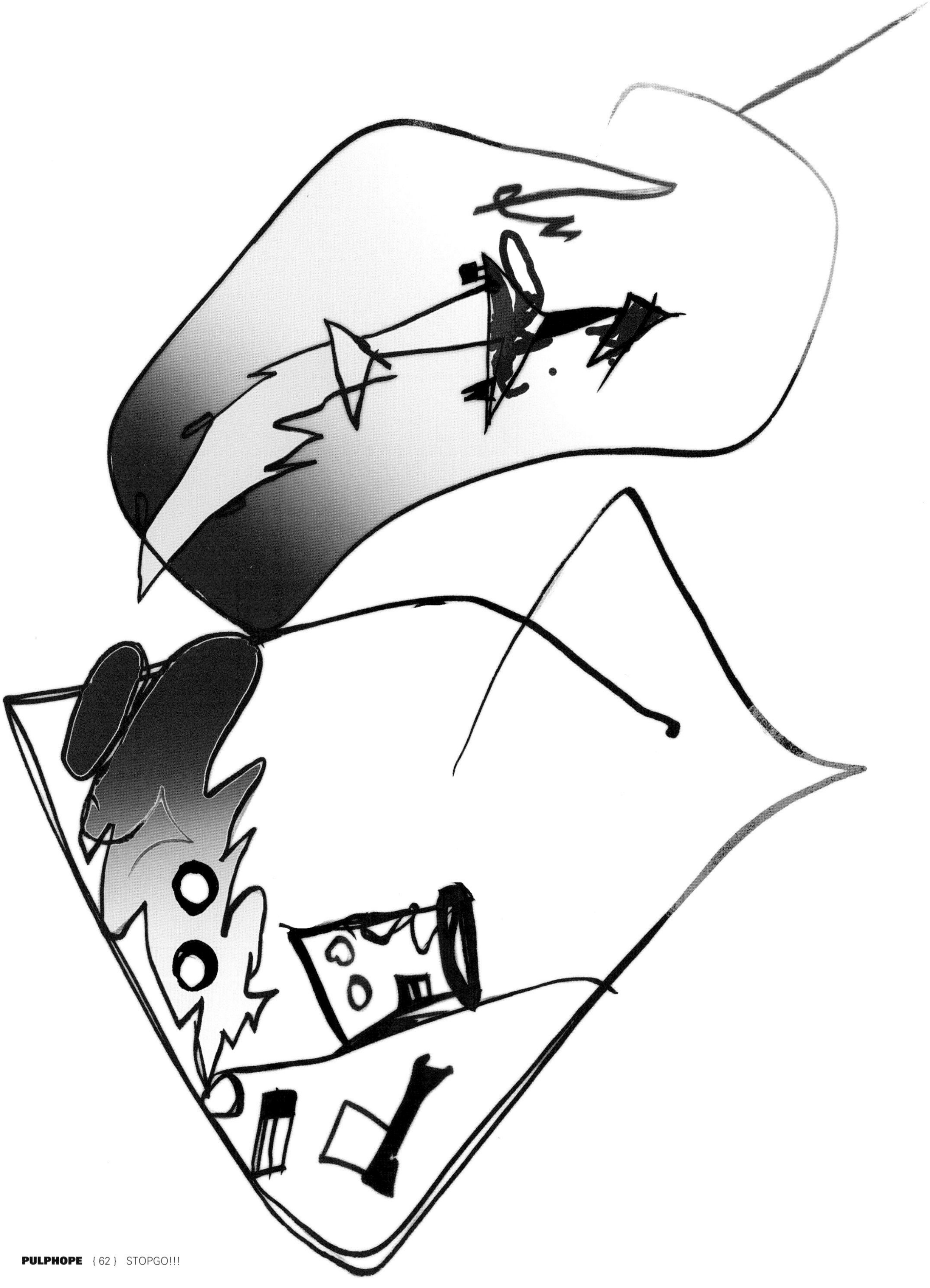

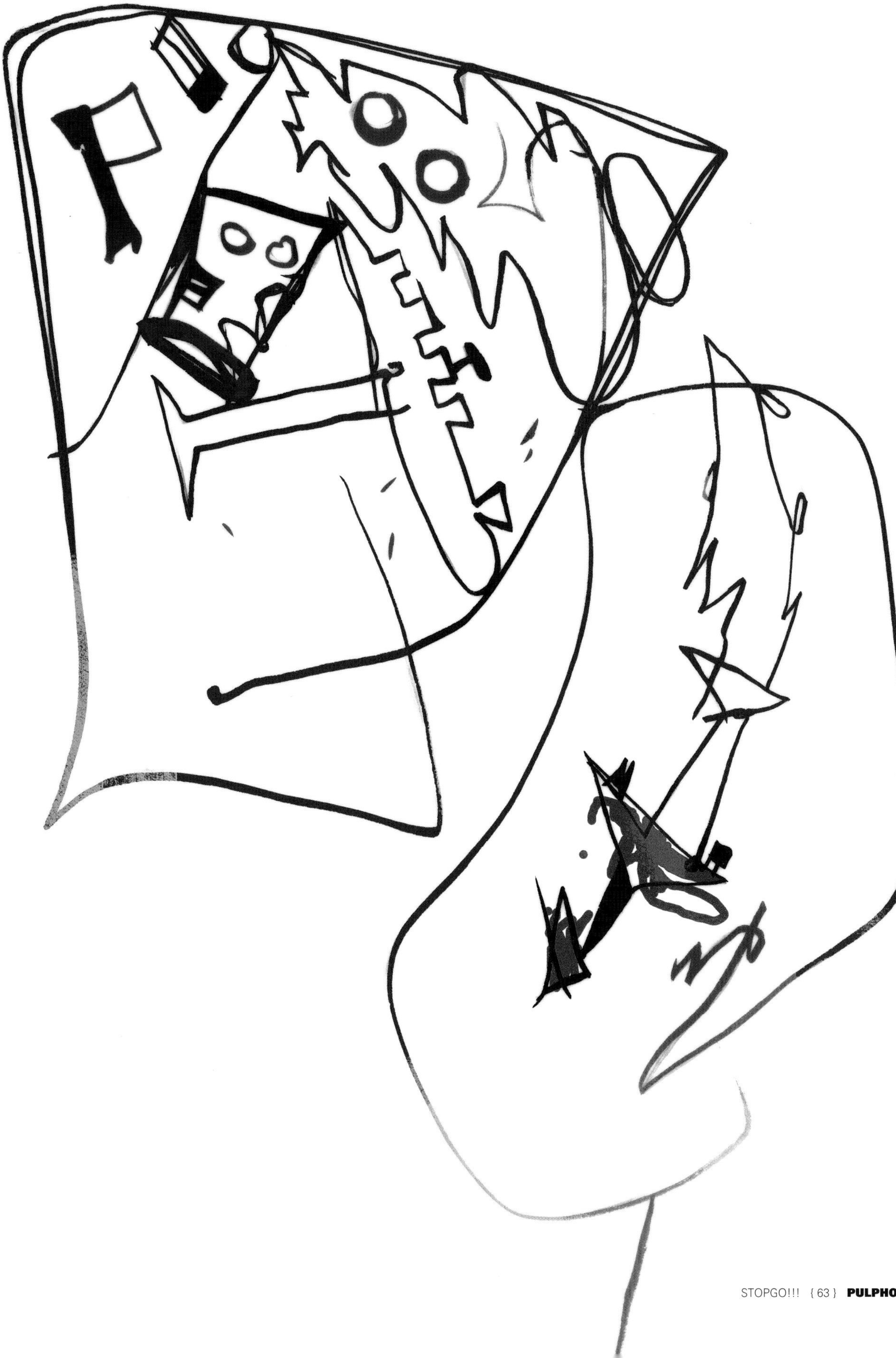

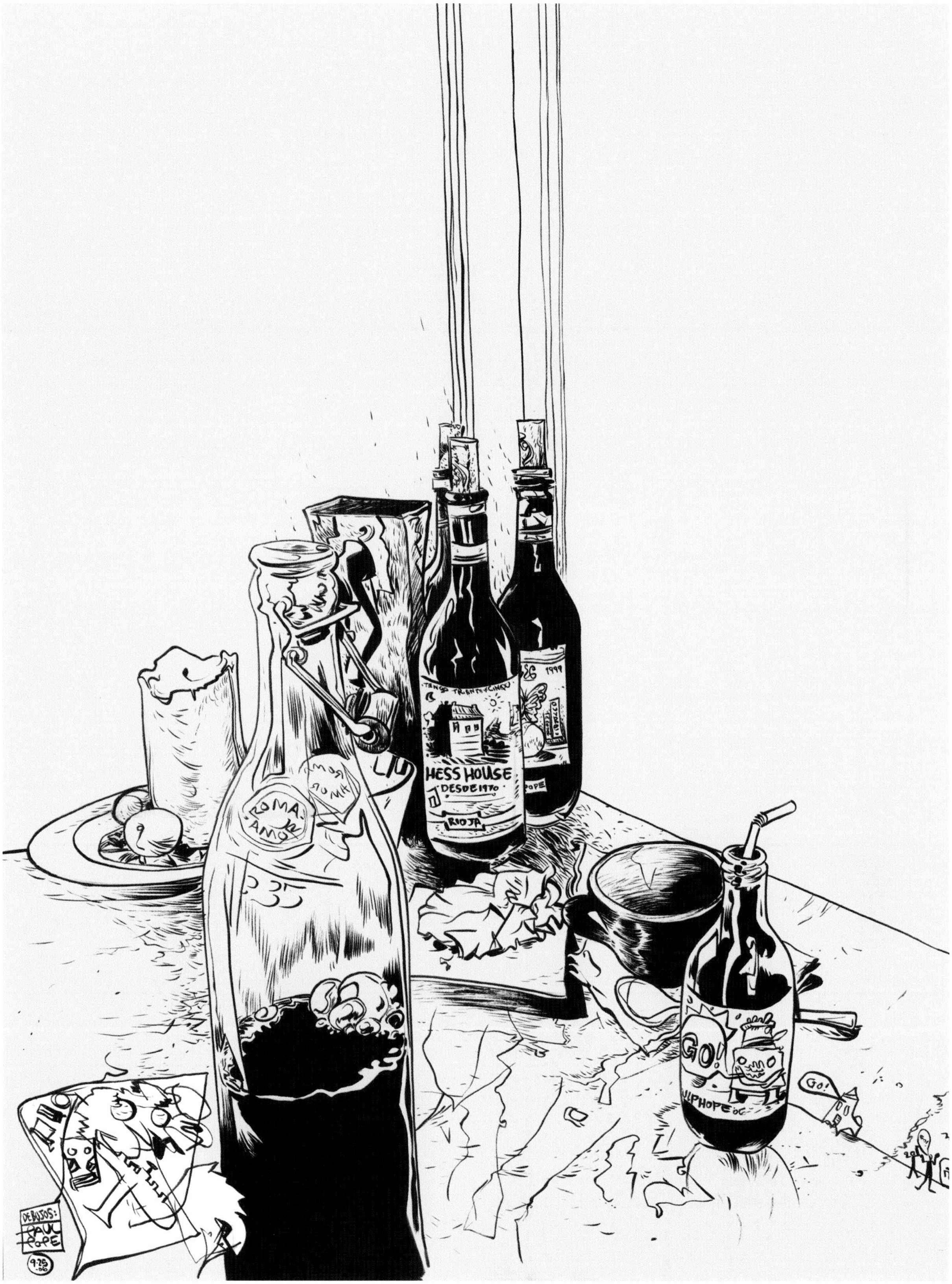
HESS HOUSE
DESDE 1970
RIOJA
1999
GO!
GO!
DEBUJOS:
PAUL POPE
9-25-00

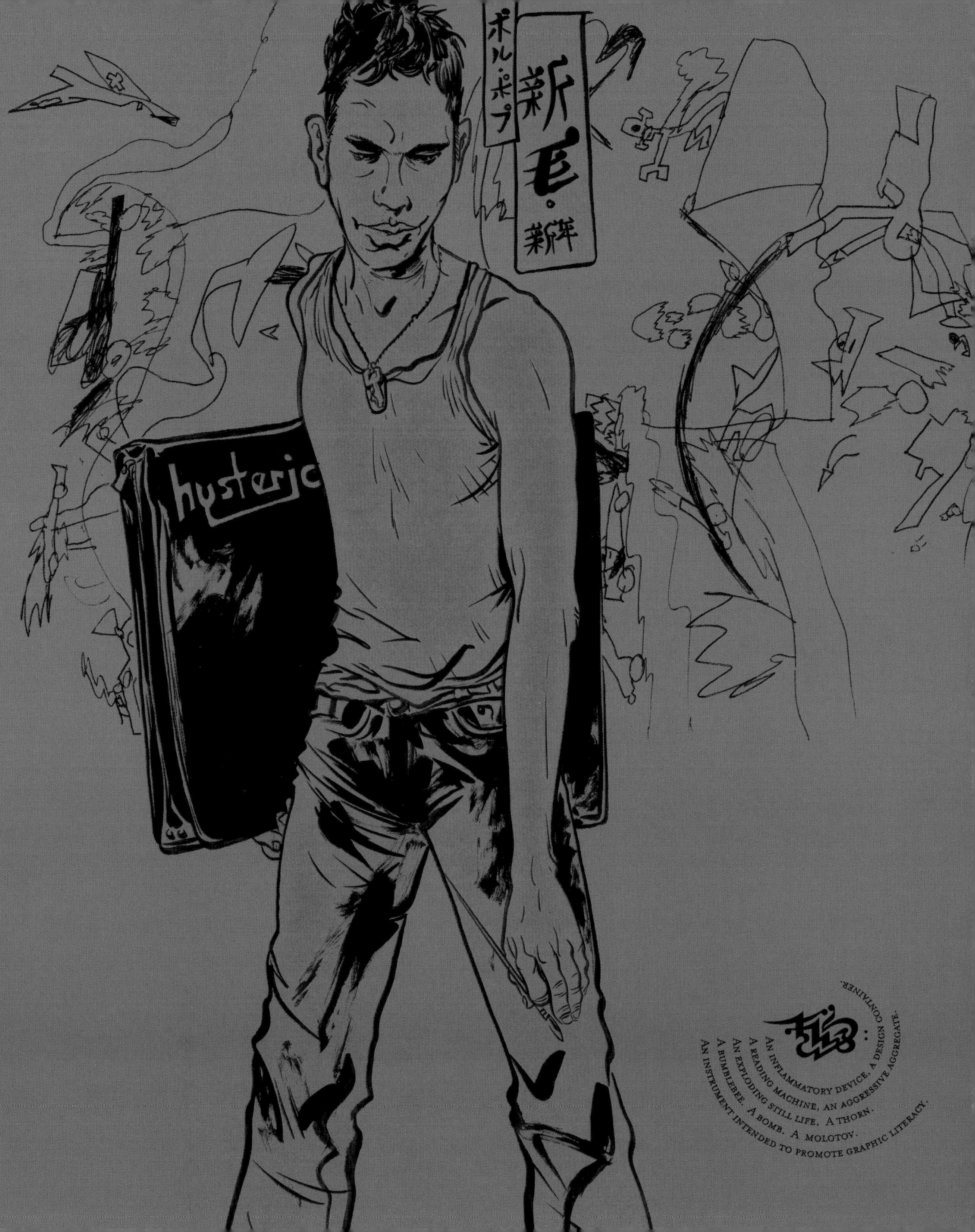
ポル・ポプ
新毛。
新年
hysteric

An inflammatory device, a design container.
A reading machine, an aggressive aggregate.
An exploding still life. A thorn.
A bumblebee. A bomb. A molotov.
An instrument intended to promote graphic literacy.

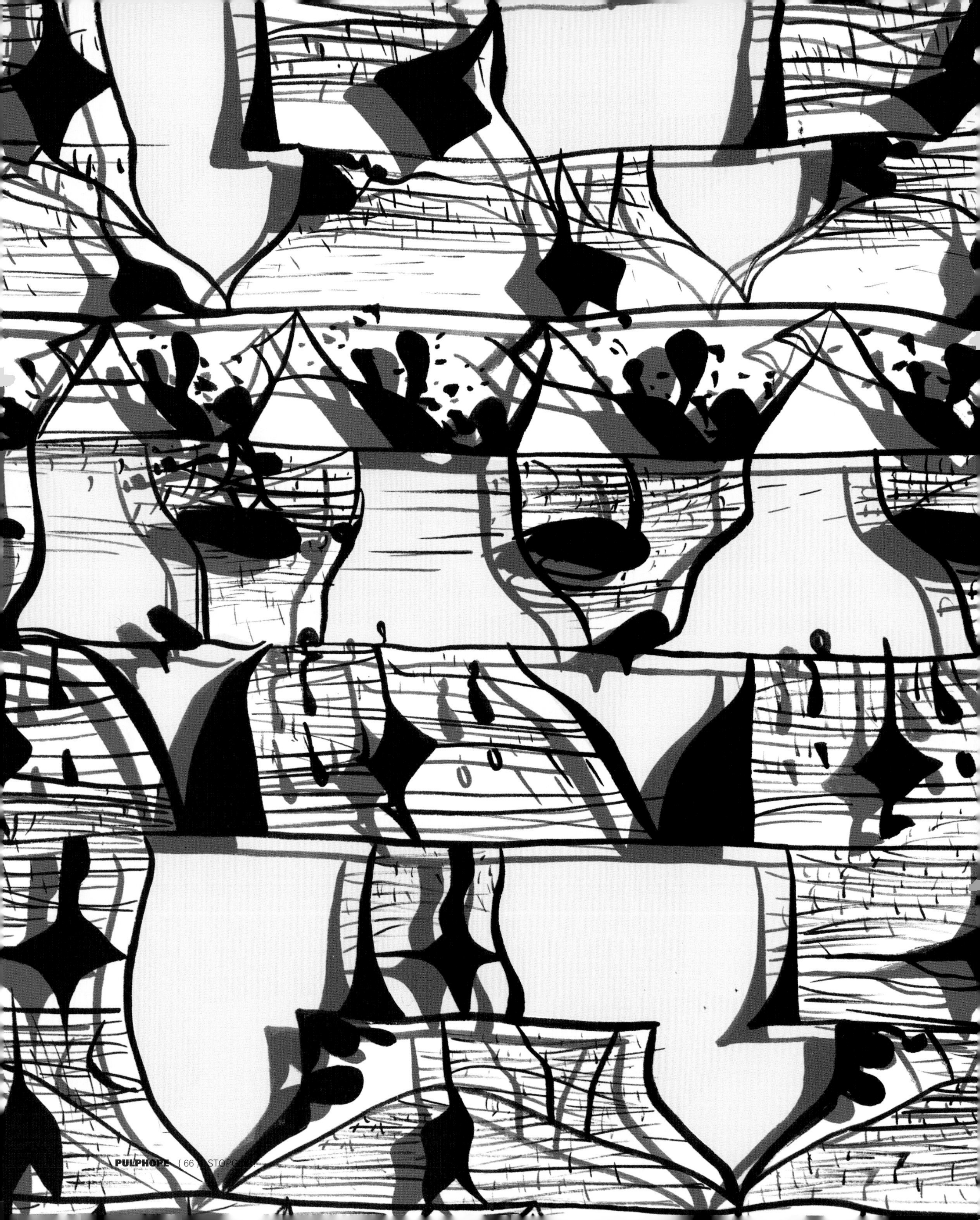

MANG

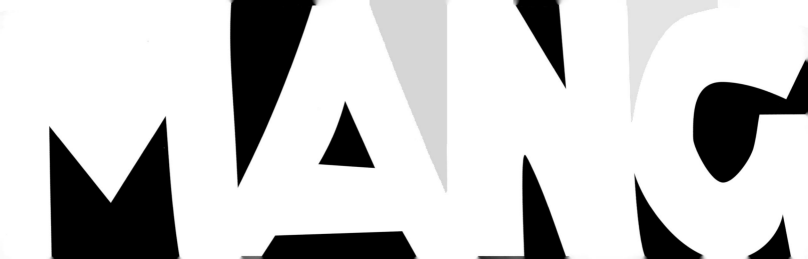

A-KA

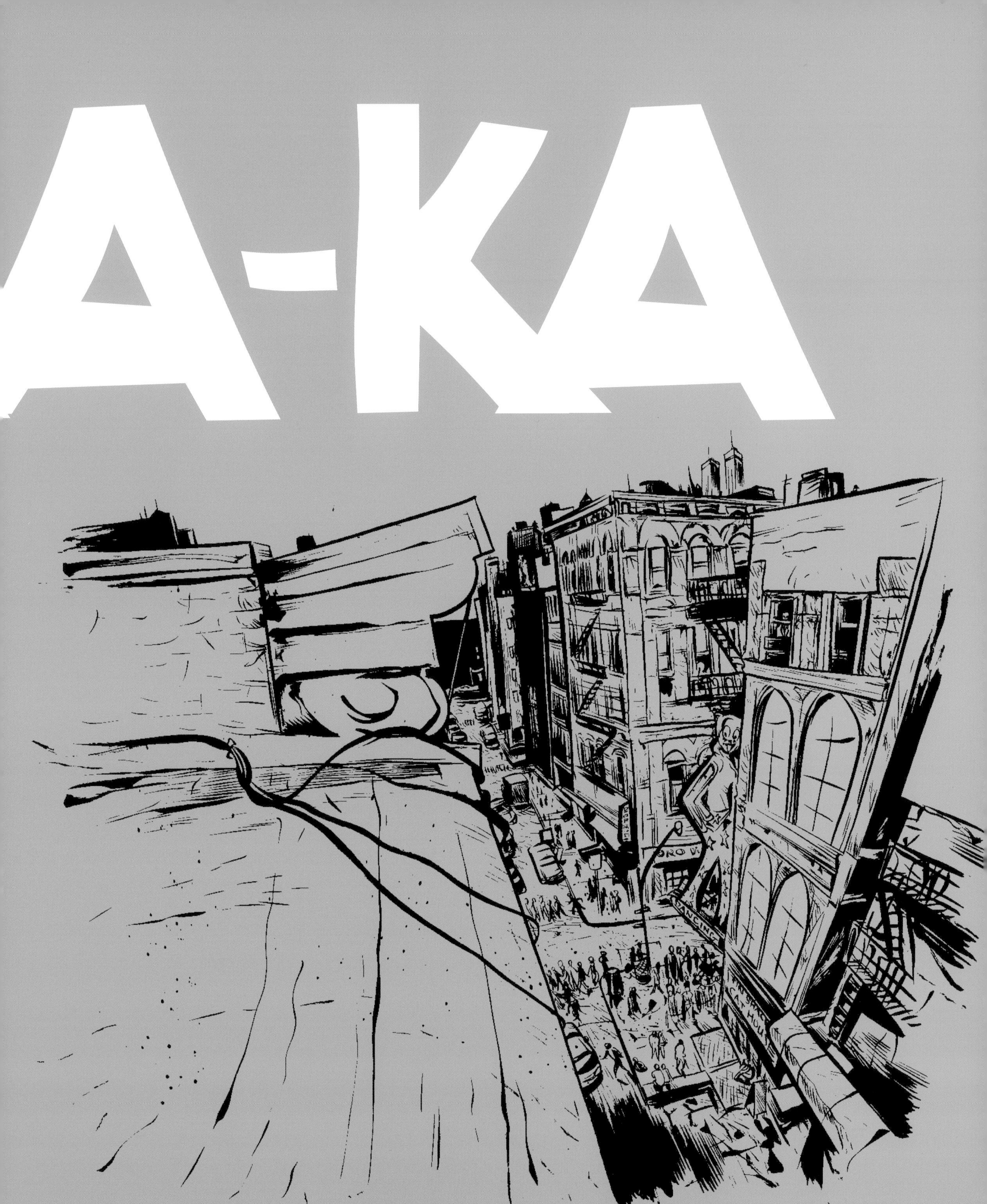
DANCING

THE BENEFITS OF THIRST

The first time I saw manga I was 9 years old going on 10. This would've been in 1980. Pac-Man was new back then. We still listened to 8-Tracks and all the girls wanted Jordache jeans. My mom had just bought a house — our first real house, in a real suburb, with nicely paved streets and manicured trees and lots of neighbors. It'd been years since my sister and I lived with our mom, and we were excited. Before that we lived more-or-less in the country with our grandparents. Our new house was on a street called Edgevale in a neighborhood called Upper Arlington. This was in Columbus, Ohio. The house was a modest one story, with white stuccoed walls and a dark brown fence. It formerly belonged to a family from Japan. I liked the miniature rock garden they built for the tiny backyard. It had a small water fountain you could turn on, although we never did. It attracted mosquitoes.

My sister Erika and I were new kids at a big school and we were both shy and as a result we spent a lot of time by ourselves. Up until then that's how it had been for us and that's how we liked it. The two sons of the Japanese couple who had lived in our house were still enrolled at our school and would be there for a few more months. After that they'd all be going back to Japan. Their parents were professors and taught something at the University. One kid was two years older than me and like most big kids I just avoided him. His little brother was 3 years younger than me, he was my sisters age, and his name was Kenji. My sister said he was crazy. Crazy Kenji. He'd say the craziest things and make jokes nobody could understand. He got into fights all the time, usually defending his friend Tekuma, another Japanese kid whose parents were there for the same reason.

Looking back on it, it seems a lot of kids got into fights at that school. Even the girls got into fights. I got into a few myself and it was the first time I got hit in the face for real (I was surprised it didn't sound like it did in the movies). One time I saw Kenji give a big kid a black eye for picking on the school's one near sighted, slightly retarded kid, Jimmy Beaver. Only the meanest kids would pick on him — knock his glasses off or give him a rough push or knock his books out of his hands — and he would cry and his little red-haired sister would come running up and it would embarrass everybody. But this one time Kenji just leapt up and smacked this big kid right in the middle of his face, one punch. Wham! The big kid fell down and the fight was over. A third grader had given a sixth grader a black eye! Incredible! It was overwhelmingly impressive and for the short time Kenji stayed at our school he became a kind of legendary figure. This made him unbearably arrogant, as if the two years of prejudices and misunderstandings he and Tekuma suffered had resulted in a kind of kingly scorn. He walked around with his arms folded and snorted at kids when they'd try to talk to him. Everybody wanted to sit with him at lunch. He'd just sit with Tekuma. If other kids sat there with them, he'd just ignore them.

I suppose this is understandable and even a little amusing, but at the time it was irritating and it confused me. Why should he react that way toward me? He didn't know me and anyway I didn't want to fight with him. Plus my mom had just bought his old house. In fact, I was sleeping in his old room. His crayon scribbles were still all over the closet walls. There were tiny glow-in-the-dark handprint stickers from a Cracker Jack box on the wall in the closet, too. Just about 4 ft. off the ground, right about where a seven year-old would put them. I left them there because I liked them. It made the place feel more warm knowing somebody had lived there before us. They left a Japanese calendar up in the basement laundry room which my mom left up too, even though it was a year out of date. Didn't that count for something?

I was curious about the other kid Tekuma, because he liked to draw and was really good at it. He had a little crush on my sister, who showed me a drawing he did for her. It was it an incredible drawing — Bugs Bunny on roller skates carrying a cake in one hand and an open umbrella with the word "Erika" written on it in the other. Bugs was skating down a paved sidewalk in a park. On the side there were daisies with smiling faces looking up at the cake. It was especially amazing because of the way Tekuma made Bugs Bunny look. You could tell who it was supposed to be, but it didn't look anything like Bugs Bunny. It looked more like a stretched out rubber balloon version of Bugs Bunny caught in a wind tunnel. Thinking about it now I can see it was simply a cartoon by a kid with above-average drawing skills, done in an imitative style of Fujiko Fujio, creator of Doraemon, a popular manga for kids. Doraemon is that

blue and white cat (actually, he's a robot cat) with a red collar and a yellow jingling bell around his neck. He has white circles for hands; maybe you've seen him. But at the time I didn't know about Fujiko Fujio or about Doraemon. All I knew about Japan could be summed up in those glow-in-the-dark handprint stickers and that out-of-date calendar in my basement. All I could see was a drawing of Bugs Bunny that didn't look like any cartoon bunny I'd ever seen before.

There was something really strange and compelling about Tekuma's drawing. I kept going back to look at it. The only thing I could compare it to at the time were drawings I saw at the public library in a book of "underground comix" drawn by somebody called Robert Crumb. Robert Crumb's comics were really unusual. They weren't like anything else in the world. But Crumb's cartoons looked shaky and wobbly to me, like scratchy outlines of burnt marshmallows. All his cartoon animals were smoking and having sex. You had to hide the book from the librarians if you wanted to look at it because it was full of dirty pictures and bad words and you'd get in trouble if they caught you. Tekuma's drawing was streamlined and simple, playful even. He stretched out Bugs' body, put it at an odd angle, gave him big wide eyes, exaggerated the front teeth, elongated the ears and put him in a wild scene doing something Bugs Bunny had never done before, so far as I could tell. It was an amazing drawing by a kid from a different part of the world who drew in a style different from anything I'd ever seen before. Erika hung it up where we could look at it every day.

It made me want to be friends with Kenji and Tekuma. Actually, they could both draw (although Tekuma was demonstrably better) and I wanted to show them that I could draw too. Maybe we could all draw together. I was a lonely new kid and I needed friends, just like they did. Couldn't they see? Didn't everybody know about how I stapled my thumbs together and knocked over a science project display of potted plants in front of the whole class on my first day of school? Or about how that

whole first week I thought the most popular boy in class, whose name was Chris, was a girl? I made everybody laugh by calling him "her". Plus, my entire wardrobe was made up of Garanimals, and Garanimals were considered ridiculous on a kid my age. It was like wearing the uniform of a clown. Garanimals were for babies — they were color-coded clothes for kids who were too young or too stupid to be able to get up in the morning and match colors and patterns on their own without help. They called me "Elvis" because I was a little pudgy and I had big hair and my clothes looked like jogging suits with wide lapels and racing stripes on the sides.

This sort of constant elementary ostracism is exactly what turns introverted kids into cartoonists. Although I guess I've since had the last laugh, at the time it was really difficult. I drew because it made me feel good — I could create in my drawings friends and people I wanted to be with and I could invent all kinds of fantastic places I'd rather be instead of where I was. It helped. Surely Kenji and Tekuma both drew for the same reasons — because they didn't have any friends? But they did already have friends, they had each other and, no, they didn't want me either. They'd just run away whenever I tried to talk to them. Tekuma never spoke to me, and Kenji's entire vocabulary consisted of the words "no" and "go away". Every lonely kid is a shipwreck survivor hiding in a little fortress on a nameless little island, guarding his conch shell and staring at his own fly-covered pigs' heads in the hot noonday sun.

One day I came across Kenji sitting alone in the yard after school. He was holding an object which to me was at the time the most amazing thing I'd ever seen. It was a kind of book, small like a palm-sized bible, but instead of tiny words it was full of drawings and it was in black and white. It was a little black and white phonebook full of comics — but it wasn't like any comic book I'd ever seen. It was like a comic book from another planet. Whatever it was, it was definitely a comic book of some kind — or else it was something like a comic book but about as thick as a phonebook. It wasn't like the scrapbook I'd made of old black and white newspaper comics I cut and pasted together when Erika and I found a treasure trove of old *Toledo Blades* some old person who lived near my grandparents threw away and we had salvaged. I had one for The Phantom and one for Buz Sawyer — old daily newspaper comics from the World War Two days, full of stories about spy planes and secret missions in African jungles, ancient temples on fire and wedding plans for princesses. Kenji's was a real book. He was holding it in his little brown hands, as he sat in his blue jacket and yellow backpack, his back turned to me and to everybody else. He was sitting on the jungle gym waiting for his Mom to pick him up, reading this thing.

Wow — what's that? I wondered. That must be a Japanese comic book! It looks kinda like it was drawn by Walt Disney. Japanese looks funny — like a football scoreboard with all the digital lights turned on at once. And what's that!? UFOs — destroying a city! What's that?!! Electrical beams shooting out of a robot's eyes, people on fire, buildings caving in! Wow! I've never seen anything like that before! Wow! I gotta see that!

I asked if I could see it but he wouldn't show it to me. I tried a couple of times. I climbed the jungle gym but he kept moving away. I could see in a couple of seconds he'd jump off and that would be that, so I stopped. I could look, not quite over a shoulder but from a few feet back. I asked to hold that thing but he said no. Please? If you would want you can hold my watch for hock. You can hold my watch for hock and time it on the stopwatch. Let me see it for two minutes...just two minutes. One minute then. But he just kept saying no.

It was frustrating. I knew kids were always teasing him and to him I was just another kid there, no different from the others. He wasn't about to let me hold his treasure. He wasn't even going to give me the benefit of knowing what it was. I would just have to suffer. He didn't care if I lived in his old house. He hated that old house! He didn't want to live there anyway. He could care less if I could draw, or that I was another new kid. He didn't even care if I lived or died.

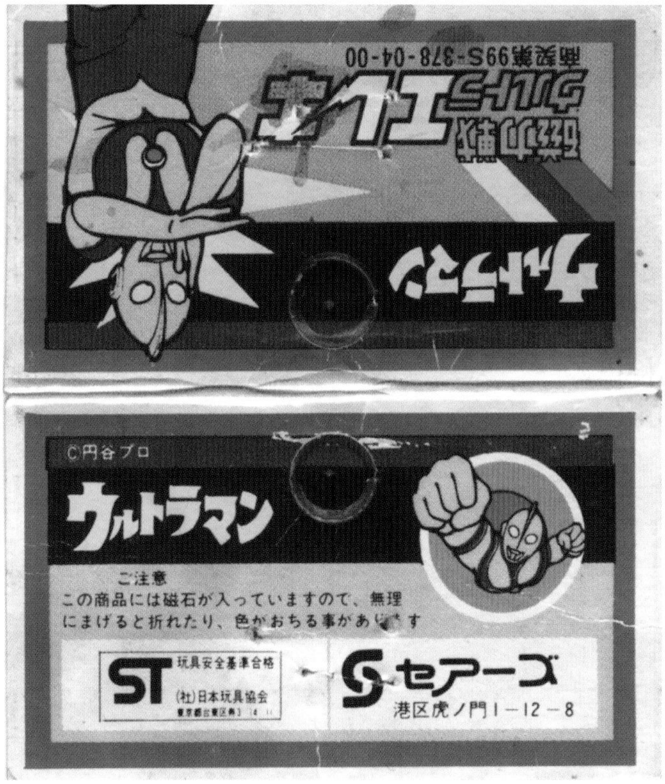
©円谷プロ
ウルトラマン
ご注意
この商品には磁石が入っていますので、無理
にまげると折れたり、色がおちる事があ
ST 玩具安全基準合格
(社)日本玩具協会
セアーズ
港区虎ノ門1-12-8

Then the honk of a car's horn and that amazing book tamped together between his little hands which gave big kids black eyes, and he leapt off the jungle gym and he disappeared into a car door and he was gone.

Soon after when Kenji, his big brother, and Tekuma were all going back to Japan the principal called a special assembly to see them off. By then I made a couple of friends and persuaded my mom I needed some new clothes and a different haircut and I learned to fit with the other kids well enough. We all sat indian-leg style and listened to the principal talk. I remember those three kids, the two tiny ones, Kenji and Tekuma, sitting up with my sister and the other second graders, and the bigger one sitting back with the 6th graders. I remember how they all stood and politely bowed to the applause our principal asked for. Kenji's bow was merely a gesture, though. You could see he didn't mean it. Both Tekuma and Kenji's brother smiled widely, but Kenji gave a cold, fierce stare across the room. His nostrils flared once and his eyes grew tighter with some private thought all his own. It was startling to see and to recognize such intensity in someone so young. He would've spared no one. His heart was metallic. He had a thick hide of leather around him. His gaze was freezing. He hated everyone. He hated all of us. His eyes shot electrical beams and everyone in the room was on fire. Giant robots stepped on the teachers. The building was caving in and UFOs hovered above us. But he was just a kid who had had enough and was fed up with being picked on. He had cursed the world he was living in and he left it to die. Where he was going he was going to be happier and he knew it. The food would be better and so would the TV and people would understand him when he made a joke. All this clapping, even mine, was nothing but a mockery, a formality. He was already gone.

And that was it. All three of them were gone the same day, along with that mysterious, wonderful book. But I thought about it a lot. I wondered about a place where such books could exist. Where does such a book come from? A comic book from Japan. That means there must be comic books for kids all over the world. Did they really have comic books in Japan? Sure, why not. They had kids in Japan, didn't they? I knew where Japan was. I looked it up on a map. Japan was on the other side of the world. It was on the right side to the lower part, under China and the USSR. Where we lived was on the left side, in the USA, which everyone knows is right between Mexico and Canada and Ohio is situated near the Great Lakes which are to the left of where the original thirteen colonies were. I had one book that was sort of like Kenji's big-thick book, although it was the size of regular comics and in color. It just had a lot more pages than a regular comic book. It was a big, colorful collection of Marvel comics my dad brought me from Montreal when I was four or five, in bed with the flu, and he was coming back from hockey camp. *Bring On The Bad Guys*, it was called. It had the origin stories of all the biggest Marvel comics supervillains. My favorites were the ones about Doctor Doom and The Red Skull and the one about the Dreaded Dormammu. The Dreaded Dormammu, he was scary. His head was made of fire.

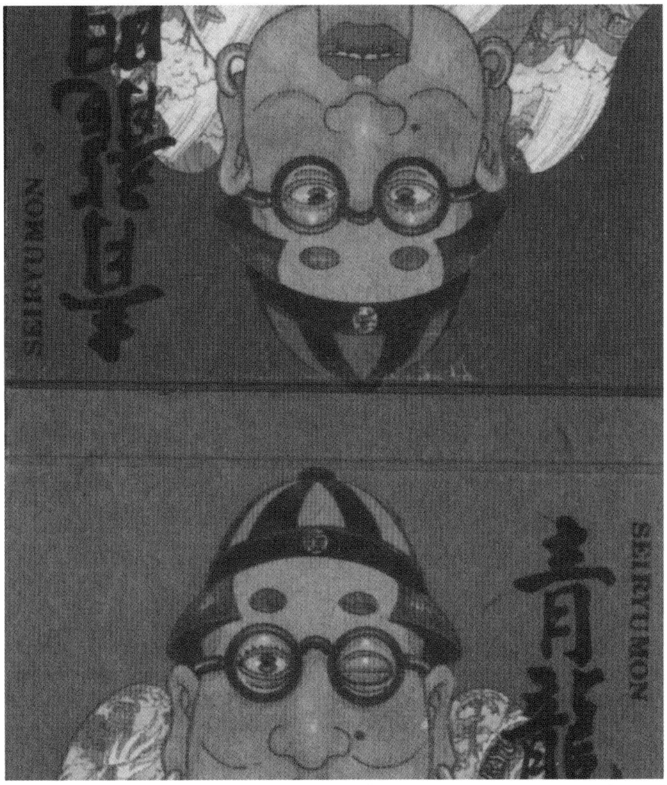
SEIRYUMON
SEIRYUMON

But Doctor Doom's was the best. I imagined telling it to Kenji. See, there's Doctor Doom and he was raised by gypsies and he lived in a circus trailer near a castle. He goes to school and he meets Reed Richards, who becomes Mister Fantastic of The Fantastic Four. This is before Doctor Doom was a bad guy. He wasn't Doctor Doom then, he was just a kid raised by gypsies who becomes a university student called Victor Von Doom. He was probably a student like one of the ones your mom and dad taught when you were here. I liked the part where he makes a mistake messing around with black magic and his science lab blows up and he is burned in an explosion and expelled from school. He sits in a bed in a hospital all wrapped up in bandages like the Invisible Man. That's where the Dean of the Department comes and tells him he is expelled. He doesn't say anything when they tell him that, he just sits there. Then he walks to Tibet to get a suit of armor made by monks which covers his entire body so nobody can see his horrible burns. It's a little like Darth Vader. Doctor Doom has a little ring on his finger on the outside of the armor which he can twist and when he does he can take off the mask. I guess so that way he can still eat. Maybe he has another ring that he can twist for when he has to go to the bathroom. The monks give him some special herbs to cover up the ring so nobody can see it. He blames the freak accident on Reed Richards and devotes his life to trying to destroy the Fantastic Four. That's the origin of Doctor Doom. I read it so many times that the cover came off and the book fell apart.

Other than that big book and the scrapbooks of Buz Sawyer and The Phantom we cobbled together, acquiring new comic books was almost impossible. Sometimes you could find them at drug stores or gas stations. My very modest stack of comics was acquired almost entirely off the single dollars my grandad gave me and my sister when we would visit. But no drug store ever had the same comics, and never two issues in a row. You didn't expect it. I didn't even really understand that the comics I had usually ended with cliffhangers so you'd want to read the next issue — I just assumed all comics ended in disaster. Only instead of saying "the end", they said "to be continued".

I remember one that had Plastic Man being tied up and knocked out and trapped in a box in a gangster's hideout, being pushed through a trap door into a freezing cold river where he would surely drown. I had another one where Captain Marvel somehow got sucked into hell, fought with the devil, almost lost, and was last seen being thrown into a volcanic pit where he would surely be burnt to a crisp. Another one had Iron Fist (a Kung-Fu fighting superhero) fighting somebody on a tightrope over a pit of sharp spikes. The rope breaks and we last see Iron Fist plummeting to a tragic and perforated end. I thought that was just the way comics were, little encapsulated morality tales without a moral; grim melodramas always ending with the hero's grit-toothed defeat. Kenji's book was sort of like that because it had all that destruction in it — people being electrocuted, buildings on fire, giant robots. But that giant thing of Kenji's looked totally different. It was full of hundreds and hundreds of panels. It was more like the newspaper comics I saved, like having a stack of comics which told one long story, with a beginning and a middle and an end, like a movie. But the newspaper comics I had didn't end either — they'd go on forever and ever. It would've taken a year to read Kenji's book from cover to cover. The ones I had were short, and you could read them in five minutes. Within five minutes it'd be Plastic Man shoved in a box and thrown into the river, over and over, to be continued indefinitely.

I eventually forgot this minor chord episode of childhood until one day while I was working for Kodansha and was in Japan, decades later. I accidentally came across the very book Kenji was reading that day all the way back in 1980. At the time I was standing in a used bookstore near Shinjuku Station avoiding a rainstorm, just waiting for it to end. April showers, even in Japan. It was murder on paper, since the climate was also humid. All the books had warped pages and undulating cover stocks. Used bookstores are rare in Tokyo — finding used anything is rare in Tokyo, I came to discover, and the smell of old books made me homesick. With the exception of old kimonos and some old bric-a-brac junk peddled at flea markets in the parks on a Sunday — old handwritten postcards and letters, cheap knock-offs of classic Ukiyo-E prints, old tarnished silverware and broken serving trays — you can't find much second hand stuff at all. Not even old T-shirts, I discovered, much to my chagrin. That was the one thing I really wanted, vintage Japanese T-shirts with cool old logos. You could find all the old T-shirts you wanted, so long as what you wanted were imported from American thriftstores and marked up about a hundred and twenty percent. Unless you're someone looking for a neon-green Michael Jordan T shirt circa 1995, these are utterly useless. Old manga collections are the only other exception to the no-old-stuff rule. You could still get old manga by the bucket full.

Over here in the US we use the generic term "manga" to refer to both the act of Japanese sequential storytelling and also the book collections of these same visual stories. This is the same as how people call a story which is made with words and pictures a "comic" or a "graphic novel" and also the object containing it a "comic" or a "graphic novel". They are conceptually interchangeable. In Japan what is considered the rough equivalent of a "graphic novel" is known by two different names and these come in two distinct sizes (with some rare and notable exceptions, such as Otomo Katsuhiro's larger-sized editions of *Akira*, published in a format imitative of US comics or European BD). A manga collection is called a tanko-bon if it is the bigger-sized editions, about the size of a mass market paperback, only a bit wider. Tanko-bons are usually first edition mass market paperbacks, and they are the standard format for Japanese comic books newly put into collection for sale in bookstores. These are more-or-less identical to all the English-language manga collections we are getting now in the States from publishers like Viz and Tokyo-Pop. Books about the size and heft of spinner-rack softcovers by a John Grisham or a Stephen King. There is also another size — a smaller book edition called a bunko. This is the size of the recent Lone Wolf And Cub editions that Dark Horse serialized. The smaller bunko size indicates that the book is a perennial best-seller, and in Japan it is considered a mark of distinction to have a book available in this smaller compact format. The reason the best-sellers are smaller is because it is assumed the reader will want to keep these books forever, and being that in Japan personal living space is always at a premium, these things tend to take up a lot of space overtime if you collect a lot of them. And so the smaller editions are designed for maximal storage potential. You can store two bunkos on a shelf for the same amount of space it takes to store one tanko-bon, and if you are a devoted manga-ensu — a manga fanatic — that makes a difference. A bunko edition is like a gold medal. I am sure this is why the Japanese publisher insisted Dark Horse released the Lone Wolf US editions at this smaller size — even if in the States it may seem counter-intuitive to make comics even smaller, and I'll bet nobody bothered to explain this to anybody over here. The English editions of Dark Horse's *Astroboy* and *Samurai Executioner* are printed at the same reduced size. It is the semiotic equivalent of saying "a million copies in print" for those who know.

Having floated across the tanko-bons, I picked a bunko off the shelf at random and flipped through it with mild interest. Unless the spine in someway caught my eye, I just picked copies at random in these used bookstores. Being completely uneducated in Japanese (I would memorize the shape and sounds of important words and phrases, making things like riding the subway and ordering food possible) there was just no other way. As with the tanko-bons, most of the bunkos were unremarkable, like reading a drab menu at a boring restaurant. Variations on a visual theme. Most were like looking at the Xeroxable equivalent of Pachabel's Canon for the nth time. But not this one. This one was good. It took a couple minutes to process why I was feeling such a sense of deja-vu looking at an old bunko I'd never seen before. Then it all came back to me in a flash. I had seen it before.

The scene with the UFOs and the people on fire and the giant killer robot was from an old episode of Osamu Tezuka's classic series *Astroboy*. All this time, it was *Astroboy* I had seen way back in the beginning. Goddamn Astroboy. No wonder it looked like a Disney comic. Astroboy is considered the Mickey Mouse of manga, as Tezuka is the Disney of Japan. I've seen this stuff a million times. I didn't recognize it because what I remember having seen was an interstitial sequence, focusing on what the badguys were doing when the pointy-haired big-eyed hero wasn't around. All this time.

Before I was able to finally look at that book without having to look over a seven year old's shoulder I had to first travel in time then follow both the book and the boy half way around the globe.

PP

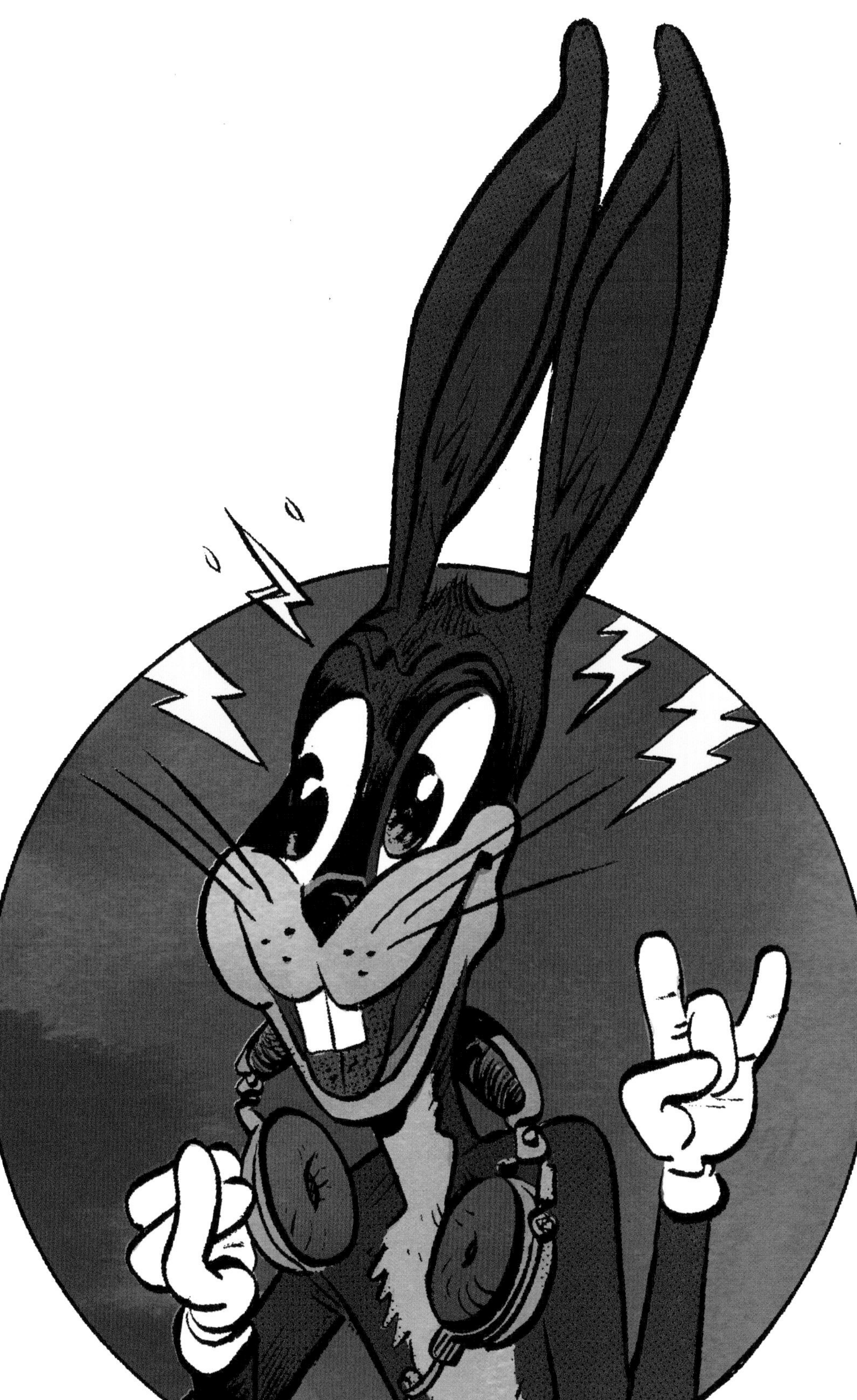

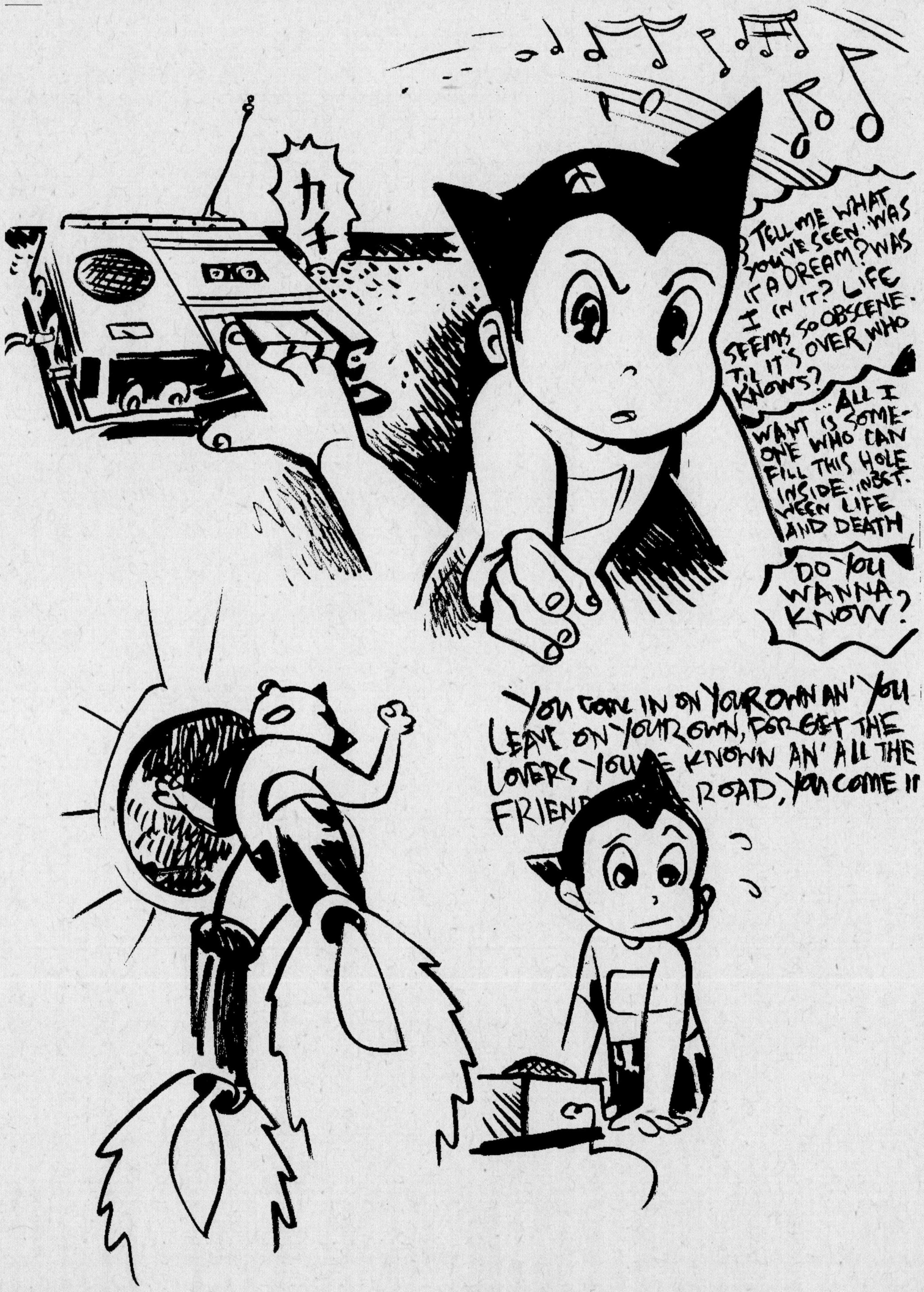
カチ
TELL ME WHAT YOU'VE SEEN. WAS IT A DREAM? WAS I IN IT? LIFE SEEMS SO OBSCENE. TIL IT'S OVER, WHO KNOWS?
...ALL I WANT IS SOME-ONE WHO CAN FILL THIS HOLE INSIDE. INBET-WEEN LIFE AND DEATH
DO YOU WANNA KNOW?
YOU COME IN ON YOUR OWN AN' YOU
LEAVE ON YOUR OWN, FORGET THE
LOVERS YOU'VE KNOWN AN' ALL THE
ROAD, YOU COME I
FRIEN

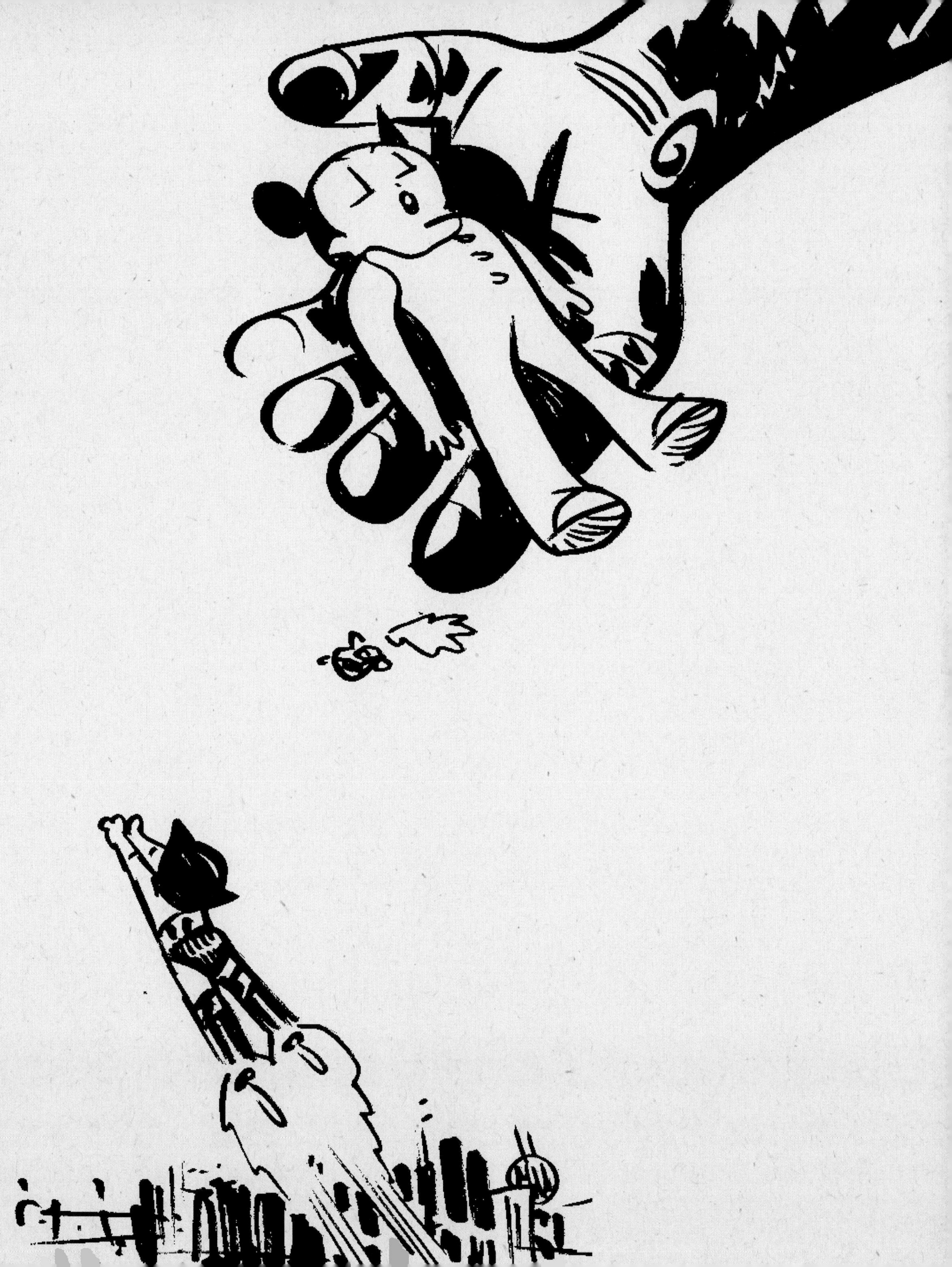

I worked for Japan's largest manga publisher, Kodansha, between 1995 and 2000. I have the dubious distinction of being the last foreign artist working for them into the 21st century, or the first fired by them in the 21st, depending on how you look at it. With the exception of the great French artists Moebius and Baru, I was the only foreigner to last more than five years working for them.

The first thing I developed for Kodansha was series called Supertrouble. This was essentially a severely simplified version of *THB,* without any of the stuff which makes *THB* what it is — they were only interested in the teenage girl characters and their haircuts, skirts, and hi-jinx. Kodansha had accepted three projects in total (Heavy Liquid, Smoke Navigator, and Supertrouble), and I had one large contract incorporating all three of them (hence the five years), but it was the all-girl/teenage cast of Supertrouble which was going to be the starting point for my work in manga. I was at

first slated to appear in a monthly magazine called *Afternoon* (long since cancelled), and eventually moved to the weekly *Morning* instead — which was fine with me, because with that, my readership went up by a factor of 3 or 4. *Morning* at that time (mid-90s) was selling around a million units!

Supertrouble had a kind of lazy formula to it — the girls hatch a silly scheme, they get into trouble, they make a huge mess, they manage to get away with it, step, repeat. This is the same sort of thing I developed with my "cutie-pie" *THB* stories such as "Footrub" and "THB vs. RHM" — except the *THB* stories were free to get strange or surreal or thoughtful or sinister if they wanted, since I had no editorial input, and no space or page count restrictions to consider. Supertrouble could only be silly — Saturday morning cartoon stuff at best. At most, it could be sexy, which wasn't necessarily my intention, either. In the end, the work was a bit lackluster, and after maybe 4 longish

episodes, totalling maybe 100 pages of finished art and another 60 or so in pencil roughs, we shelved Supertrouble and moved onto a story with a contemporary urban hipster in the lead role — Smoke Navigator.

The Japanese editors I worked with at Kodansha were primarily interested in the visual aspects of manga. They really didn't care what you wrote about or what your intentions as an artist were, so long as whatever you produced looked good and would sell like hotcakes in Japan. Even though I was a foreign manga artist, I insisted on working in the same way a Japanese manga-ka would. This was the only way you could ever have a shot at having a real, bonafide hit in Japanese comics. You have to work very closely with your editors, it's just a fact of manga life. The editor functions much more like a big Hollywood film producer does in relation to a director, very hands on, and the publishing house is like a studio. Even Go Nagai, one of Japan's biggest manga artists, had to work under these conditions. Nobody who makes it big in manga is hands off. It just doesn't happen. And a hit in mainstream Japanese comics is a big deal, too. You can have a million weekly readers, and the contract for the merchandise spin-offs, stuff like TV shows and toys and clothes, etc., can make you filthy rich. You can do a lifetime of personal work off the money made from just one popular manga title. There are plenty of rich and famous (and young!) manga-ka in Japan — it's just that none of them happen to be foreigners (the exceptions are manga-ka from Korea and China, who, at the end of the day are foreigners, but not Western foreigners). Luckily, I had good editors who were considerate and cared a lot about my projects and who cared about manga, so all the hoop-jumping was never a problem, rather it was a benefit.

Kodansha published other foreign manga artists from all over. There were dozens from Asia, Europe, a few from America, maybe one or two from South America, and with the majority of those, the editors remained hands off, allowing the artists to do whatever they wanted, with minimal editorial input. They tended to treat foreigners as expensive experimental test tube babies, to be tolerated and indulged, at times nurtured, always to be studied and observed. After a few years, it became clear to them, while the editors and the artists were happy, the manga done by foreign talent wasn't hitting a popular chord with the usual manga readers. It was just too different, too strange for the maddeningly conservative manga readership. The sales weren't equalling sales from new manga developed by home-grown talent. Knowing that, I decided to work as closely as I could within the accepted Japanese model, with all the delays and false-starts, the team of editors, and all the multiple conference meetings and translation hold-ups prior to putting a single line of manga on paper. This commitment also meant working on many projects in different states of development progressively. In this way, over the course of five-plus years, I produced hundreds of pages of material of which maybe 16 actually saw print. At times it felt like being in a Kafka novel.

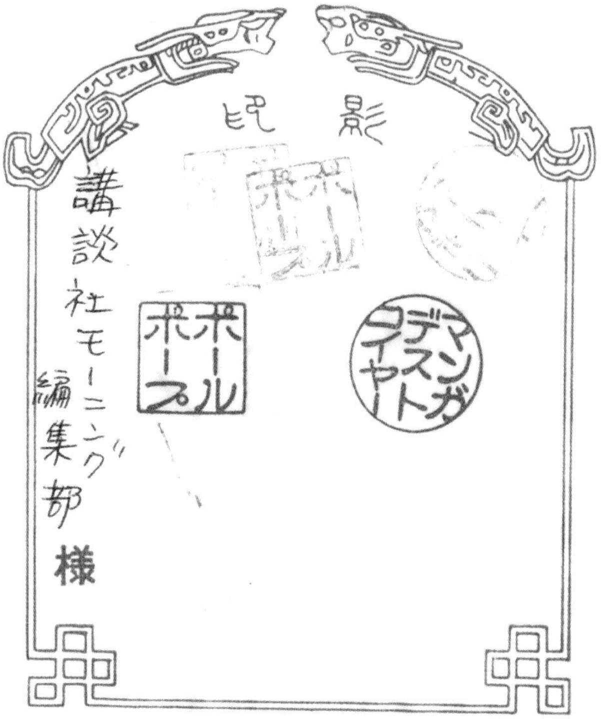
講談社モーニング編集部様
ポールポープ

When developing a story, I'd sit down with my editors and we'd hammer out an idea — we'd do this over the phone through our consultant if I wasn't in Japan or Los Angeles, where Kodansha worked with consultants from a US/Japanese company called Dyna-Search. From the initial pitch meetings, I'd go and draw out the script as a rough little comic, emphasizing all the visual cues. This handmade comic, which I faxed back to Tokyo, was what the editors looked at and approved. These manga roughs like the kind of comics I did in high school — using just a stack of typing paper and a felt-tip, I'd whip off stories without too much polish or grace. Once I got an approval, I'd go off and do the actual story for print. Since this stuff was intended for Japanese publication, I did all the artwork so that it read right-to-left, the opposite from how we in the west read things on a page. It was difficult at first, but eventually I got the hang of it, a facility which has been a big help since. This "magic marker" method, as I called it, is tedious and repetitive, but it works, especially if the others on the team speak English from fairly well to very poorly.

The story which began as Smoke Navigator went through many phases, from a moody romantic tale, to a hardboiled crime story, to a light-hearted coming-of-age story. When Kodansha dropped the project and paid me a severance for breaking contract, Smoke Navigator had developed into a pretty straightforward love story. Toward the end of my manga tenure, I was working on a version of Smoke Navigator which was romantic and more light-hearted than the others, drawn very quickly. The idea was for me to produce 18 finished pages a week. A week! Which I did for about a month before they thankfully shelved this version too, because the art was suffering due to the demands of such a high rate of production. This wandering process taught me how to be flexible with a story theme — how to bend an idea, twist it, let it be elastic and green with life. "Smoke Navigator" is the backbone for the "John and Daisy" thread of my book *100%*, significantly reworked for the better; and ultimately published by DC/Vertigo.

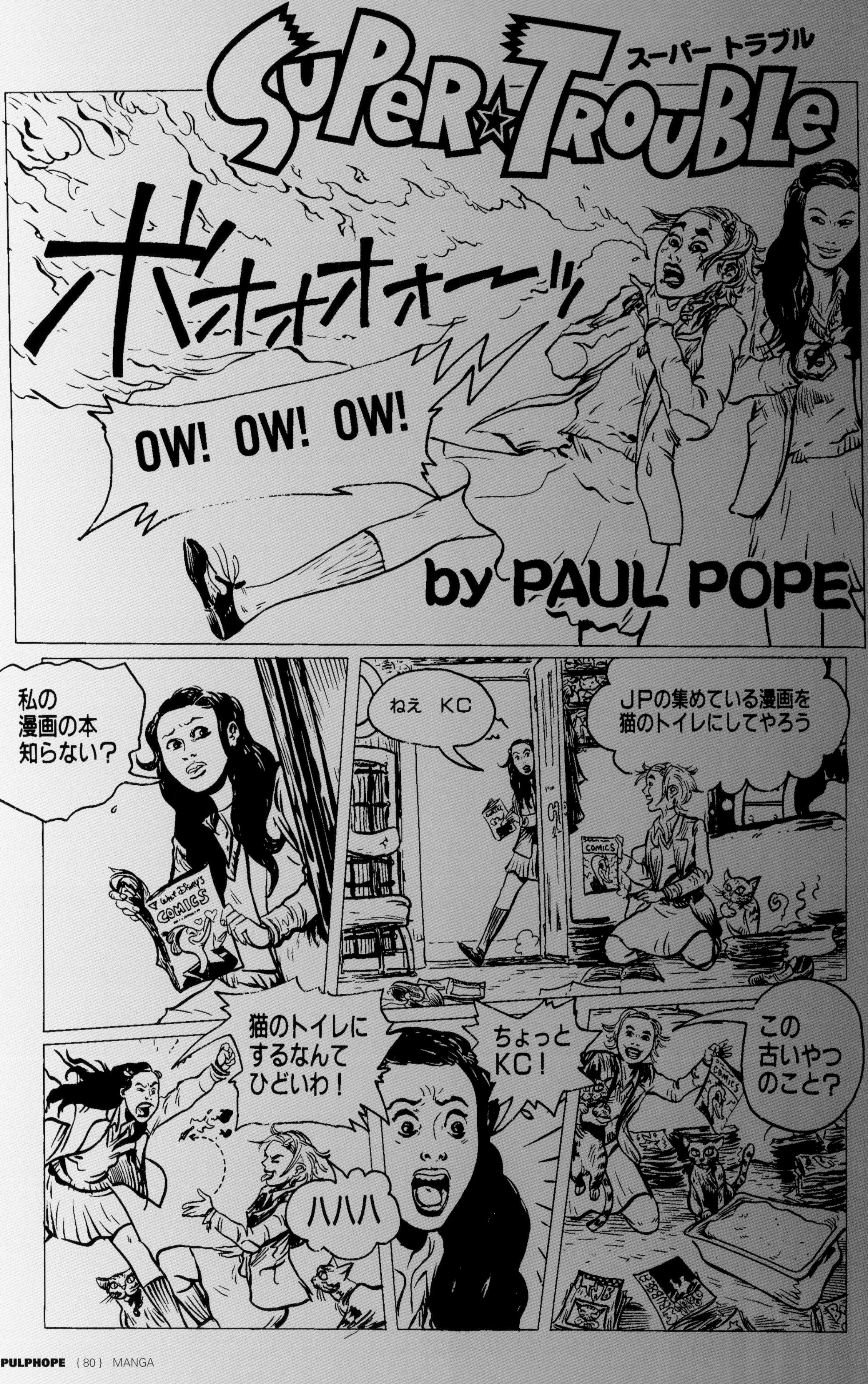
SUPER☆TROUBLE
スーパー トラブル
ボオオオオーッ
OW! OW! OW!
by PAUL POPE
JPの集めている漫画を猫のトイレにしてやろう
ねえ KC
私の漫画の本知らない？
この古いやつのこと？
ちょっとKC！
猫のトイレにするなんてひどいわ！
ハハハ

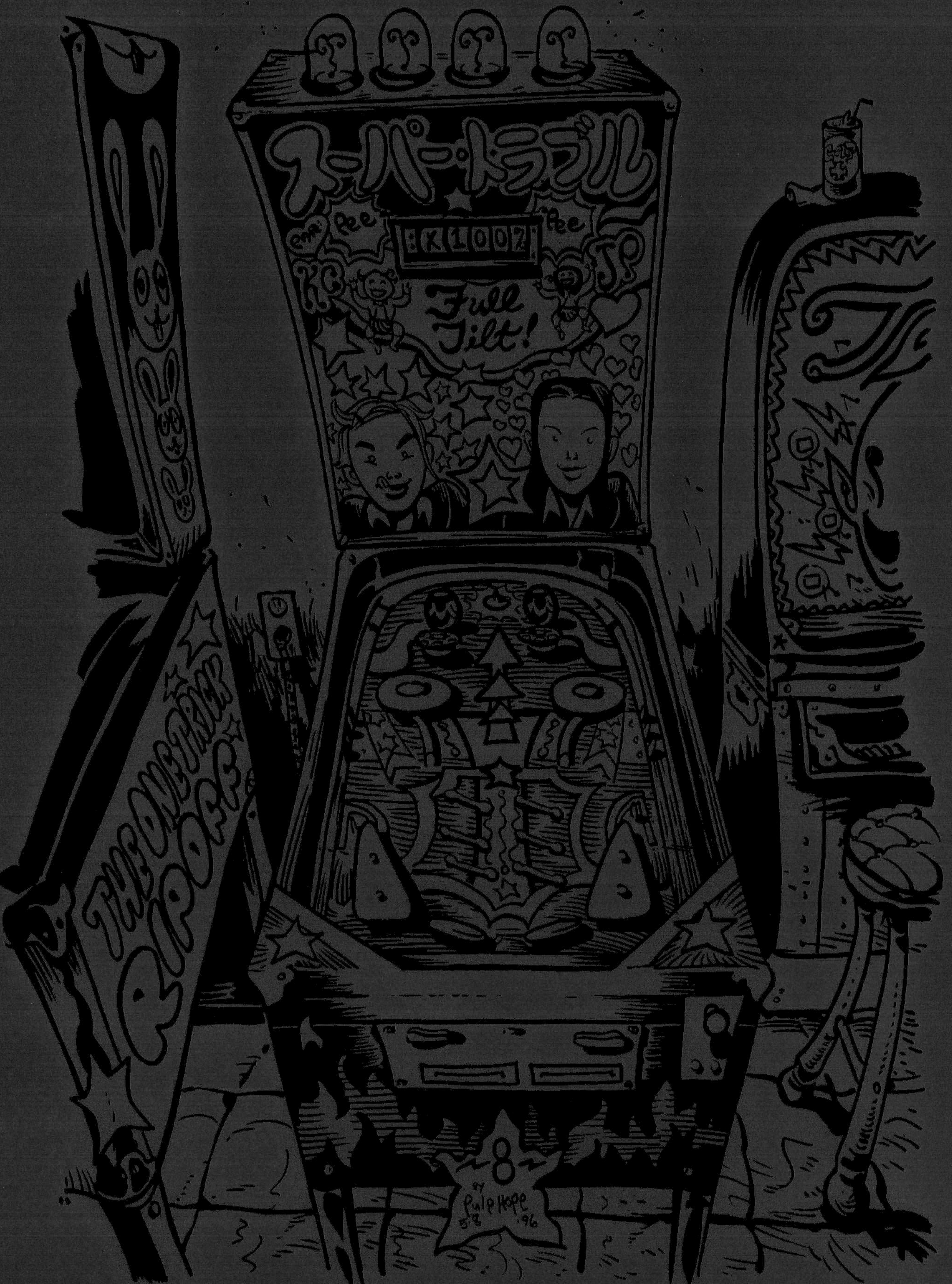
スーパー・トラブル
Full Tilt!
THE ONE TRICK RIPOFF
8
Pulp Hope
5.8 .96

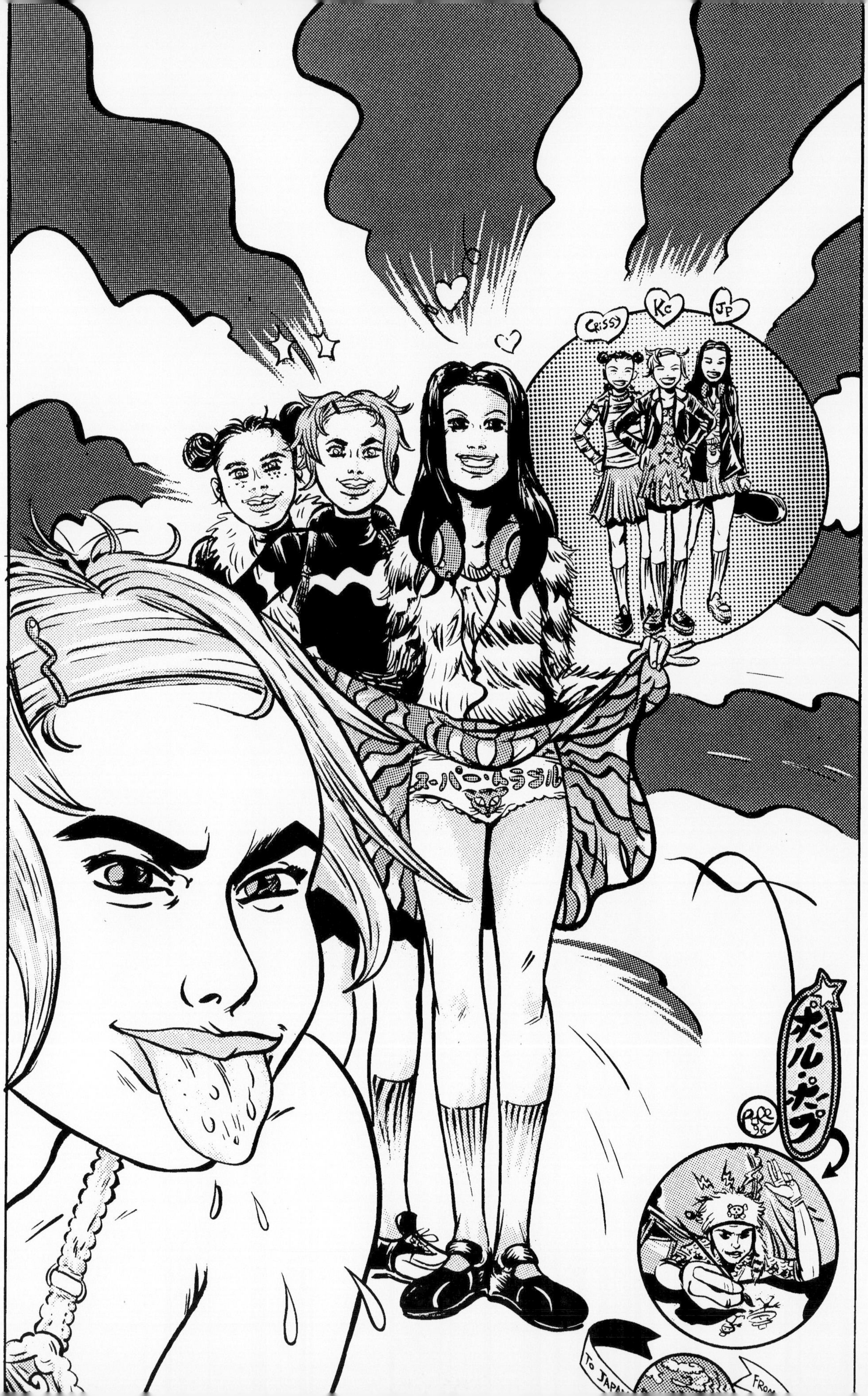
CRISSY
KC
JP
スーパー・ムラガル
ポール・ポープ
TO JAPA
FROM

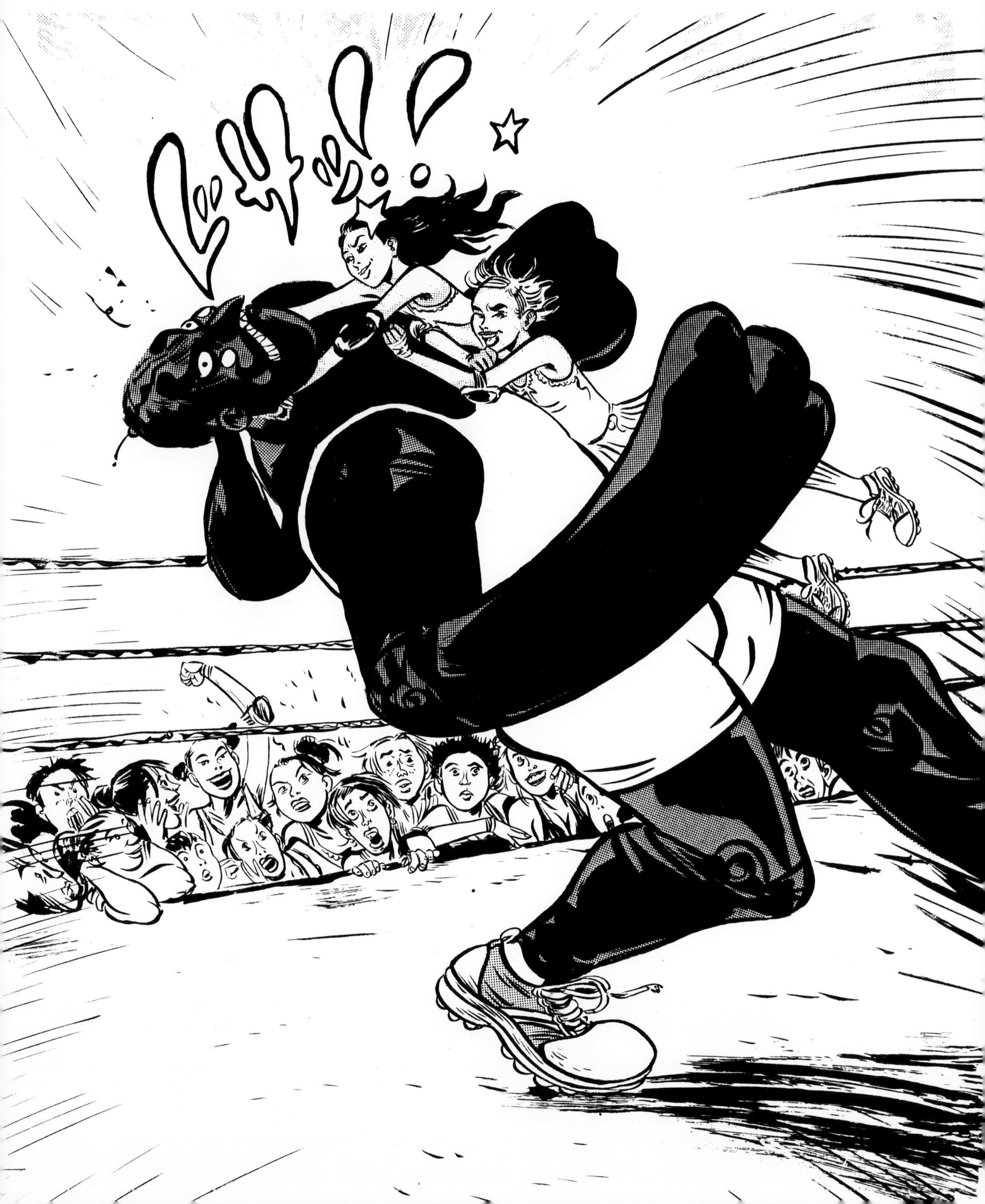

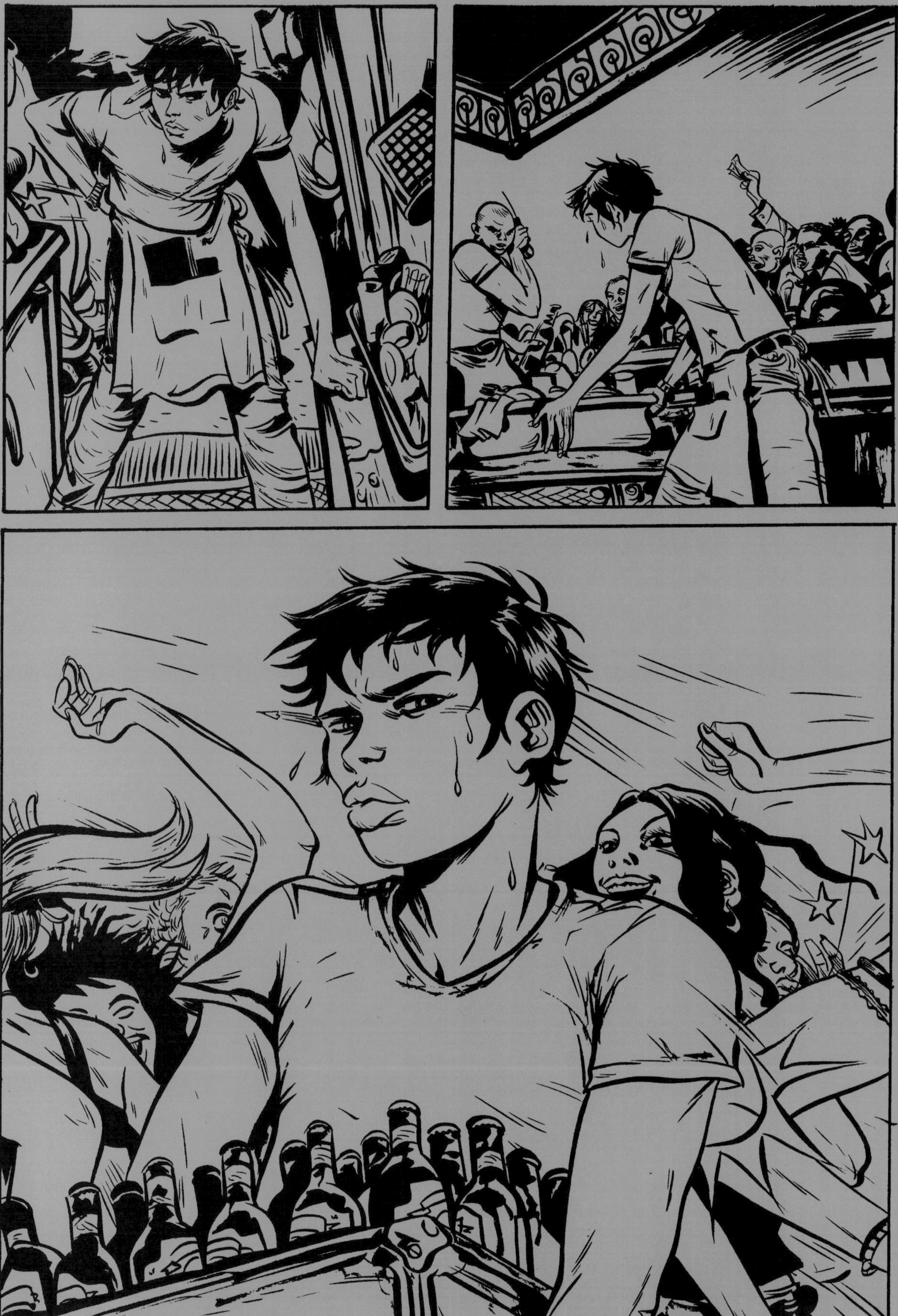

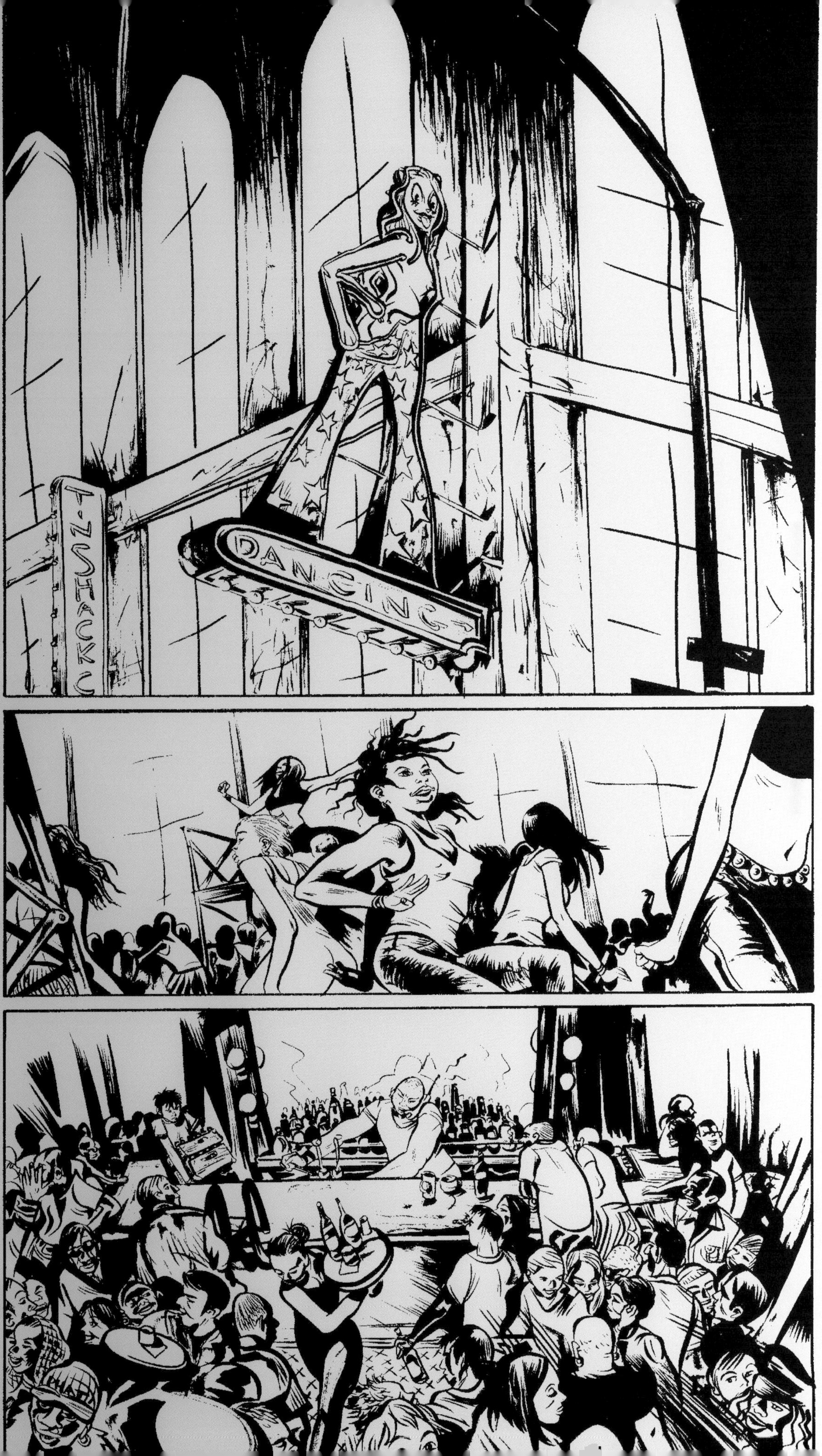
T-J SHACK C
DANCING

UKIYO-E

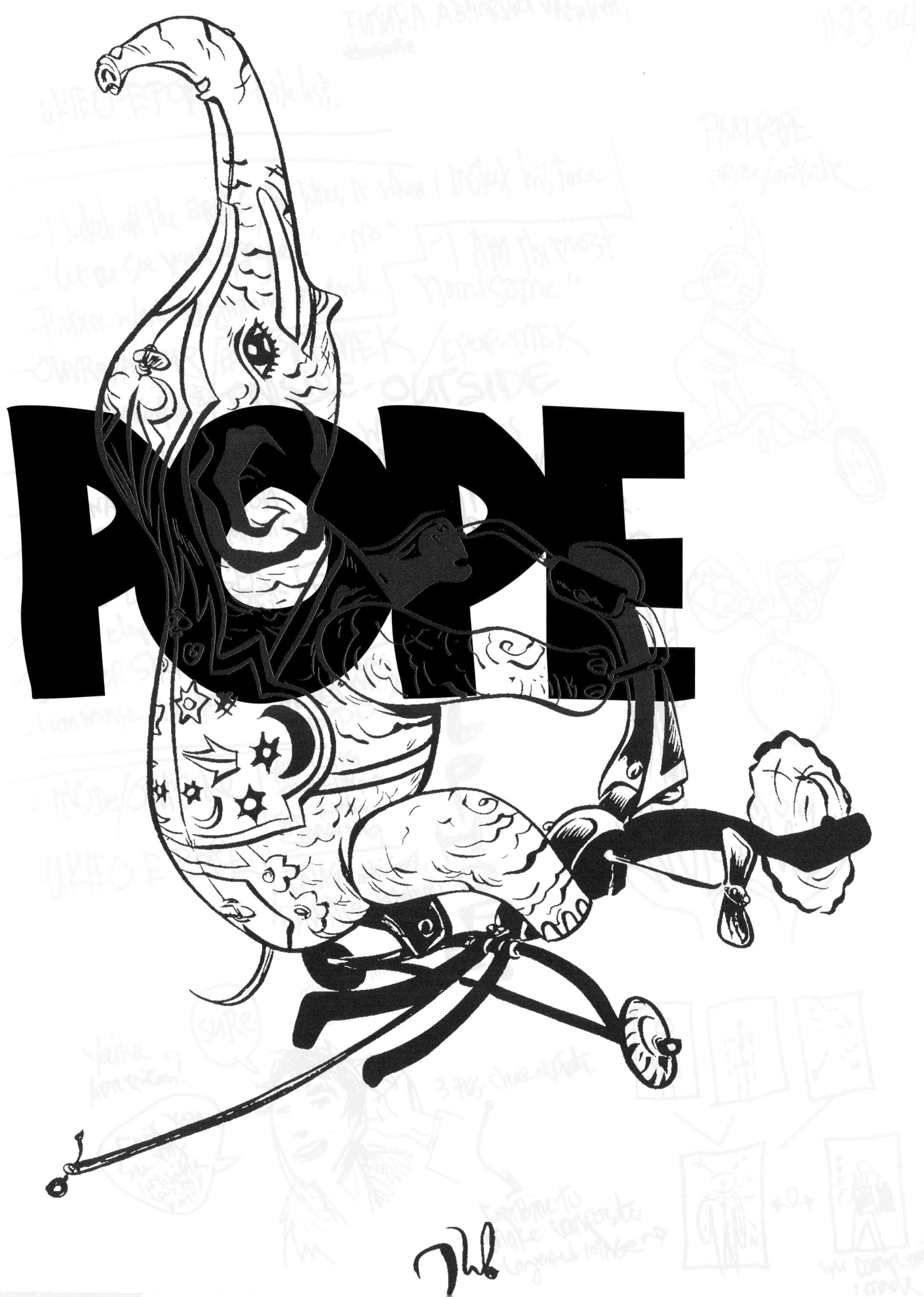
POPE

PICTURES OF THE FLOATING WORLD

"Ukiyo-E" means literally "pictures of the floating world" and it's the name given to the traditional Japanese woodblock print. These are the pictures you'll see offering three-quarter views of Japanese women or maybe orange carp floating in a pool of water, accompanied by Japanese type, often embellished with a small red or gold signet stamp in the corner. Japanese woodblock printing dates as far back as the 16th century, however the most famous Ukiyo-E work didn't occur until the late 1700's. In 1765 the first polychromatic Ukiyo-E prints were produced by Suzuki Harunobu. These were privately commissioned picture calendars featuring a wide range of images accompanied by decorative design motifs and arcane hidden symbols relating to numbers and dates of the month. In 1835, the celebrated Ukiyo-E master Hokusai made what is probably the most famous Japanese woodblock print —

"the hollow of the deep sea wave" — which is that image of a giant blue wave with white frosting caps, rising like a curving palm above the surface of the water, a small skiff caught in its rise, Mount Fuji in the distance. Hokusai, coincidentally, also coined the term "manga" (meaning "humorous sketches"), and published small books of his fanciful drawings of monks, animals, and monsters engaged in battles.

The Ukiyo-E print gradually came into popularity during a two hundred year period (1603-1868) of general prosperity called the Edo, during which time Japan saw the rise of a merchant middle-class able to support an artistic culture independent of the cloistered aristocracy of the royalty. The richer the middle class, the richer the arts. This was a time when Kabuki theater, Sumo wrestling, and popular music were becoming available to the

average citizen. Inexpensive printing methods allowed for the spread of books and posters, and Ukiyo-E prints were often used to advertise theater events. Private collectors helped spur on an exuberant sense of competition among Ukiyo-E artists, and from this creative climate many exciting Ukiyo-E images were accomplished in an accelerated space of time. The prints originally focused on things such as portraits of famous Kabuki actors and courtesans, genre landscapes, floral arrangements, and various expressly erotic images.

The "floating world" of Ukiyo-E referred to the world of the courtesan, the Geisha. The brothel. Every source I've seen relating details of the Edo period suggests there was a healthy escort service industry available to entertain male clients, and many authoritarians complained of the general air of debauchery and decadence in the larger cities. In fact, among all of the classic Ukiyo-E prints, you will find the official stamp of a government censor's seal, crucial for a print's public display or distribution. There was a somber Buddhist reading intended in the underlying meaning of what the Ukiyo-E images represented, and it was appropriate to feature so many images relating to the pleasures of the flesh. The didactic message is the dour reminder that the things of this floating world are transitory and do not last. I've always found the Buddhist notion of sexual intercourse as being somehow metaphorically linked to weightlessness fascinating, as if implying physical suspension and the act of love making share a common psychological-physiological route. A Japanese phrase for ejaculation dating from this time is "the moment of rain and clouds".

I've seen many outrageous erotic Ukiyo-E prints from this era, including images of men and women making love while an old pervert looks through a window, masturbating. I've seen one print depicting two young women masturbating with a huge, phallic vegetable. I've seen another in which a courtesan is lubricating her pussy with the oily secretions of an almond. These were the Edo-era equivalent of stag films. The majority of these traditional erotic prints will depict the sex organs enlarged or exaggerated to shocking proportions, and often if a man is shown coming inside a woman, rivers of sperm are gushing out heroically. These symbolic distortions are really no different in kind from the mannerized pornographic exaggerations of today, which often features men with monstrous dicks and women with artificially enlarged breasts, stupendous come shots which cover a woman's face like icing, and other Olympic sex acts. It seems like people's fascination with the extremes of sexuality and the amplified depiction of the sex act have always been with us.

Relief printmaking of the sort used for these old prints is easy to control if the design of the drawing and the placement of the colors are simple, clear, and minimal. The reductive, economic use of drawing favored by the Ukiyo-E masters, streamlining gestures to little more than a few lines defining contours' and edges, developed largely as a result of the fact that the original, hand-made design needed to be transferred to a block of cherry wood, then carved with a knife before a print could be taken. Over time, master printers developed more and more sophisticated printing techniques and the later Edo period of Ukiyo-E printwork often featured prints with as many as twenty colors. The quality of linework and minimal, overlapping color printing methods of the Ukiyo-E

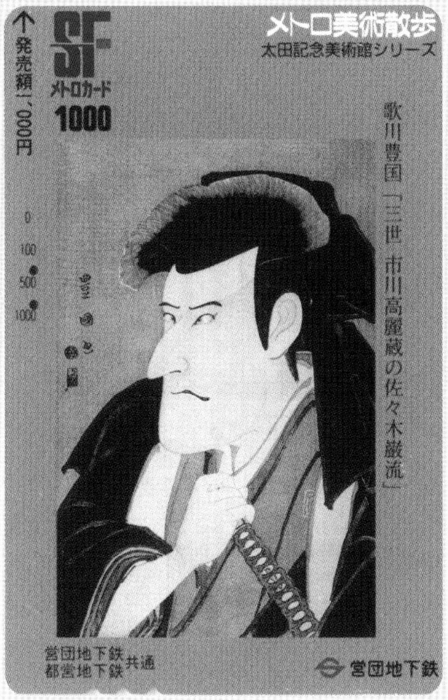
メトロ美術散歩
太田記念美術館シリーズ
SF
メトロカード
1000
発売額1,000円
歌川豊国「三世 市川高麗蔵の佐々木巌流」
営団地下鉄
都営地下鉄
共通
営団地下鉄

share many of the qualities we like to see in comics. Both blend elements of 2-D graphic design, mannerized draftsmanship, and personal artistic expression, within the express intention of producing a popular, mass produced commercial object. And to people of today, so inundated with advertising art and digital-print media in general, there is something appealing and strangely contemporary about Ukiyo-E print imagery. Like the warmth of an old solo recording of Skip James (such as *Cypress Grove Blues*) or the ponderous intimacy of Rachmaninov's *Prelude in C Sharp Minor*, there is something undeniably organic and immediate about hand-printed images. Very often, as with comics or blues music, the Ukiyo-E print is the product of a single artist's hand.

As pop art came into being in the 1950's and 1960's, and artists such as Jasper Johns and Roy Lichtenstein were stealing liberally from comics and advertising, a similar movement was beginning to develop in Japan. Inspired largely by pop music and art, and especially the exuberant graphic design work of Milton Glaiser and the Push-Pin group in New York, many young Japanese artists bent their thoughts in similar directions. In the 1960's the great printmaker and designer Tadanori Yokoo pioneered a pop art style which borrowed images and drawings considered by the Japanese to be untouchably kitsch. Things such as lotus flowers, the rising sun, geisha girls, and certain Meiji-era Imperial court motifs appeared in his work. For Yokoo and other young artists, this embrace of traditional Japanese forms was an attempt to reclaim a national visual identity by aggressively resisting the clean lines and sharp edges of what is called international modernism. Yokoo pulled the anonymous "Made In Japan" seals off cheap incense packets and placed them prominently within the picture compositions he'd create. Using these clichéd visual tropes within his compositions and color arrangements, Yokoo sought to evoke a sense of the classic prints of the old masters of the Ukiyo-E. Whereas they used woodblock printing, Yokoo and others used serigraphy or silk screens, but the common factor they shared was the quality of handmade design. The established post-war design community dismissed his work but the younger audiences hailed it. Yokoo illustrated portraits of movie stars, famous baseball players, writers, and politicians for popular magazines throughout the 1960s. He worked closely with Japanese avant-garde theater groups, and like the Ukiyo-E masters before him, created playbills and posters for the live stage. Others young Japanese artists who were Yokoo's contemporaries included Uno Akira and Keiichi Tanaami. This new Japanese pop art movement was given the name "Ukiyo-E-Pop" because, like the traditional Ukiyo-E prints of the old masters Hokusai, Utamaro, and Hiroshige, Yokoo and his fellow illustrators worked for a popular (i.e. non-academic) audience. Yokoo's pop imagery employed emotionally-charged signs and symbols familiar and recognizable to everybody, and he focused on the mass production of single art images which could easily be obtained and cheaply purchased. He became famous in the West in the late 60s after winning an international competition sponsored by the Metropolitan Museum in New York to design a poster for their *Word And Image* exhibition, featuring poster and print art from around the world. The Metropolitan Museum has a nice collection of his prints in its permanent library which are available for viewing upon request, and you can still find some 3rd or 4th generation copies of Yokoo's first edition prints for under $100.

Around the same time, Yokoo did a very powerful series of prints which were a particularly interesting variation on the traditional theme of the classic erotic Ukiyo-E. Cribbing pornographic photos from contemporary girlie magazines and blowing them up to epic proportions so that the texture and grain of the halftone printing process itself was as much a part of the image as the subject matter presented in the photos, Yokoo created a new body of erotic pictures. He flattened and obscured the sexually graphic images through the use of dramatic sillouhettes and solid day-glow color tones, reformatting the explicit photographs so that all the action was cloaked behind a wall of black. The effect made the images more clinical and alienating, more shocking, anonymous and displaced. On one level, he was creating some very exciting pop art pieces. On another, he was cleverly commenting on the then-contemporary government policy toward pornographic imagery. Censors would literally scratch-out or blacken-over the naughty bits in pornographic photos with a magic marker. By placing pornographic images within the framework of the traditional Ukiyo-E format, Yokoo found a wry way to publically display pornography by changing it so it legally fit within the strict government standards.

郵便はがき
NIPPON
50
NIPPON
20
年賀
AIR MAIL
Street, Apt.#9
New York, NY 10012
USA
Mr. Paul POPE
(再生紙はがき)
平成12年

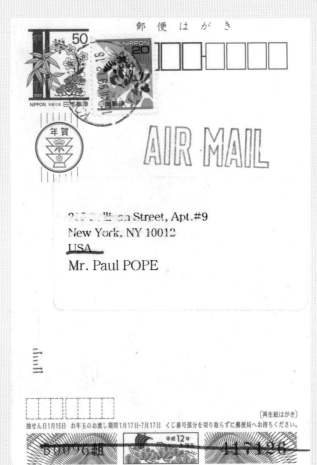

Comics and the Ukiyo-E share many historical similarities. Both were relatively cheap and easy to produce and obtain, and both were widely distributed and available to a non-academic, non-aristocratic audience. Both remain valid art media which initially had been considered low-brow. Not all Ukiyo-E prints depicted images of explicit sex. Some celebrated events from the stories of heroes and gods in much the same way comics do. Both comics and Ukiyo-E contain images of boldly colored, fantastic characters illustrated in highly mannered, highly caricatured drawing styles, incorporating text elements into the overall graphic design. Well into the 70s, Yokoo designed covers for popular manga weekly titles, including the "underground" manga *Goro,* as well as 9 covers for *Shonen* magazine. Also, in the late 1970s Katushiro Otomo — who would later go on to create the manga masterpieces *Domu* and *Akira*, as well as direct many popular anime movies, created some Ukiyo-E pop posters for the playwrite Yamamoto Kiyokazu.

In preparing the material for *Pulphope*, it occurred to me my study of manga/comics/BD and years of practice within the international publishing field has also been dual-paralleled by a patient study and gradual application of lessons learned from the Ukiyo-E tradition. If Yokoo and his contemporaries sought to smash the boundaries of modernism by aggressively applying a purely pre-modern artform, maybe today we can transcend the tyranny of the digital through an aggressive application of the analogue. I am not anti-computer — they were used in making this book after all. I am merely suspicious and unsatisfied. There is an elastic, dynamic energy in the hand-made gesture which no computer can touch. As we move further and further in the 8-bit virtual, and people spend more time in front of a screen or with a piece of plastic plastered against their ear, this seems more and more apparent to me.

I call my work inspired by Tadanori Yokoo's print-design work "Ukiyo-E-Pope" or "Ukiyo-Epop". He has been as great an influence on my artistic thinking as has Jack Kirby, Roy Crane, or Moebius.

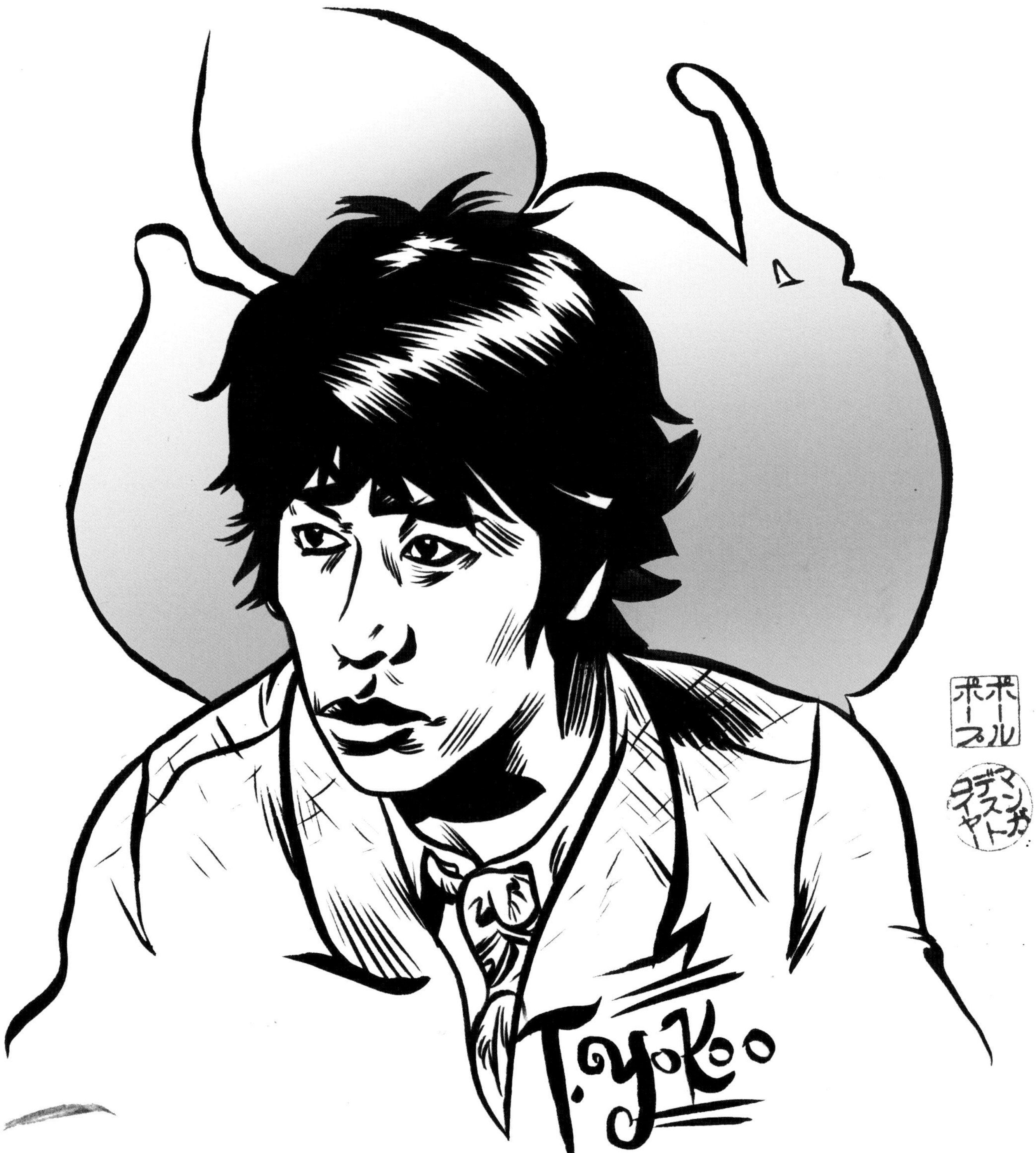
ポール
ポープ
マンガ
デスト
ロイヤー
T.Yokoo

UKIYO-E-POPE

The initial proposal for the Ukiyo-E-Pope series was to create a group of drawings based loosely on compositional elements and visual themes borrowed from traditional Ukiyo-E prints. The objective for this exercise was to (hopefully) acquire valuable lessons learned from a diligent graphic-visual study of the masters of traditional Japanese woodblock printing. I knew that for a cartoonist, there would undoubtedly be much to learn from a "sibling" medium such as classic Japanese woodblock printing, which values a simple use of line coupled with flat, abstracted patterns organized into various pleasing, asymmetrical compositional arrangements.

It is easy to simply take the visual surface or feel of classic Japanese prints (or any other type of art) and incorporate those into your work, in the same way a lot of young cartoonists have taken the superficial mannerisms of "manga" and consider that adequate for an understanding of Japanese comics. Rather, I hoped to glean something richer and deeper. My goal was therefore not to merely ape the style of classic Japanese print artists, but to explore the inherent image-making values of the Ukiyo-E with the practical purpose of discovering new visual storytelling techniques.

The format I chose was to create a series of drawings using explicitly vertical or horizontal compositional arrangements employing whatever aesthetic values I could borrow from the Ukiyo-E print. Where useful, I decided to incorporate specifically Japanese typographical elements in some graphically complimentary way (something I wouldn't do now, and

haven't for a long time, as explained below).

Borrowing an idea from the Dadaist sculptor/painter Jean Arp (who in turn, had borrowed it from the I-Ching), I randomly placed 37 tear sheets into a hat, each containing one suggested word, phrase, or sentence which could lend itself to erotic inter-pretation. From this, I would draw forth 16 random samples which would serve as the basis for all subject matter. For each Ukiyo-E-Pope image, I would utilize where appropriate the "found" sentences or phrases, and, if it seemed warranted, add a text element in kanji or katakana. The hope was that using this process, I might actually create a series of new and valid Ukiyo-E pictures. Whether I succeeded or not, I don't know, but the experiment has been a useful laboratory of image-engineering. Coincidentally, I later learned that Brian Eno and David Bowie also used this method for coming up with lyrics for the album, *Station To Station*, and they derived this idea from the same source. That gave me some encouragement.

The list of the original 16 words or phases from the experiment were:

(to be) jealous of Ray Hanson's pants.
"I am more terrible than you."
carnivorous/cavernous
made-in/invade-in
panty dispenser
sherbert/summer
ouvre/amour
kitchen antics
Big Jim
tandoori thighs
lovely specimens
obese banana

foot-licker
Jim
vagina constellation
the specter of death

...based on these suggestions, I derived the first group of Ukiyo-E images. Not all of the pictures were erotica, as it turned out. Sometimes the pictures wanted to go in other directions.

When I returned to the Ukiyo-E-Pope series later, I decided the new batch of pictures would be thematically more open-ended, not necessarily required to be of erotic subject matter, or for that matter, of anything in particular, at all. They could be pictures of just about anything. Since having read Ira Progoff's book *At A Journal Workshop,* I have more recently become interested in trying to describe through visual imagery things which are impossible to describe easily through words, and so there is in this new series more of a pre-occupation with personal dreams and subjective memories as subject matter. Also, as I ultimately believe the role of design in human culture is to communicate meanings, I now regard using Japanese for pictures such as these Ukiyo-E-Popes to be a kind of typographical fetish, in which I must admit I'm no longer very interested. I have also tried to allow in this new series a further exploration of any other spontaneously "unconscious" imagery which might appear, such as the repetition of Napoleon Bonaparte-related themes. I really have no idea from where that comes.

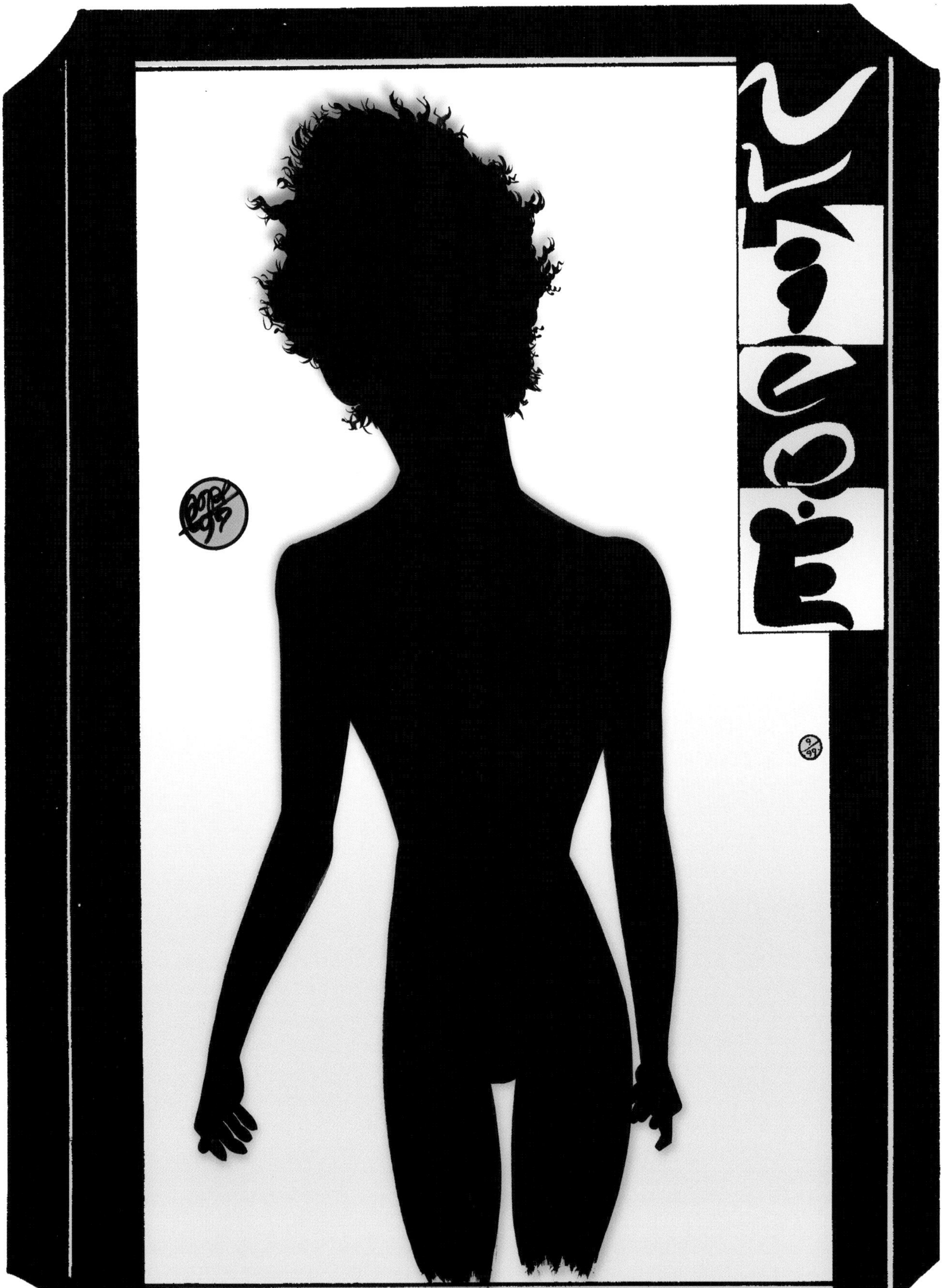

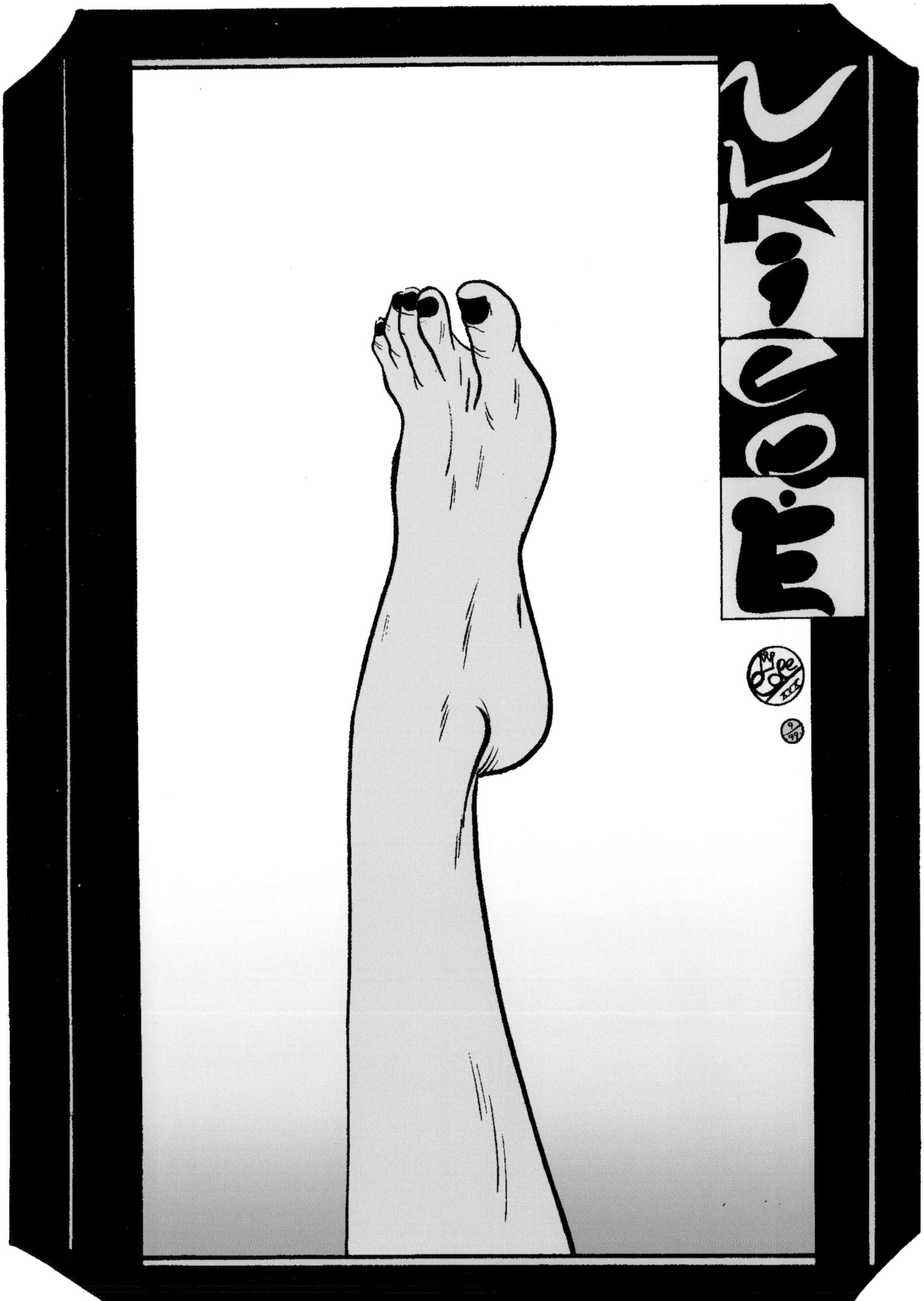

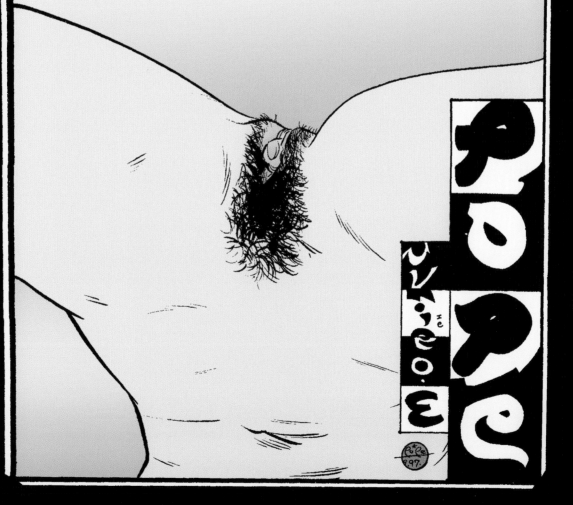

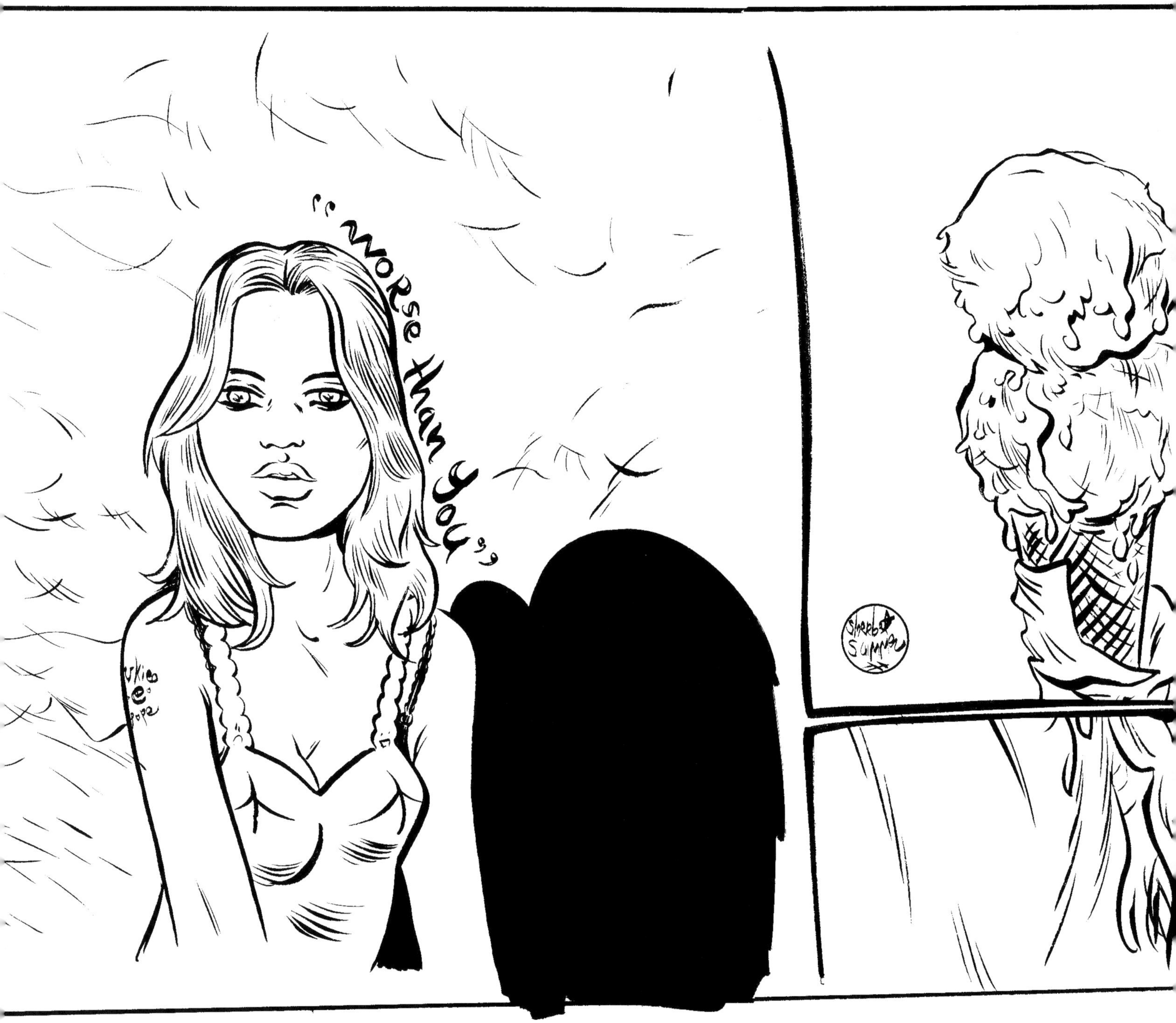
"worse than you"

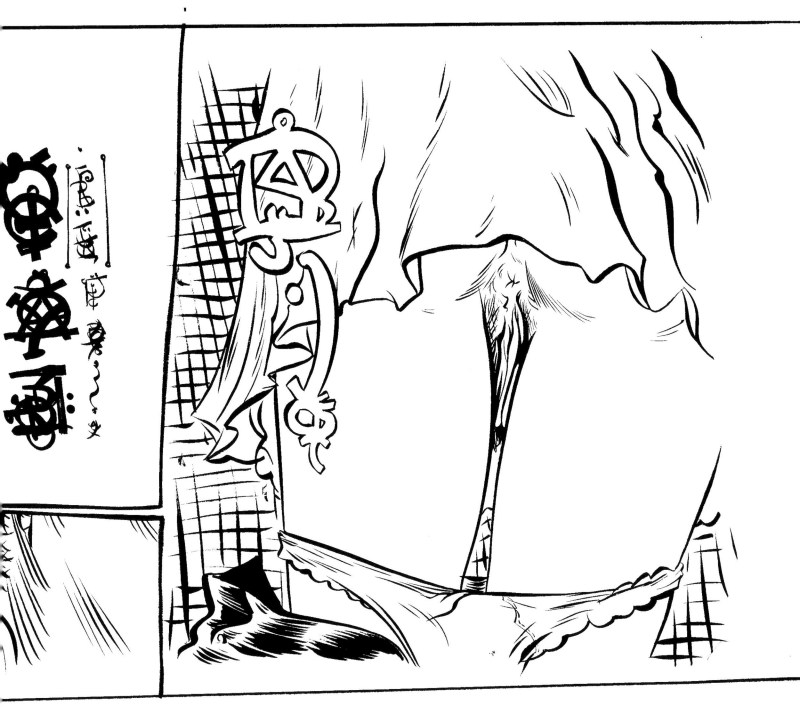

"UKiEO.E.Pope"
xxx 9.08.97

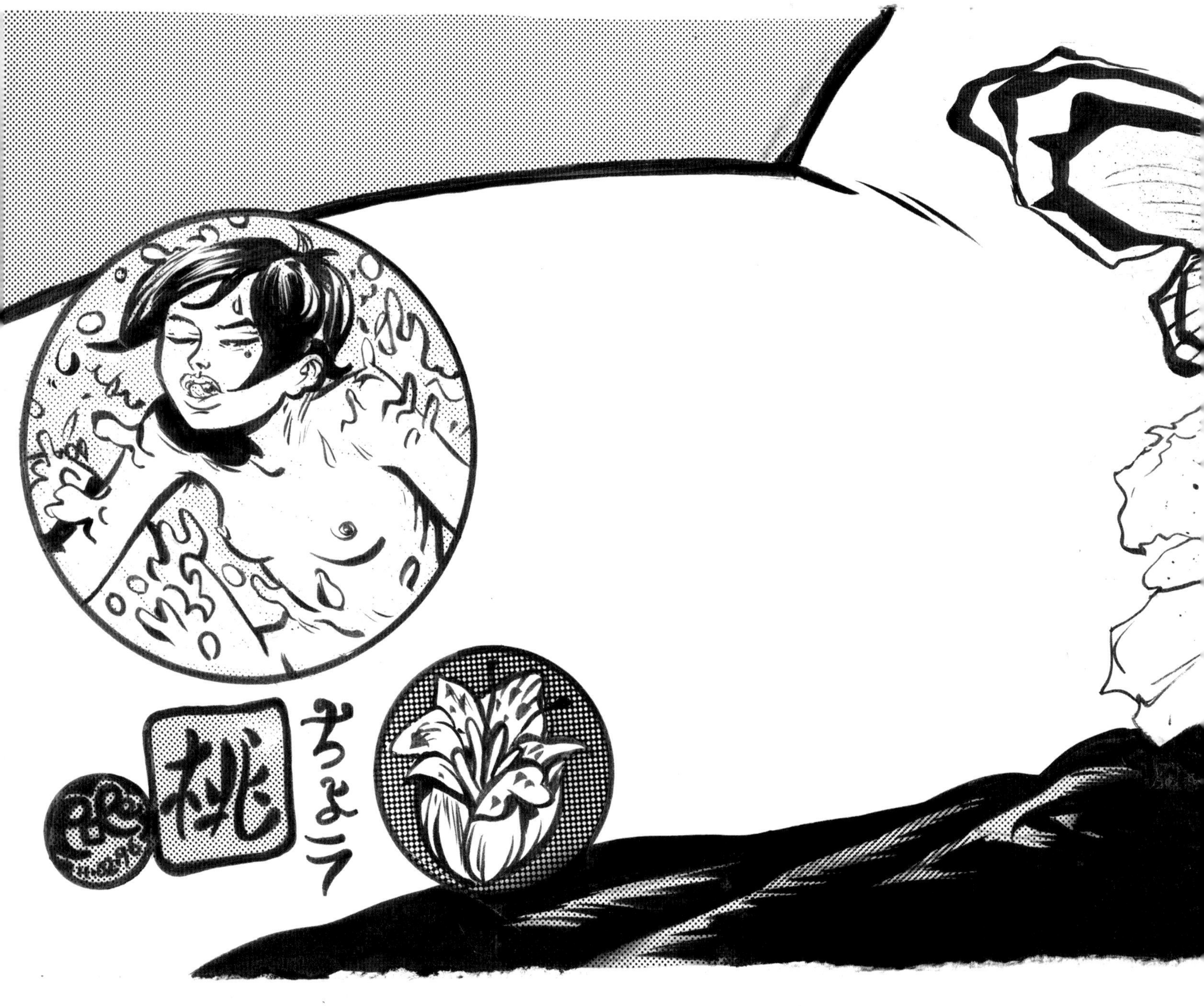
桃

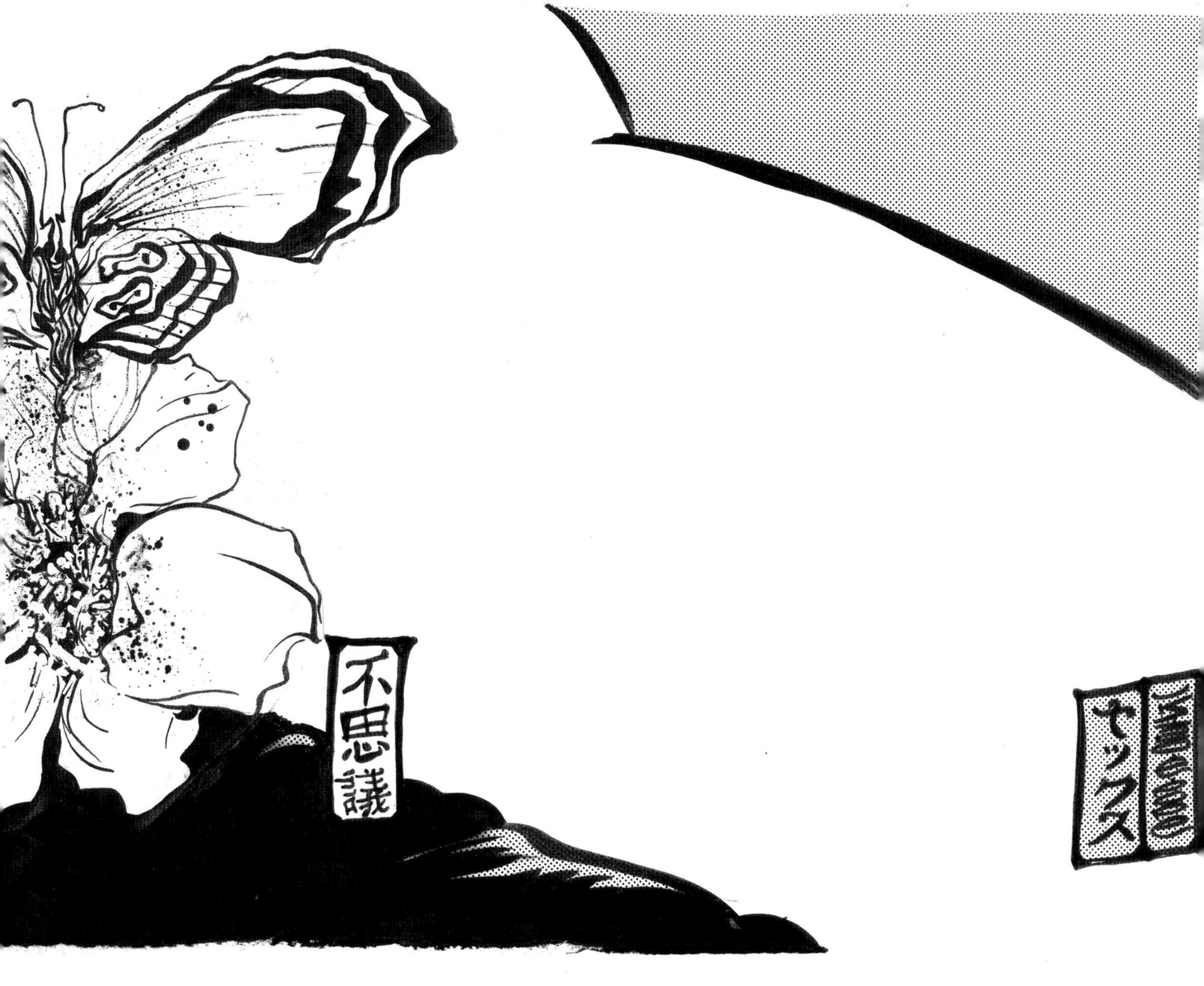
セックス
不思議

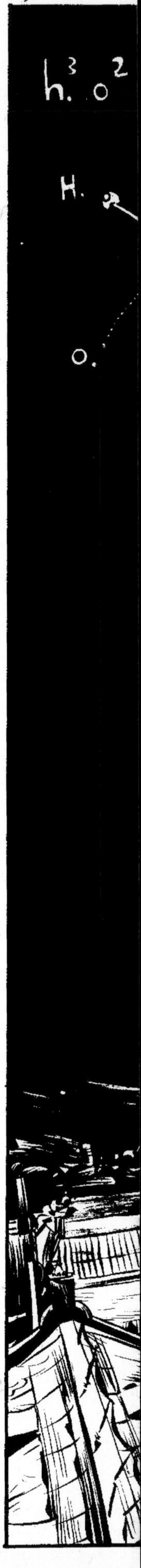
h3 o2
H.
O.

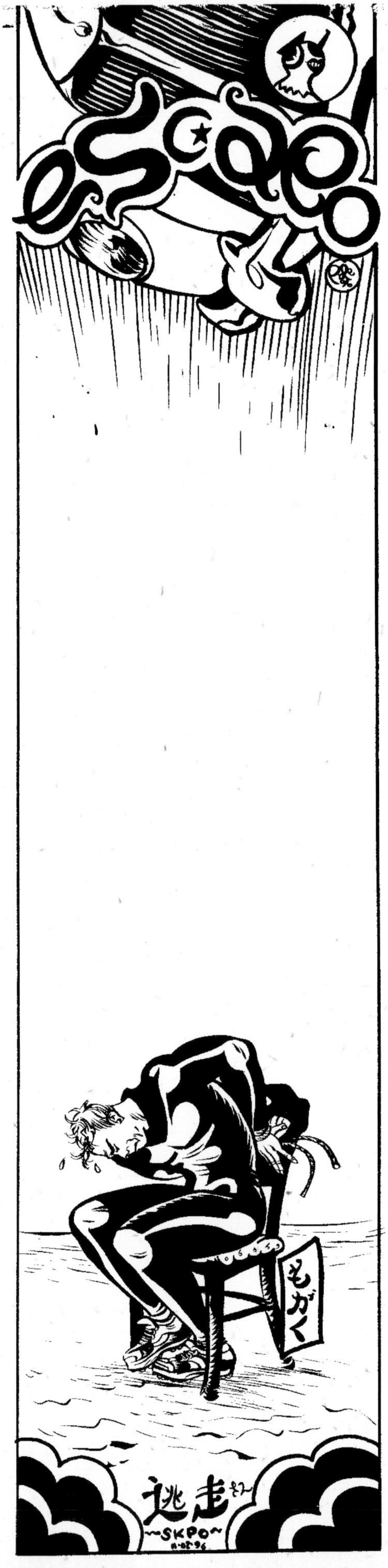
もがく
逃走
~SKPO~

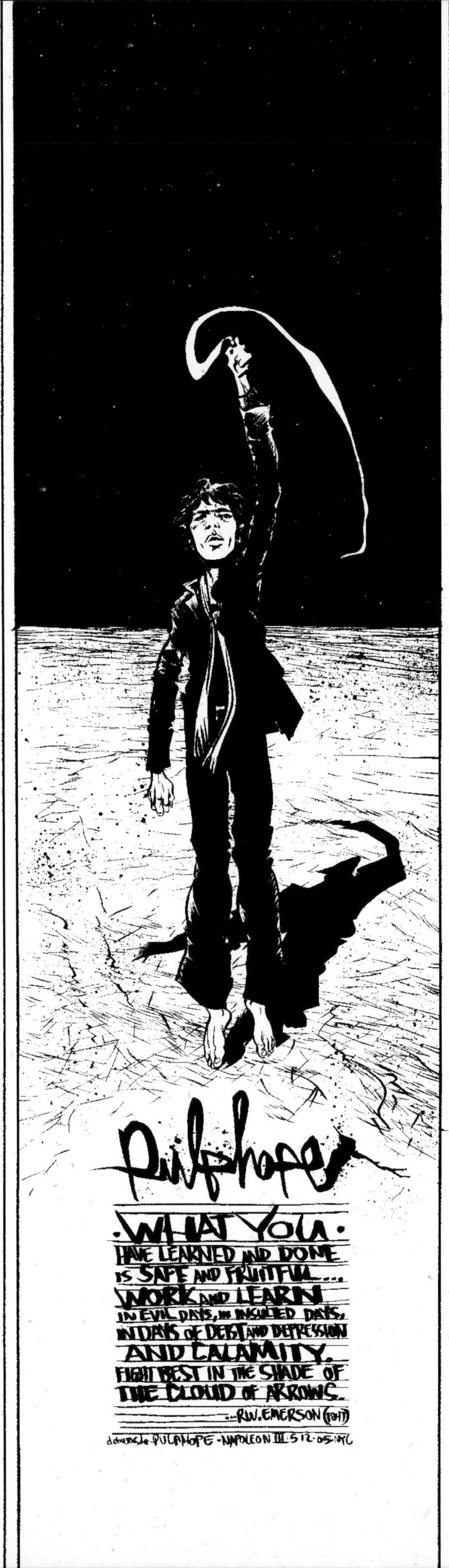
pulphope
·WHAT YOU·
HAVE LEARNED AND DONE
IS SAFE AND FRUITFUL...
WORK AND LEARN
IN EVIL DAYS, IN INSULTED DAYS,
IN DAYS OF DEBT AND DEPRESSION
AND CALAMITY.
FIGHT BEST IN THE SHADE OF
THE CLOUD OF ARROWS.
...R.W. EMERSON (1847)
PULPHOPE - NAPOLEON III 5.12.05 NYC

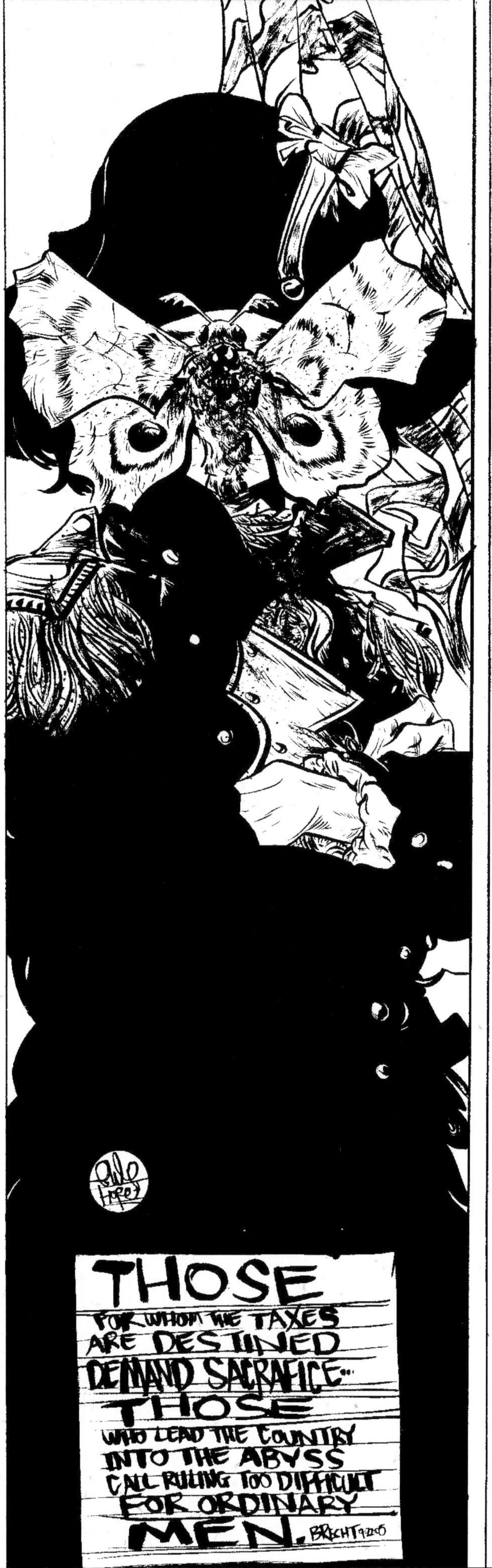
THOSE
FOR WHOM THE TAXES
ARE DESTINED
DEMAND SACRAFICE...
THOSE
WHO LEAD THE COUNTRY
INTO THE ABYSS
CALL RULING TOO DIFFICULT
FOR ORDINARY
MEN.
BRECHT 9-22-05
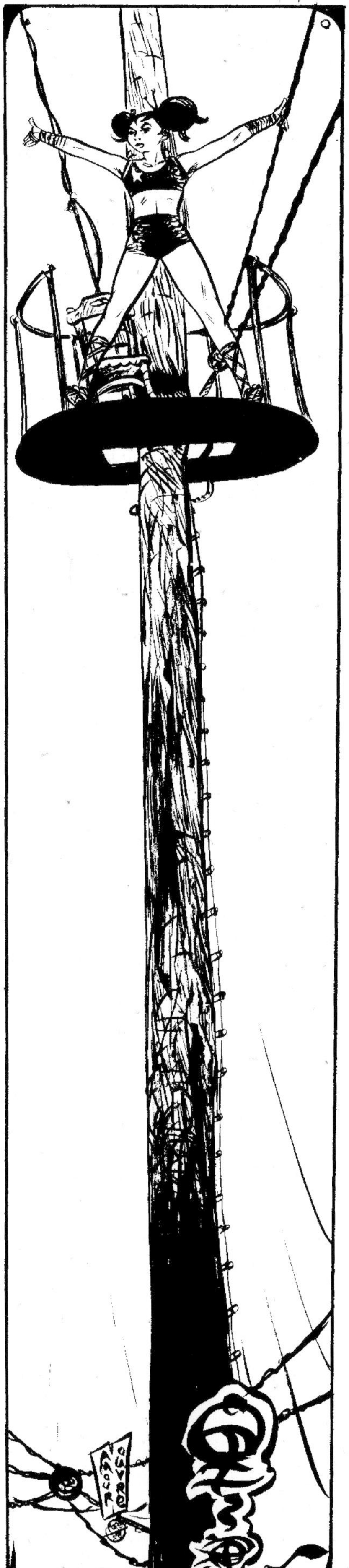
AMOUR
OUVRE
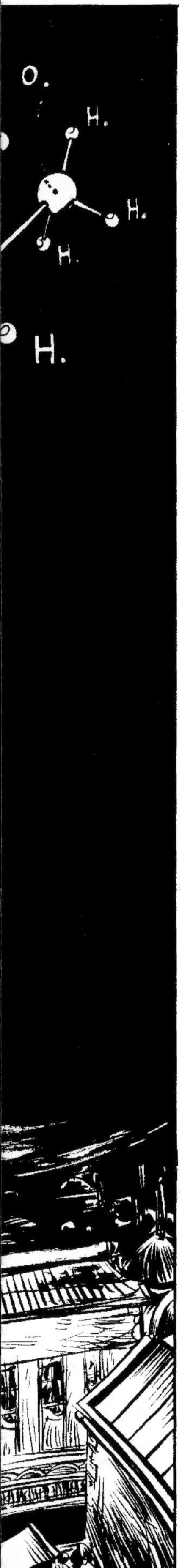
O.
H.
H.
H.
H.

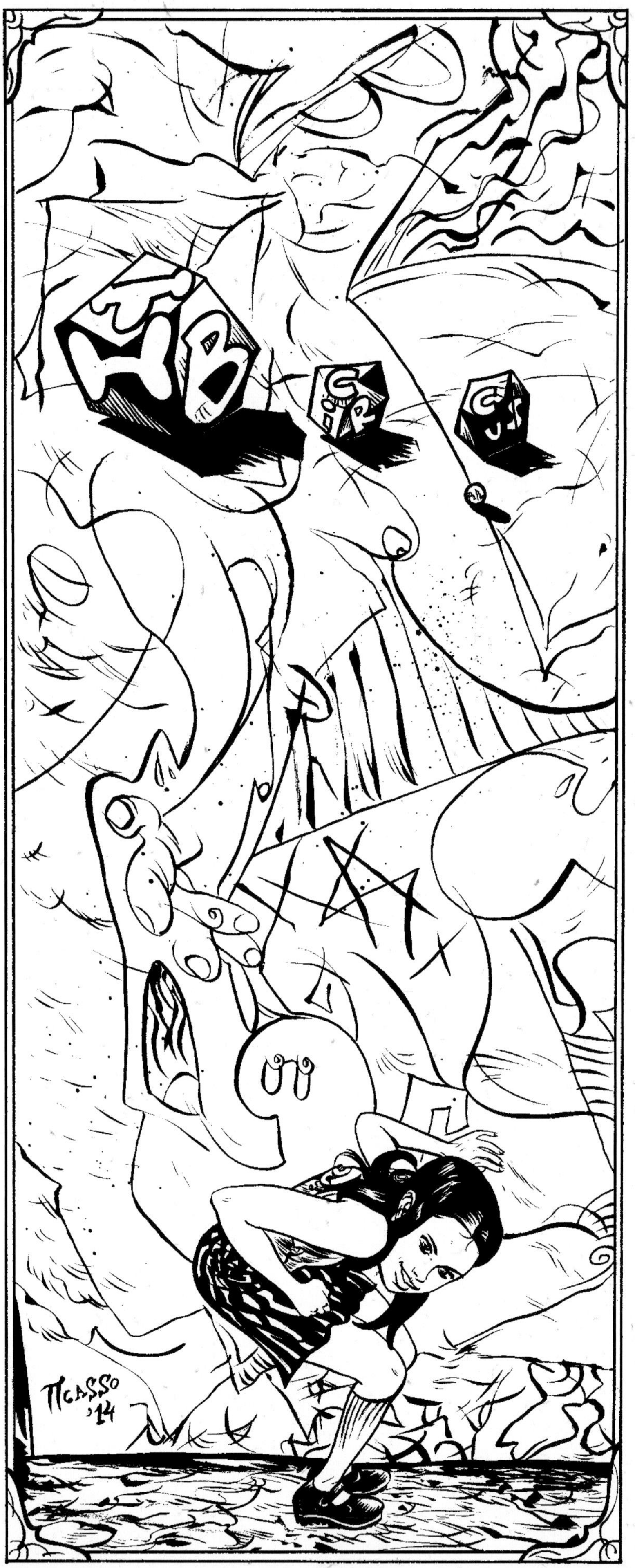

ΠCASSO
'14

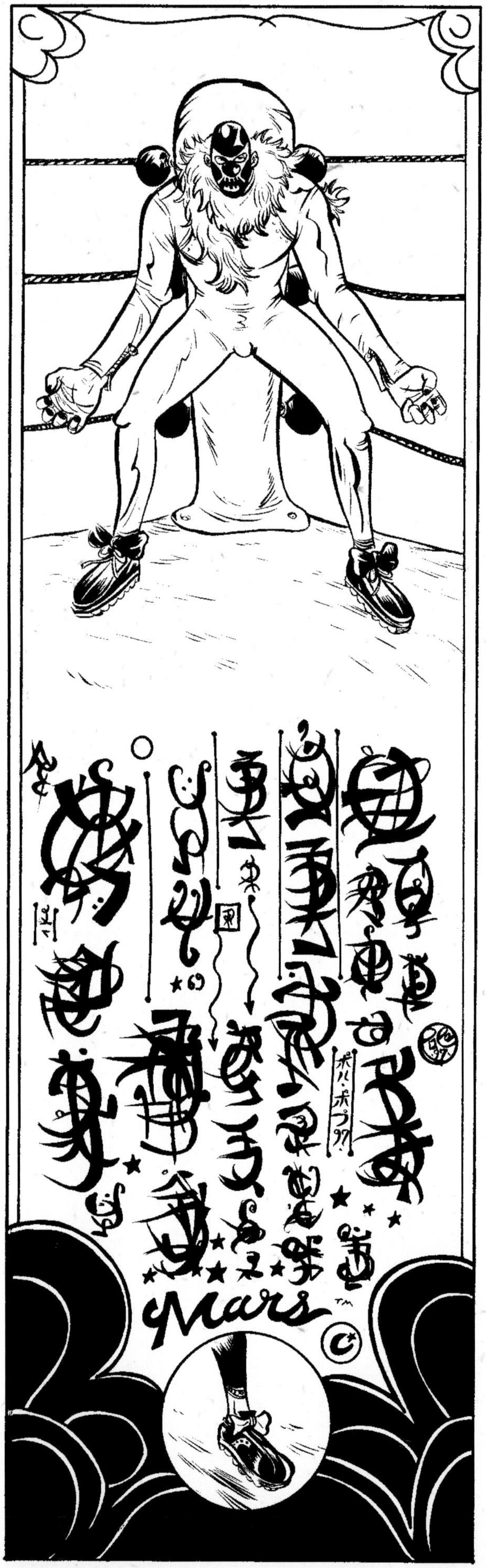

ポハ・ポプ97
Mars ™

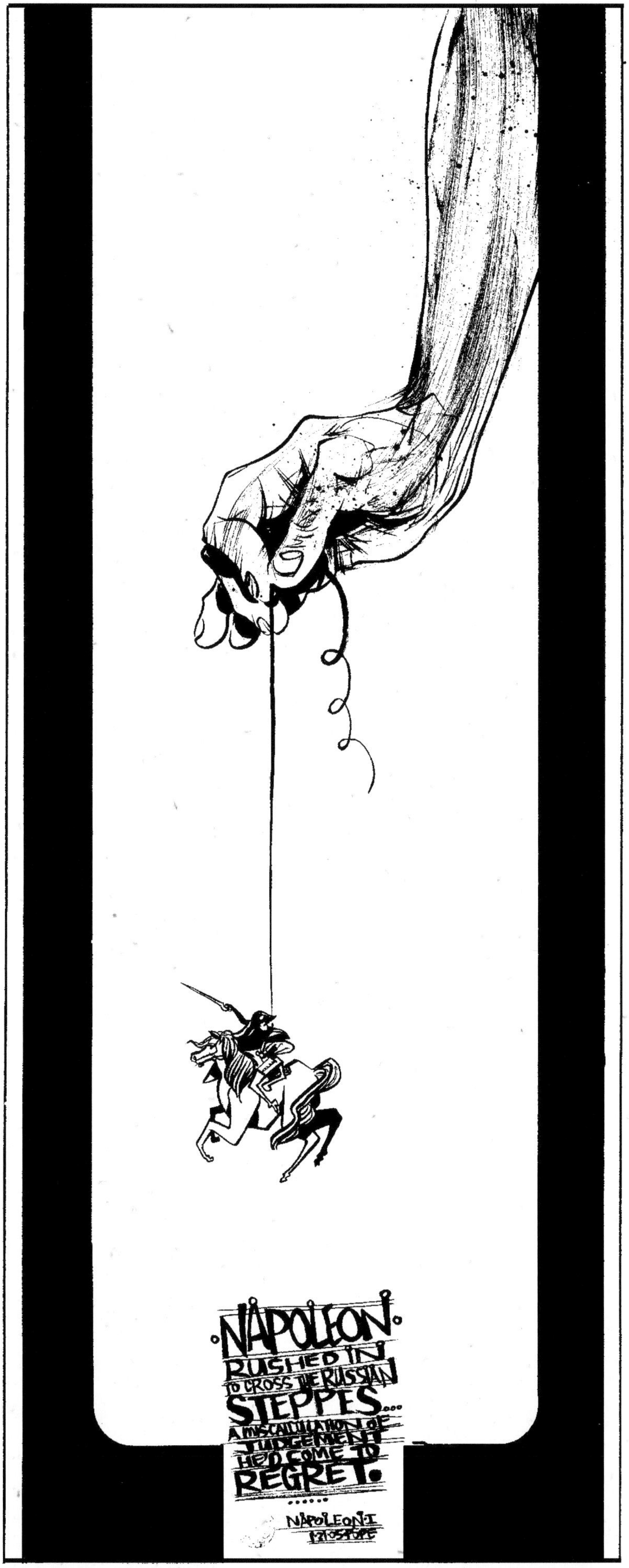
NAPOLEON
RUSHED IN
TO CROSS THE RUSSIAN
STEPPES...
A MISCALCULATION OF
JUDGEMENT
HE'D COME TO
REGRET.
NAPOLEON·I
1·21·05·POPE

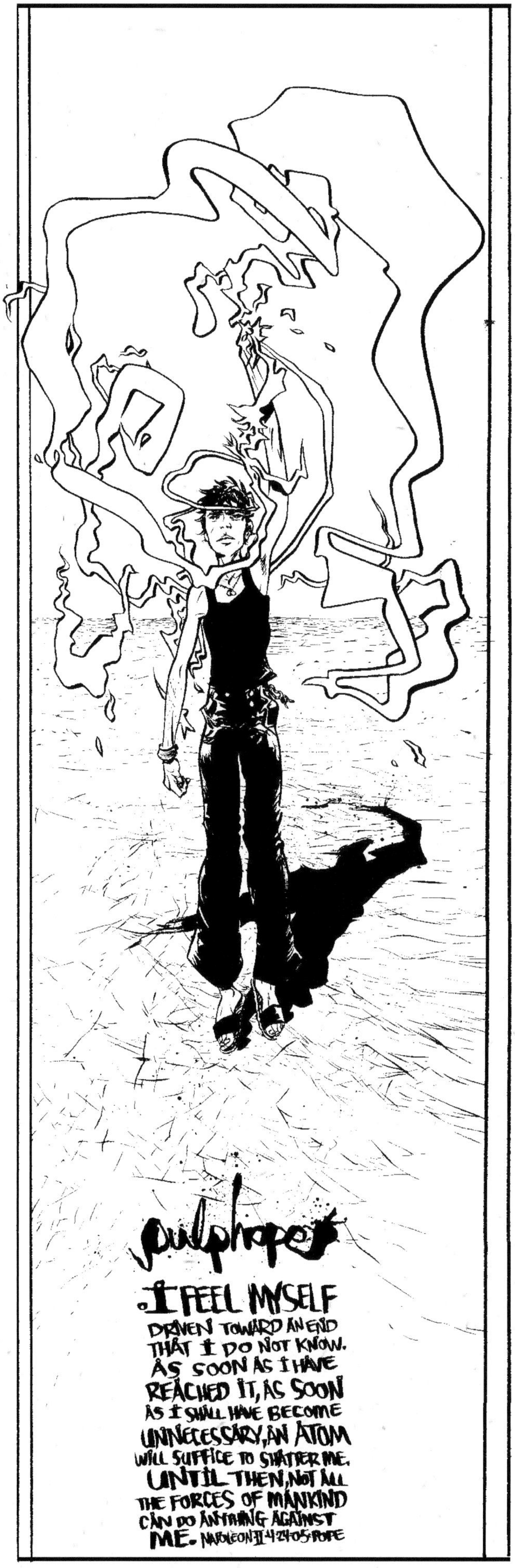
pulphope
I FEEL MYSELF
DRIVEN TOWARD AN END
THAT I DO NOT KNOW.
AS SOON AS I HAVE
REACHED IT, AS SOON
AS I SHALL HAVE BECOME
UNNECESSARY, AN ATOM
WILL SUFFICE TO SHATTER ME.
UNTIL THEN, NOT ALL
THE FORCES OF MANKIND
CAN DO ANYTHING AGAINST
ME.
NAPOLEON II 4·24·05·POPE

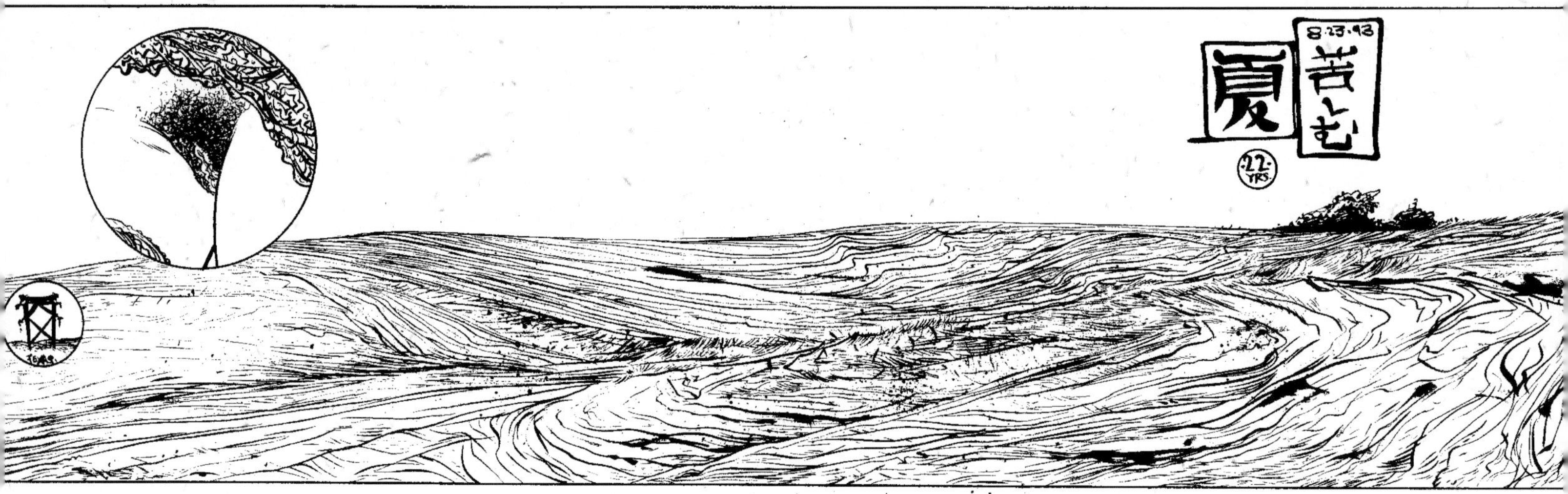
8.23.93
夏
22 YRS

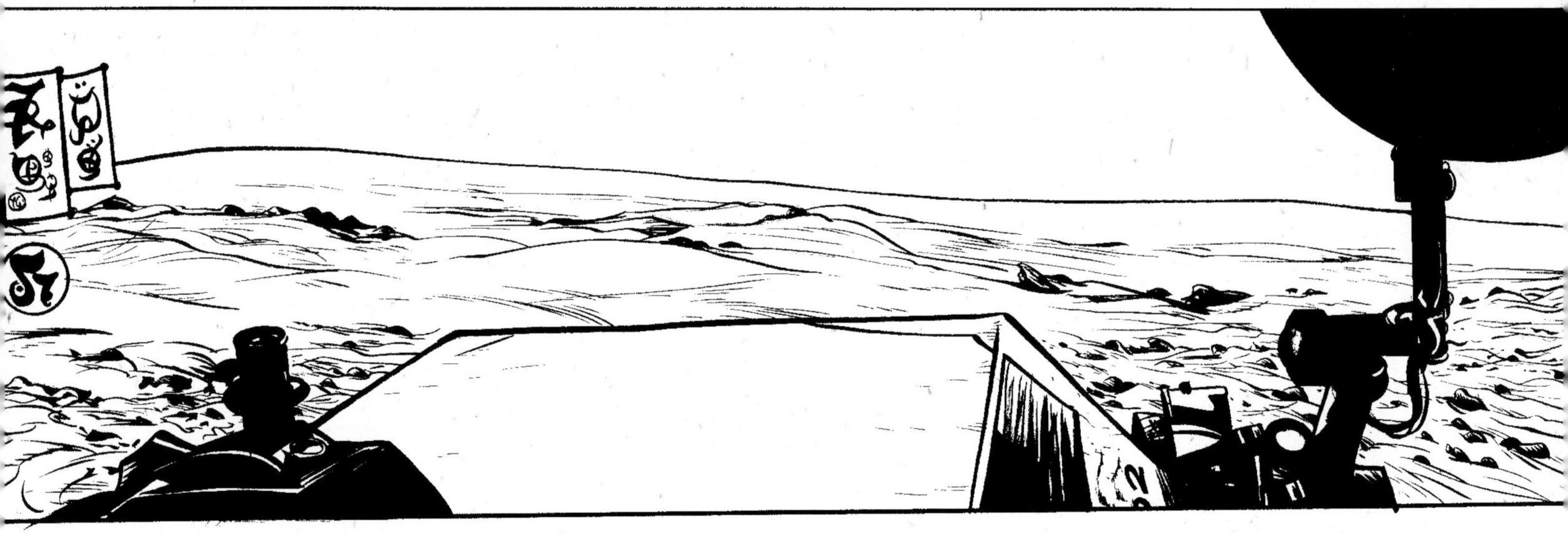

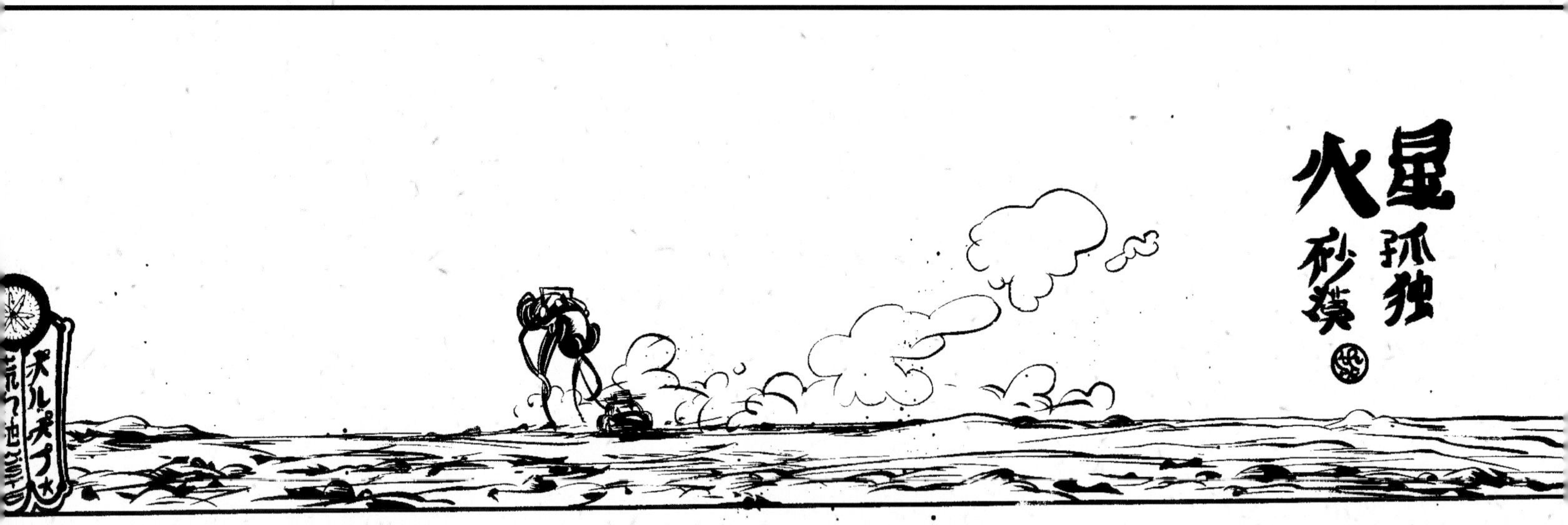
火星
孤独
砂漠

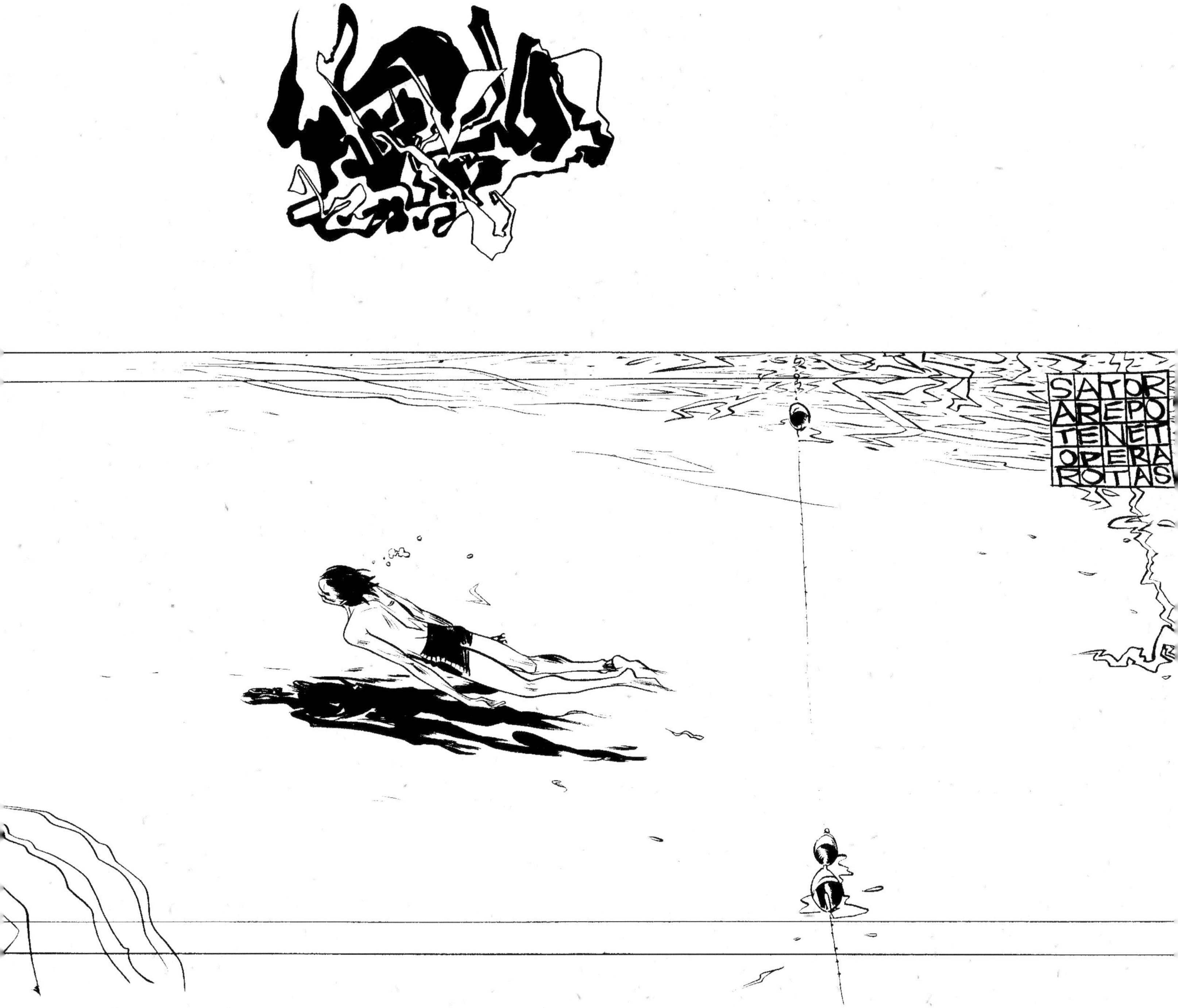
SATOR
AREPO
TENET
OPERA
ROTAS

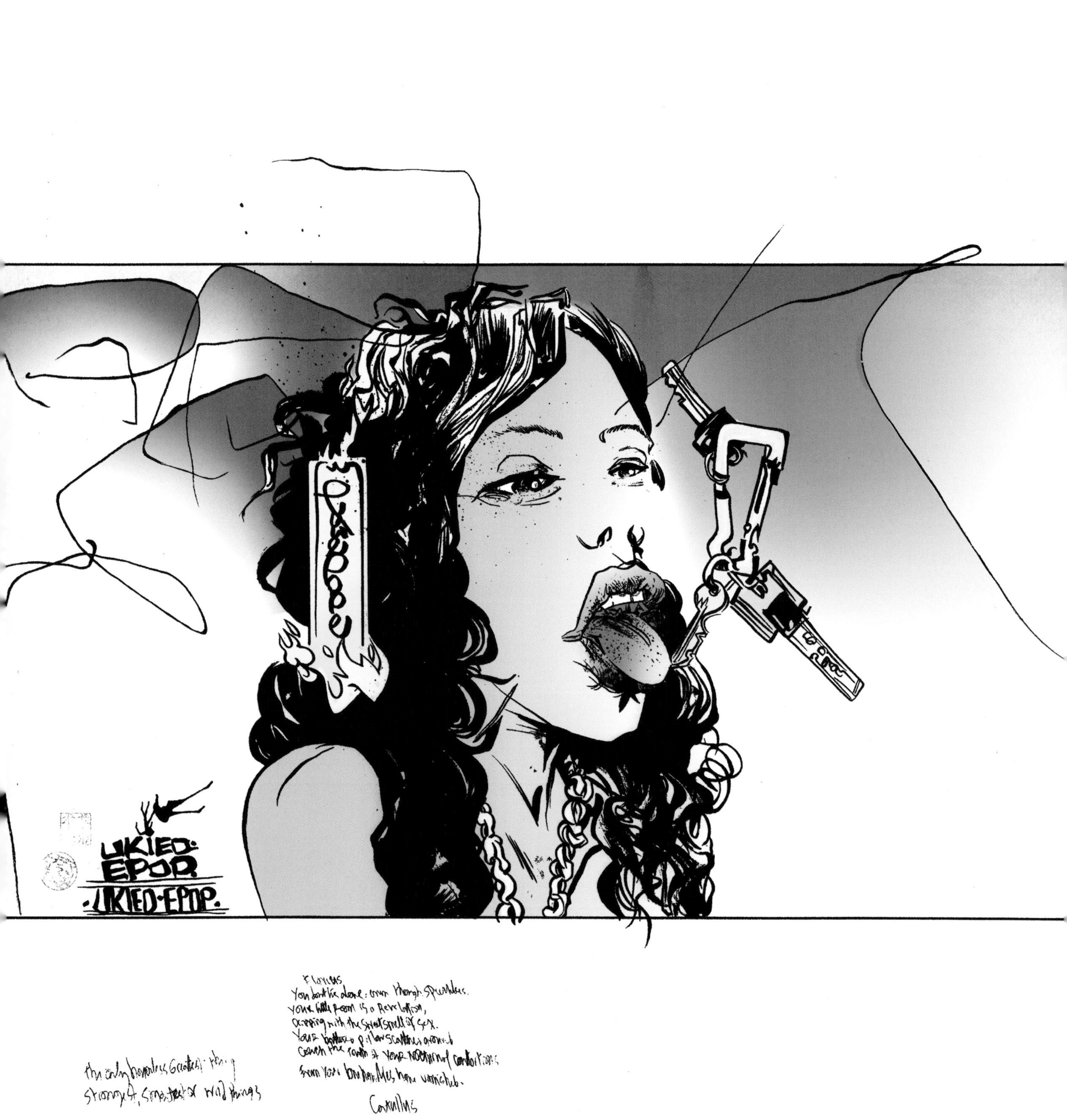
UKIED-EPOP.
-UKIED-EPOP-
Your little room is a Revelation,
Catullus

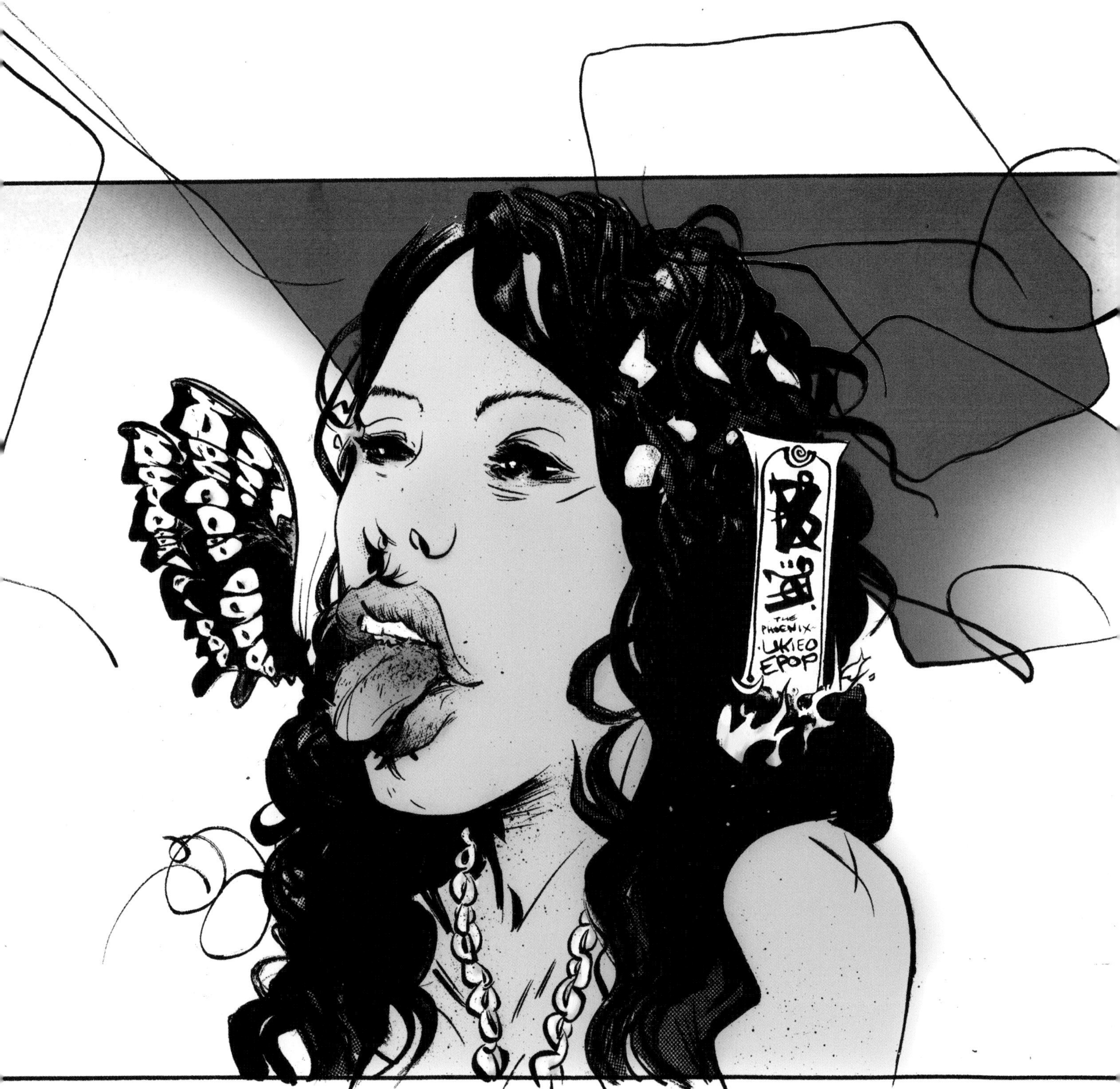
THE PHOENIX
UKIEO EPOP

COMBAT.

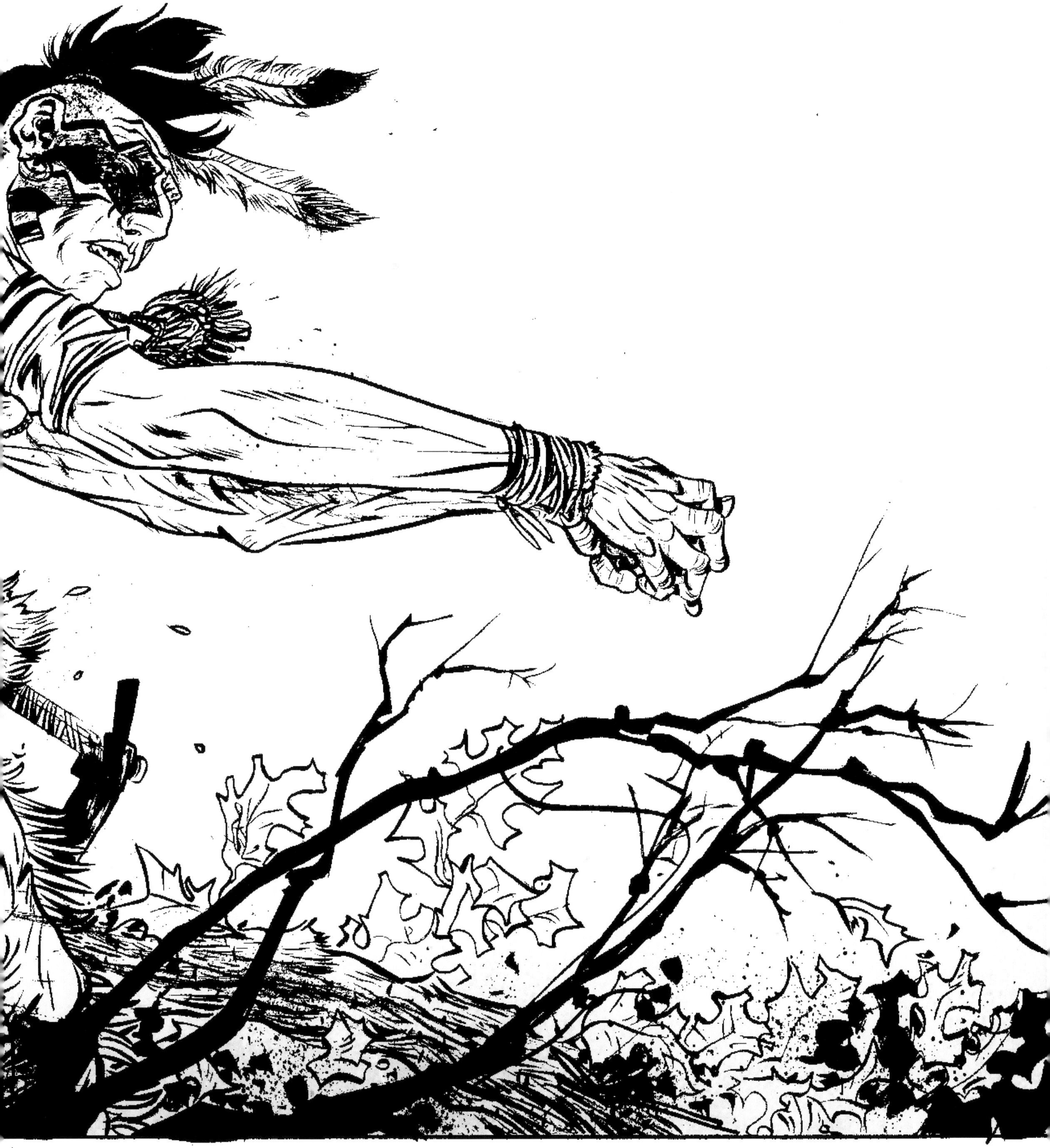

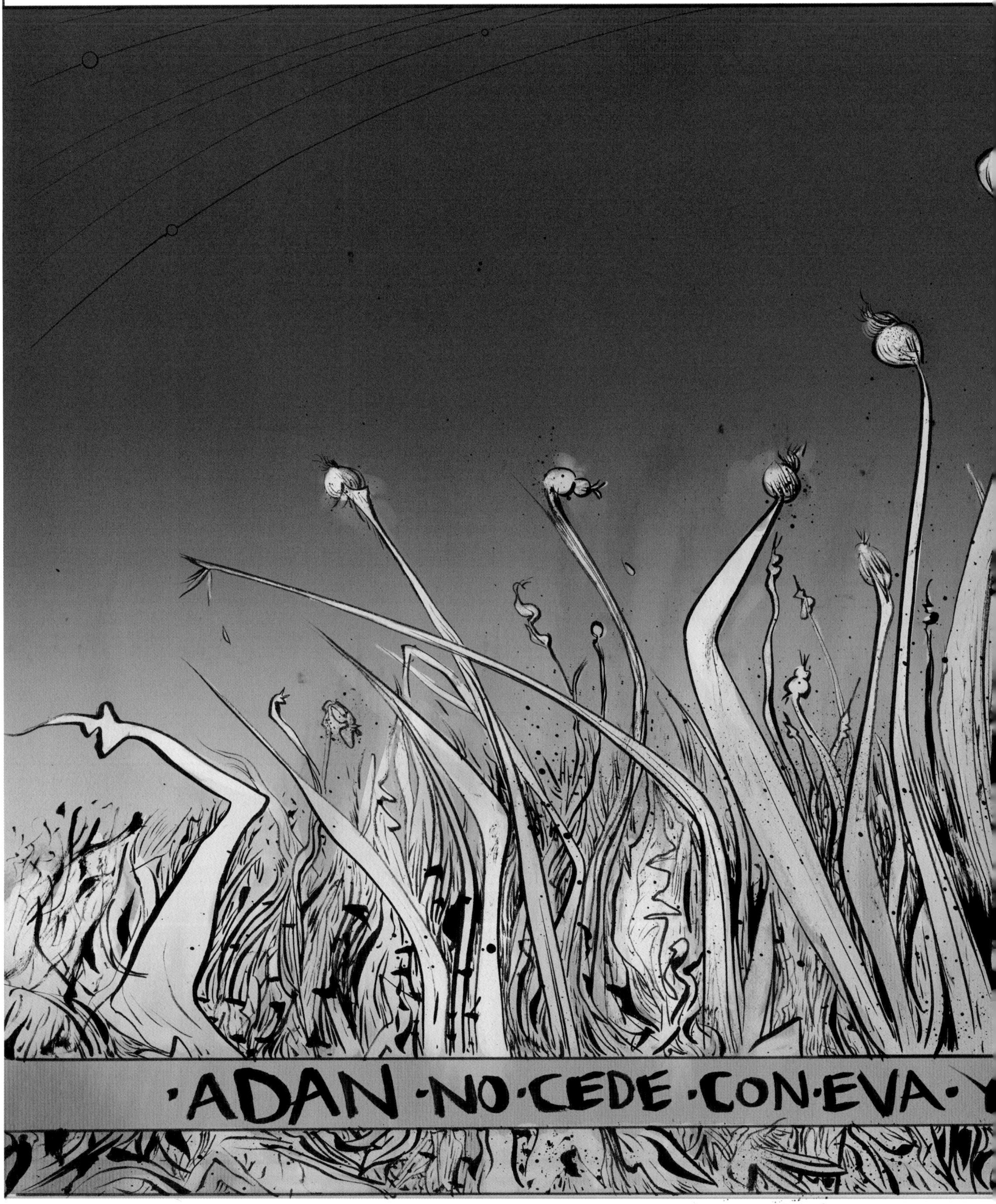
·ADAN ·NO·CEDE ·CON·EVA·

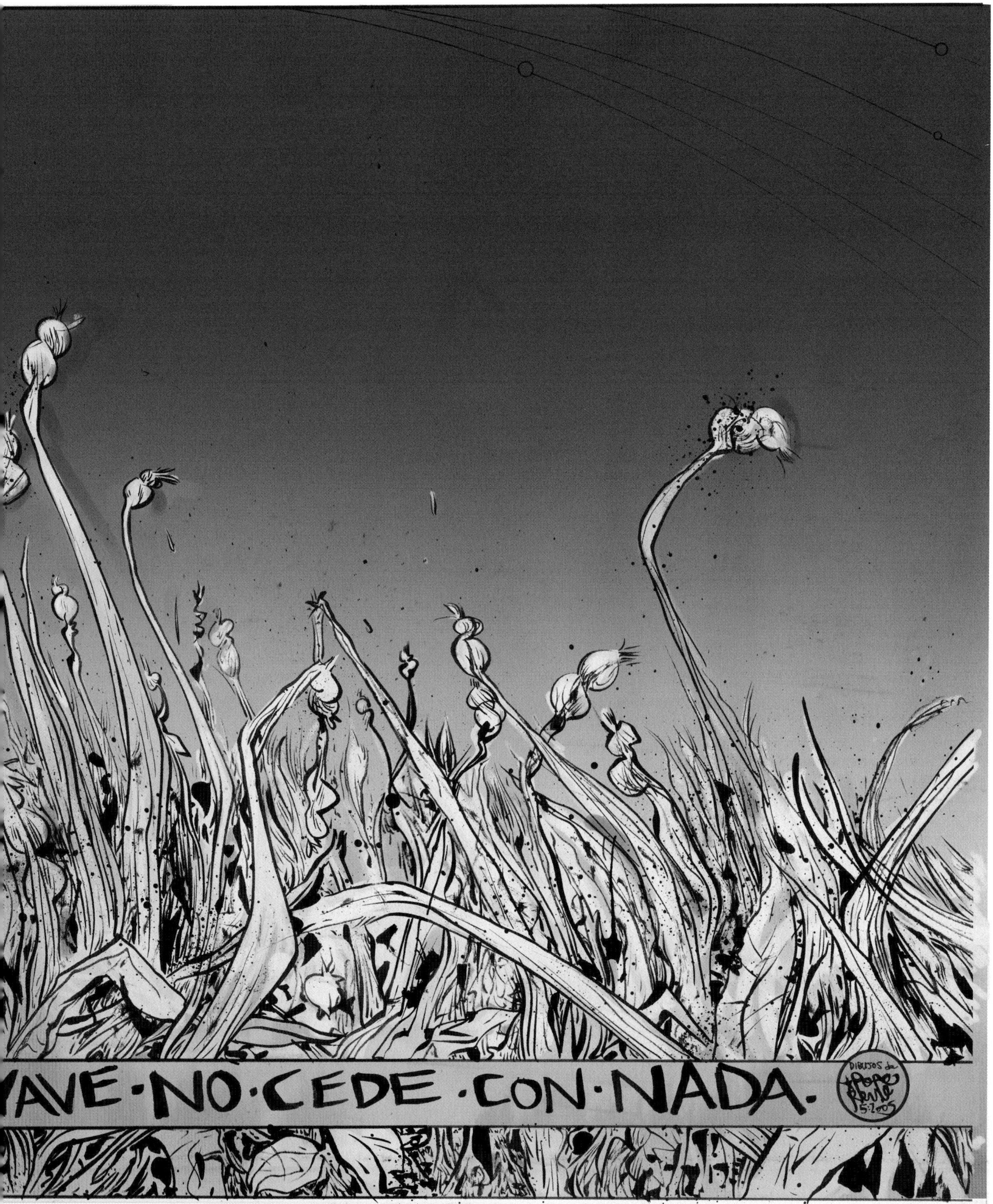
YAVE·NO·CEDE·CON·NADA·
DIBUJOS de Pope
5·2005

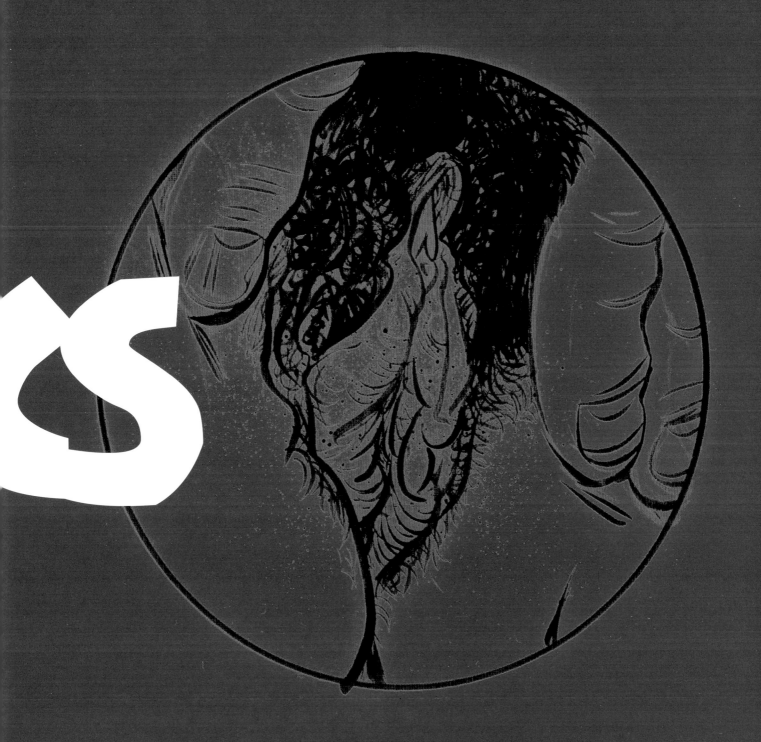

In March 2004 I was contacted by someone at Suicide Girls about doing some art for a new men's magazine. They wanted a girlie pin up poster, along the lines of the old *Playboy* centerfolds. The guy on the phone told me they were planning on launching something called "*Pin-Up*" which was to be their foray into brown paper bag, hold-it-with-one-hand publishing, featuring articles and reviews sandwiched between photo spreads of naked girls. Their big idea was to get an artist to do the centerfolds rather than publish large pin-up photos of a playmate of the month, ala *Playboy* — the old staple in the navel, three-sheet gatefold thing. Along with the centerfold pullout, each artist would be given a feature piece showcasing some of their other art, along with a short interview or article. They were looking at Kozik and Fafi for future issues, plus some hip-hop graffiti artist I'd never heard of, and James Jean if he wanted it, so that was the company I was to be keeping. They also said they had Nick from Yeah Yeah Yeahs on board as the record reviewer for the first issue, which I thought was cool. I had met Nick by then, and did a tour poster for his band and I was happy to be involved in some project with him again, even at this tangent. They said they wanted to keep that up every issue — have an actor or director reviewing films, a musician reviewing music, a writer reviewing books, etc. So in this magazine you'd get articles and

reviews, some spreads of naked chicks, and doubtlessly ads for cars, cigarettes, liquor, blow-up dolls, Russian wives, Spanish fly, Ben-wa balls and penis pumps. And in addition to all this, a nice, big, three-sheet centerfold illustrated by a different artist every month, something you could take out and hold with one hand or stick up on your wall.

The pay was OK, not great. If it had been a call from *Playboy*, it would've been great pay. But this was reasonable pay, which, when added to the fact that they'd be publishing a companion article with artwork, added up. Exposure is part of the hustle, afterall. The magazine would undoubtedly be reaching a lot of people who'd never heard of me, some of whom might be moved to go buy some comics after seeing something I did. I'd make time for it, why not? Plus, I thought it was a pretty intriguing idea, illustrating a centerfold for a girlie magazine. I'd never done anything like that before. The idea presented lots of interesting creative possibilities. The guy on the phone said they were planning on printing something around a half-million units for their first issue, pretty decent numbers for a debut newsstand magazine even if you figured he doubled the number for exaggeration purposes, and their list of advertisers was pretty good. Absolut vodka was the only one I remember, but there was some big

car company in there too. They clearly weren't thinking of this as some fly by night samizdat mimeograph, they were looking at getting into the ring with heavyweights like *Maxim, Penthouse, Leg Show,* and of course, *Playboy*. I told the guy I'd work up a few ideas and get back to him the following week. Then I got off the phone, realizing I had no idea what Suicide Girls is.

Suicide Girls? No, I'd heard of it someplace. Yes, they sponsored a party once which I never went to. Something about female wrestling in a tub of oil in a club on the Lower East Side. Never did find out what Suicide Girls was. I assumed it was some crap punk-pop band, like Blink 182 or something, only shittier. That or some slick downtown guerrilla start-up advertising/design company. I looked online.

Oh, it's this kind of thing — a subscription based porn site with some all-access content over here on the free side. Interviews with Woody Allen and Grant Morrison. They had some free photos of girls, too (of course). Scary goth chicks with pink hair and nose rings. Mid-90s Rob Zombie tattoo parlor lollapalooza babes with striped stockings holding baby dolls. Postgraduate-looking, clipped-hair librarian types posing in a kitchen someplace, showing just enough curvature and skin to qualify as half naked and provocative in a coldly academic, Gertrude Steinish way, like a self-aware Cindy Sherman rip-off. A few Lolitas.

Well, I guess this must be "alternative" porn. I found it largely uninteresting. Who was their target audience, I wondered? Record store clerks at indie rock stores? Burning Man veterans? 13 year-olds in ankle length black jackets in Colorado? Women's studies majors at Sarah Lawrence? Seminary students?

With a couple more clicks, I swerved straight into some hard-core sites. Big butts, big tits, BBFs, trannies, twinks, bears, MILFs, threesomes, foursomes, hairy girls, DPs, ridiculous pages of scat and pee, Bukakke. Anything you want and a lot of stuff you don't, two or three clicks away. It's all so ridiculous. Who has time to look at all this? Are you kidding? Nobody does — it's all just a whole bunch of unconnected, normal, regular everyday law-abiding people looking at it without knowledge or regard for the other — it's people working at the DMV, people on the street, kids in libraries, the person sitting right next to you, your best friend, your boss, you, me. Who would ever admit to it, let alone what they're really into? It's all sexual fantasy, it's all play. It's possible people don't even know why they're attracted to the things they're attracted to, regardless of whatever anyone else might think. Fetishisms, locked-box desires, boredom, a momentary reprieve from the grinding banality of everyday living.

Porn is the big embarrassed elephant in everybody's living room. Everybody looks at it and nobody talks about it. Is that because it's boring? No, it's because it would be embarrassing to talk about it. Its personal. It's really nobody else's business. Looking at porn seems harmless enough to me. Porn is a business, with contracts and legal obligations and payrolls and accountants, like any other. I'm sure there are plenty of crooks and people getting burned. Sometimes there are tragedies. But most of the porn industry seems voluntary and consenting to me, people move in and out of it, some regret their time in it some don't, some get rich off it,

some go broke. For the most part, the people involved seem to know what they are doing.

When it comes to porn I take the cynical view. I don't have a problem with it and would generally say I like it. But fundamentally I see it as yet another way to separate people from their money. It's not sex, it's menu reading. It's other people's bodies. Somebody's making a lot of money off all these naked bodies. Some of it's getting back to the girls, and that's good. Some of it's getting back to the photographers, and that's good. A lot of it goes back to the publishers and the retailers and the rest goes to players like Time Warner and other big media distribution matrixes. Time Warner also broadcasts all sorts of products to the entertainment world which are nominally for children, such as Spongebob Squarepants and Scooby Doo. They also happen to be the parent company of DC Comics/Vertigo, who, among other things, are the publishers of my books *Batman Year 100, Heavy Liquid,* and *100%.* At Vertigo, you could publish drawings of people's brains spurting out of the backs of their skulls, bullets flying out of people's faces along with an eyeball and some teeth, you could publish drawings of people sticking needles in their arms, people getting plowed over by steamrollers, electrocuted, mauled by tigers or sharks. You could show somebody getting his arm sawed off while watching his daughter being raped. You could publish burning crosses and swastikas and all kinds of other things that are not pornography. You could even publish drawings of people having sex (as long as it was cleverly obscured with shadows or a sheet or something). The one thing you couldn't publish was drawings of engorged human genitalia. Never mind *The Watchmen's* naked, blue-skinned superhero Doctor Manhattan — he is the one full frontal exception I can recall. The only time I was ever told I couldn't do something at DC/Vertigo was when I wanted to draw exposed, explicit human genitalia within the context of a sex scene in *100%.* They didn't like that, and it was the last time I'd seriously considered publishing x-rated artwork. *Batman Year 100* certainly

didn't need or call for any, and that project occupied my thoughts for well over two-and-a-half years.

I certainly didn't blame Vertigo for not wanting to publish pornography — it isn't their defined business plan and it never was. Even if Vertigo comes close to nasty sometimes (some of Azzarello's scripts for *100 Bullets* immediately come to mind, bless 'em), they've never wanted to compete with Bob Guiccone or Larry Flynt. In the case of my book *100%,* the challenge gave me the chance to consider whether I really wanted to do a comic with pornographically explicit sex scenes. In the end I chose to sublimate the visual depictions of sex in the story, to pull away from graphically explicit and focus more on mood and characterization, and it seems to me to be the better choice. For one thing, it allowed the book to be published by Vertigo. It would've probably been possible to get *100%* approved as it was originally conceived, but it would've been an embarrassing nightmare for all involved and we would've wasted a lot of precious time. More importantly, publishing it in a toned-down hard-R rather than X format allowed *100%* to get into the hands of a much wider audience. As it is, I still managed to get a scene in with a guy stealing a girl's sweaty panties. Pulling it back from X to R didn't change any of the idea content or the emotion — only the way they were presented on the printed page. Sexually explicit imagery wasn't really needed to help convey the themes of *100%* so it wound up getting cut.

Suicide Girls didn't want sexually explicit images either. I think what they wanted was a modern-day Vargas — a young artist who could create tastefully sensual, exciting erotic images. Suicide Girls wasn't about promoting any extreme sex at all, and as far as I could tell, it wasn't even really porn. It was more like a stylized porn simulation, half way in the deep end, half out. It seemed to me to be a kind of elaborate visual-rhetorical game for people who are likely very media savvy and also very likely tired of porn, people looking for something else, some variation. Their magazine wasn't going to be hardcore anyhow. You might not want to get your mom a subscription, but it certainly wasn't going to be the worst out there. All this thinking I was doing was more to understand the thing through contrasts, which is something I often do when I am searching for boundaries. All right then, so that was the playing field. Forget pornographic comics. Forget porn. This is a pin up poster for an alternative girlies mag with wide newsstand distribution and OK, but not great pay. Well, it could be interesting anyhow. It could be really cool. Some of my favorite graphic artists used erotic themes in their work. Artists such as Tomi Ungerer, Guido Crepax, Istvan Banyai, Masami Teroaka, Tadanori Yokoo, Silvio Cadello, Blutch, Guy Peelart, Rene Gruau. Picasso. Not to mention the masters of the Ukiyo-E. I too was interested in creating strong single image visual statements using erotic themes combined with dynamic drawing.

Coming up with interesting single images to use as the subject for the poster proved pretty hard. Everything I came up with seemed derivative or horribly ironic. Cliched variations of Betty Page in some vintage sexy hula-skirt pose (so boring I couldn't bring myself to draw any of them) or else some sly comment criticizing porn while simultaneously making it (worse, this approach was cowardly, Camille Pagalia with false teeth). Then there was the compromise between the two — things like imagery of superhero girls who looked like Betty Page, placed in subtly ironic poses (boring and cowardly). Nothing was clicking. Out of frustration I turned back to internet porn in the hopes of coming up with the germ of an idea for something more interesting than what I was coming up with on my own — something more edgy, more topical. I had never looked at porn purely for the sake of research. My eyes glazed over as I skimmed cartographic maps of flesh with half-hearted interest. I never considered how mercilessly repetitive porn imagery is. After a couple minutes of clicking through shots of naked girls, I stumbled across something interesting. What's this? Images of a female gymnast doing a balancing bar routine in a g-string. It was Corina Ungeraneau, one of the true heroines of girlie mags. Cornina was a prize winning athlete on the Romanian gymnastics team who lost her gold medal after posing nude for *Playboy*, a sort of soft core figure of rebellion and defiance. I loved her story — but more for her symbol than her image.

Reading about her, it suddenly struck me that I had never once had an aesthetic or creative thought while looking at porn in my entire life. Not once, never. With Corina, what I was responding to her was the excellence and athleticism, not the T&A. It occurred to me porn does not stimulate my creative impulses, my artistic synthetic-analytic process at all, and it never did. It only stimulates in me a desire to have an orgasm. This was the only reason I'd ever looked at it in the past, and it was the only affect it was having on me then. In rare instances, porn sometimes inspires in me a fleeting sense of the mysterious, of the undulating ineffabilities of the female body. This is a slightly nostalgic and adolescently romantic feeling similar to the sudden percolation of poetry. But it fades fast, an aesthetic fuse connected to nothing. All those shots of boobs and butts and pussies and mouths over all the years, although they were all very nice and sexy, not one got me from the neck-up.

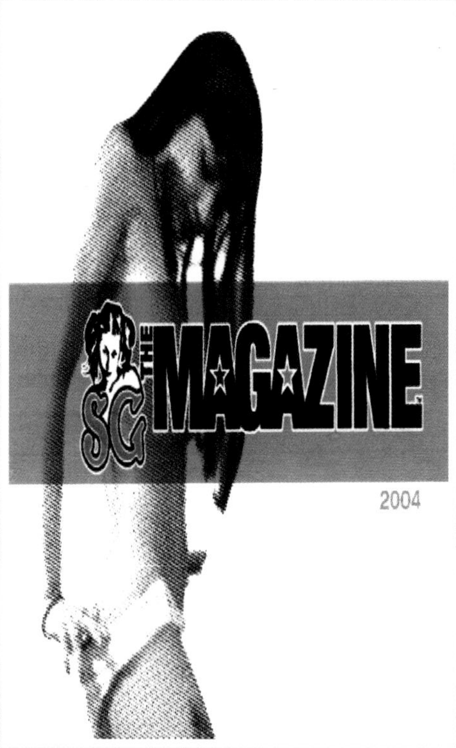
SG
THE
MAGAZINE
2004

Well then, what turned me on in an aesthetic way? Memory, mostly. Music. Some passages in Salvador Dali's purported autobiography, *The Secret Life* (the stuff where he first gets to Paris, and also where he is seeking a companion for his 'Parsival'). Some of Anais Nin's short stories in *Delta Of Venus*. Guido Crepax's *Valentina*. Shuehiro Maruo's sick-manga. These things are not technically porn. I guess they would be considered erotica.

Erotic comics and erotic illustration are two different things with two different audiences and traditions, however both incorporate explicit drawings, both are intended to titillate the audience, and at times both have been really successful and/or effective. I spent an adolescence reading *Heavy Metal*, so I'd seen plenty of erotica before I ever saw a naked girl for real. *Heavy Metal* in the 80s was one of the best sources for continually excellent comics material. The late, great Lou Stathis's *Dossier* section featured lots of great album reviews and interesting interviews with film directors, painters, musicians, writers, and other artistic types. True, *HM* also featured a lot of tits and asses — the drawings just happened to occur within the panels of some of Europe's best bandes-dessins. To be honest, I didn't even notice the naked women too much — I was more turned on by the drawings, stories, and color.

In Japan, it seems to me erotica is considered more mainstream, more on the coffee table rather than under it. This might be because of the proud tradition of the Ukiyo-E print and its place in Japanese culture. Be that as it may, the Japanese widely understand a drawing to be an idea of a thing, not the thing itself. This is one reason their manga can be so explicit. One of my favorite manga — Egawya Tatsuya's brilliant *Tokyo University Story* — is a long running, charming boy-meets-girl-boy-keeps-on-losing-girl-(for-three-thousand-episodes) series, full of constantly inventive visual narrative techniques. The series is so popular, it has spawned a TV series in Japan and firmly established Tatsuya as a well-known pop culture figure, regularly seen on TV talk shows and in magazines, sort of how Frank Miller is viewed over here (and over there, for that matter). For years, Tatsuya and his assistants have, in my opinion, consistently produced some of the most exciting manga being made today, full of charm and style and graphic invention. The series also features extended sequences which can only be described as straight-up, sweat-drenched manga-smut, and it seems to switch tracks without warning. In one scene, you have two characters sitting in a cafeteria talking for page after page after page over dinner, complete with page after page of detailed drawings of the various dishes they're eating. You practically think you're looking at a cookbook. At one point, Tatsuya drew a famous sequence with two guys endlessly playing ping-pong — this game went on for weeks and weeks, unfolding 18 pages at a time, followed immediately by week after week of the loser on a bike chasing a couple in a car, and it was breath-takingly exciting. Tatsuya also wrote and drew whole seasons' worth of two lovers in bed — actually, a few different sets of two (or sometimes three) lovers in bed. *Tokyo University Story's* cast is pretty large and Tatsuya's created a few interconnecting soap-operatic subplots in this winding narrative — and as with the ping-pong match, some of the various sex matches would go on and on and on. Marathon sex scenes. World class rave-ups. This series was serialized in the pages of *Big Comics Spirits,* a manga weekly published by Shogukan, Kodansha's biggest rival. I'd pick it up when I could, but inevitably you wind up missing a few weeks at a time. Who has the diligence or the dedication or the money to keep buying a weekly Japanese import week after week after week? Not me. Even when I was in Japan, I couldn't keep up with the weeklies. Kodansha would send me their magazines for years on end, and I read them every week or every month (some of the bigger titles were monthlies), until I had precarious stacks of them piling up in my closets. But Kodansha had nothing like *Tokyo University Story* in their publications. They had pornographic manga and they had well-drawn manga, and they had manga that would go on and on and on, but in my opinion they had none which had all of those together in the same way Tatsuya's work hit you. Tatsuya's work on *Tokyo University Story* was ceaselessly bold and daring. Pick up *Big Comic Spirits* a month later and there those lovers still are, in bed. Not even five minutes have passed in their world. She's still giving him head, he's giving her head, he's still buried face-first, so is she. A month long sixty-nine — revealed week by week through a series of sequential segments featuring dynamic page compositions and excellent draftsmanship.

There was something about it I found so liberating, so fresh, so unorthodox, and I freely admit it was a big influence on my book *100%. Tokyo University Story* always seemed more real to me than other comics and other manga, it always seemed more the way personal life really is — somehow within the confines of this manga, you could kick off your shoes and socks and sometimes even the rest of your clothes, the way you really do in real life, and sometimes spend a few well-deserved hours under the covers on a rainy day with somebody you love. It had lazy, laconic passages, it had action. It had humor and loss and it had sex. And somehow, the sex, while explicit, didn't seem pornographic at all — it was heart-felt and sort of charming. The only American comic I can think of which could do this is Los Bros' early-to-mid-period work on *Love and Rockets.*

Never during all those years of reading *Tokyo University Story* did I ever think I was looking at pornography. While a drawing or a prose piece can be explicit or even vulgar, I don't believe either is categorically capable of being pornography. I believe only literal depictions of actual individual human beings filmed or photographed can be pornography. Somehow, perhaps, erotica (whatever that is) — written or drawn depictions of the human sexual experience — comes closer to the truth of sex than does porn. Erotica is more about the idea of sex than the object of sex. That would certainly explain the logic behind getting an artist to do the debut pin-up poster for a men's magazine rather than publish a large gatefold shot of an actual girl in a provocative pose. I wouldn't say I prefer erotica to porn and I neither would I seek out erotica for sexual gratification. For sexual gratification I would choose pornography over erotica any day. But at the same time, I can't see myself tearing out a big centerfold of an actual girl and hanging it on my wall to look at from time to time. And therein lies the contradiction. It was a conundrum really, and in the end it didn't help make the job easier. It made it harder.

In the end I copped out, after trying a number of different ideas, none of which were any good, anyhow. I guess I just didn't identify with or care much for the kind of image Suicide Girls promotes and I didn't want to be associated with them because of it. Just not my thing, no offense. I sent them a re-colored image I had previously done for Uglytown's crime novel *By The Balls.* A sexy girl in a negligee. Very tame by SG standards. I felt like I failed.

In the end it didn't matter, because after invoicing and sending the image over to them, they called back and told me *Pin-Ups* wasn't going to happen. Suicide Girls pulled the plug on the project. They never did pay me and they never did say why they killed the project. Que sera sera.

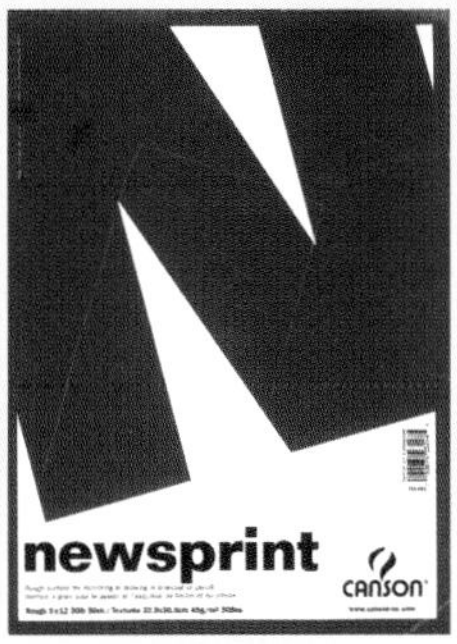
newsprint
canson

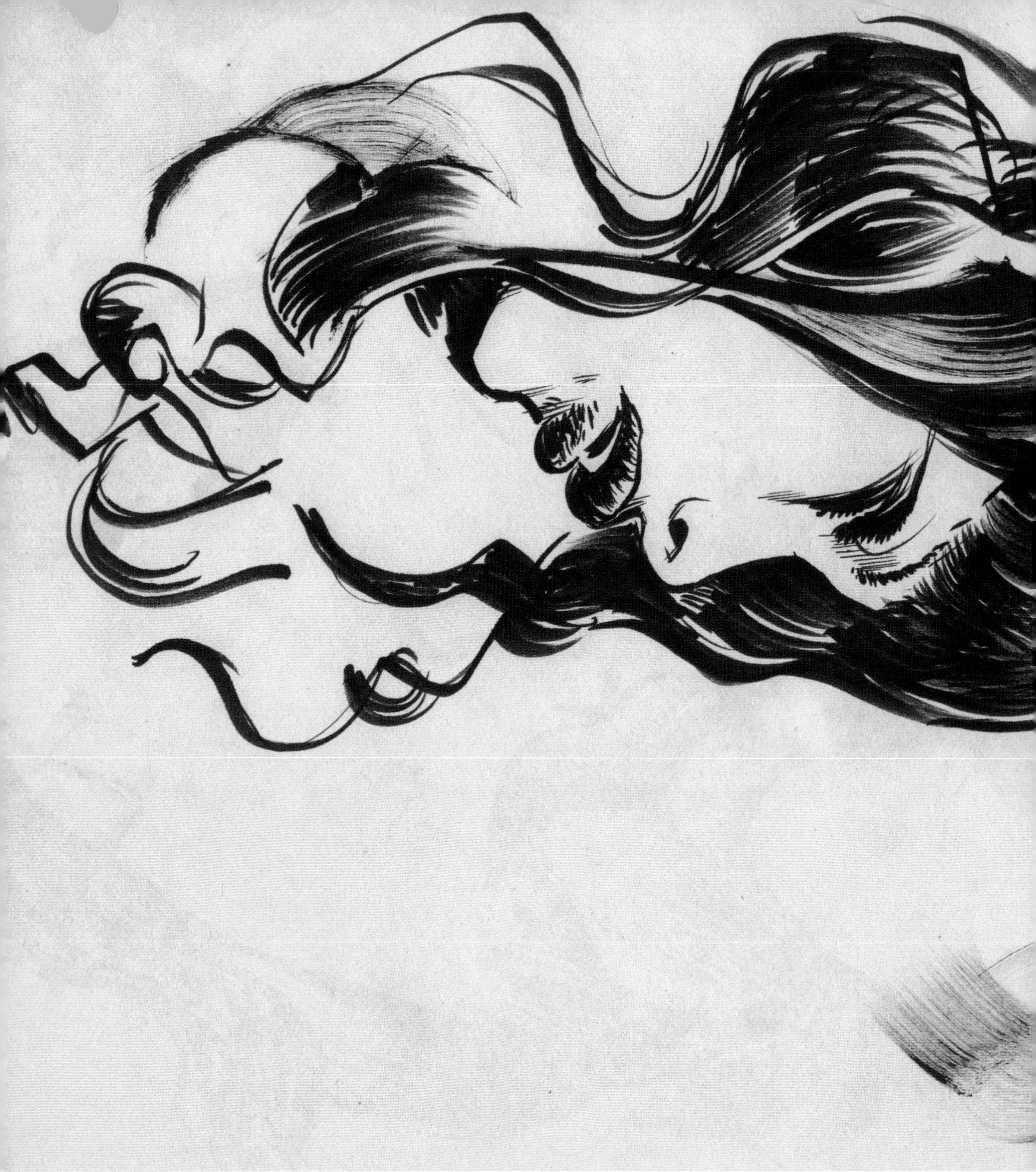

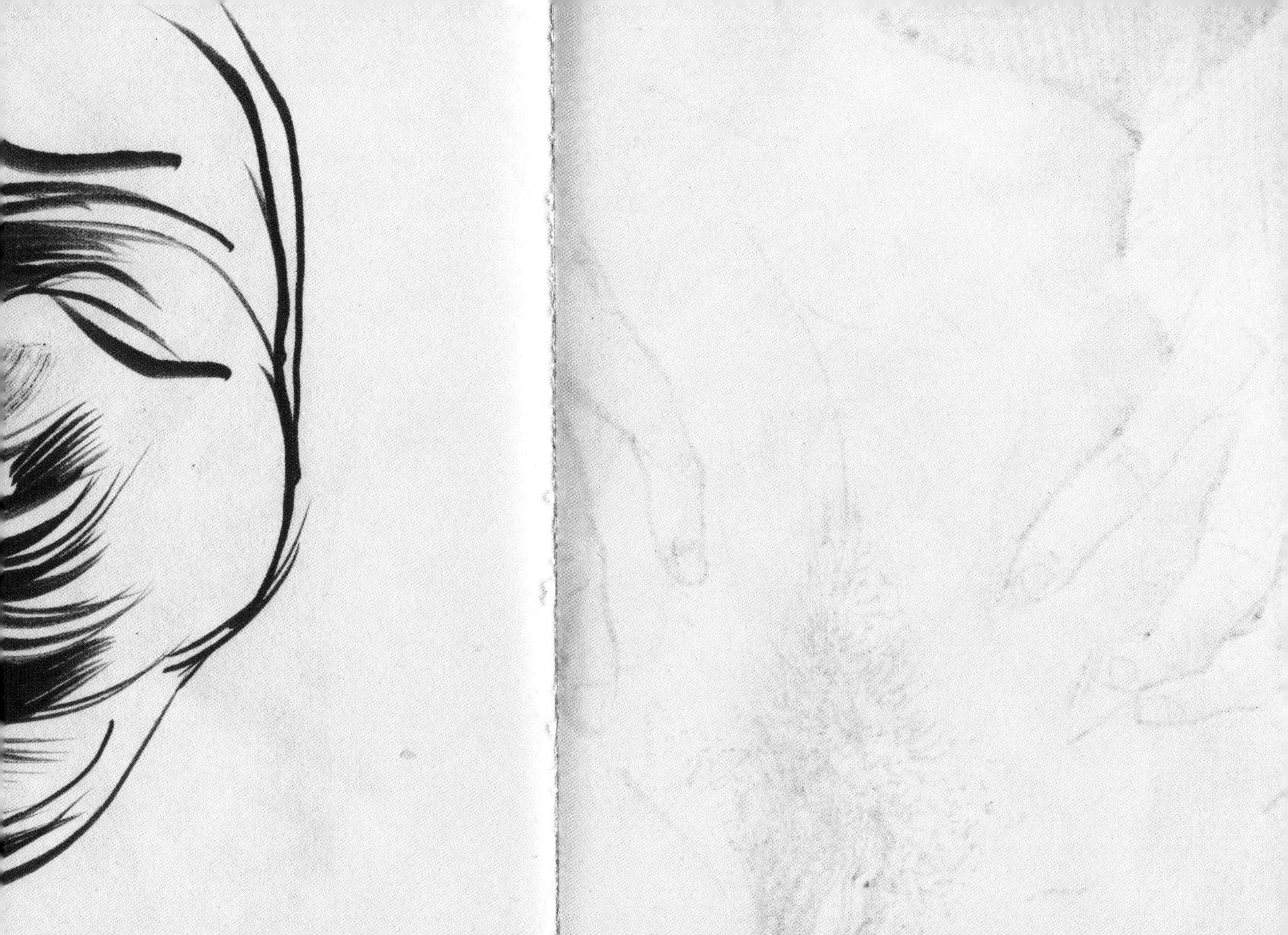

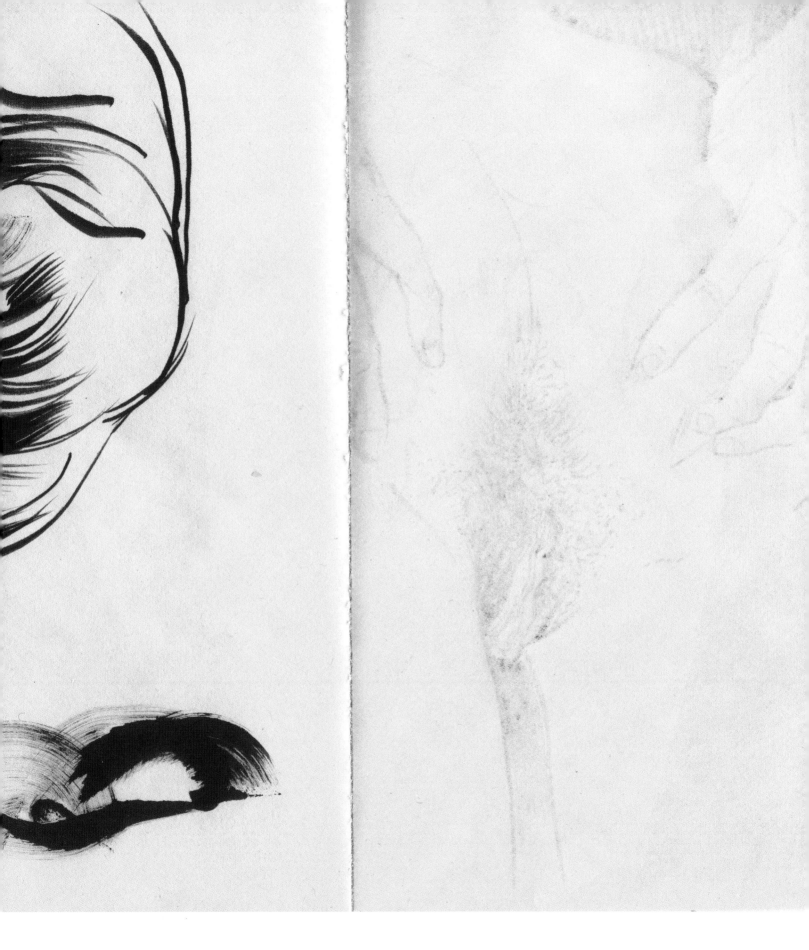

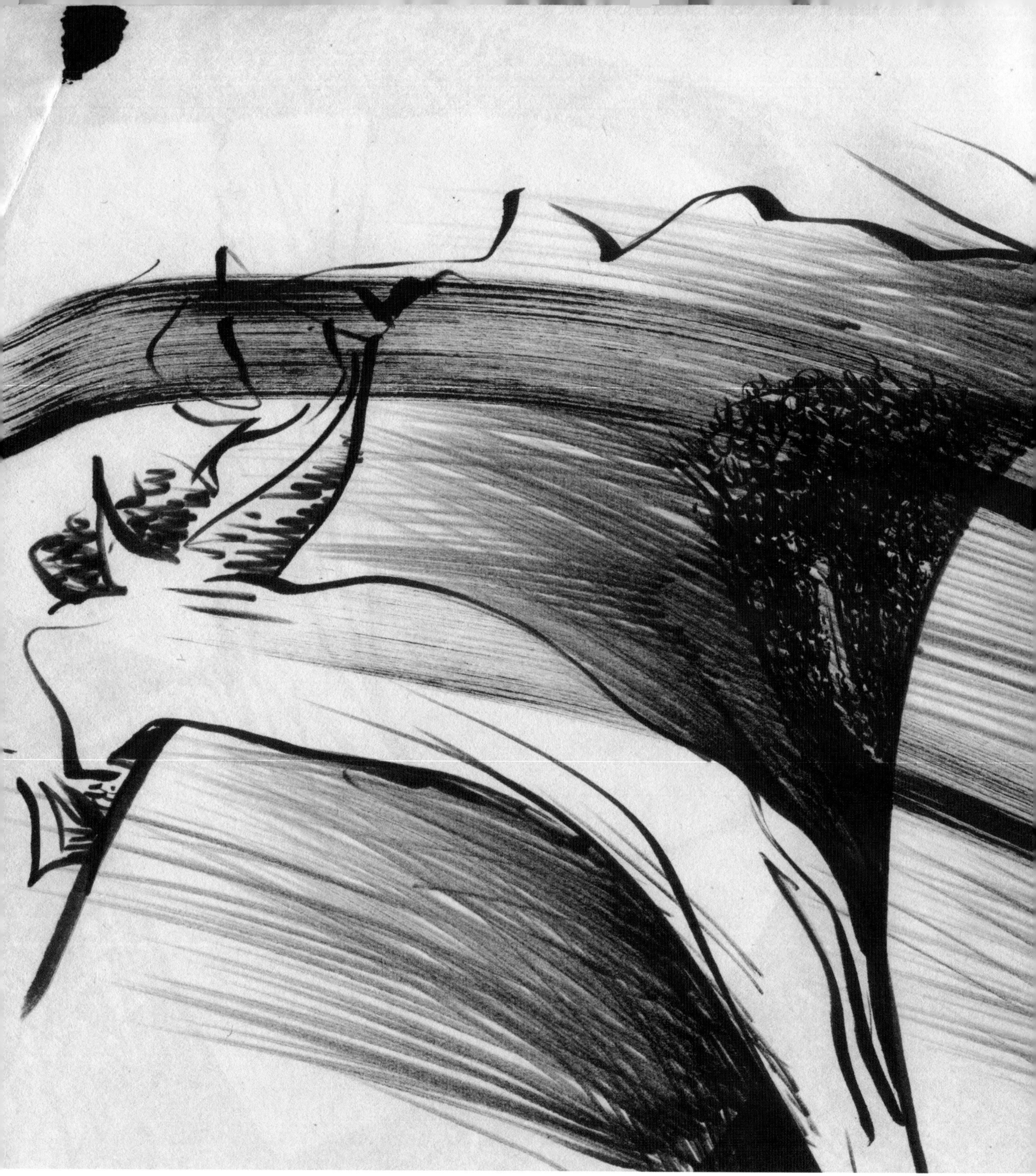

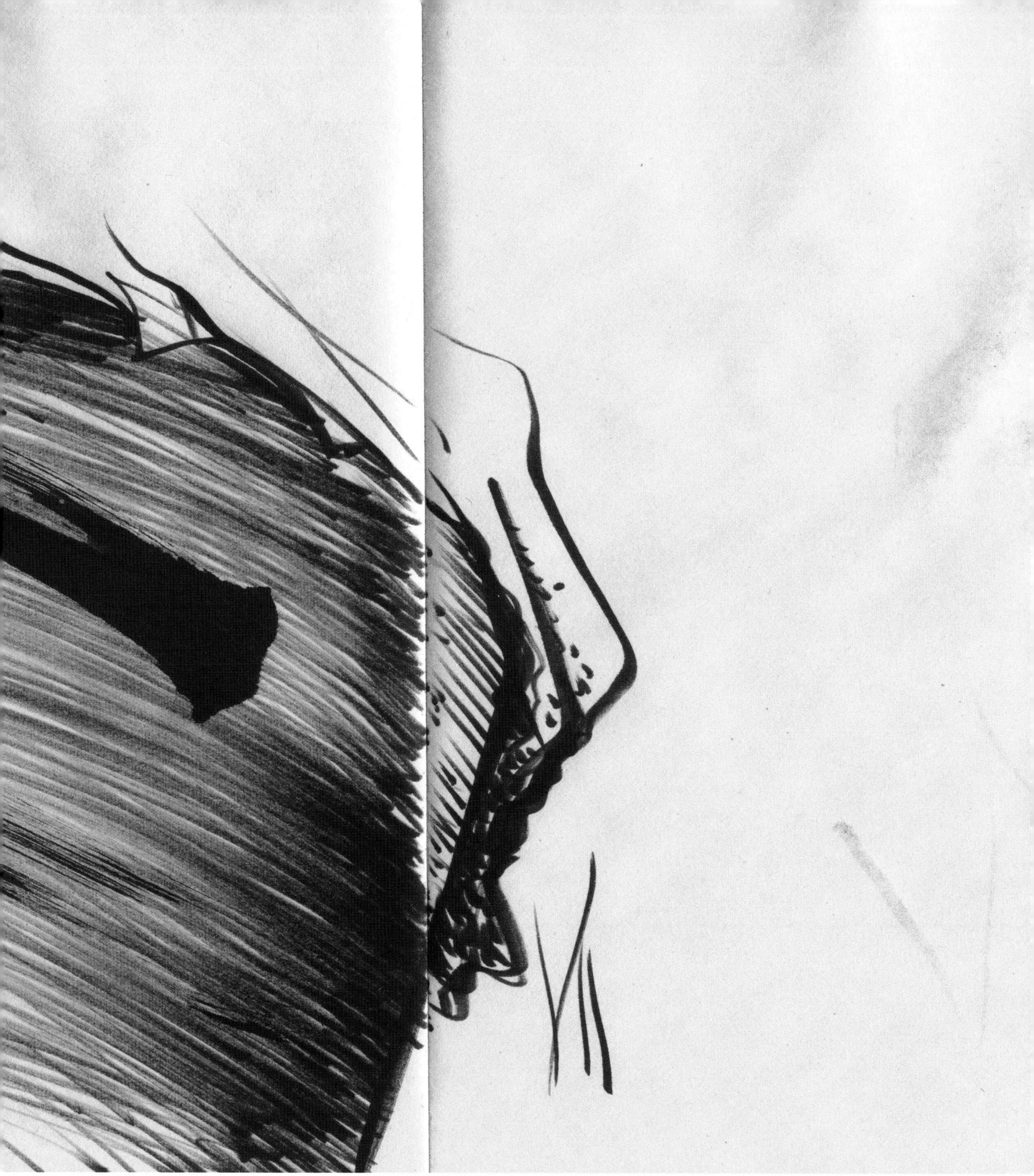

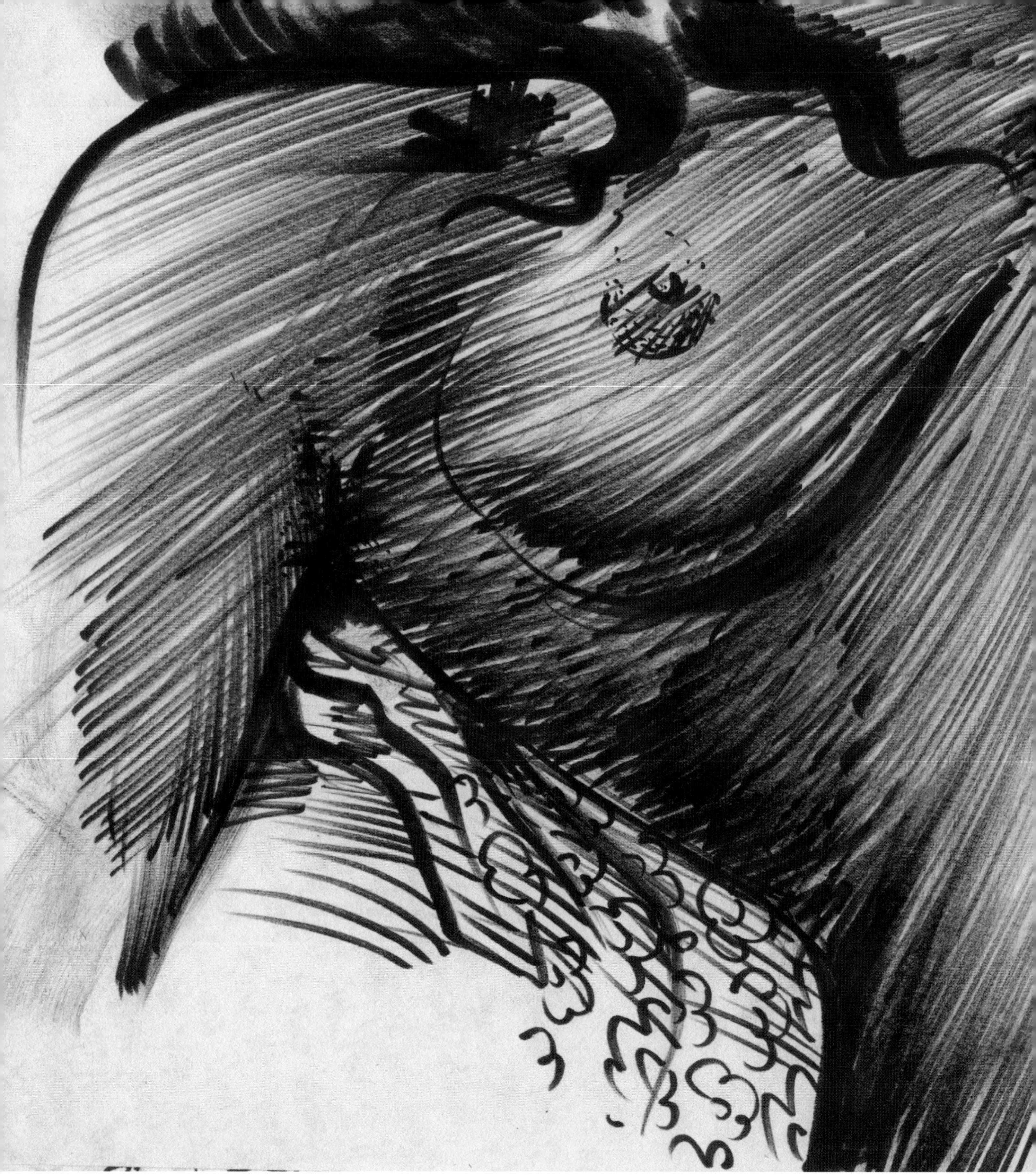

Why keep an erotic sketchbook?

All these are all well done copies of pornographic photos cribbed from DIRTY MAGAZINES... well, on an immediate level, I am not having sex and I seek a way to express my sexual desires and thoughts in some way more creative than simply masturbating. These Drawings often do not even lead directly to sexual stimulation. It's a more mental process...

In a way, I'm experimenting with some techniques I'm interested in exploring. Some new ink approaches learned from looking at Sam Weber and Yuko... Also, Flesh is excellent. Yeah, Flesh is Excellent. There is nothing like it in the world.

Reduction, simplicity, observation, exaggeration, imagination.

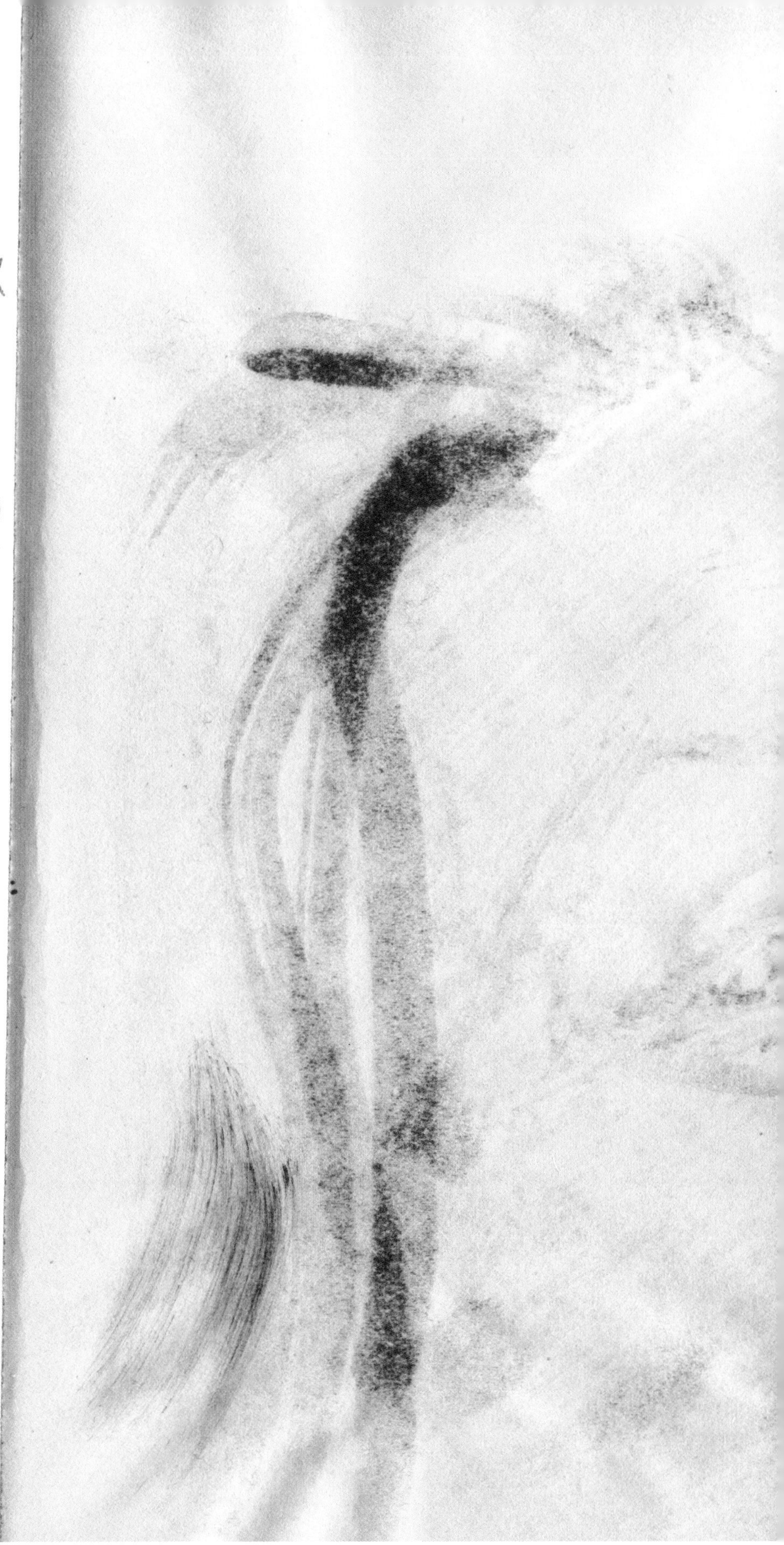

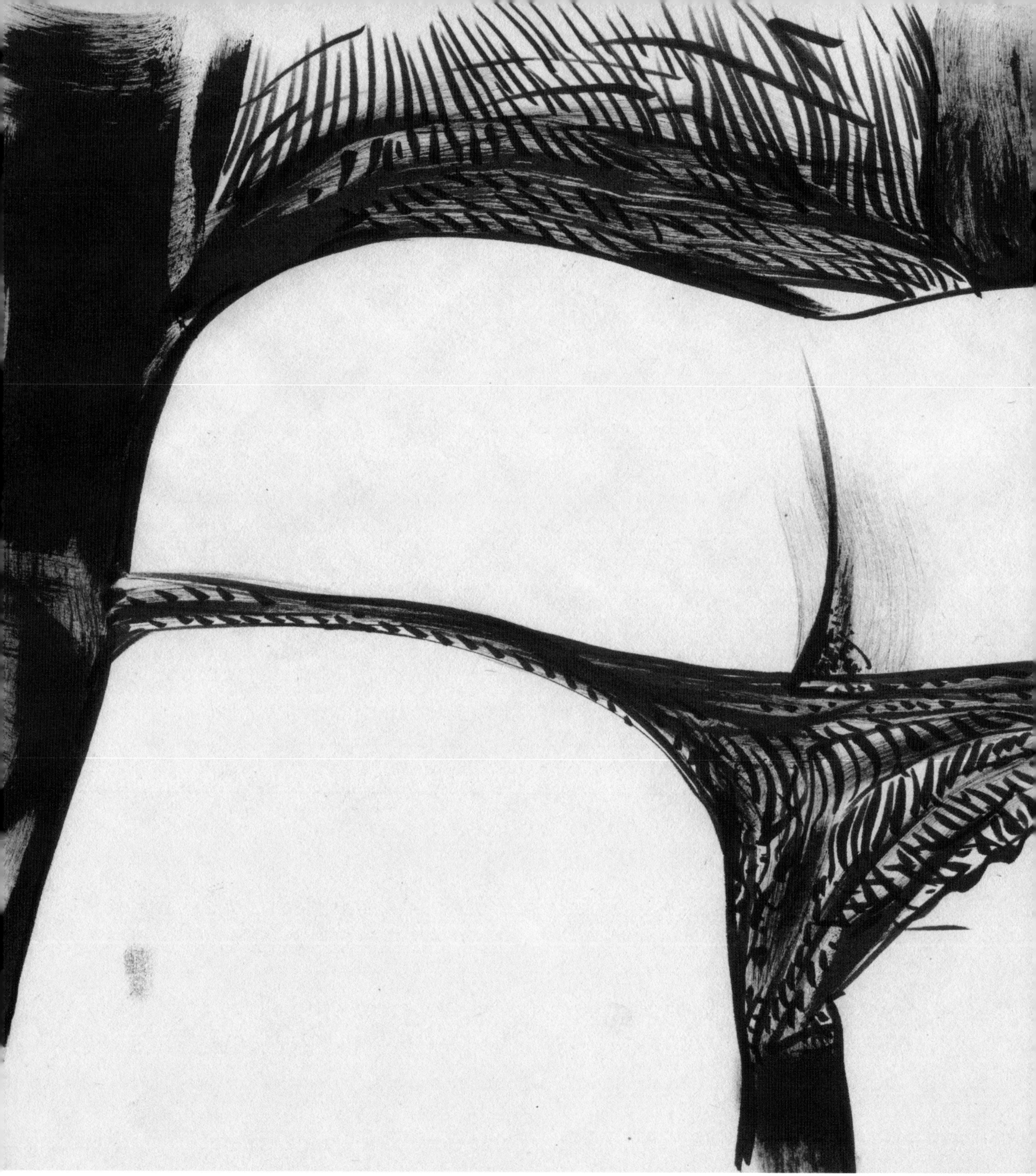

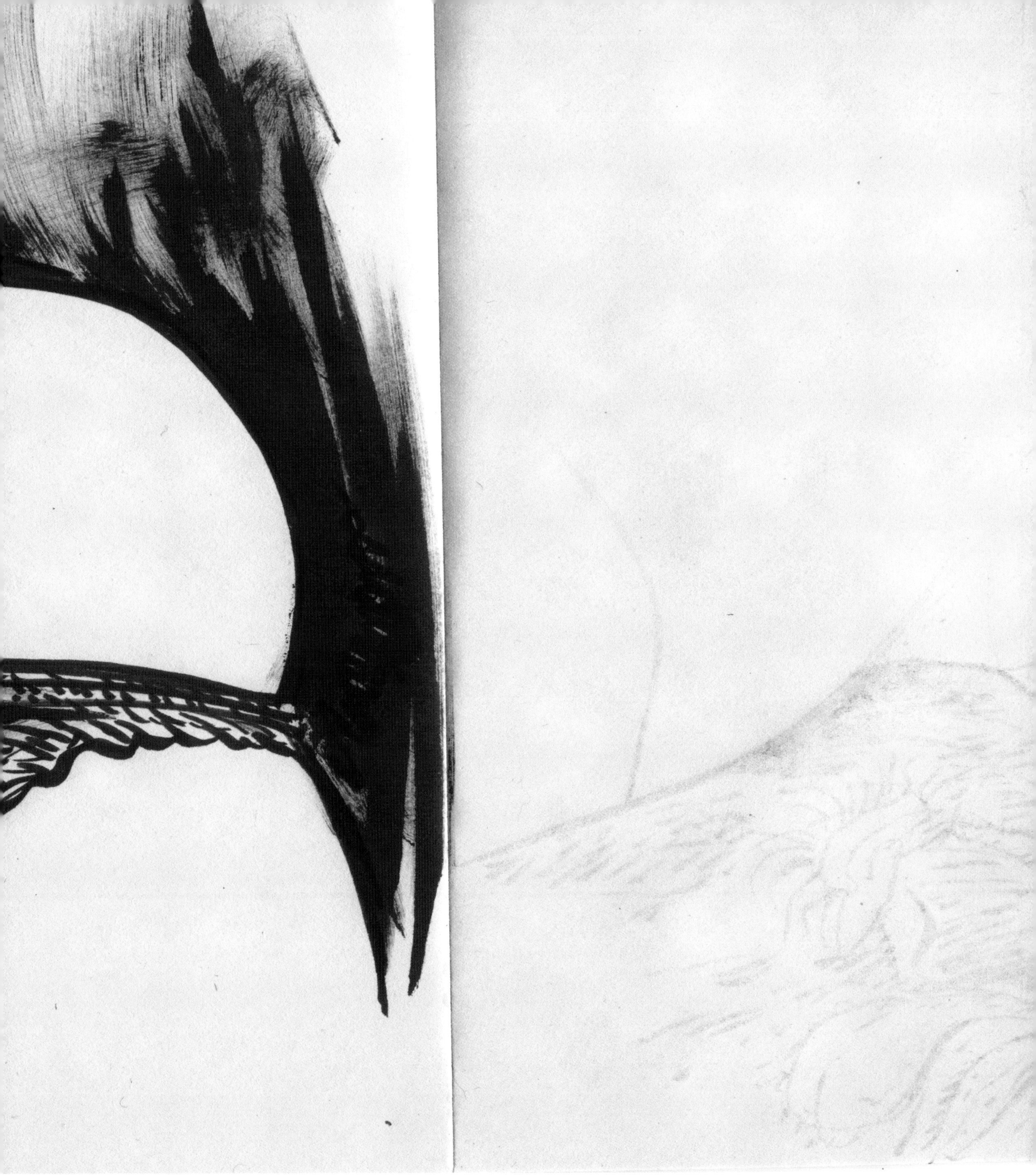

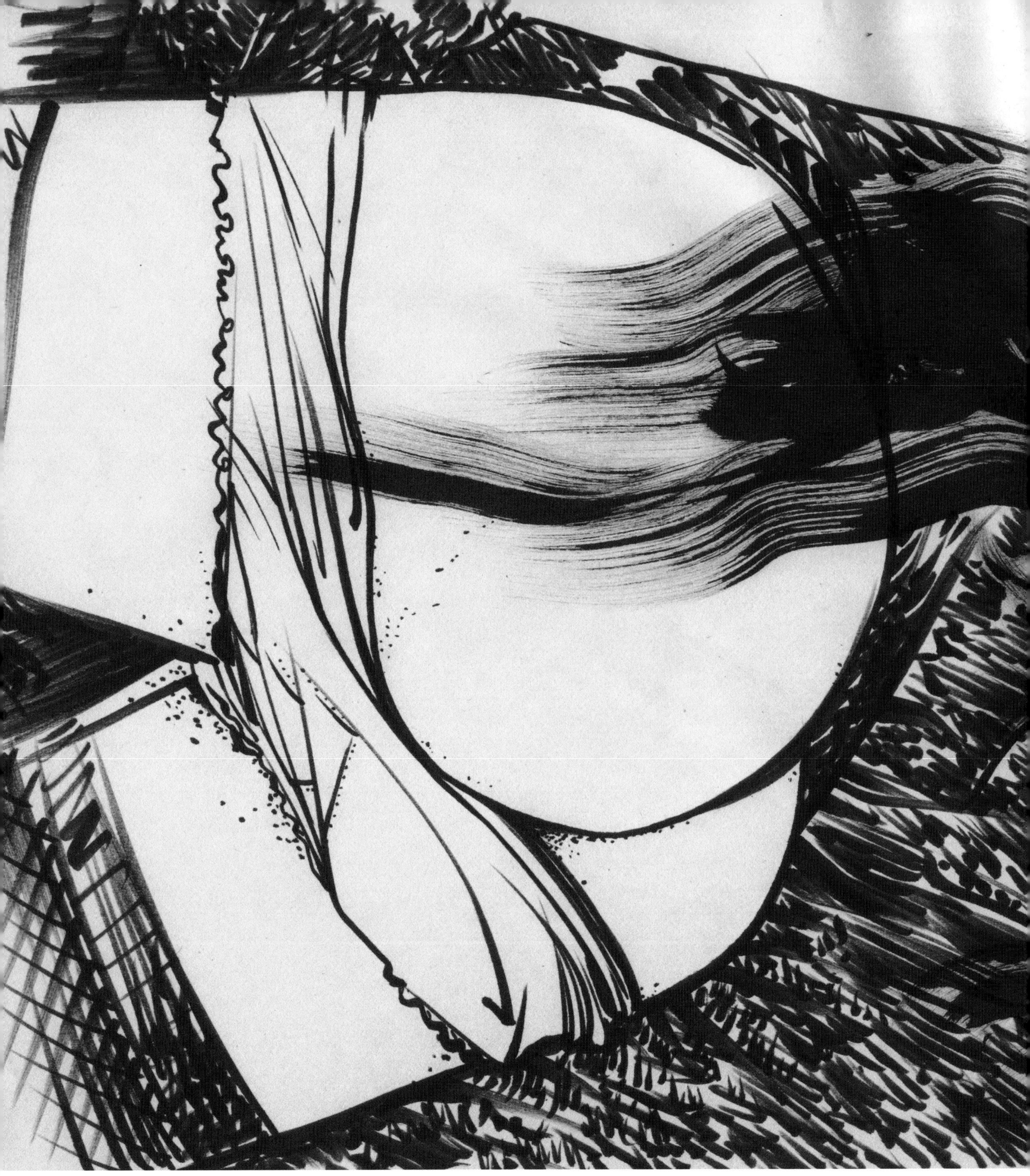

PIN UPS 2

There's a secret hidden somewhere in the difference between photography and drawing which gives erotic art a special dynamic power. The difference between erotica and pornography seems less obscure.

James Joyce defined pornography as anything intentionally designed to elicit a purely visceral response in the viewer without also eliciting any aesthetic reflection. I like this definition because it is wide enough to include all sorts of things, such as the images of casual violence we often see in movies. I would argue images of explicit violence are pornographic. Joyce's definition also is wide enough that it could be said to include some video games and also these stupid "reality tv" shows such as *The Real World, Survivor,* and *American Idol,* which I consider to be not only porn but bad porn, and a kind of cultural cannibalism as well. I would rather have people looking at pictures of naked bodies.

I think the reason pornography is so overwhelming is because it serves as a sexualized testament of actual living bodies. It allows the viewer to gaze upon another's form as if it were an object capable of being possessed. What's under her dress? What's inside his pants? How wide can she open her mouth, etc? These things the viewer wants to, and is forbidden to know, certainly without invitation. The only invitation you need from pornography is to behold it. A pornographic photo is a kind of literal-visual treatise, expertly and specifically calculated to sexually stimulate the viewer. Subjects presented in pornographic photographs or on film are actual

living human beings, each with an actual individualized sexuality, posing in an actual place at an actual time. A pornographic photograph is a kind of deliated document of specific, temporal, sexualized human nature. However, whereas a photo of a specific person's eyes and lips, shoulders and hands could be capable of expressing any number of subtle gestures belonging to that particular person, a photo of that same person's engorged genitalia expresses rather a very basic, very simplified idea. There are few if any distinguishing characteristics identifying, say, a vagina as belonging to a particular women. A photo of a particular model's sex organs becomes a kind of universal idea-box. The pornographic image becomes an object of sex, literally a sex-symbol. In truth, a pornographic picture is an accelerated, obsessive visual meditation on the object of the viewer's intended sexual gratification. It is in fact not at all a portrait of this-or-that specific model. It is a symbolic mirror of the thoughts of the viewer. The model becomes a temporary object of sex in the mind of the viewer.

By contrast, an erotic drawing is something else entirely. A drawing is not an actual visual document of a specific person, place, or event at all, but rather a symbolic image abstrued from the mind of a particular artist. An erotic drawing does not presume to capture the actual document of specific human sexuality which a model in a photo embodies, and it is incapable of reducing a particular person's anatomy into a kind of flattened sexual objectivity. Even if an artist attempts to copy an explicit photo faithfully, or to draw the

erotically provocative gesture of a posed live model (I'm thinking here of Egon Shille's stunning erotic watercolors), or even if an artist attempts to faithfully render an erotic memory, the drawing is still nothing less and nothing more than a visual document of the artist's expression based on his or her selective aesthetic values. Whereas a pornographic photograph functions much like a pervy medical report, detailing with clinical precision all the proportions and colors and contours of human anatomy, an erotic drawing functions more like haiku. Using a reduced number of gestural lines, the artist is suggesting meaning without documenting it directly, saying as much with what he leaves out as with what he leaves in. The power of any drawing is in its brevity, it's selectivity, its invitation to subjective involvement. The viewer is invited to fill in the gaps — so to speak — of a drawing's dynamic reorganization of observed reality. As with all drawing, an erotic drawing is an art-argument of individual style, an artistic framing device through which we see not reality, but rather artists vision of reality.

"Are drawings more powerful than photos?" asks Michele Houellebecq in his introduction to Tomi Ungerer's book *Erotoscope*. "Something about sexual emotions does seem very difficult to capture on film... you might think that a breast, a pubic bush or a vulva might, if sensitively rendered, add to the sexual charge of work. Well, no. And in this department the superfluous is a turnoff. You can film the joy of lovemaking lighting up a woman's face, but the essential thing, the kernel of sex, is invisible, inaccessible

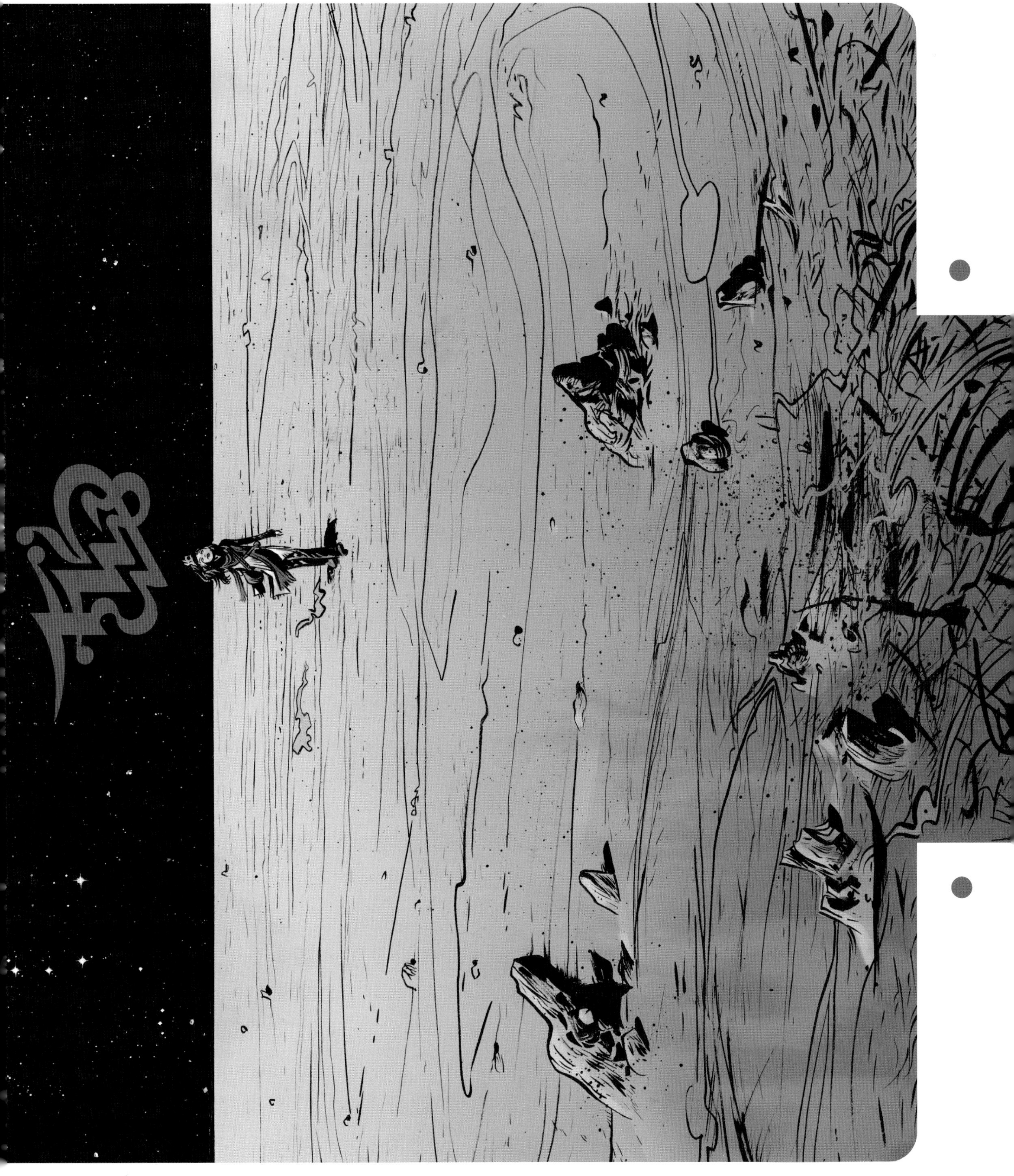

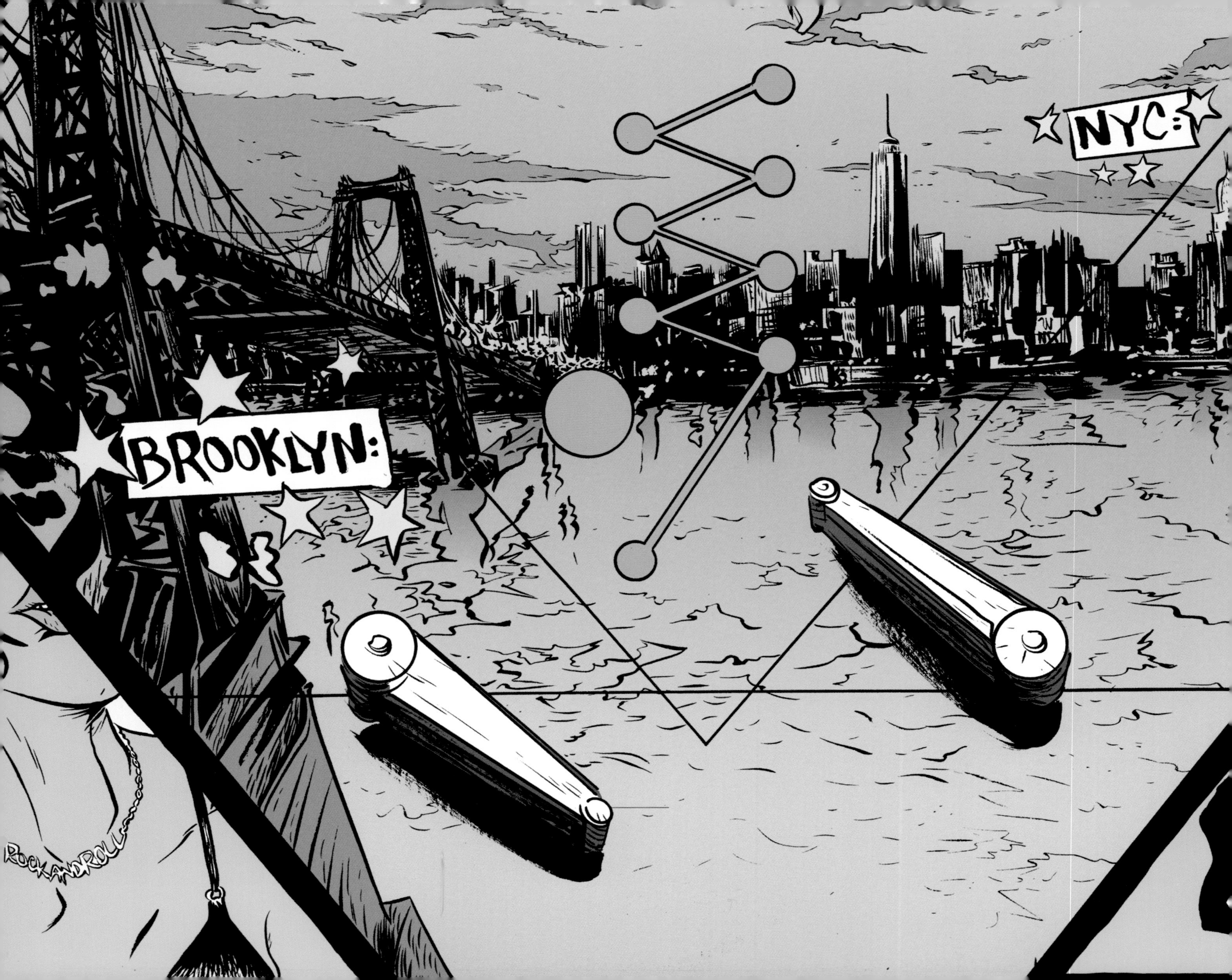
NYC:
BROOKLYN:
ROCKANDROLL

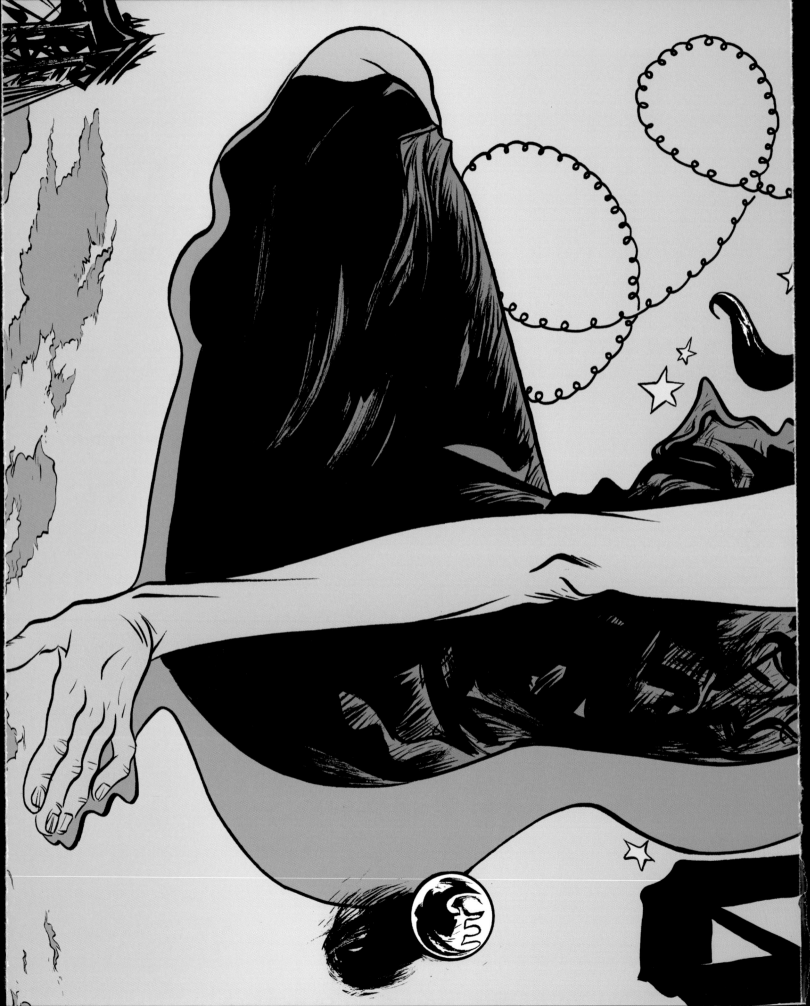

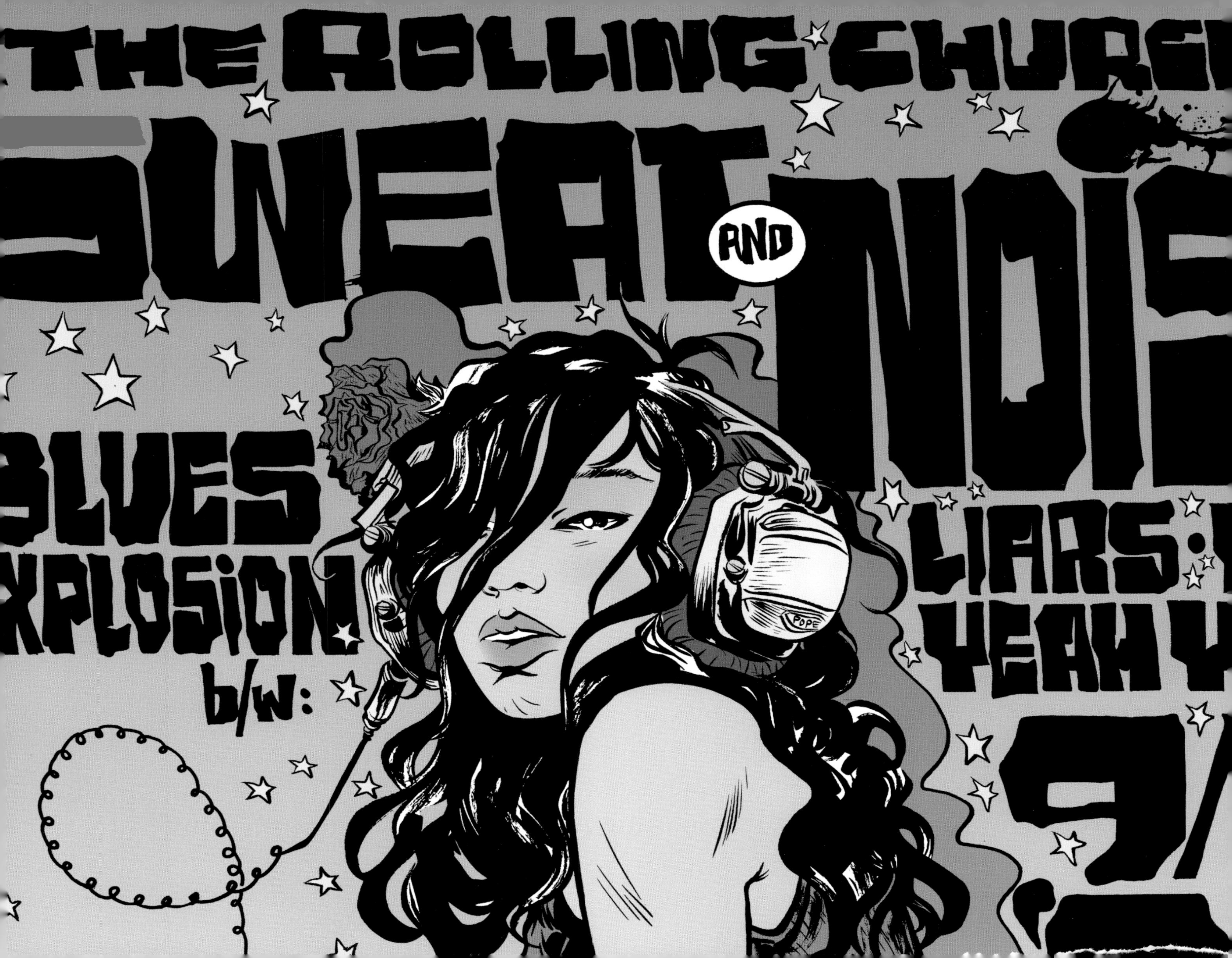
THE ROLLING CHURC
SWEAT
AND
NOIS
BLUES
XPLOSION
b/w:
LIARS:
YEAH Y
POPE
9/

to the camera. In the field of erotic fantasy, drawing is manifestly superior."

The "manifest superiority" which drawing has over film may lie in the possibility that through drawing we come closer to what it is to actually see — to perceive — than we ever can through photos. By momentarily adopting the eyes of an artist, it may be that we move into the realm of what we might call the mystery of vision. When we look at a drawing — when we look into a drawing — we are seeing the world through the eyes of another who has reduced perception to the points he wants us to consider. These he represents as lines on a page. While a photograph does contain an image, it is not a reduced construction, as is a drawing, but rather a construed reduction. A photographic image is a composition which a photographer has framed, containing the elements captured as impressions of light through a lens. Certainly, photography can be art, and often is. However, the power of the photographic medium, it seems to me, lies in its ability to journalistically capture actual elements undiluted — what makes something powerful in photography is the documentary evidence captured, the preservation of reality, of the actual. It is almost impossible to imagine any drawing doing a better job of conveying the reality of, say, the chemical plant explosion in Bhopal India or the collapse of the World Trade Towers than a photograph could. It is also the reason photography has superceded painting as the medium of choice for portraiture. The impression of captured light is the bedrock of Hollywood — the movie star would be nothing without it. It would also be absurd to imagine a drawing doing at all what a photograph can do when it comes to blackmail or litigation.

Whereas photography reveals, drawings embody. A few curves, two dots, two dashes and a sensuous, wavering line for a mouth — these can make up the face of a woman. By reducing a subject to a brief visual statement, we somehow remove from the specific everything which is not the general. This abstracting quality

is also one of the secrets of cartooning, erotic or otherwise. For erotica, it seems to me this quality serves to stimulate both memory and desire in a way no photograph can. Subject matter in drawing exists in a kind of timeless reality all its own, never aging, never getting tired or bored, never needing to get paid, never wanting to leave, never quitting.

Personally, I prefer to look at old *Playboys* and *Penthouses* if I am going to look at images of porn for anything other than pure sexual gratification. I prefer the curvy women shot in grainy soft focus, the unfixed tits, the big black triangles, the ostrich feathers and silk bandannas. I even like the old ads for Winston cigarettes and Myer's rum. I know it is largely nostalgia, a product of having been born in the 70s, and I don't care. The women in those old magazine looked like what I imagined women would look like when I was finally old enough to be involved with some. Those old pictures will for me forever be the symbols of that youthful speculation. The pictures left something to the imagination and I was happy to fill in the rest myself. For me, they contain some added idea content above the depiction of sexualized bodies.

As an adult, I find that when I look at pornographic photos, particularly ones in more or less cheap quality porno mags, I sometimes feel a sort of alienating sadness when I notice accidental details captured by the camera, such as scuffs on the bottom of a woman's high heel or other random elements. A curling corner of astroturf, a band-aid, a box of tissues or a cheap lamp edging into the corner of the picture frame, things like this distract from the nominal purpose of the picture, the intention it is purportedly designed to serve. Although captured by the lens, these incidentals are not intended to be in the image. It may be that the photographer is simply not very good, but never the less it ruins the effect, for me at least. It makes me wonder where the photo was shot. Was it in a hotel room or maybe somebody's apartment? Was it in Miami? Cleveland? Queens? It makes me consider that particular woman

wearing those particular shoes with those particular scuffs, whether she bought them one day when she needed them or wanted them, and whether she walks around them in her everyday life. It makes me wonder how old the photo is. For all I know, it might be ten years old and the girl in the picture might not even look like this anymore. This photo might have been appearing in magazines for years and years, passed from one agent to another, from one cheap magazine to another. It makes me wonder how much the model was paid, things like that. This has happened to me often enough that now I can never lose the understanding that this particular photograph of this particular naked person I am looking at is a real person, and moreover, that she is a total stranger, and that as I look at her I am not supposed to be considering these things. Maybe that day she was photographed she was in a good mood, maybe not. Maybe it was a day she won't remember in 10 years anymore than I will remember looking at her, maybe its all just more grains of golden sand slipping through our fingers to the deep. Maybe that day she had a headache and all she can think of is aspirin — although in the picture she looks like what you one a beautiful woman to look like when she's on all fours, looking at you from over her shoulder. Often the models are presented with names like Candy or Vivid, or Nova or Vivica but we all know these are not their real names. These are stage names. These girls don't want us to know their real names. They don't want anything to do with us. They don't want us to know who they are or where they live. They don't want us to ever see them on the street or in a store buying something or out on a date with whoever they really have sex.

By contrast, everything you need to know about the character of a drawing is found within the drawing itself. Drawings don't need names, fake or otherwise. "Untitled" will do.

PP

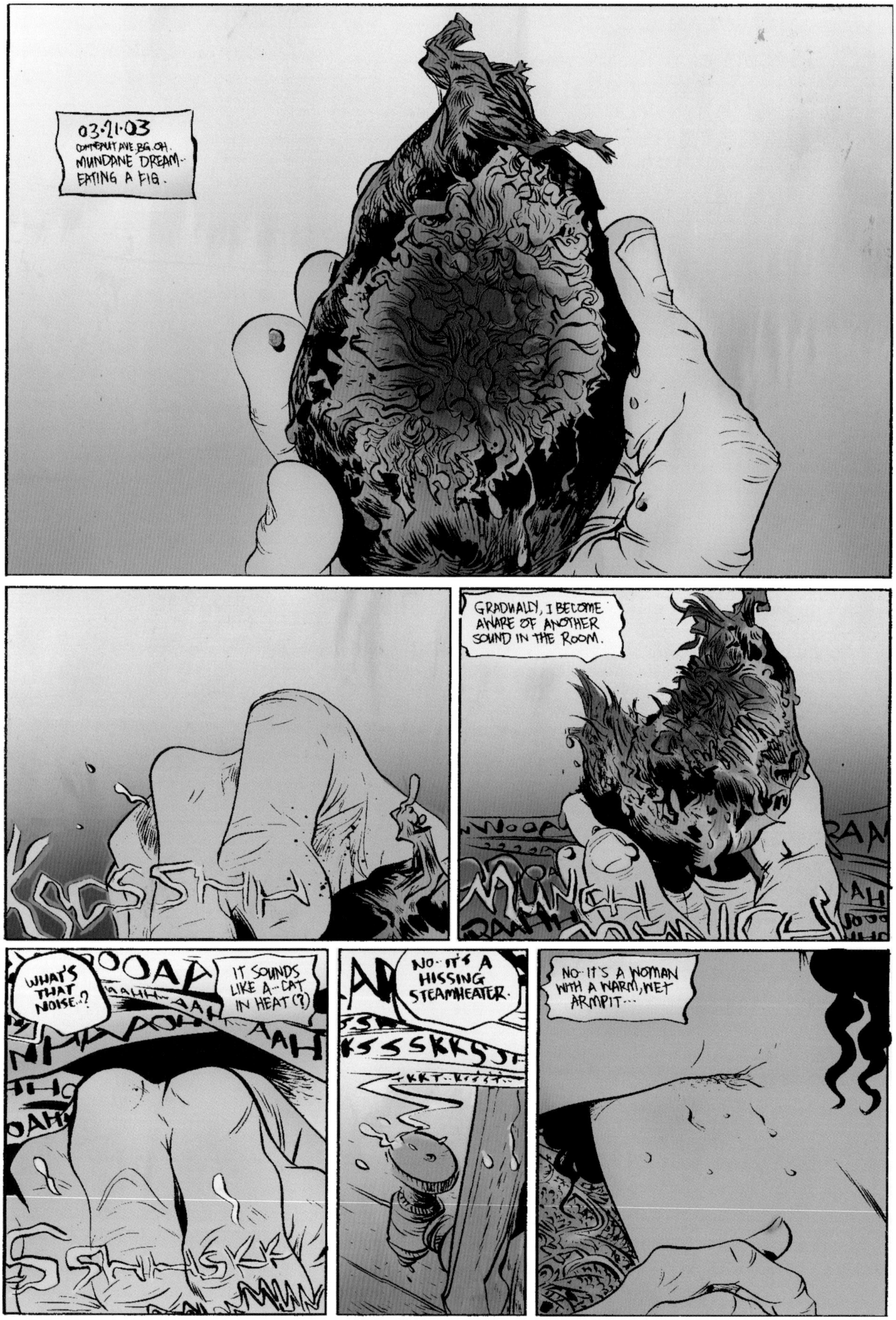
03·21·03
CONTINENTAL AVE. BG. OH.
MUNDANE DREAM--
EATING A FIG.
KSSSHH
GRADUALLY, I BECOME AWARE OF ANOTHER SOUND IN THE ROOM.
WOOAA
MUNCH
WHAT'S THAT NOISE..?
IT SOUNDS LIKE A...CAT IN HEAT (?)
AAH
SSHHSKK
NO...IT'S A HISSING STEAMHEATER.
KSSSKKSS
NO...IT'S A WOMAN WITH A WARM, WET ARMPIT...

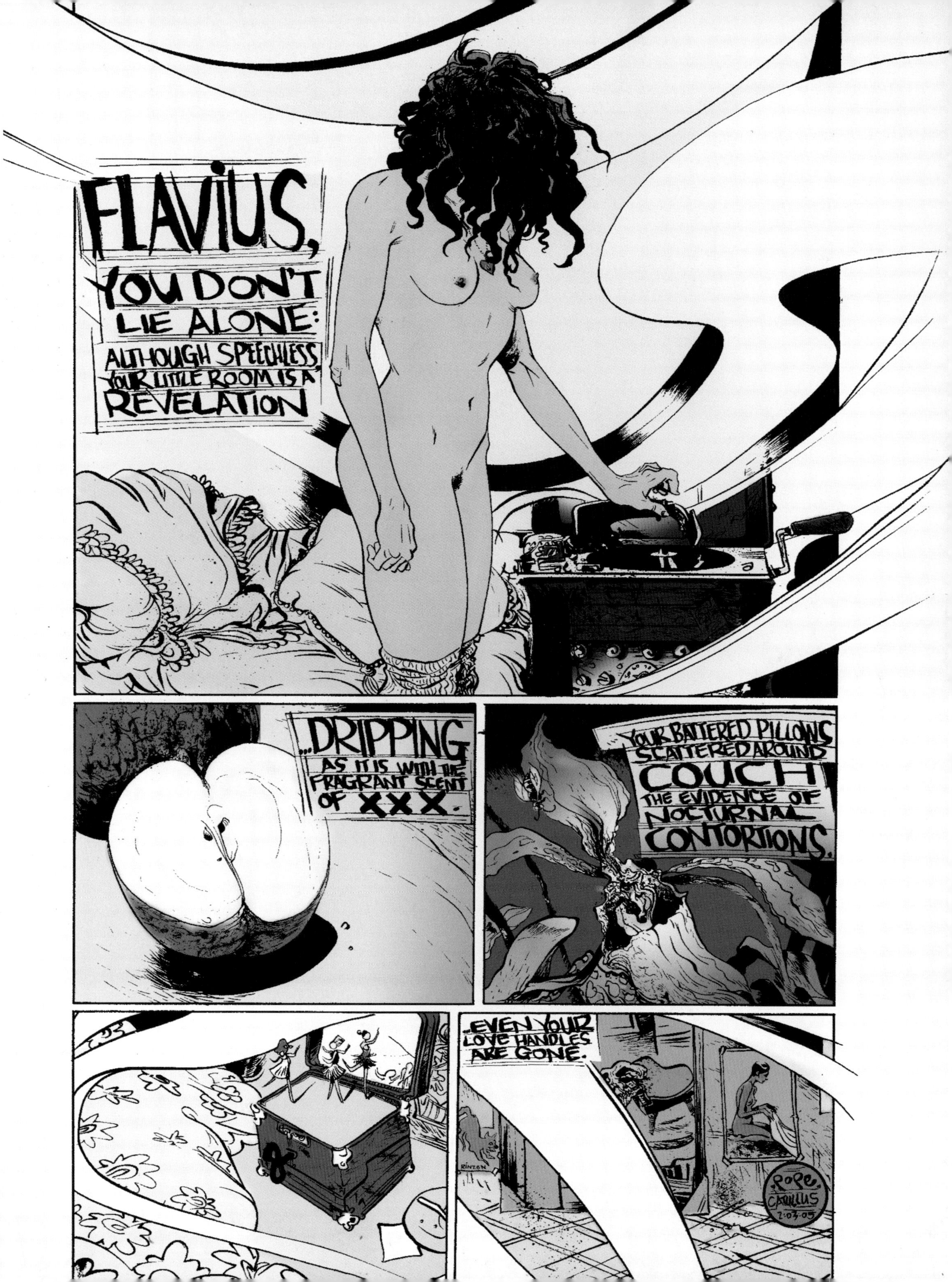
FLAVIUS,
YOU DON'T
LIE ALONE:
ALTHOUGH SPEECHLESS
YOUR LITTLE ROOM IS A
REVELATION
...DRIPPING
AS IT IS WITH THE
FRAGRANT SCENT
OF XXX.
YOUR BATTERED PILLOWS
SCATTERED AROUND
COUCH
THE EVIDENCE OF
NOCTURNAL
CONTORTIONS.
...EVEN YOUR
LOVE HANDLES
ARE GONE.

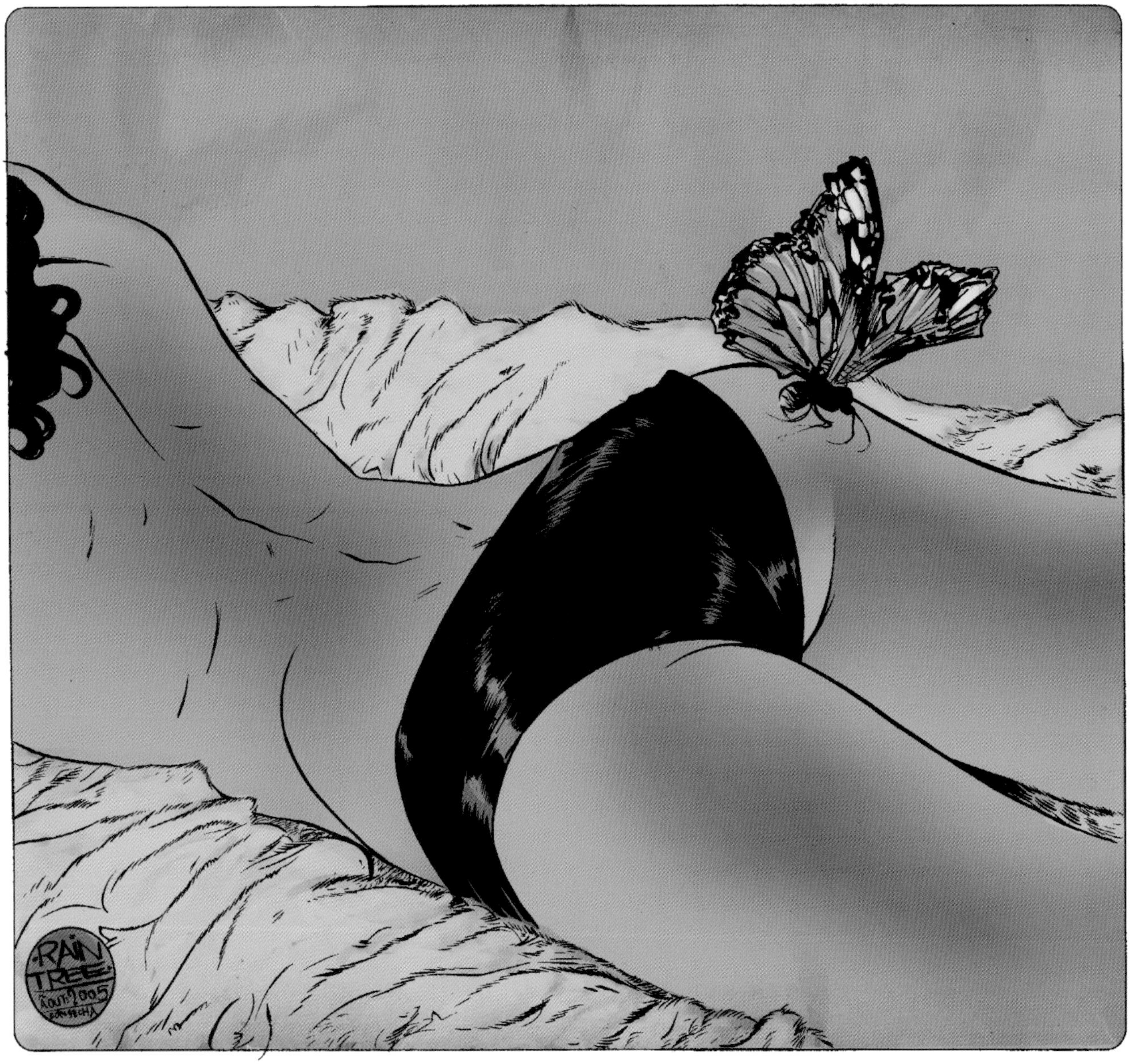
RAIN
TREE
AOUT 2005

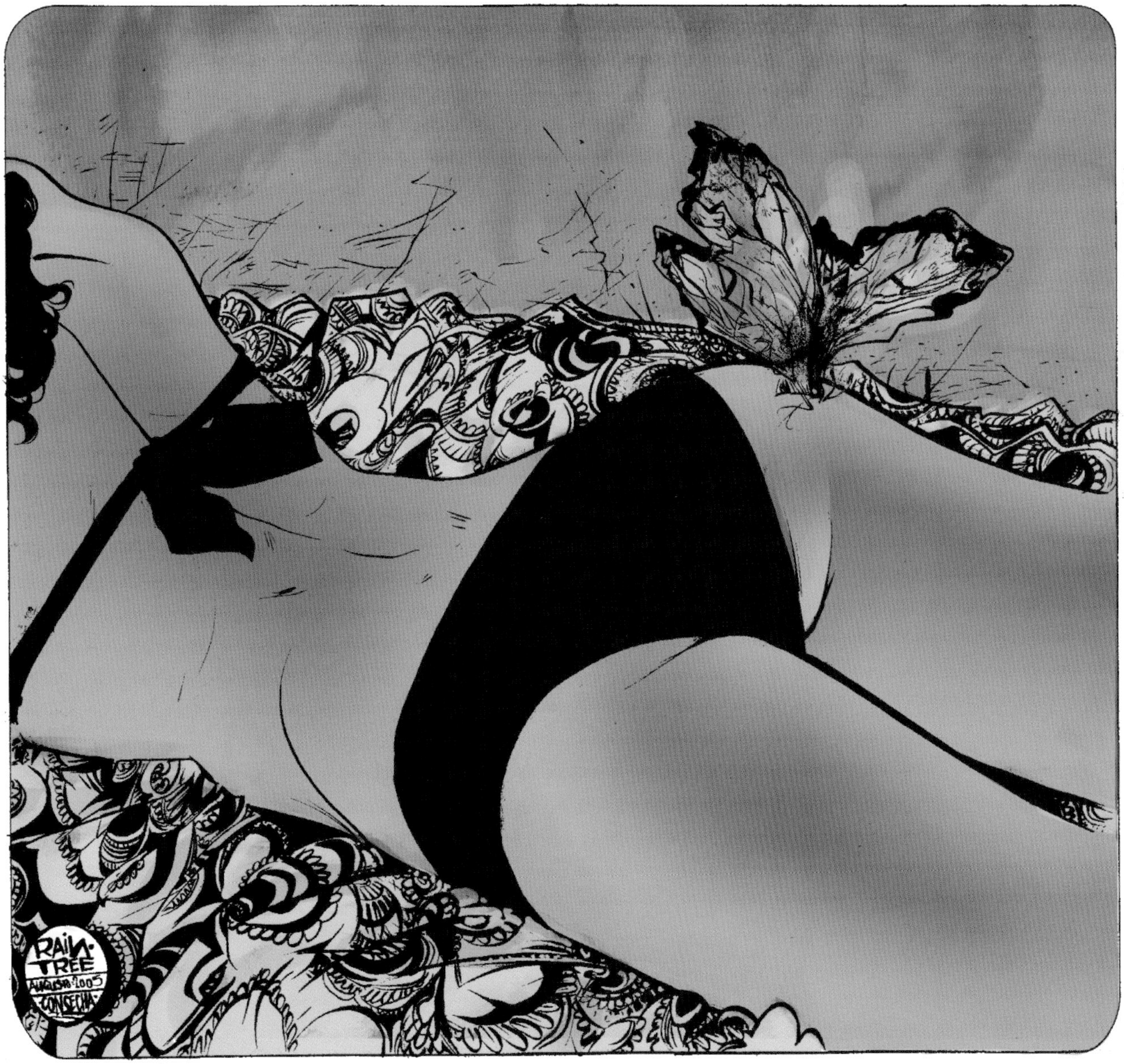
RAIN·TREE
2005

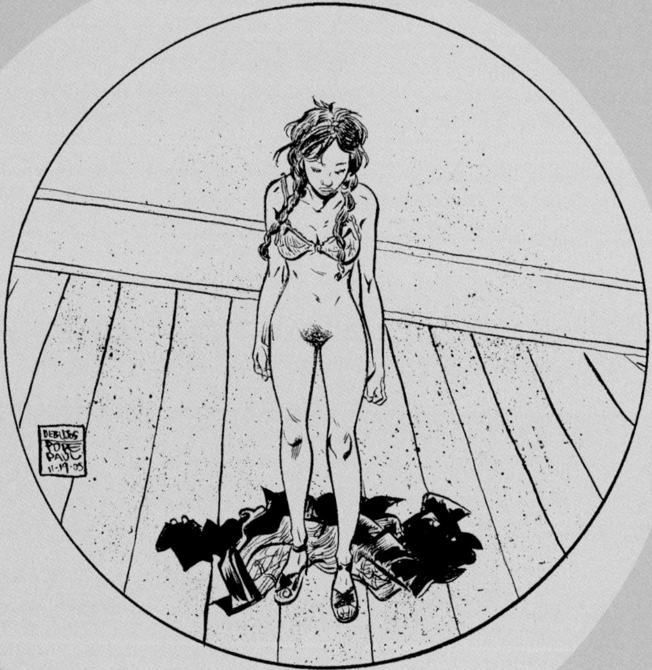

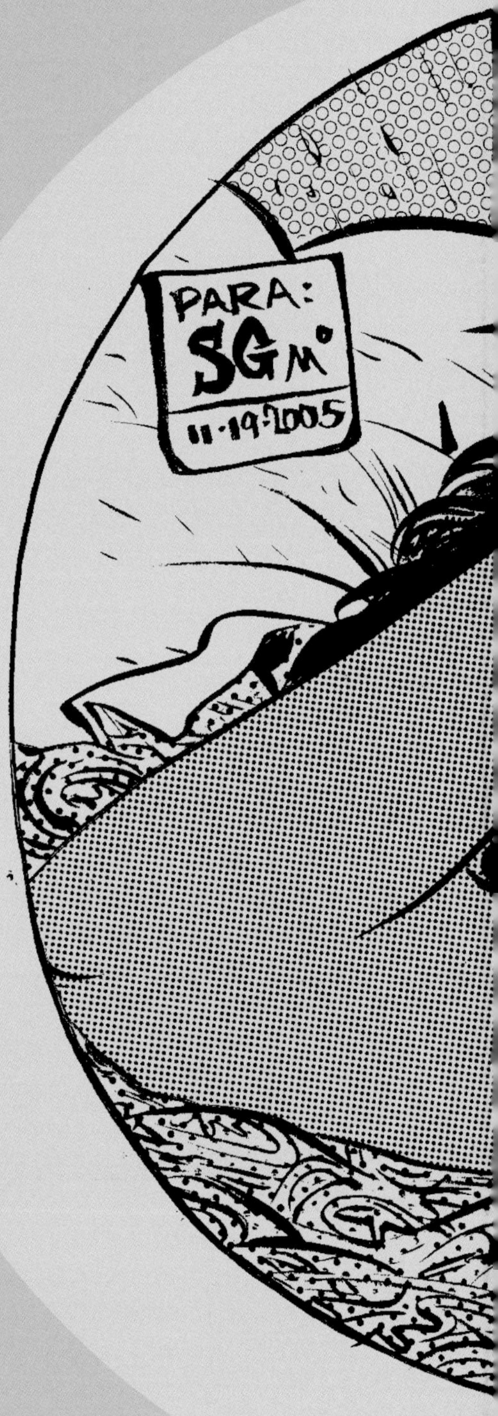
PARA:
SG M°
11-19-2005

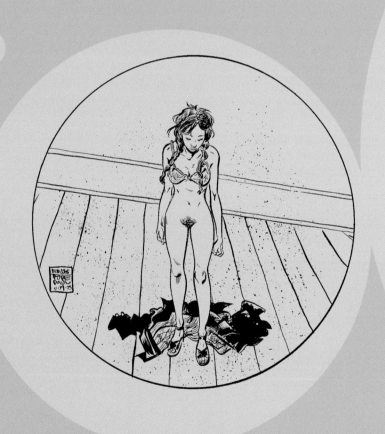

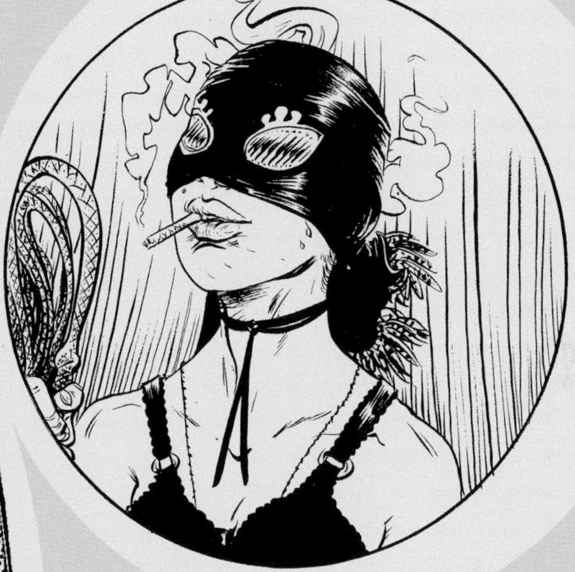

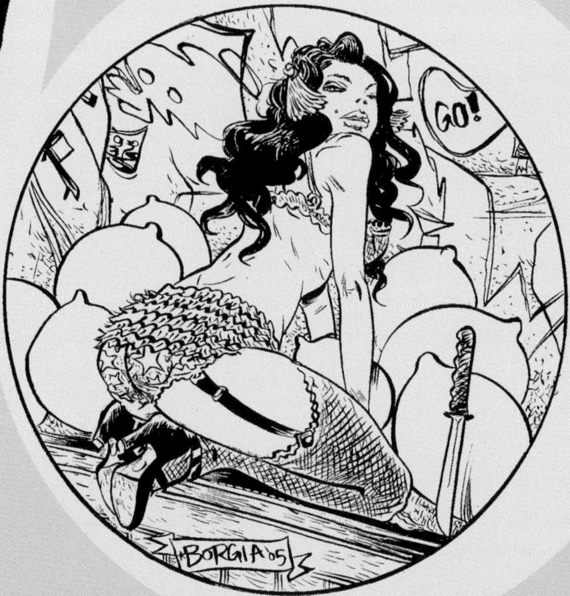
GO!
BORGIA '05

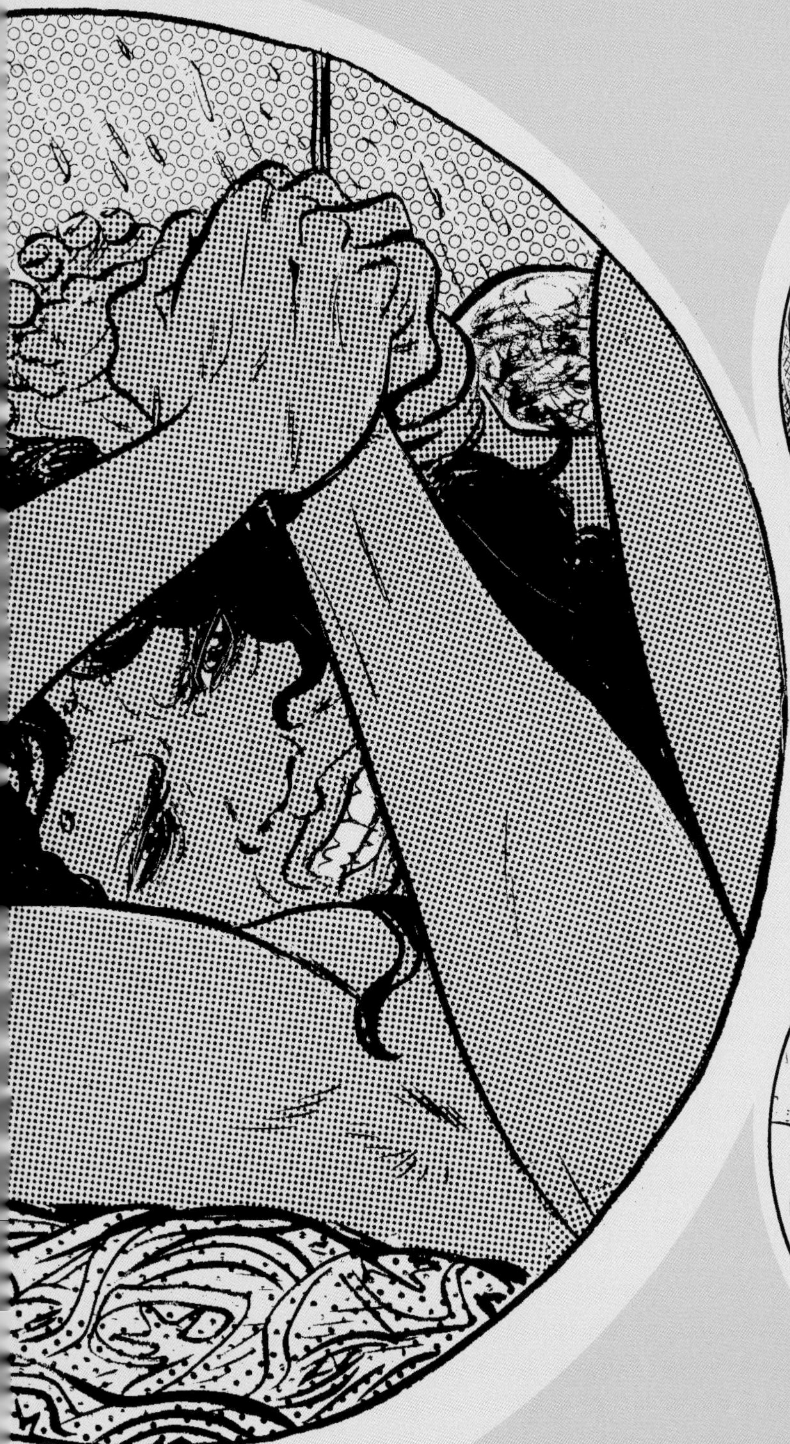

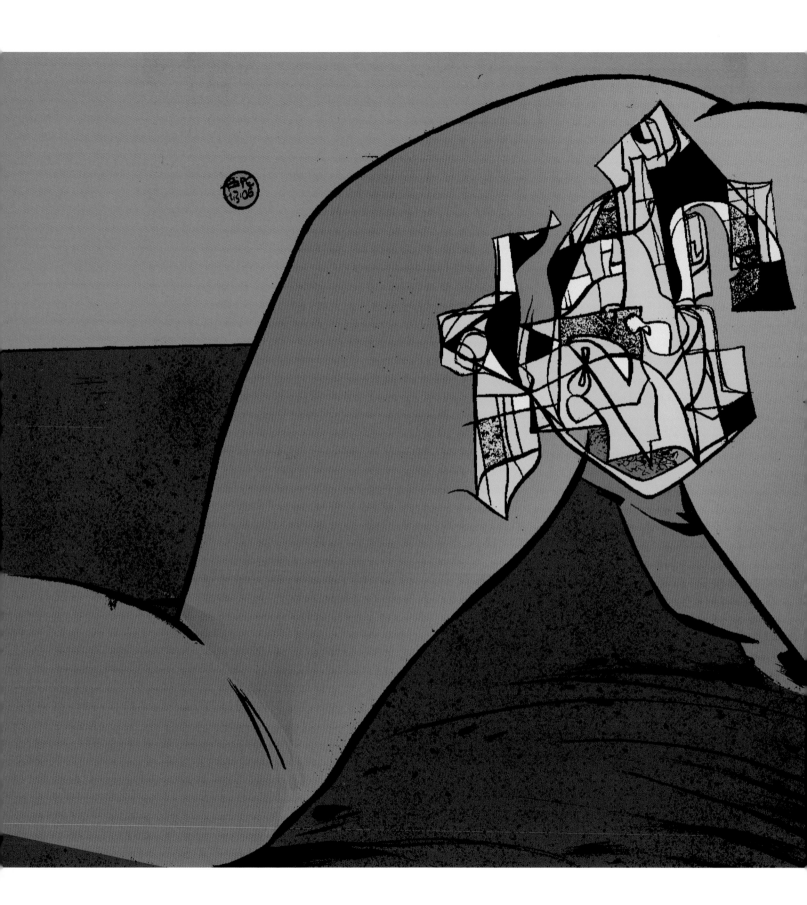

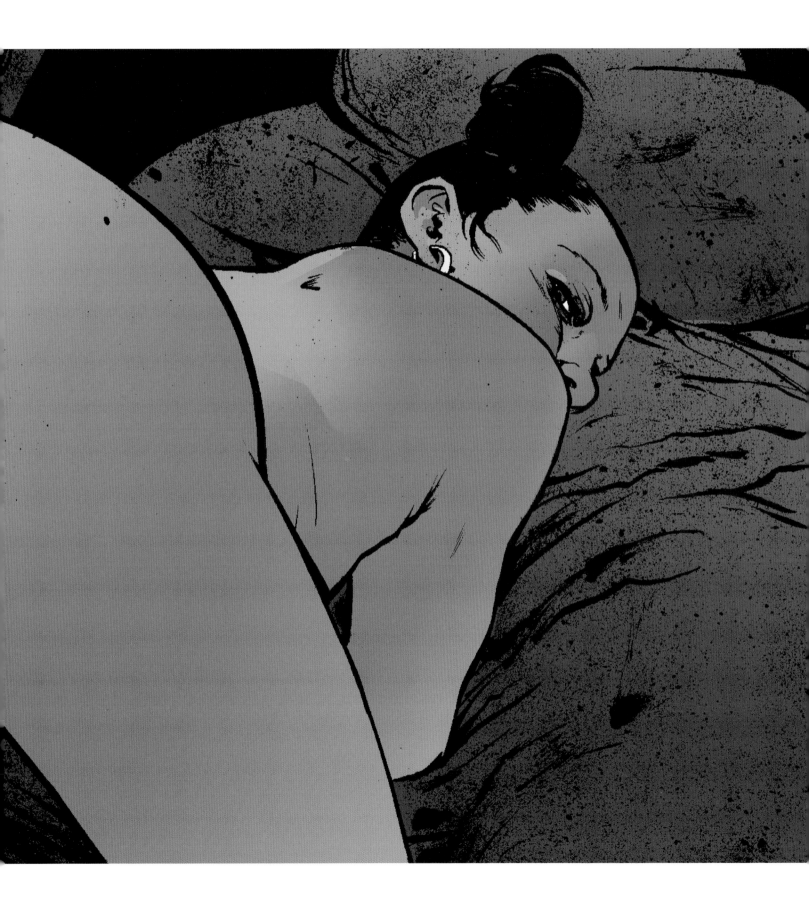

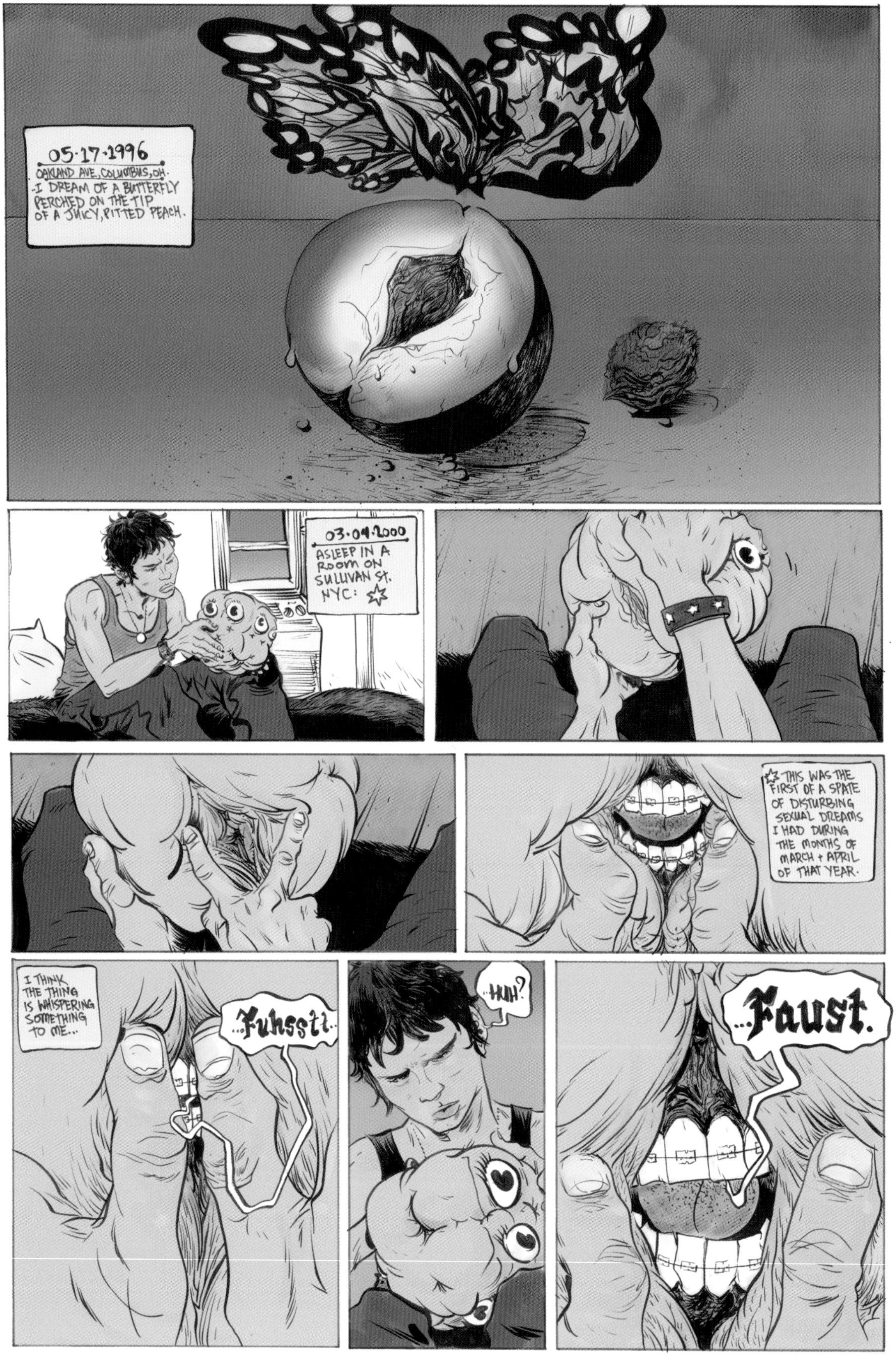
05·17·1996
OAKLAND AVE, COLUMBUS, OH.
-I DREAM OF A BUTTERFLY PERCHED ON THE TIP OF A JUICY, PITTED PEACH.
03·04·2000
ASLEEP IN A ROOM ON SULLIVAN ST. NYC: ☆
☆ THIS WAS THE FIRST OF A SPATE OF DISTURBING SEXUAL DREAMS I HAD DURING THE MONTHS OF MARCH + APRIL OF THAT YEAR.
I THINK THE THING IS WHISPERING SOMETHING TO ME...
...Fuhsst...
..HUH?
...Faust.

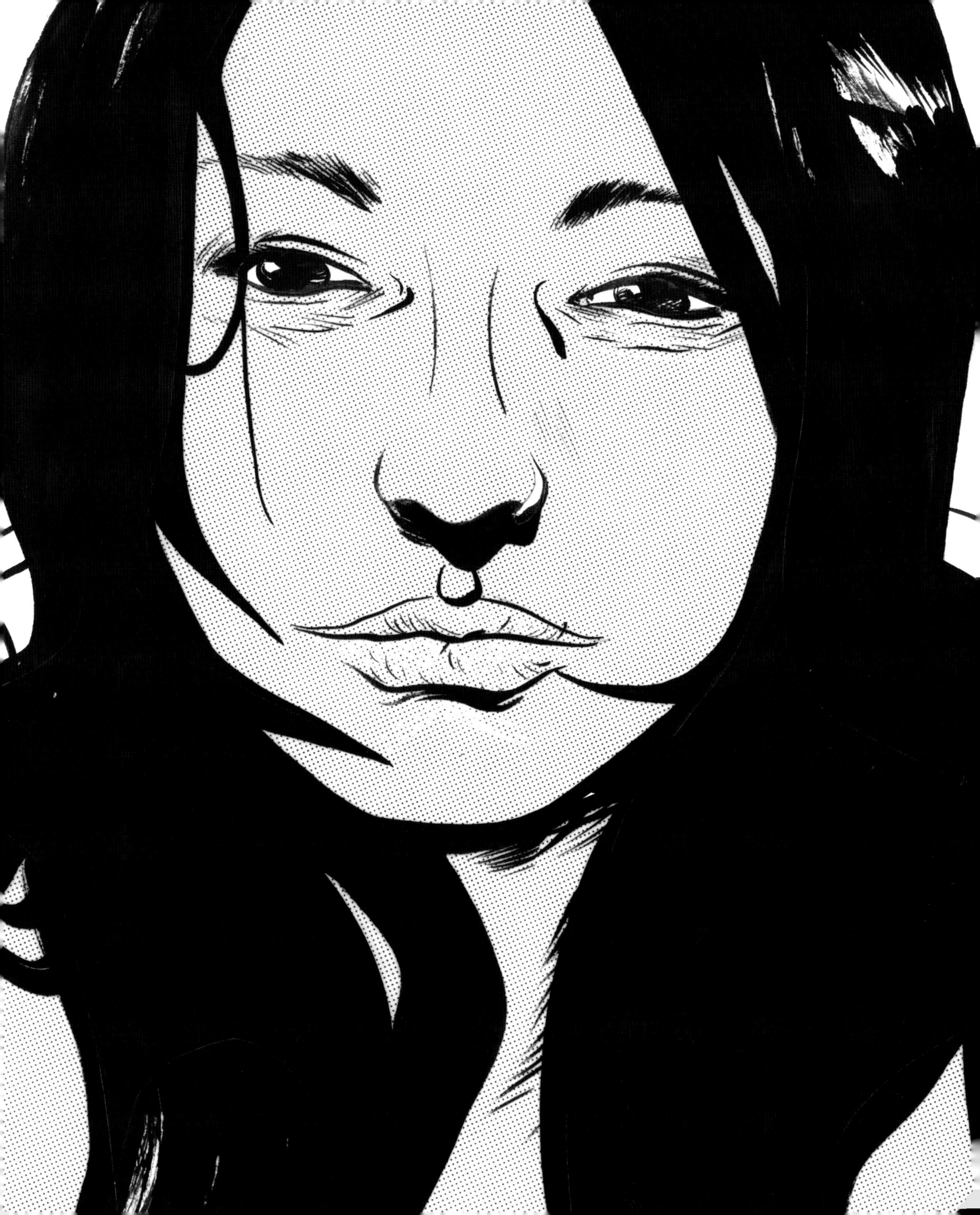

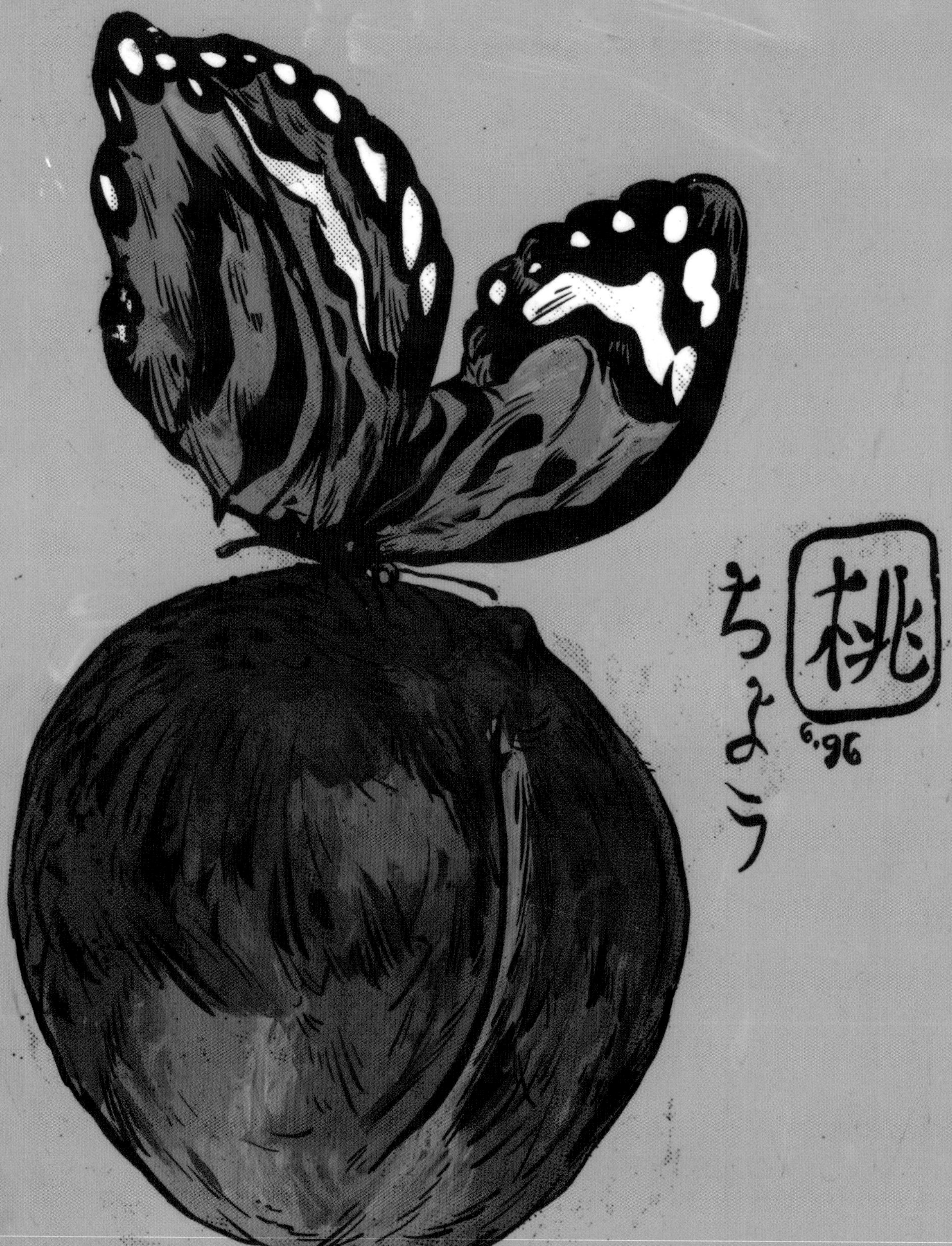
桃
6.96
ちょう

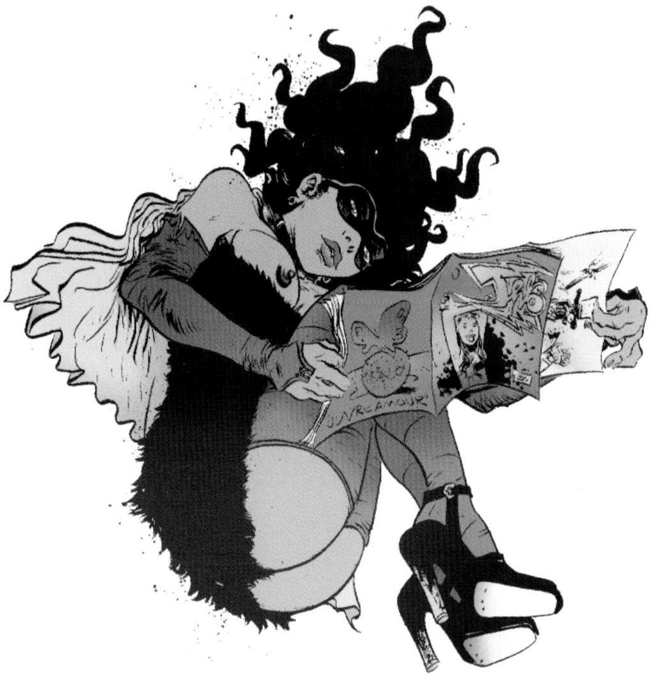

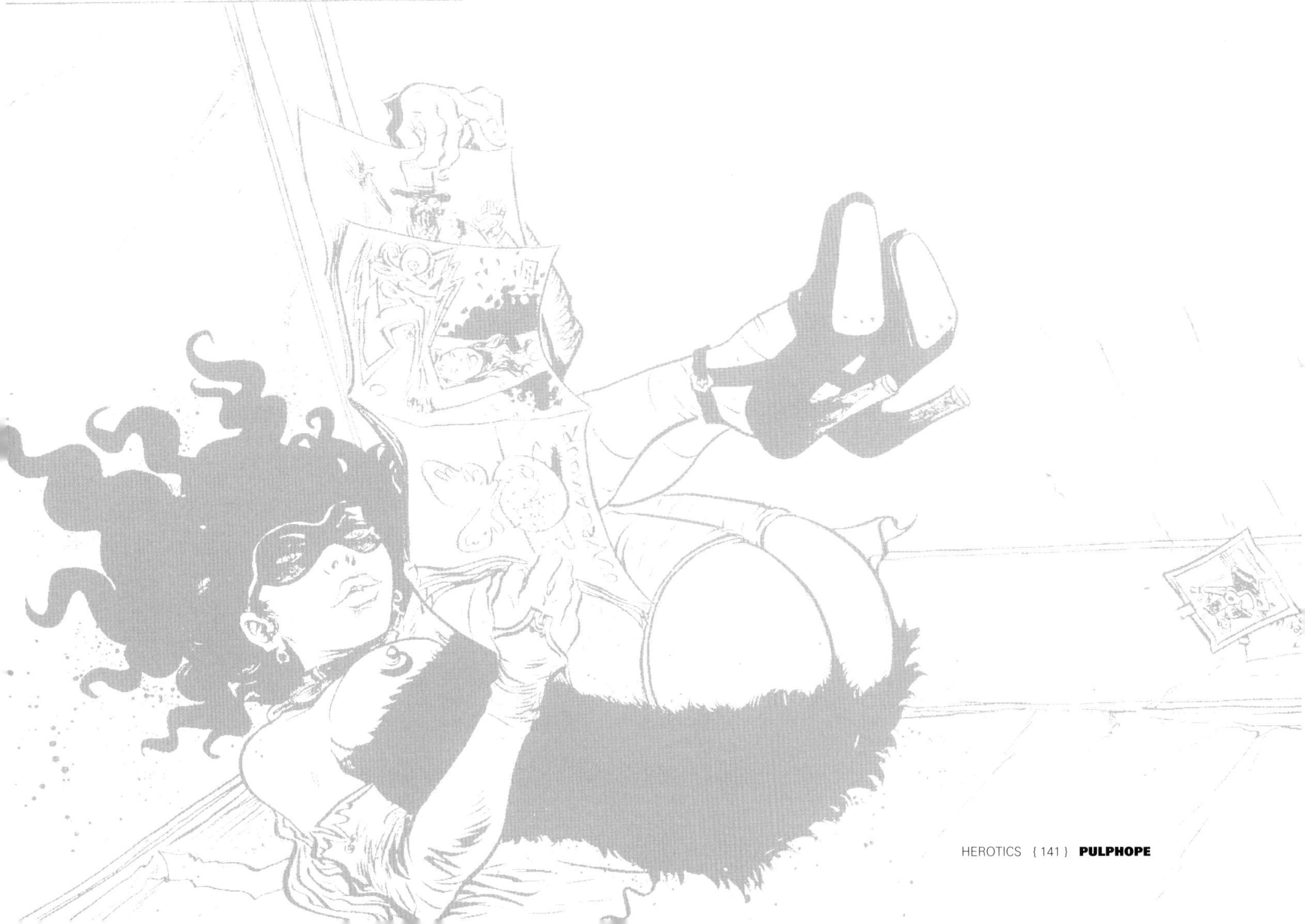

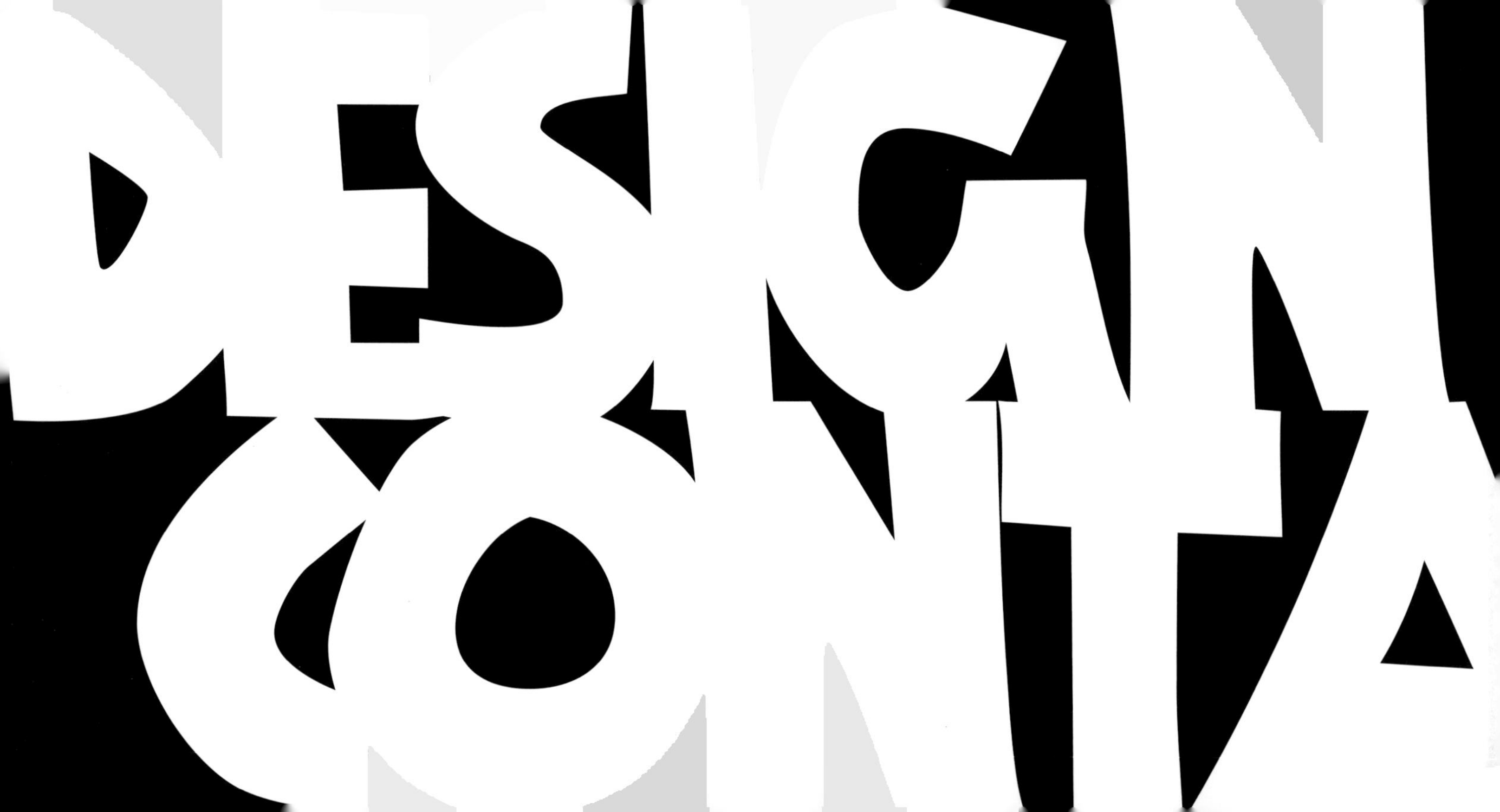
DESIGN
CONTA

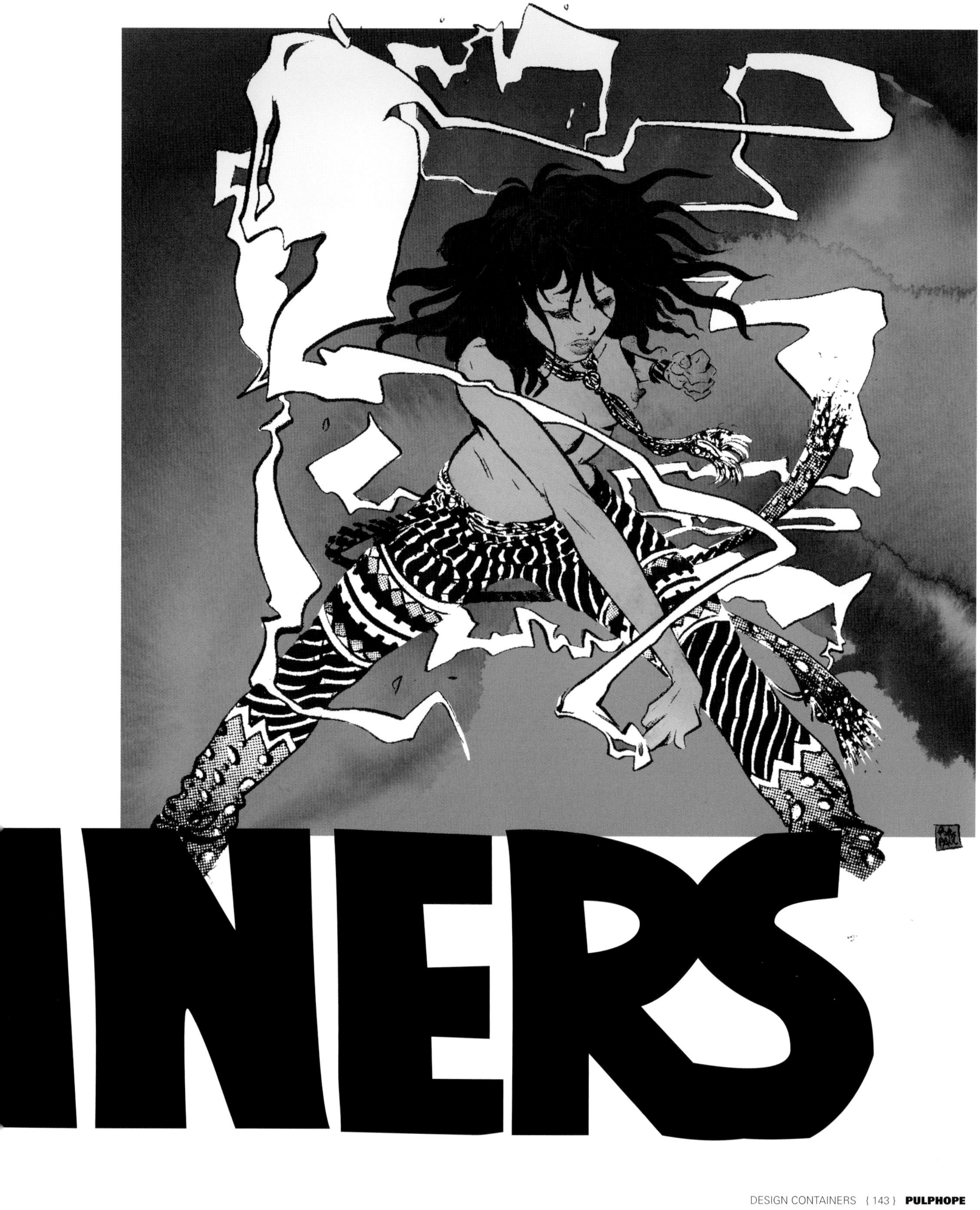

INERS

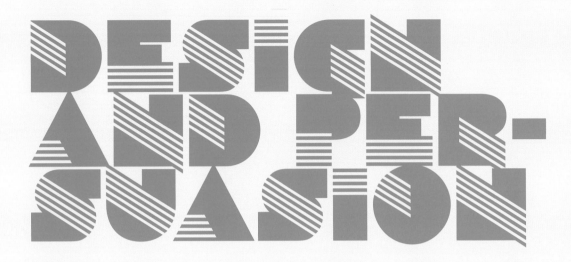

DESIGN AND PERSUASION

Despite their immediate differences, comics and all other forms of graphic design are attempts at persuasive visual communication through the use of consciously applied combinations of words and/or images, presented in the form of coherent compositions. Comics is more strictly of graphic design than graphic design is of comics, and this is the reason I like the term bandes dessines, or, what the French call comics... "designed strips". Bandes dessines has buried in its heart the very word "design". Regardless of subject matter, for a thing to truly be comics, it must contain a series of at least two pictures or images (either alone or combined with text elements), organized in some narrative or thematic sequence. This "two panel" rule is specific to comics and need not apply to the wider field of graphic design, or for that matter, to the art of cartooning, although all are essentially instances of applied visual communication. That much they share.

I began to consider the function of design as it relates to the wider field of communication only in college, long before I got serious about comics (or bandes dessines).

Studying Rhetoric, with its tight emphasis on logic, persuasion, and the effectiveness of various argument forms, I began to understand how the mechanics of discourse, how what you are trying to say, is only half of the argument. The other half is how you say it, or inversely, how the other person hears what you're trying to say. Naturally, having the capacity to speak effectively is crucial for demonstrating the soundness of some particular view you're trying to expound on this-or-that subject, and it is essential if you hope to be understood clearly. There is the message and there is the delivery. How to make these two things work in harmony is the problem Rhetoric addresses. Harvard University Emeritus I.A. Richards, author of *How To Read A Page* as well as many other books on this subject, says, Rhetoric is ultimately the study of misunderstanding... and its remedies. He asks the (literally) rhetorical question, "How much and in how many ways does good communication differ from bad?" George Orwell's frightful, excoriating essay "Politics and the English Language", touches on a similar theme — the uses of obsfucating speech. In this firebrand piece, Orwell mercilessly demonstrates the

inherent insincerity of political speech, and shows how words can be used to disguise meanings as easily as uncover them. In this essay, Orwell also makes an eloquent argument for the importance of using fresh metaphors in one's rhetoric in order to most effectively communicate a point boldly and memorably. He heaps contempt on tired cliched speech, reserving his greatest contempt for politicians who deliberately manipulate through the use of bland, hackneyed phrases in order to disguising the violence they intend to perpetrate on others. This concern of his was more than just a Rhetorical exercise — two years later, in 1948, he wrote his masterpiece, *1984.*

If a metaphor is understood to be a function of speech (from the Greek metapherin, "rhetorical trope") in which two or more seemingly unrelated subjects are compared indirectly, then it makes sense how a strong command of metaphor is necessary for effective, persuasive speech. In the case of the artist, or more generally, people interested in picture-making or picture-reading, whether its drawing/painting /printmaking/web design or through some other medium, these preoccupations could suggest why discovering and using effective visual metaphors is essential to good design . One of my favorite authors, Rudolph Arnhein, in his book *Visual Thinking,* defines a visual metaphor as “a complex symbolic association observed through visual cues and/or physical signs”. One of my own conscious early attempts at applying a visual metaphor (at the time, I thought of it as a “visual pun”) was a comics page I drew in which two characters having a philosophic argument are literally wrestling, arms and legs locked in battle. This is maybe a somewhat obvious way to represent a heated debate through pictures, but you have to start somewhere. In the hands of a great illustrator/designer, such as Istvan Banyai, we see visual metaphors applied expertly, often to humorous ends, such as in his 1981 cover design for the band Poco. On their album *Cowboys & Englishmen,* Banyai presents a tiny cowboy standing in the middle of what appears to be dusty-ochre negative space, as if in the middle of a sandstorm. This tiny figure — a Sheriff (we can see the starred badge on his vest) — is walking in a classic, bow-legged gait, perched over a slight shadow at high noon. The figure is drawn in a somewhat fusty, mock Victorian style, floppy hat, frumpy shirt, mustaches and all. In the shadow we see a reverse reflection, an optical illusion, as if all this time we’ve been looking at the face of a playing card and didn’t know it. Flipping the design over, we see what at first glance appeared to be a shadow or a reflection in a pool of oil, but is actually another fusty, funny drawing — this time a cliched Englishman, complete with walking cane, bowler hat, a slight, reddish Van Dyke beard on his chin. The words “Poco” and “Cowboys” are both presented in widely space, old west-era tin type, the kind of thing you think of as being on an old circus poster benefitting a Mister Kite. Along the bottom of the picture, as if a scribbly afterthought, we see “& Englishmen”, in a decorative, slightly campy, cursive script. Considering the word “poco” means “small” in Spanish, and the Cowboy and English men are as small as ants in the brownish dusty colorfield, we have a complete visual play on words transcribed through pictures.

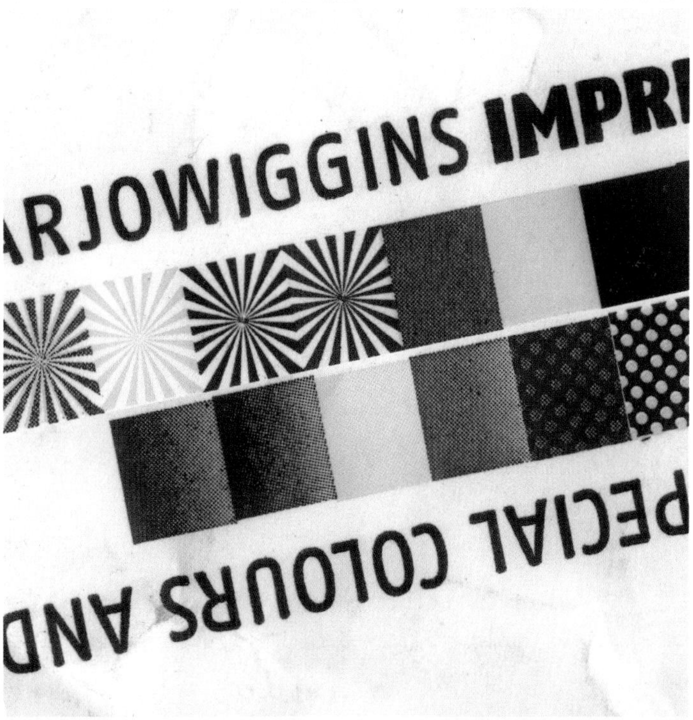
ARJOWIGGINS IMPR
PECIAL COLOURS AND

To be effective in this way through design — and in this wide net I am including comics storytelling — I believe it is necessary to have as broad an awareness of names, likenesses, images, sounds, and even other pictures, as you possibly can, all the visual symbols which will be familiar to your intended audience, no matter how large or how small (Afterall, how many people really get the meaning of the infamous T-shirt design which reads, “Han shot first”?). Those things, boiled down into symbols which your audience will more or less easily understand, are your tools. It is further necessary to find ways to combine these different elements visually so that they can convey more than simply their immediate, obvious meanings. Effectively applied visual metaphors uncover the hidden relationships which exist between unrelated subjects. The thing that is new in the combination is the association implied by your visual metaphors, and, borrowing from Orwell, the fresher and more unique your visual metaphor, the more persuasive your design argument. The best visual metaphors are those that unlock vague or heretofore unobserved associations between things, and when done well this has a real communicative power, unlike anything else.

Lately, I’ve begun to regard graphic design as a kind of “container”, as a non-linear atmosphere built to keep ideas boyant and alive. Design lends a deliberate surface to an idea or object, it helps to powerfully distinguish a thing from others of its kind, and it also amplifies certain ineffable, non-verbal meanings, moods or attitudes, relating back to the thing itself. I would go on to say that I believe the designer has primarily only one special aesthetic consideration — he ought to strive to create legibility when giving form to ideas. A designer must be conscious of his design choices. Communicating a graphic message effectively could be called design legibility, or design persuasion. Even the choice to leave in a “happy accident” is a conscious decision. Let the best design be the one which visually best communicates, or best contains, the idea.

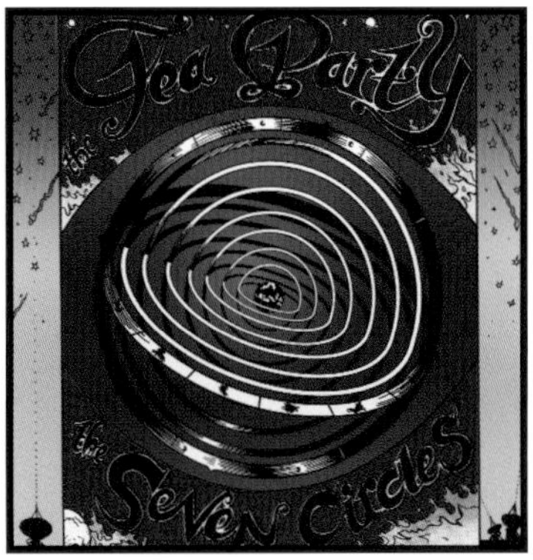
Tea Party
the
the Seven Circles
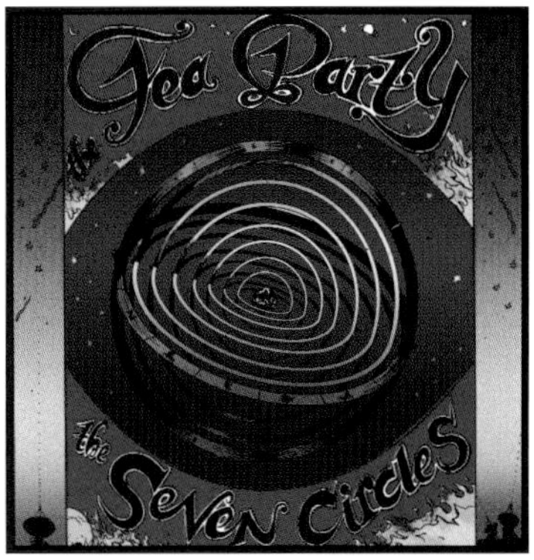
Tea Party
the
the Seven Circles

Tea Party
the
the Seven Circles

Tea Party
the
the Seven Circles
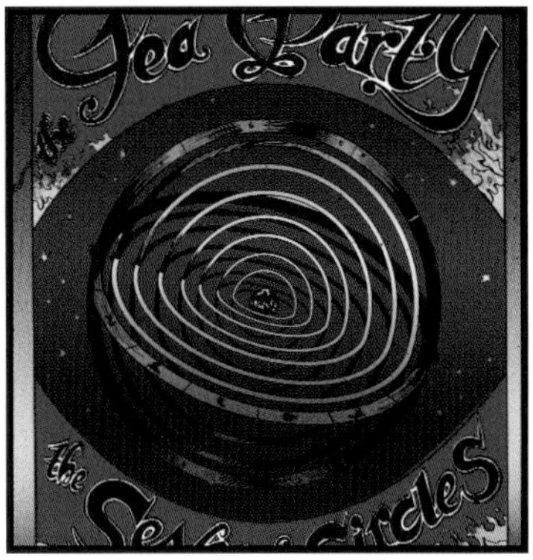
Tea Party
the
the
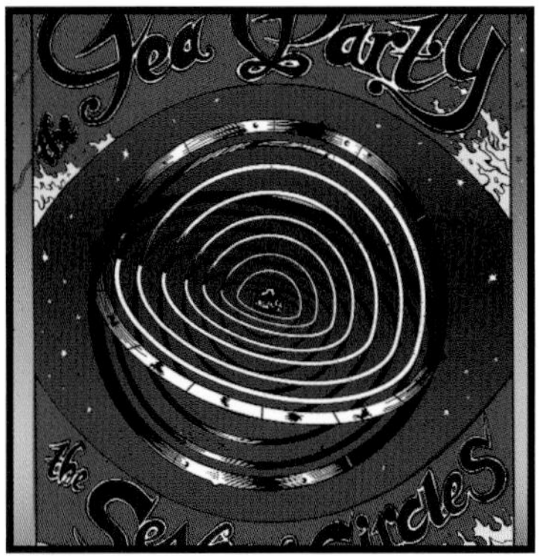
Tea Party
the
the

Tea Party
the
the Seven Circles
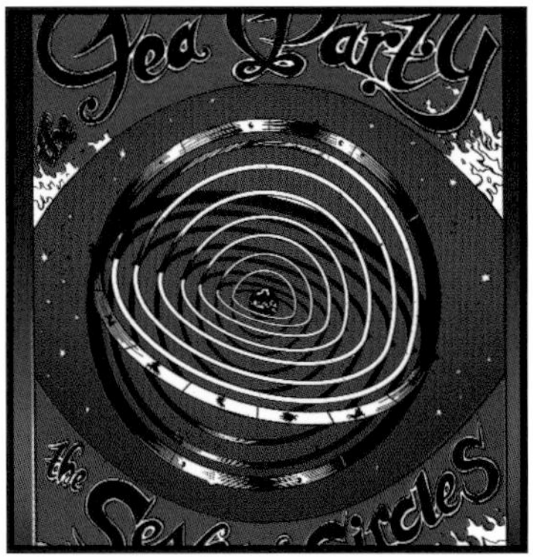
Tea Party
the
the
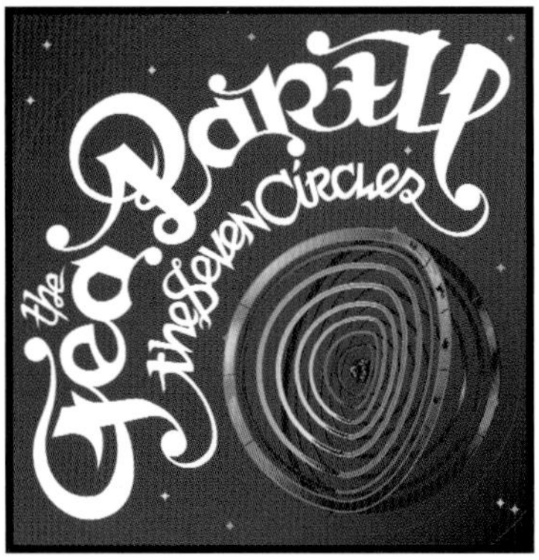
the Tea Party
the Seven Circles
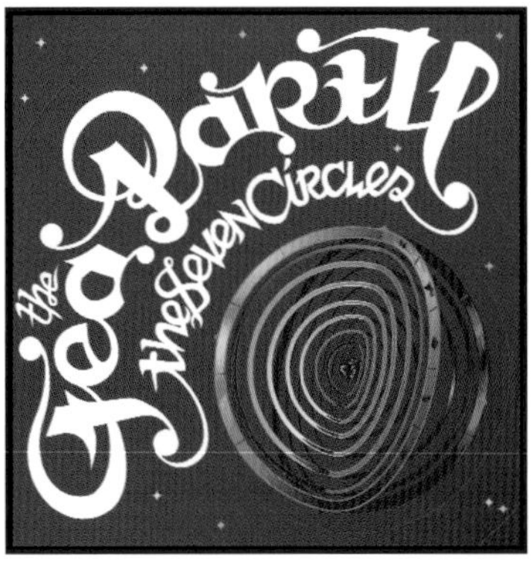
the Tea Party
the Seven Circles

the Tea Party
the Seven Circles
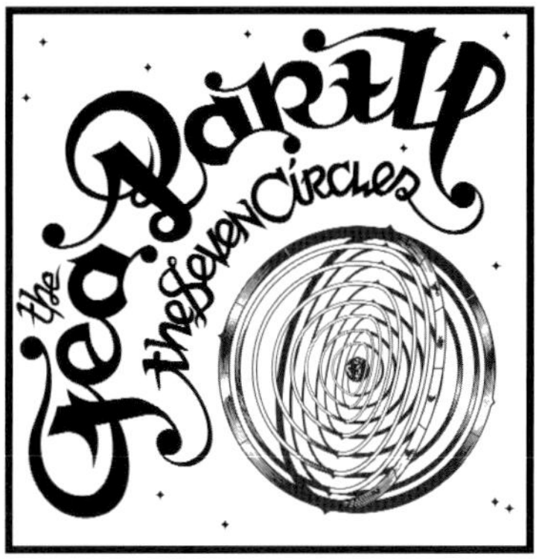
the Tea Party
the Seven Circles

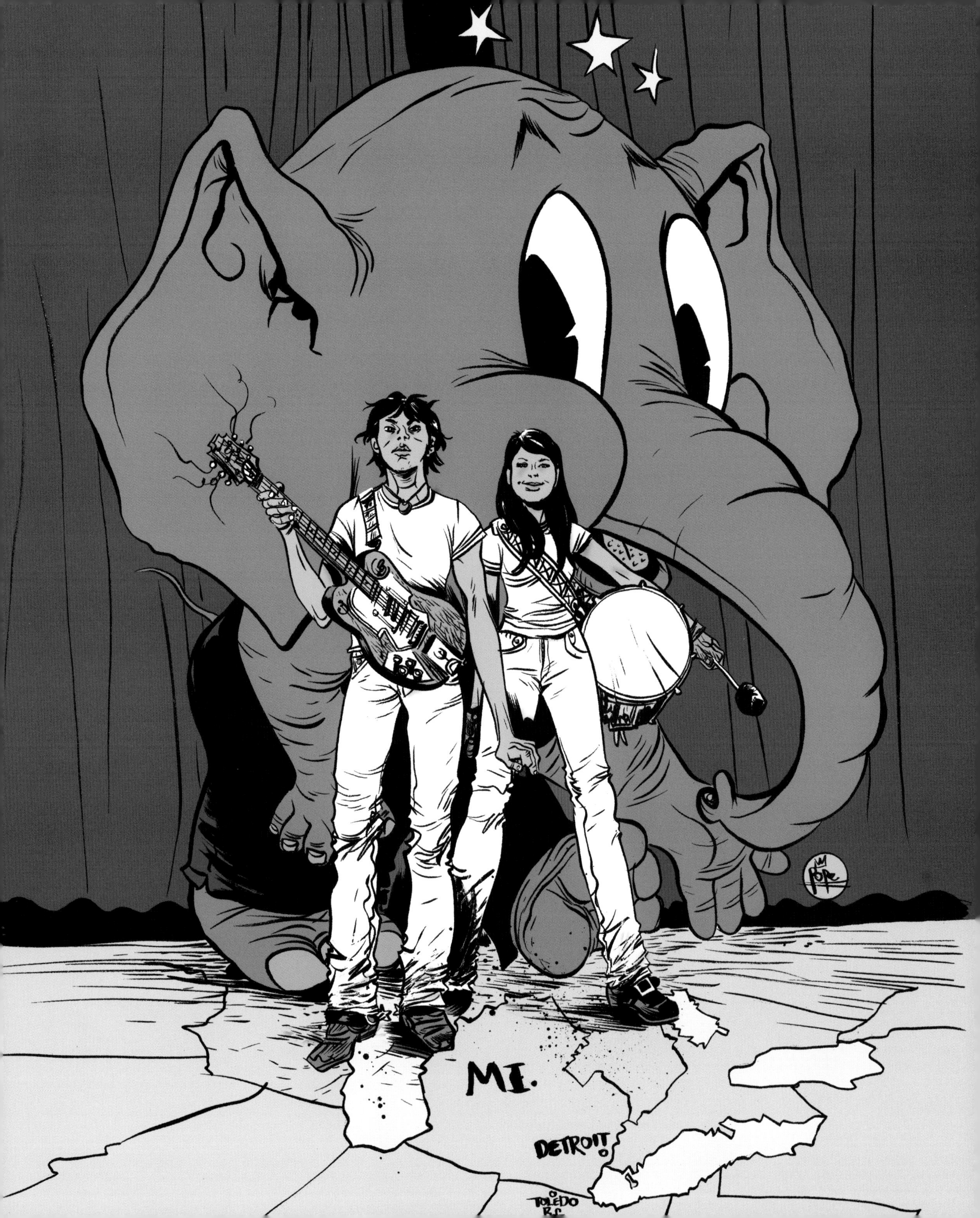
MI.
DETROIT
TOLEDO

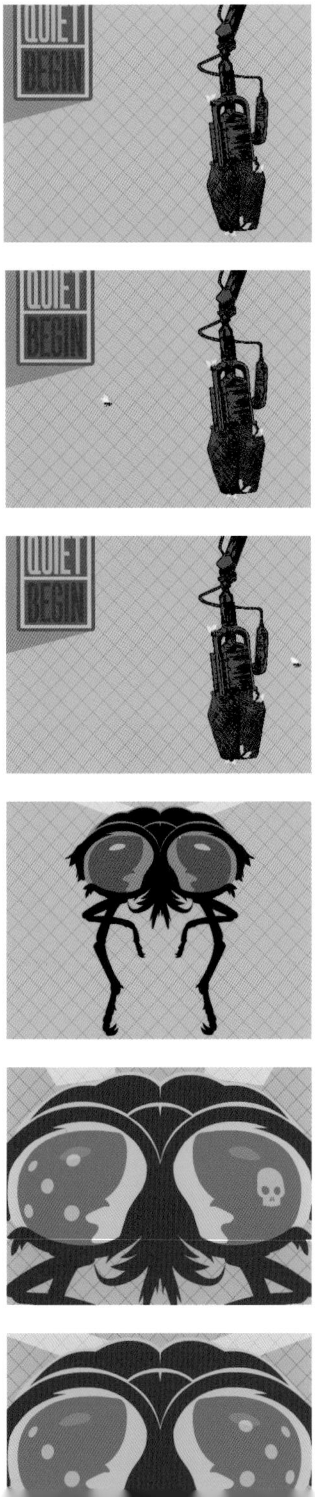
QUIET BEGIN
QUIET BEGIN
QUIET BEGIN
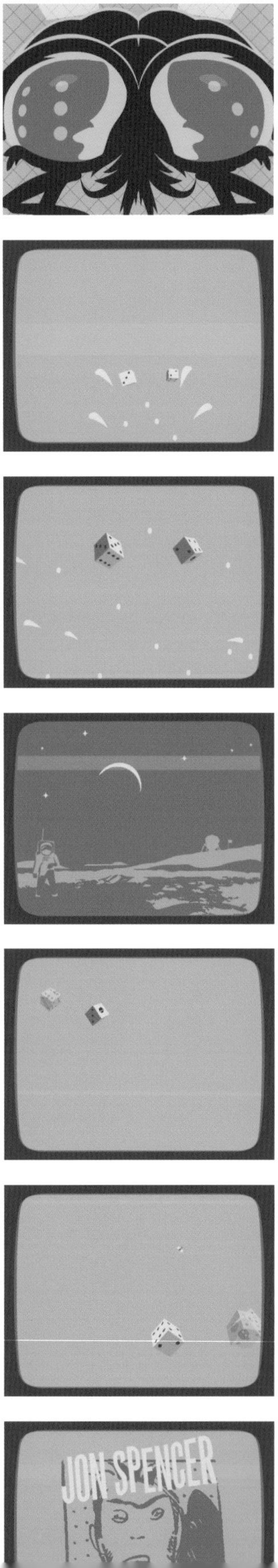
JON SPENCER
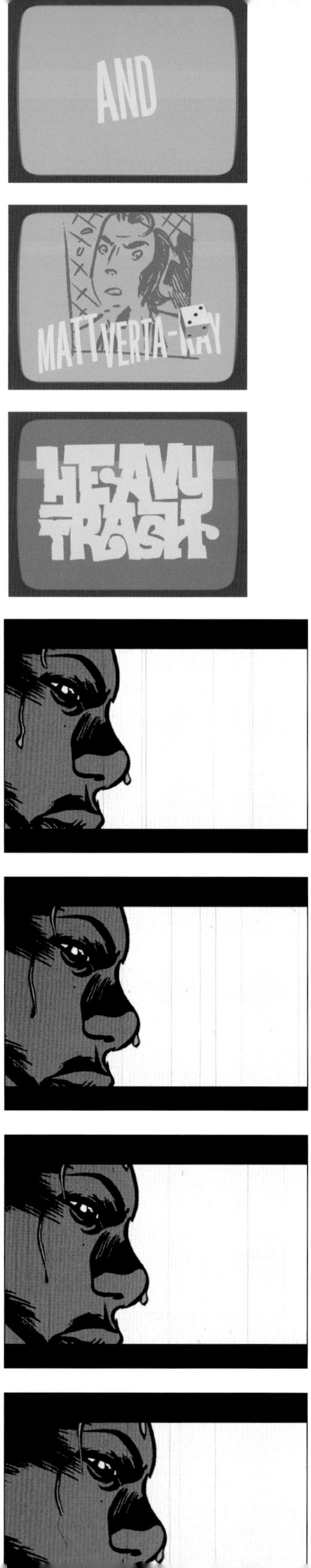
AND
MATT VERTA-RAY
HEAVY TRASH
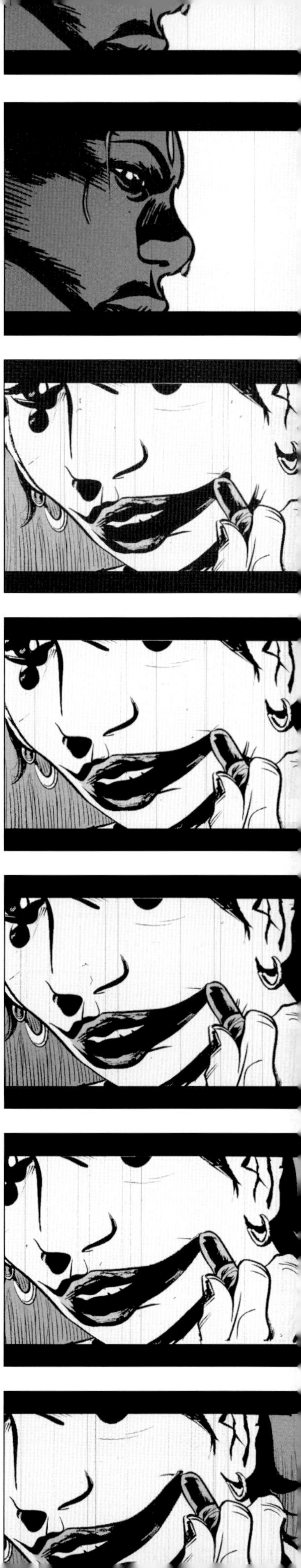

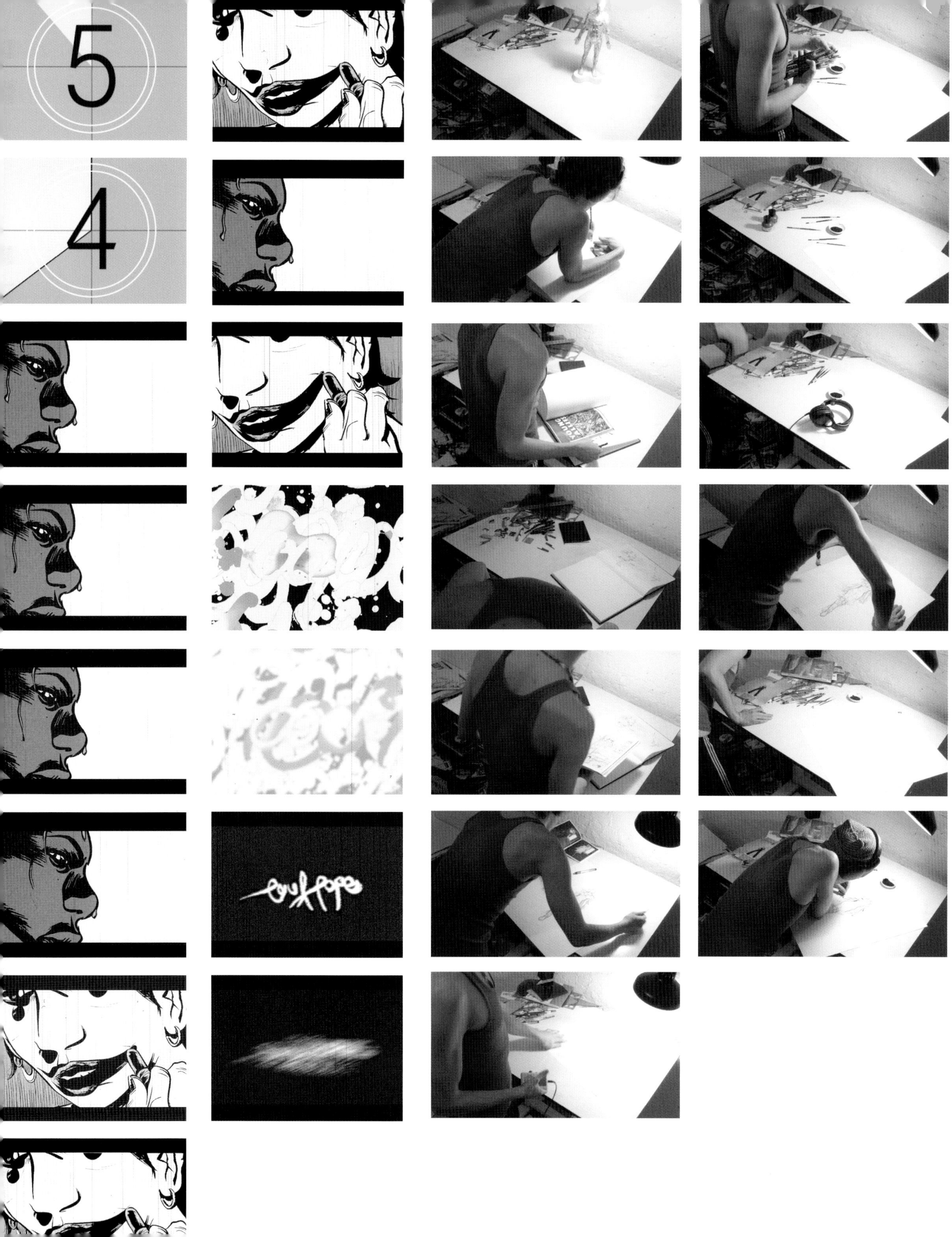
5
4

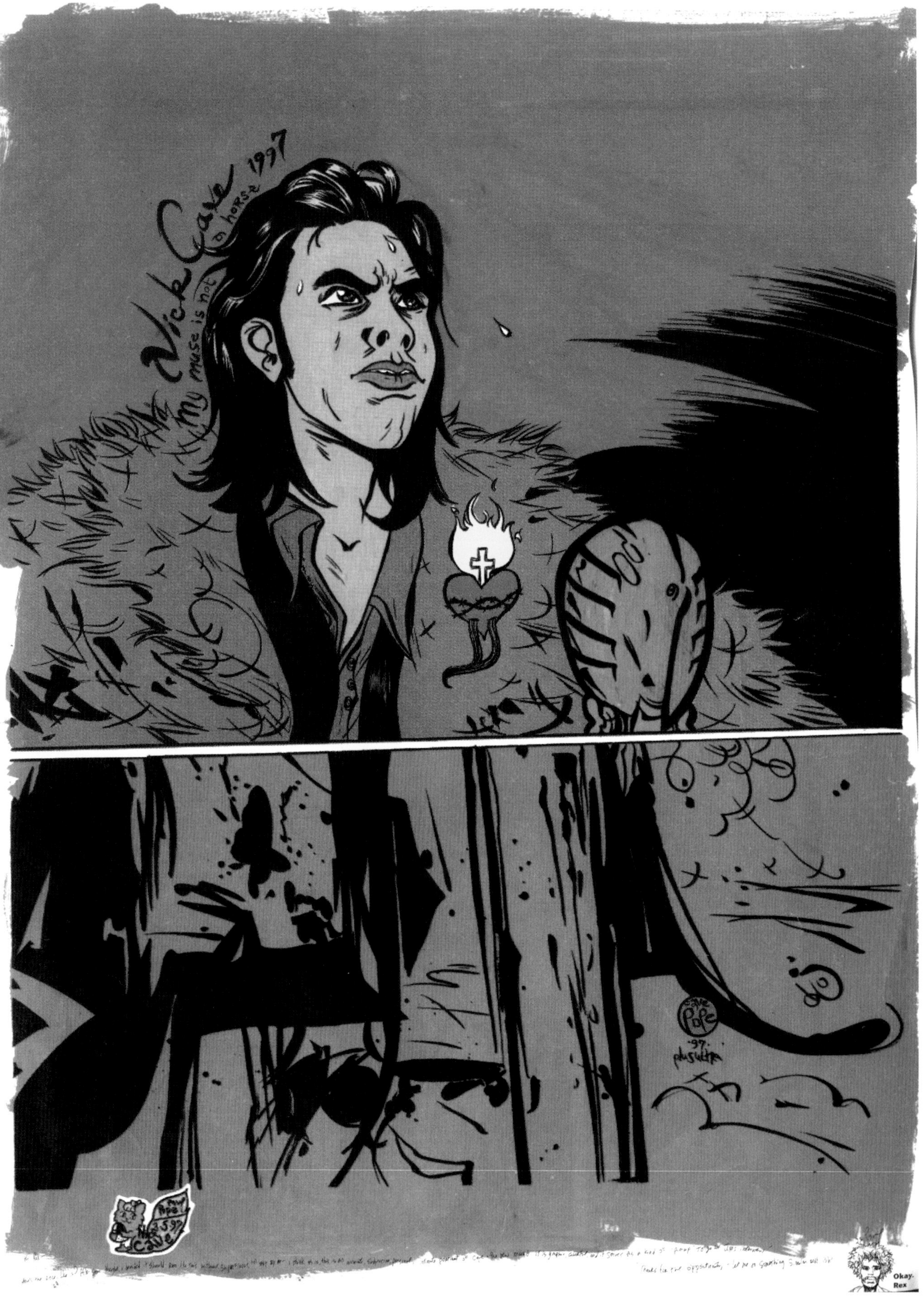
Nick Cave
my muse is not a horse
1997
Steve Pope
'97
plusultra
Okay-
Rex

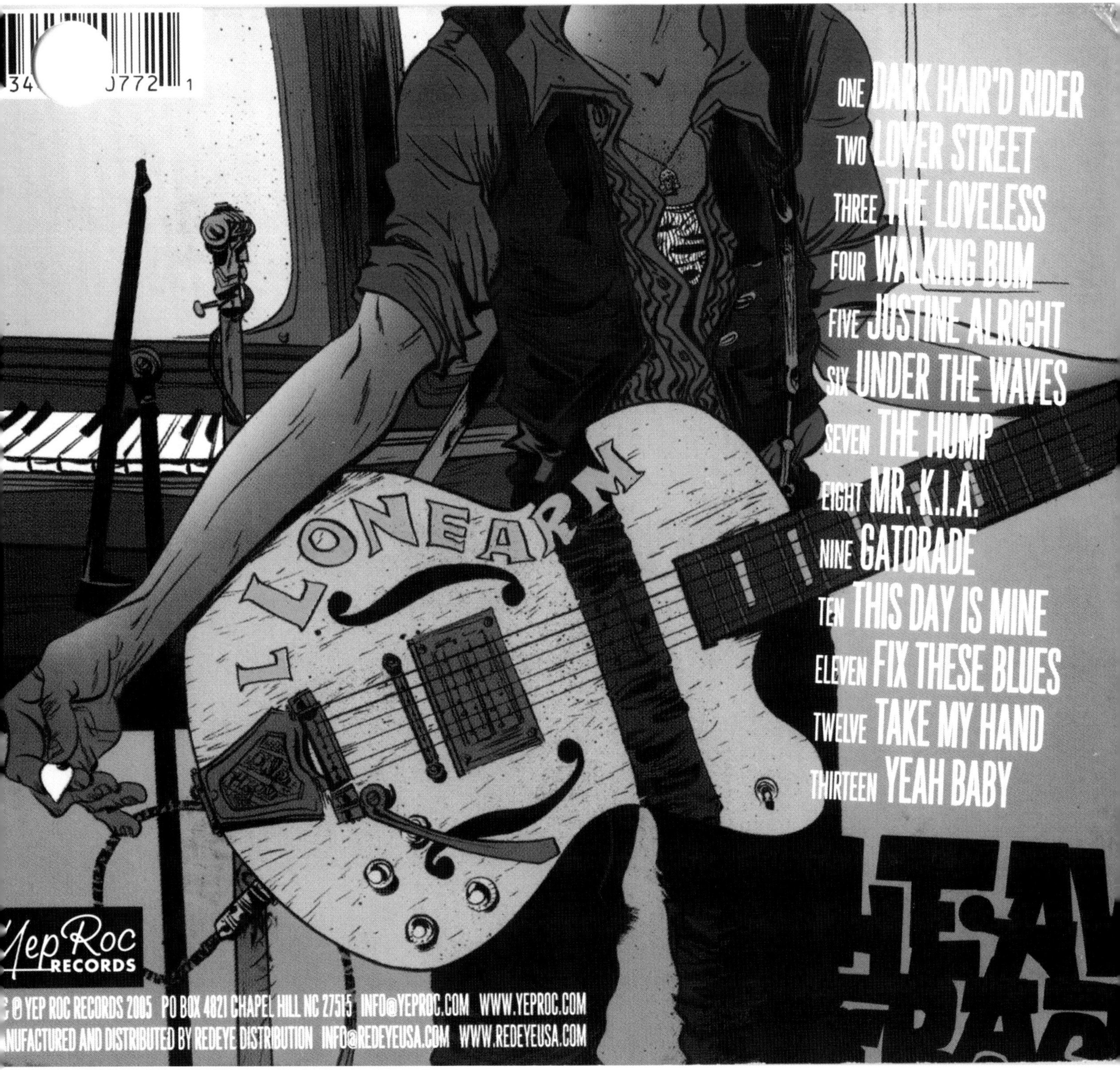
ONE DARK HAIR'D RIDER
TWO LOVER STREET
THREE THE LOVELESS
FOUR WALKING BUM
FIVE JUSTINE ALRIGHT
SIX UNDER THE WAVES
SEVEN THE HUMP
EIGHT MR. K.I.A.
NINE GATORADE
TEN THIS DAY IS MINE
ELEVEN FIX THESE BLUES
TWELVE TAKE MY HAND
THIRTEEN YEAH BABY
LONEARM
YepRoc RECORDS
℗ YEP ROC RECORDS 2005 PO BOX 4821 CHAPEL HILL NC 27515 INFO@YEPROC.COM WWW.YEPROC.COM
NUFACTURED AND DISTRIBUTED BY REDEYE DISTRIBUTION INFO@REDEYEUSA.COM WWW.REDEYEUSA.COM

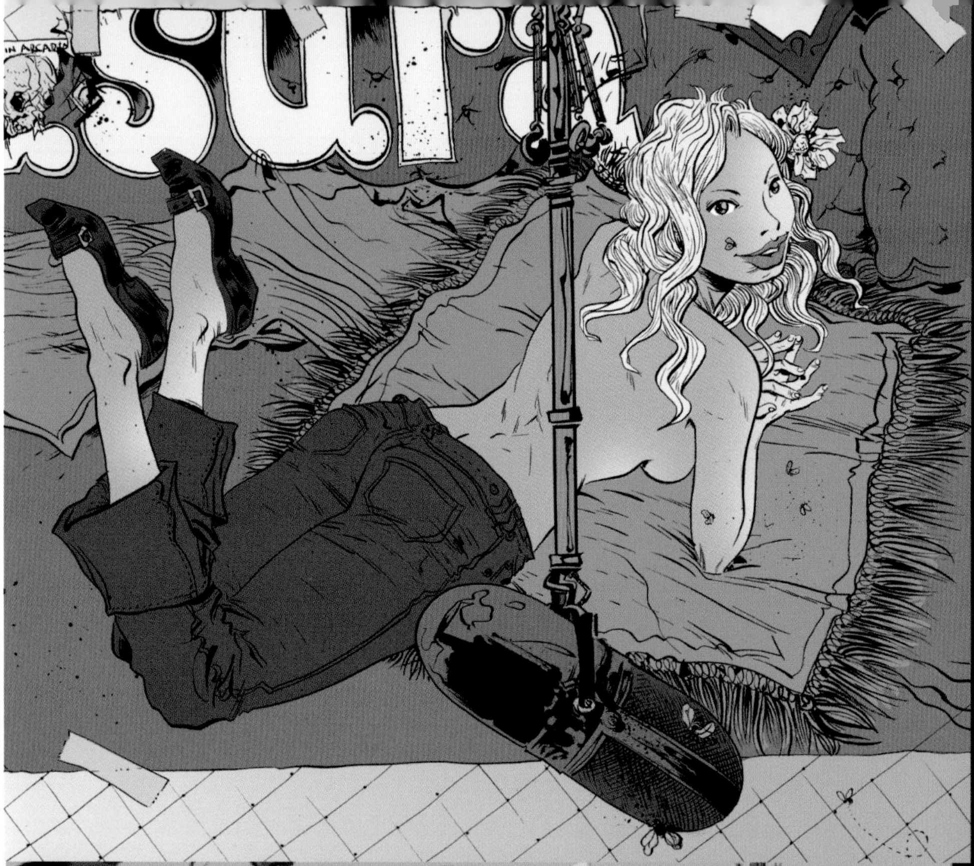

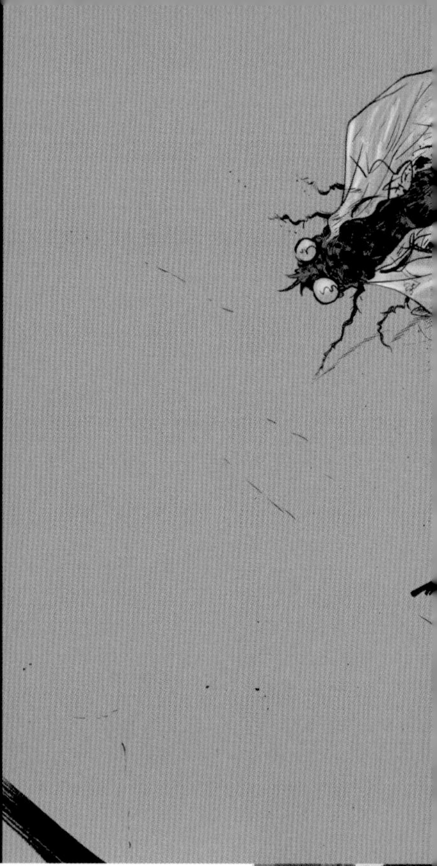

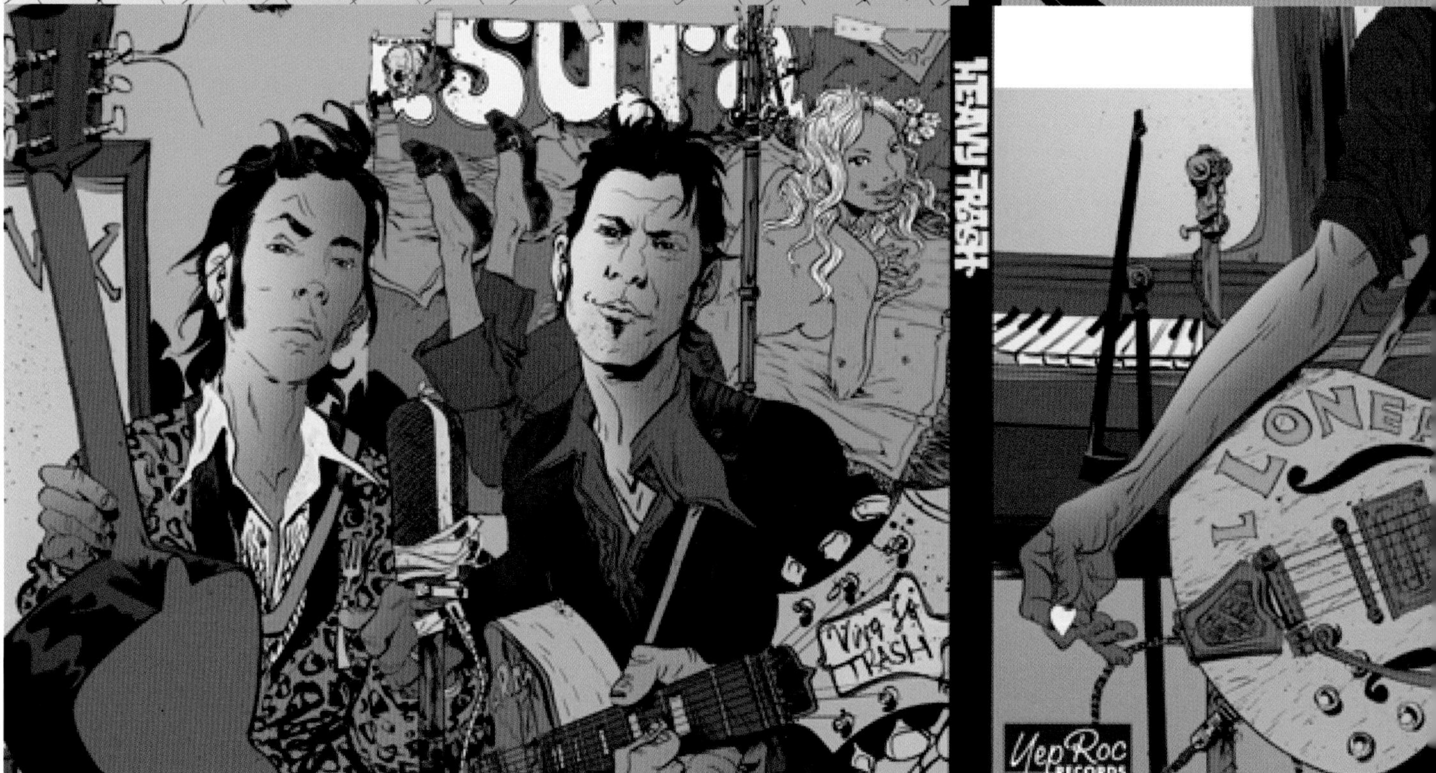
HEAVY TRASH
Yep Roc
RECORDS

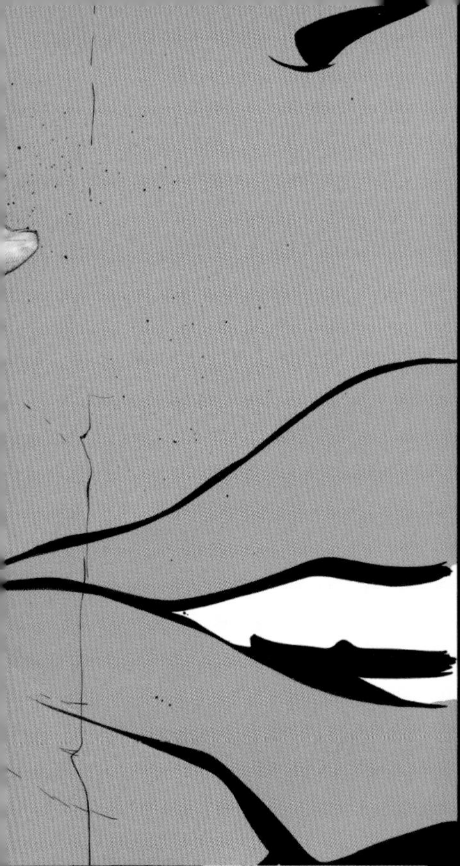

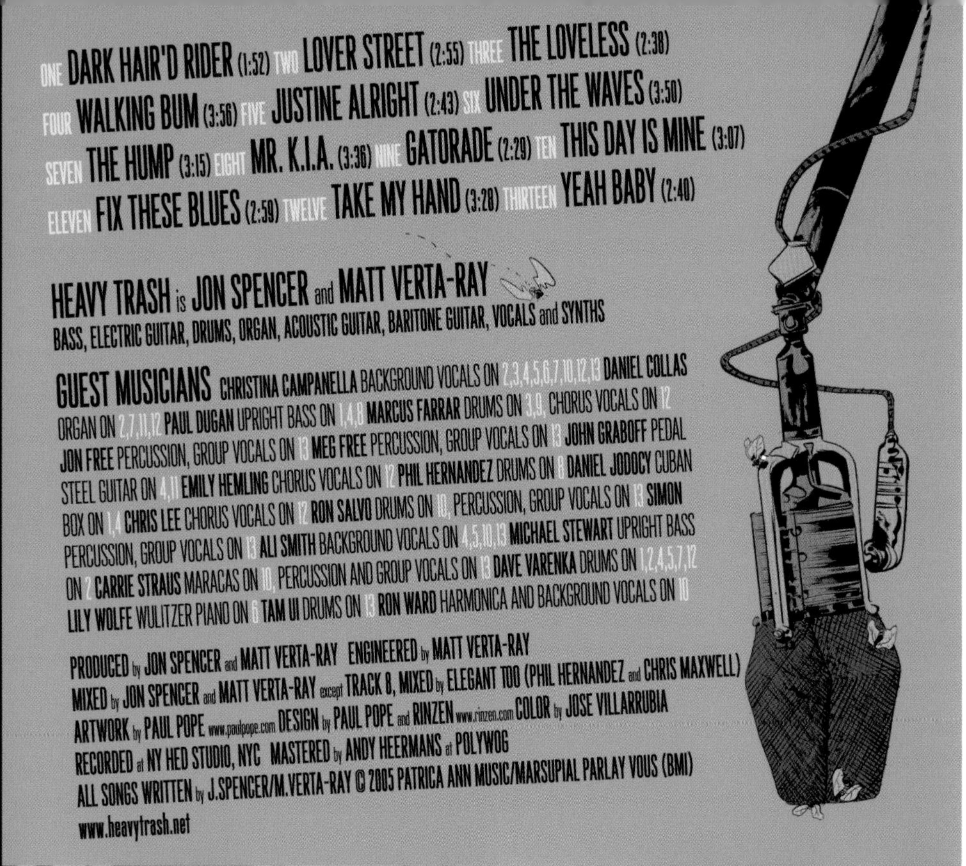
ONE DARK HAIR'D RIDER (1:52) TWO LOVER STREET (2:55) THREE THE LOVELESS (2:38)
FOUR WALKING BUM (3:56) FIVE JUSTINE ALRIGHT (2:43) SIX UNDER THE WAVES (3:50)
SEVEN THE HUMP (3:15) EIGHT MR. K.I.A. (3:36) NINE GATORADE (2:29) TEN THIS DAY IS MINE (3:07)
ELEVEN FIX THESE BLUES (2:59) TWELVE TAKE MY HAND (3:28) THIRTEEN YEAH BABY (2:40)
HEAVY TRASH is JON SPENCER and MATT VERTA-RAY
BASS, ELECTRIC GUITAR, DRUMS, ORGAN, ACOUSTIC GUITAR, BARITONE GUITAR, VOCALS and SYNTHS
GUEST MUSICIANS CHRISTINA CAMPANELLA BACKGROUND VOCALS ON 2,3,4,5,6,7,10,12,13 DANIEL COLLAS ORGAN ON 2,7,11,12 PAUL DUGAN UPRIGHT BASS ON 1,4,8 MARCUS FARRAR DRUMS ON 3,9, CHORUS VOCALS ON 12 JON FREE PERCUSSION, GROUP VOCALS ON 13 MEG FREE PERCUSSION, GROUP VOCALS ON 13 JOHN GRABOFF PEDAL STEEL GUITAR ON 4,11 EMILY HEMLING CHORUS VOCALS ON 12 PHIL HERNANDEZ DRUMS ON 8 DANIEL JODOCY CUBAN BOX ON 1,4 CHRIS LEE CHORUS VOCALS ON 12 RON SALVO DRUMS ON 10, PERCUSSION, GROUP VOCALS ON 13 SIMON PERCUSSION, GROUP VOCALS ON 13 ALI SMITH BACKGROUND VOCALS ON 4,5,10,13 MICHAEL STEWART UPRIGHT BASS ON 2 CARRIE STRAUS MARACAS ON 10, PERCUSSION AND GROUP VOCALS ON 13 DAVE VARENKA DRUMS ON 1,2,4,5,7,12 LILY WOLFE WULITZER PIANO ON 6 TAM UI DRUMS ON 13 RON WARD HARMONICA AND BACKGROUND VOCALS ON 10
PRODUCED by JON SPENCER and MATT VERTA-RAY ENGINEERED by MATT VERTA-RAY
MIXED by JON SPENCER and MATT VERTA-RAY except TRACK 8, MIXED by ELEGANT TOO (PHIL HERNANDEZ and CHRIS MAXWELL)
ARTWORK by PAUL POPE www.paulpope.com DESIGN by PAUL POPE and RINZEN www.rinzen.com COLOR by JOSE VILLARRUBIA
RECORDED at NY HED STUDIO, NYC MASTERED by ANDY HEERMANS at POLYWOG
ALL SONGS WRITTEN by J.SPENCER/M.VERTA-RAY © 2005 PATRICA ANN MUSIC/MARSUPIAL PARLAY VOUS (BMI)
www.heavytrash.net

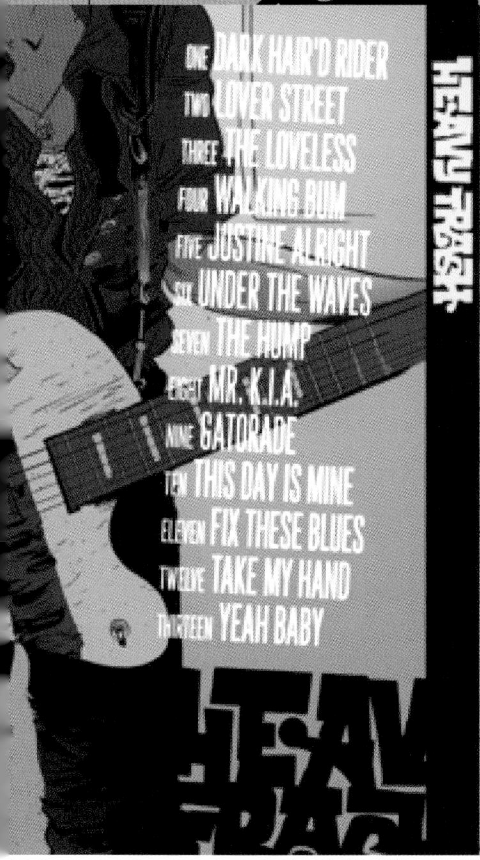
ONE DARK HAIR'D RIDER
TWO LOVER STREET
THREE THE LOVELESS
FOUR WALKING BUM
FIVE JUSTINE ALRIGHT
SIX UNDER THE WAVES
SEVEN THE HUMP
EIGHT MR. K.I.A.
NINE GATORADE
TEN THIS DAY IS MINE
ELEVEN FIX THESE BLUES
TWELVE TAKE MY HAND
THIRTEEN YEAH BABY
HEAVY TRASH

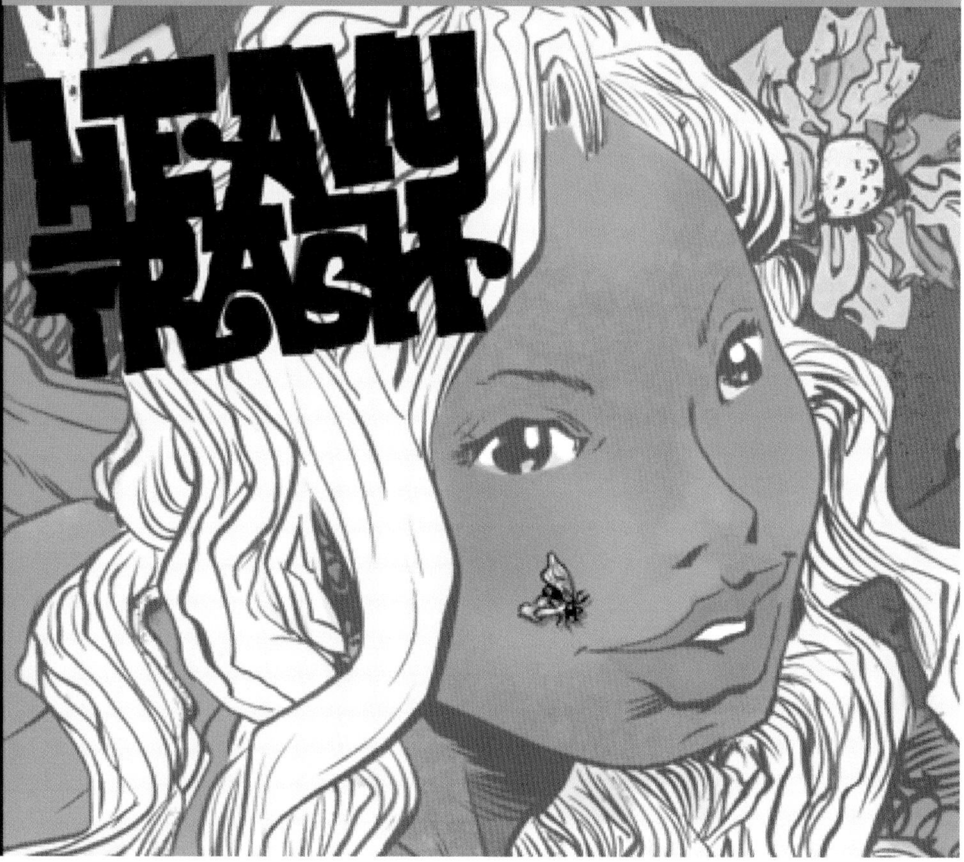
HEAVY TRASH

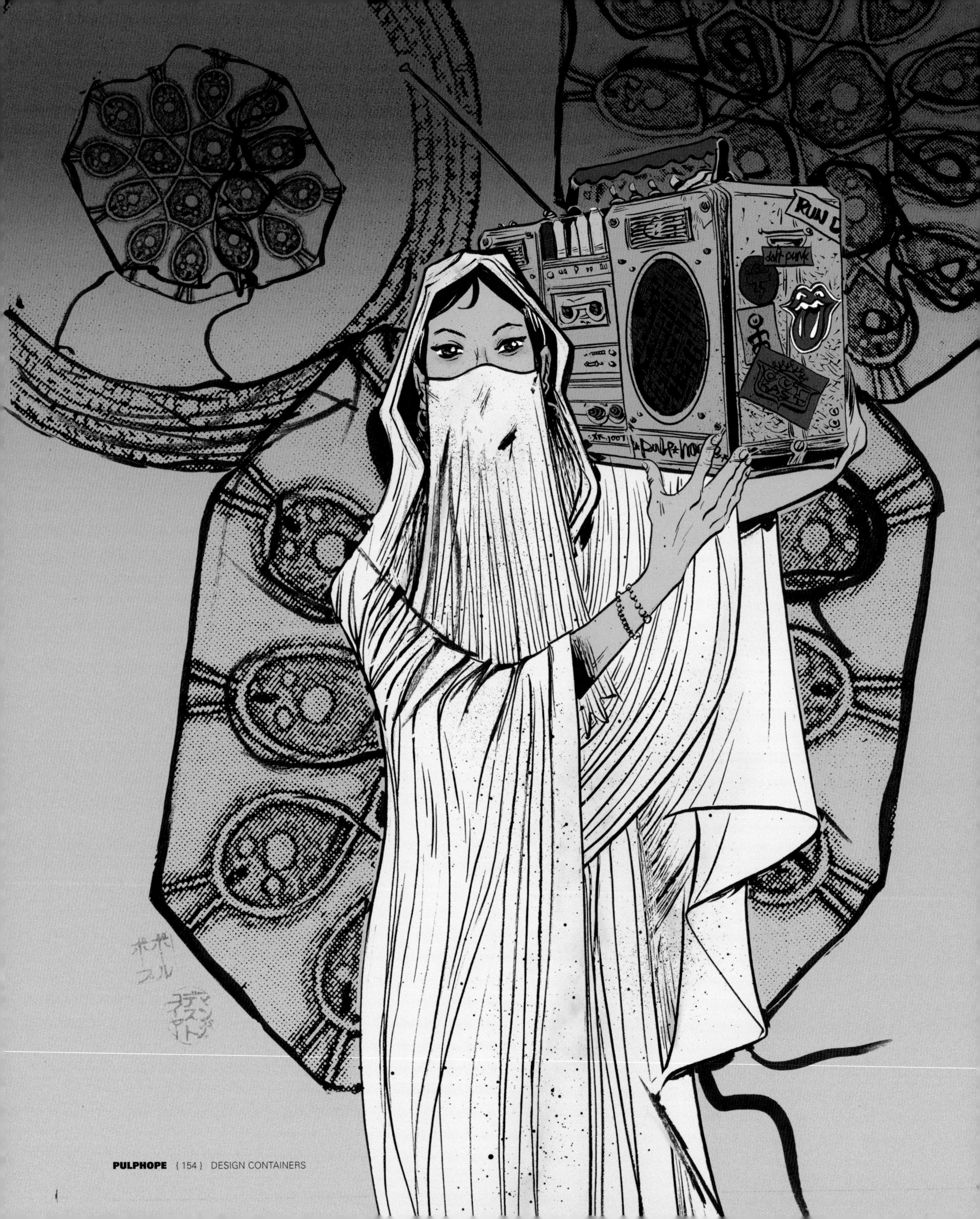
RUN D
daft punk

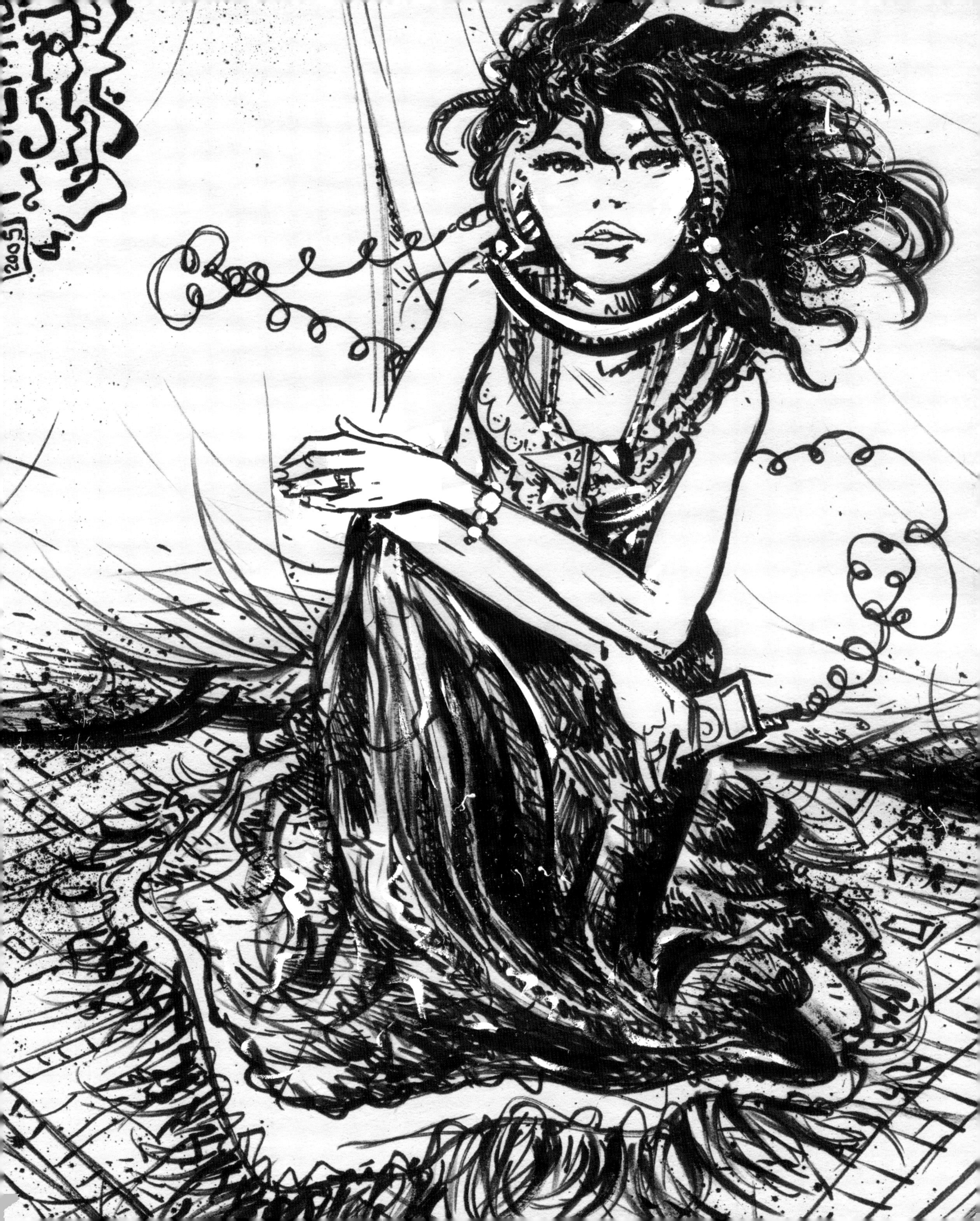

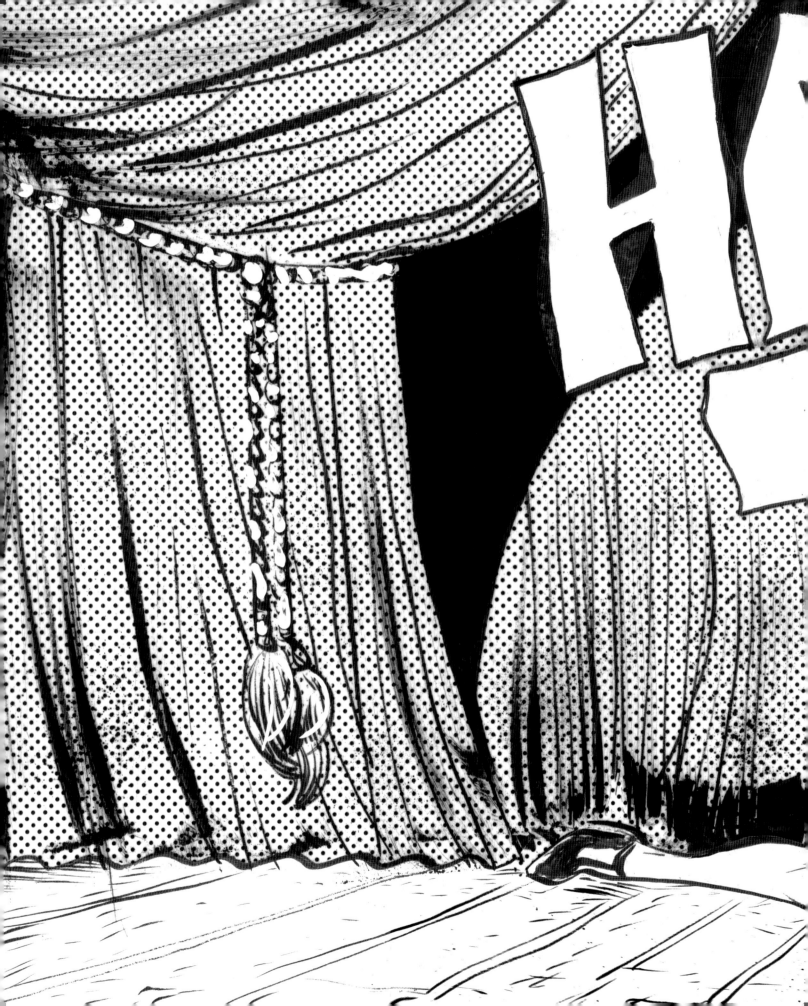

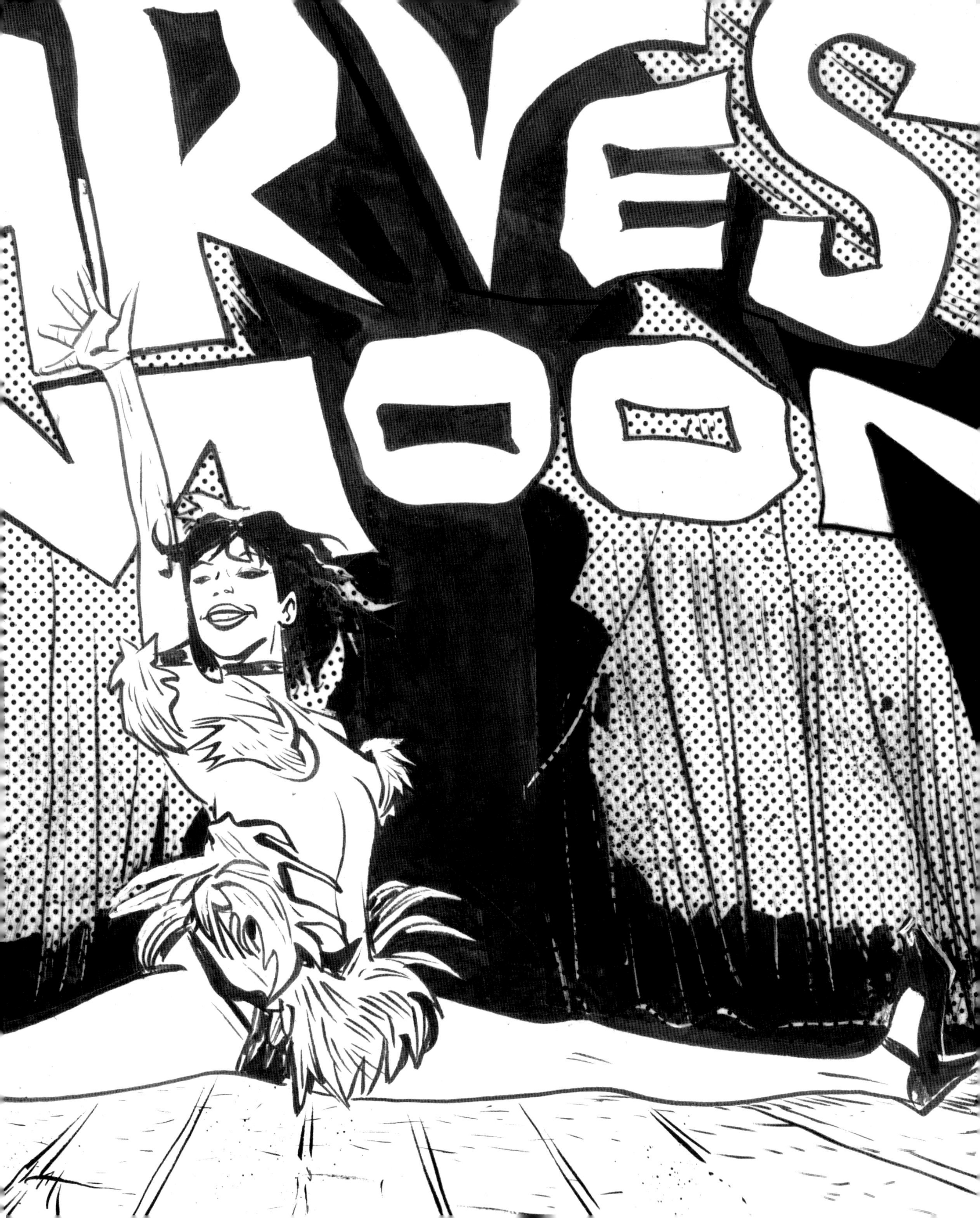

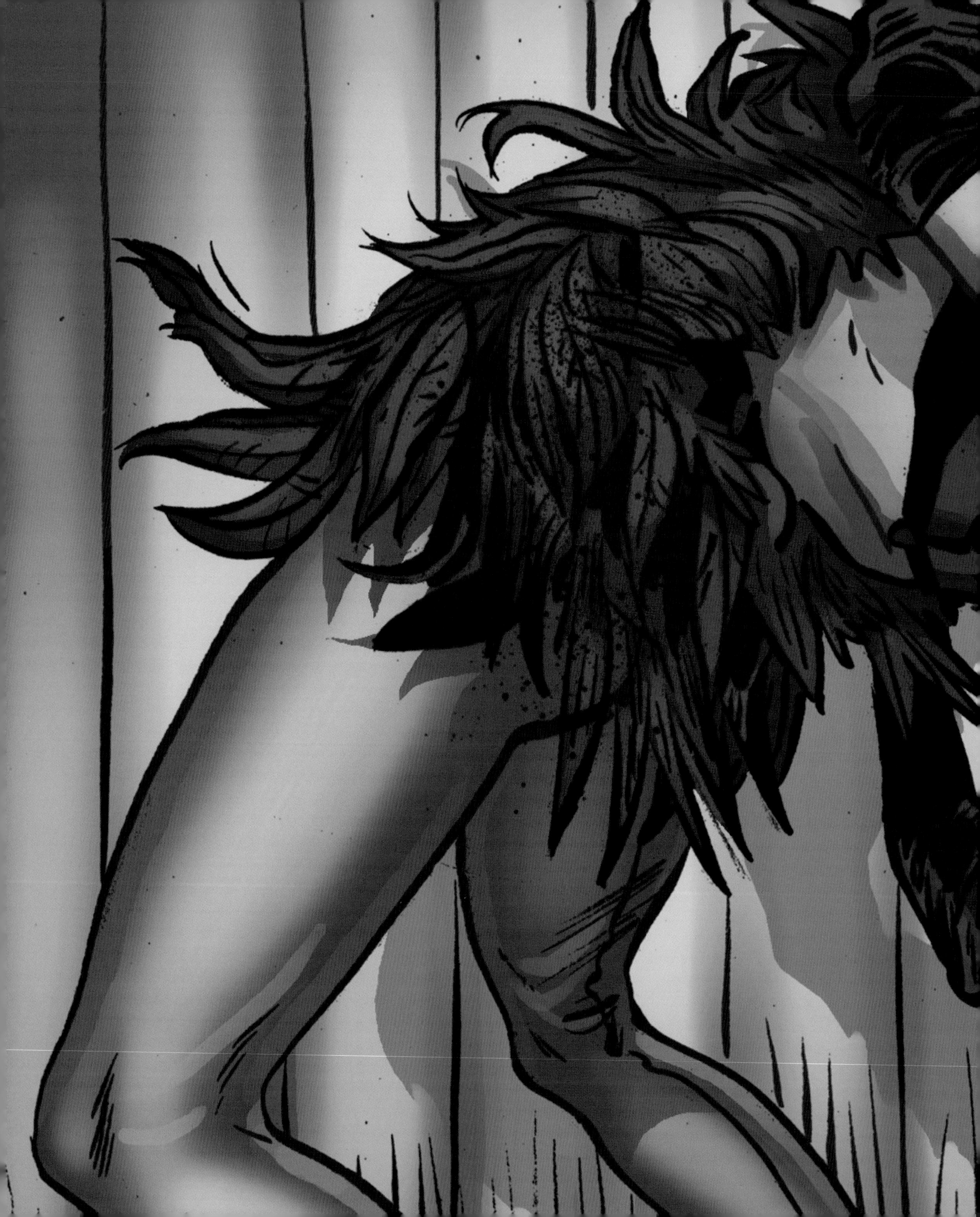

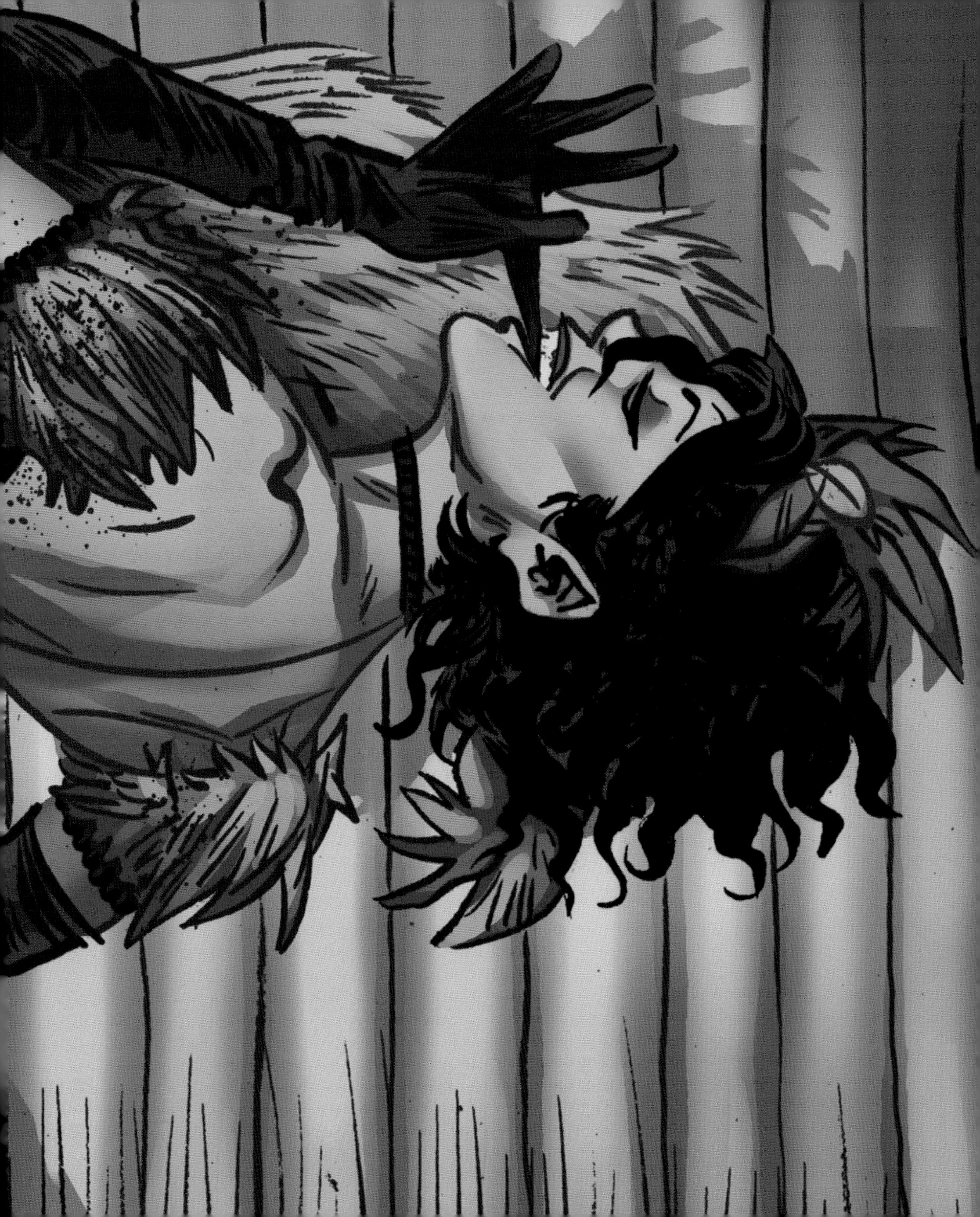

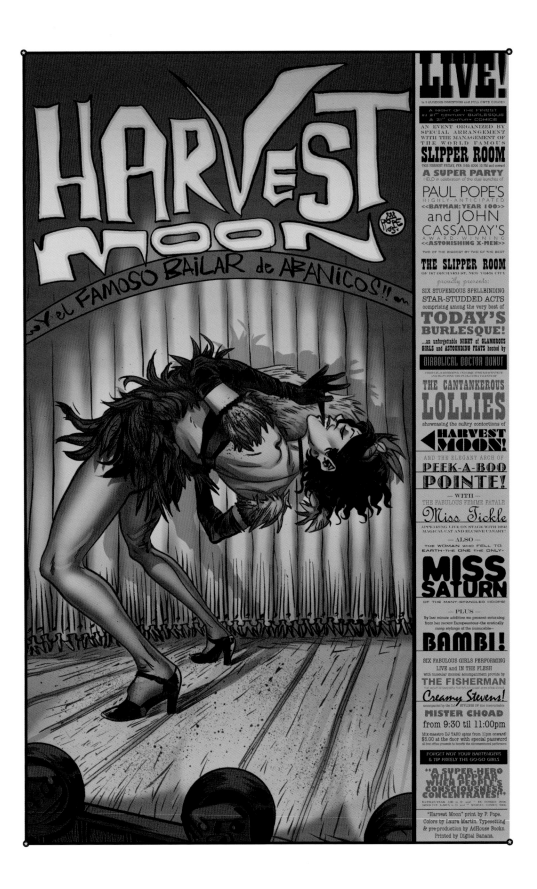

LIVE!

In 3 GLORIOUS DIMENTIONS and FULL CMYK COLOR!!

A NIGHT OF THE FINEST IN 21ST CENTURY
BURLESQUE & 21ST CENTURY COMICS

AN EVENT ORGANIZED BY SPECIAL ARRANGEMENT WITH
THE MANAGEMENT OF THE WORLD FAMOUS

SLIPPER ROOM

THIS PRESENT FRIDAY, FEB. 24th 2006 10 PM and onward

A SUPER PARTY

HELD IN CELEBRATION
OF THE DUAL
LAUNCHES OF... JOHN
CASSADAY'S
AWARD-WINNING
<<ASTONISHING X-MEN>>
& PAUL POPE'S
HIGHLY-ANTICIPATED
<<BATMAN: YEAR 100>>

TWO OF THE BIGGEST BY TWO OF THE BEST

THE SLIPPER ROOM
OF 167 ORCHARD
ST. NEW
YORK CITY

proudly presents:

SIX STUPENDOUS SPELLBINDING STAR-STUDDED ACTS
comprising among the very best of
TODAY'S BURLESQUE!
— ALSO —

...an unforgettable NIGHT of GLAMOROUS
GIRLS and ASTOUNDING FEATS hosted by

DIABOLICAL DOCTOR DONUT

CRIMINAL-MASTERMIND AND LOQUA-
TIOUS RACONTEUR AND FEATURING
THE PLUS-ULTRA TALENTS OF

THE CANTANKEROUS
LOLLIES

showcasing the sultry contortions of

HARVEST
MOON!

AND THE ELEGANT ARCH OF

PEEK-A-BOO
POINTE!

WITH
THE FABULOUS FEMME FATALE

Miss Tickle

APPEARING LIVE ON STAGE WITH HER
MAGICAL CAT and ELUSIVE CANARY!

[THE LIKE TESTING #8 IN LEFT COLUMN RIGHT ANSIDE]

THE WOMAN WHO FELL TO
EARTH—THE ONE THE ONLY-

MISS
SATURN
OF THE MANY-SPANGLED HOOPS!

PLUS

By last minute addition we present—returning
from her recent European tour—the exotically
camp stylings of the inimicable—

BAMBI!

SIX FABULOUS GIRLS PERFORMING
LIVE and IN THE FLESH
with muscular musical accompaniment provide by

THE FISHERMAN
THE NIGHT BEGINS WITH THE GO-GO SHAKE of the FABULOUS

Creamy Stevens!
accompanied by the DJ STYLING OF the inscrutable

MISTER CHOAD
from 9:30 til 11:00pm

Mix maestro DJ TARO spins from 11pm onward!
$5.00 at the door with special password
all box office proceeds to benefit the aforementioned performers

FORGET NOT YOUR BARTENDERS
& TIP FREELY THE GO-GO GIRLS

**"A SUPER-HERO WILL APPEAR
WHEN PEOPLE'S CONSCIOUSNESS
CONCENTRATES!"**

BATMAN: YEAR 100 is © and ™ DC COMICS 2006   ABSOLUTE X-MEN is © and ™ MARVEL COMICS 2006

"The Hoops of Saturn" by J. Cassaday. Colors by Laura Martin.
Typesetting and pre-production by AdHouse Books. Printed by Digital Banana.

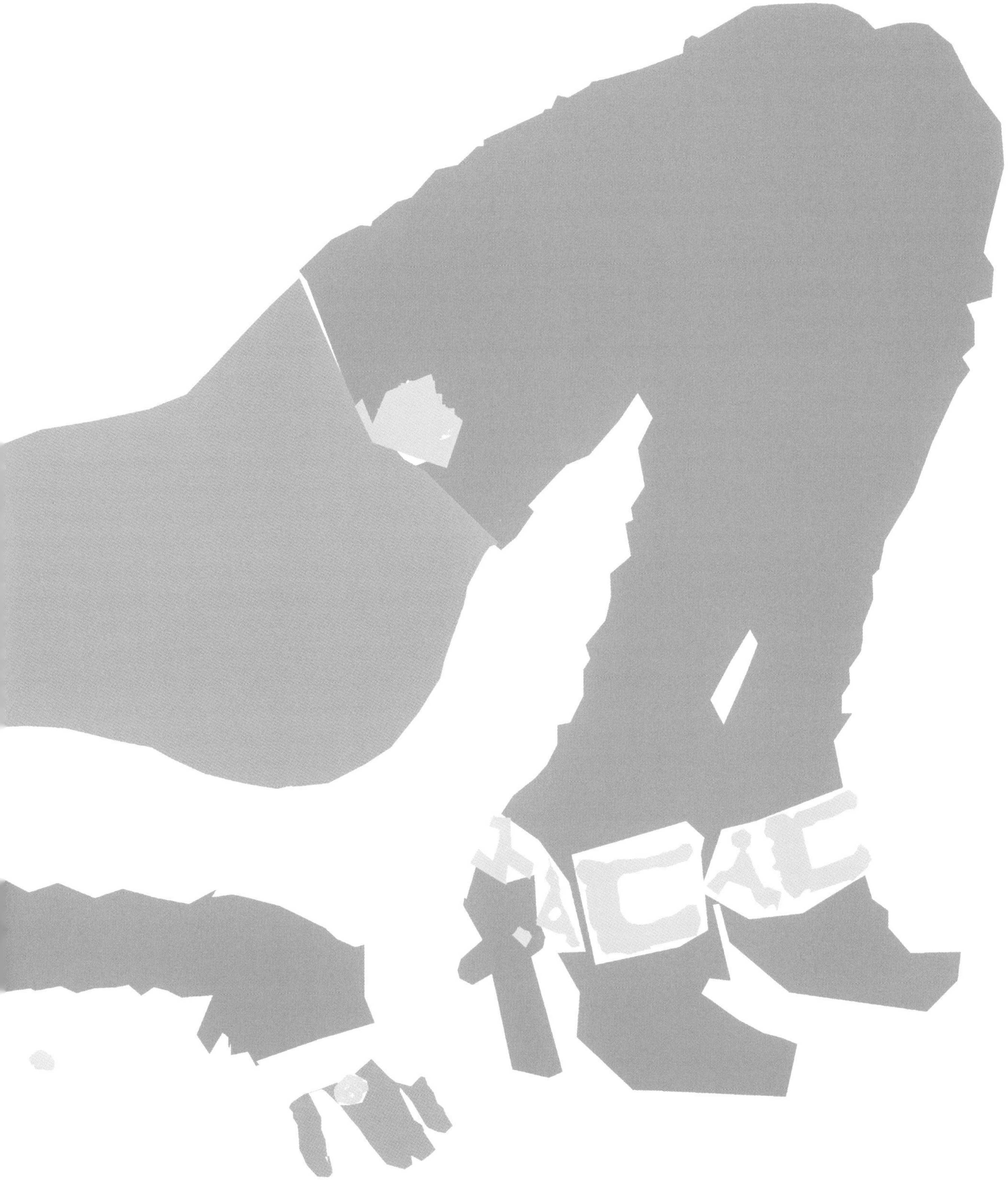

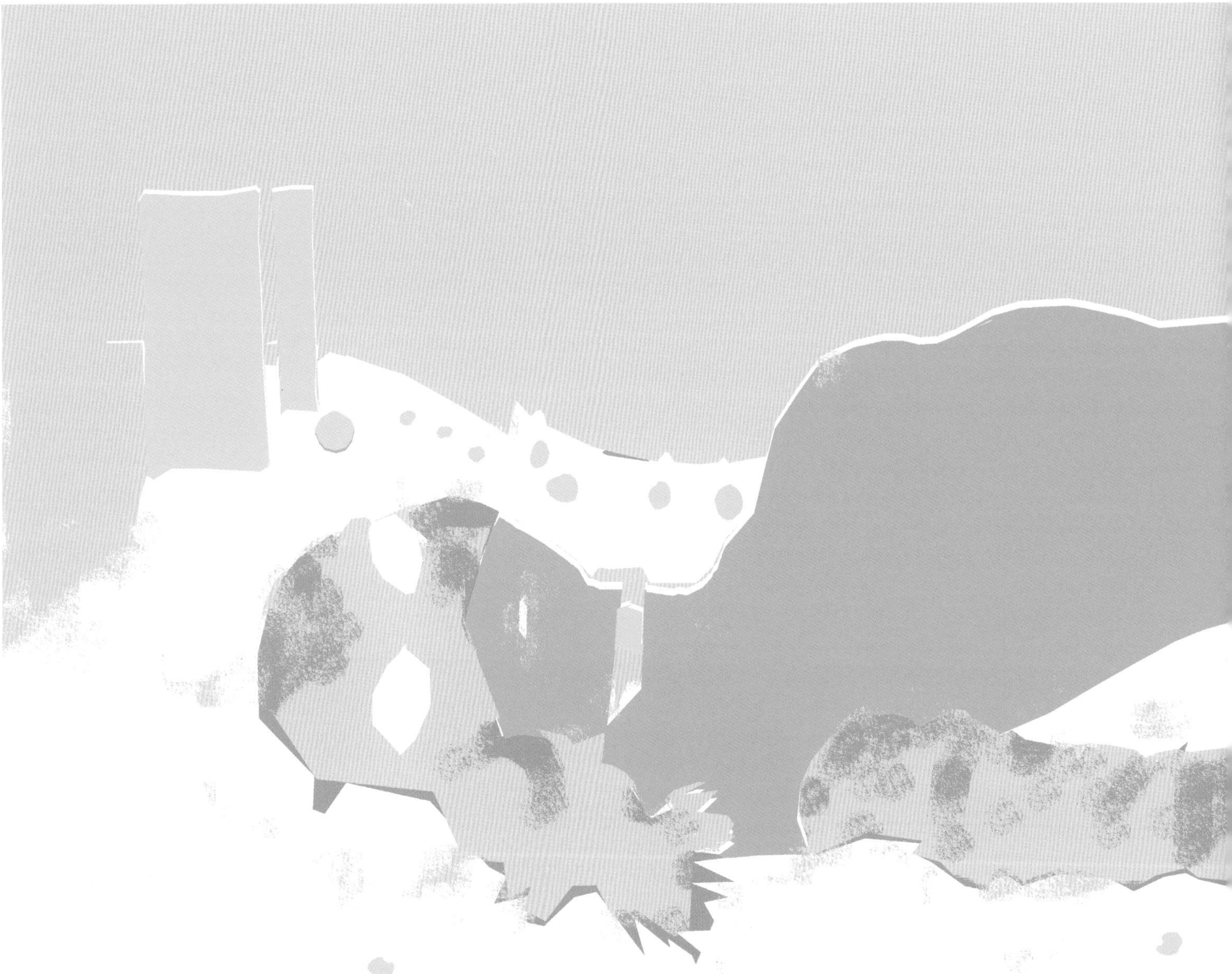

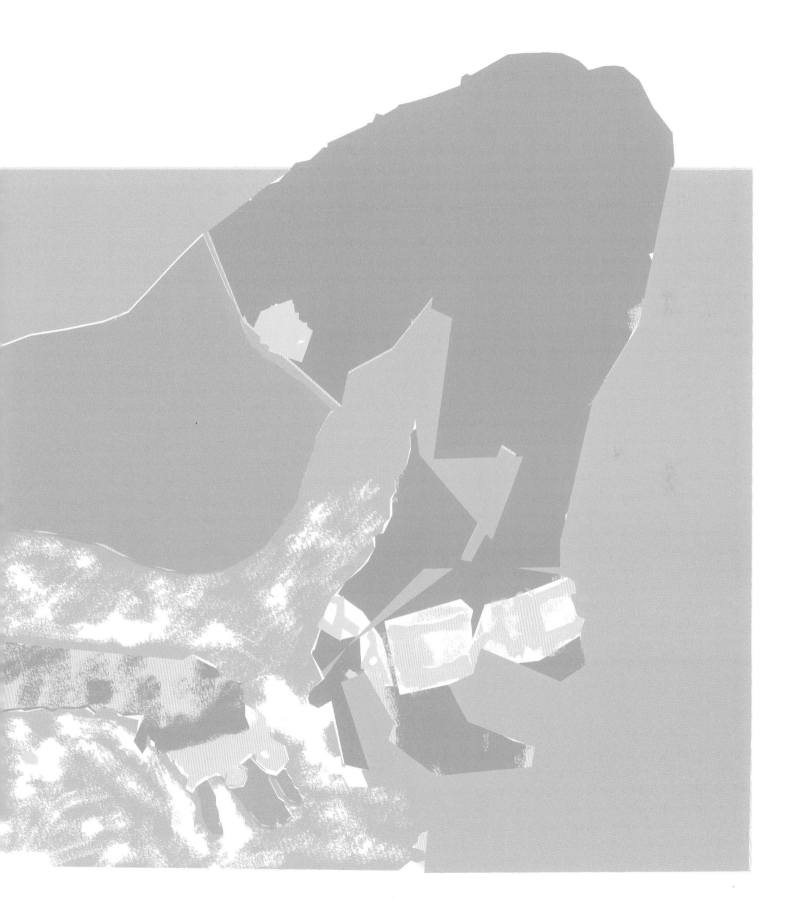

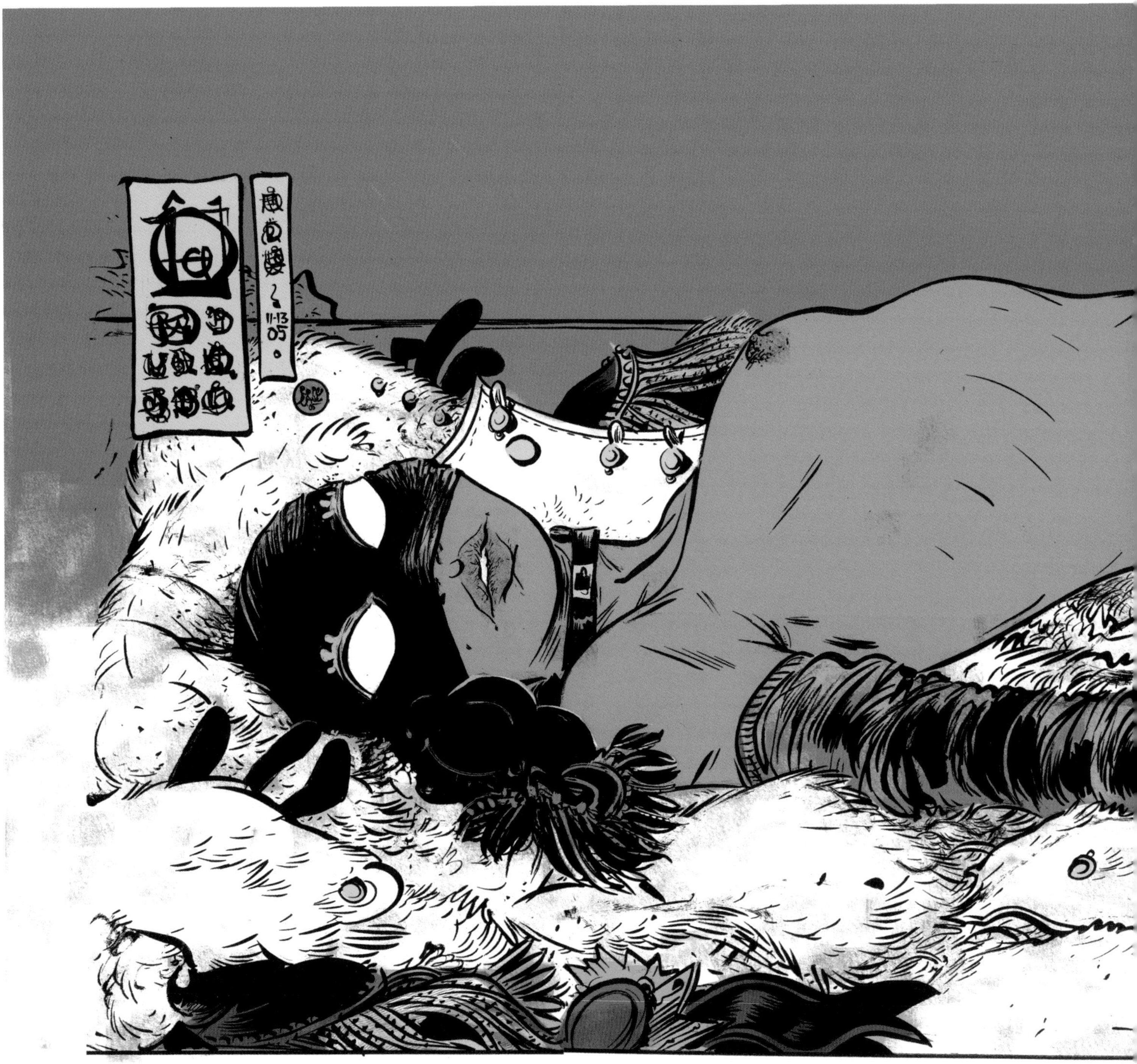
11-13
05

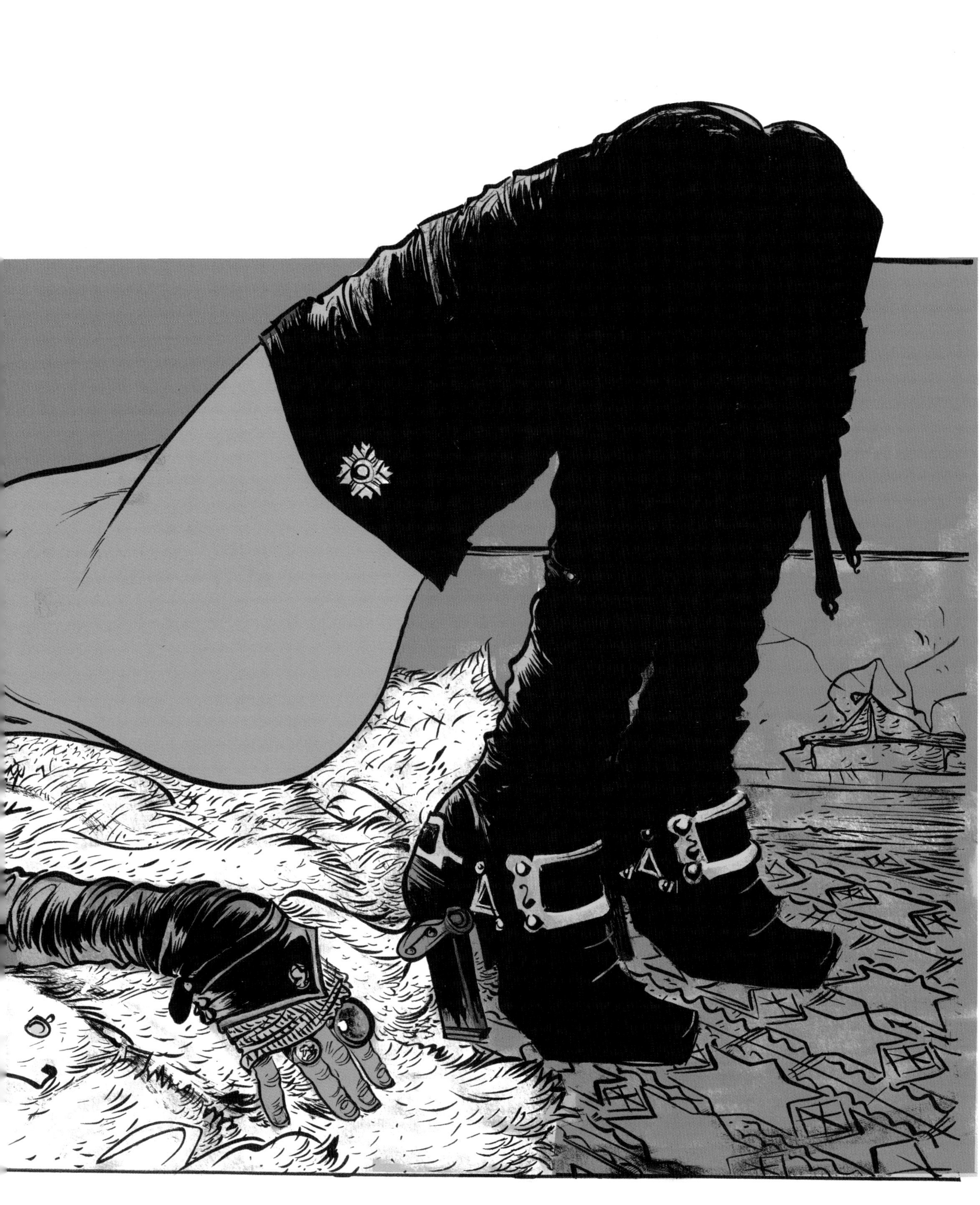

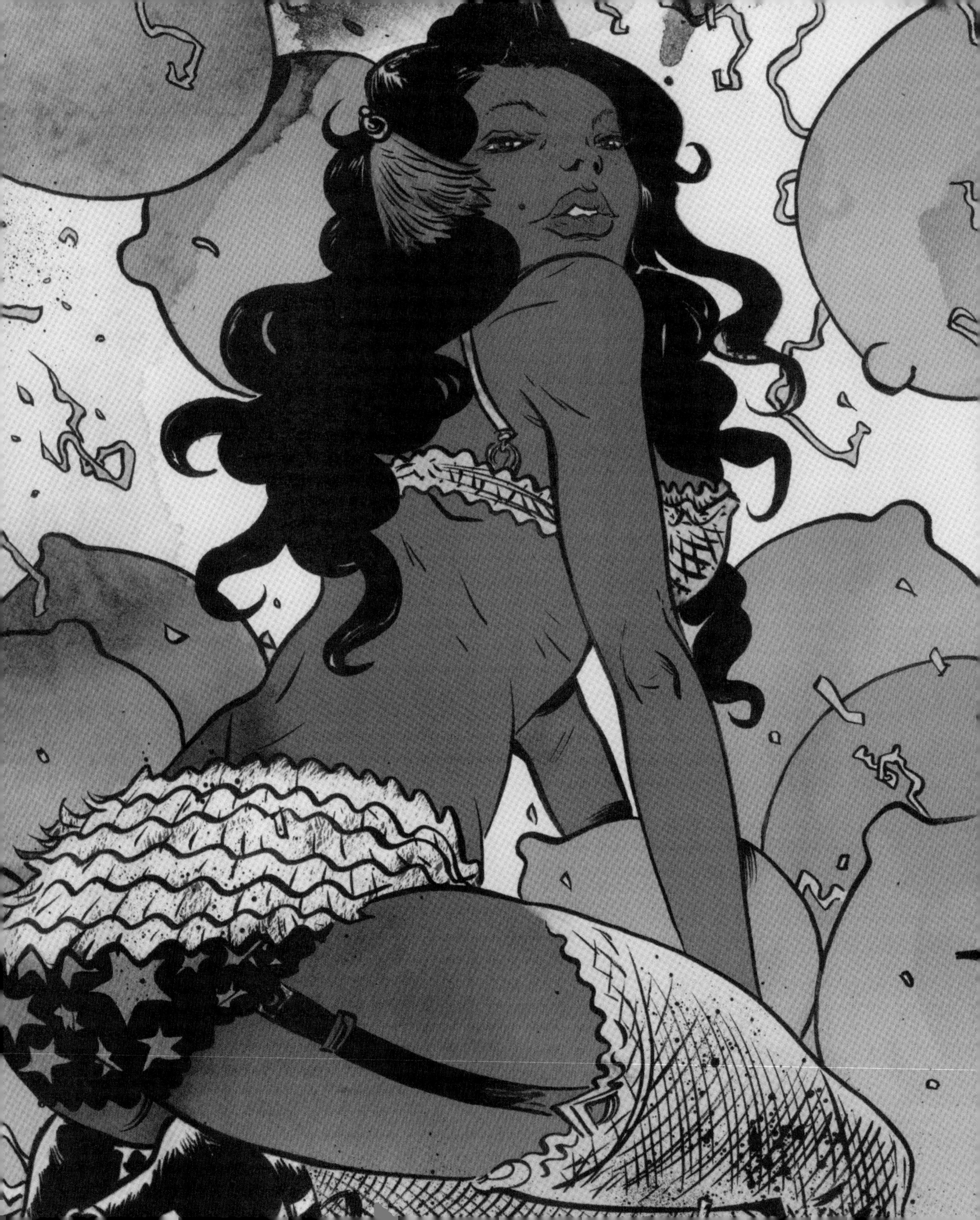

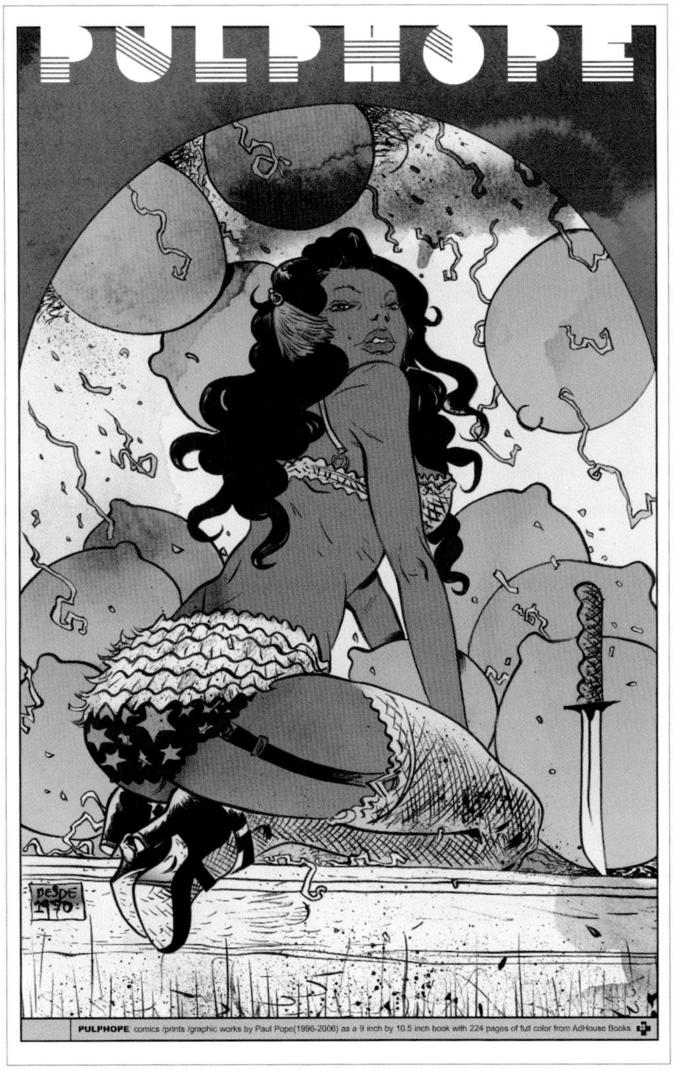
PULPHOPE
DESDE 1970
PULPHOPE: comics /prints /graphic works by Paul Pope(1996-2006) as a 9 inch by 10.5 inch book with 224 pages of full color from AdHouse Books

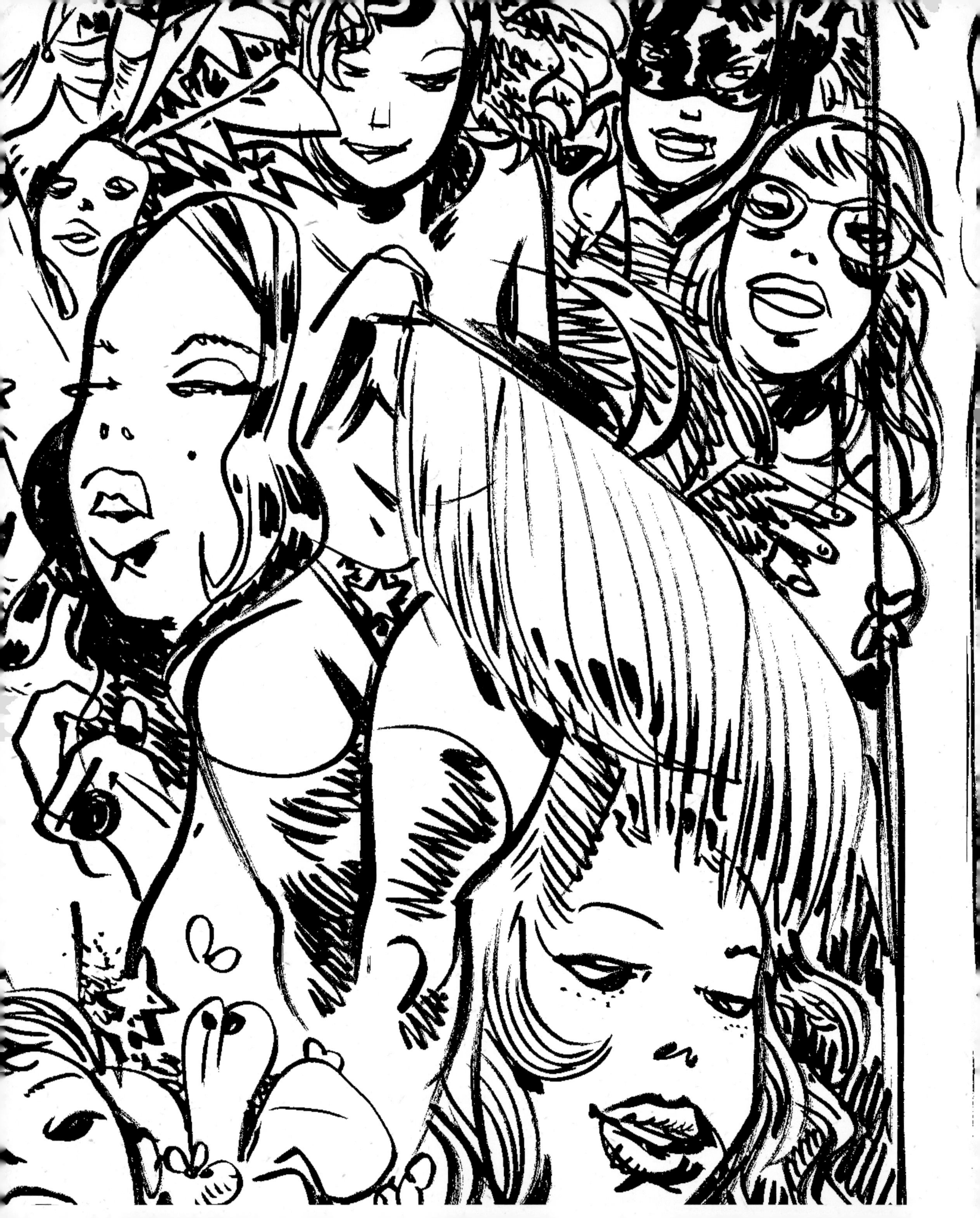

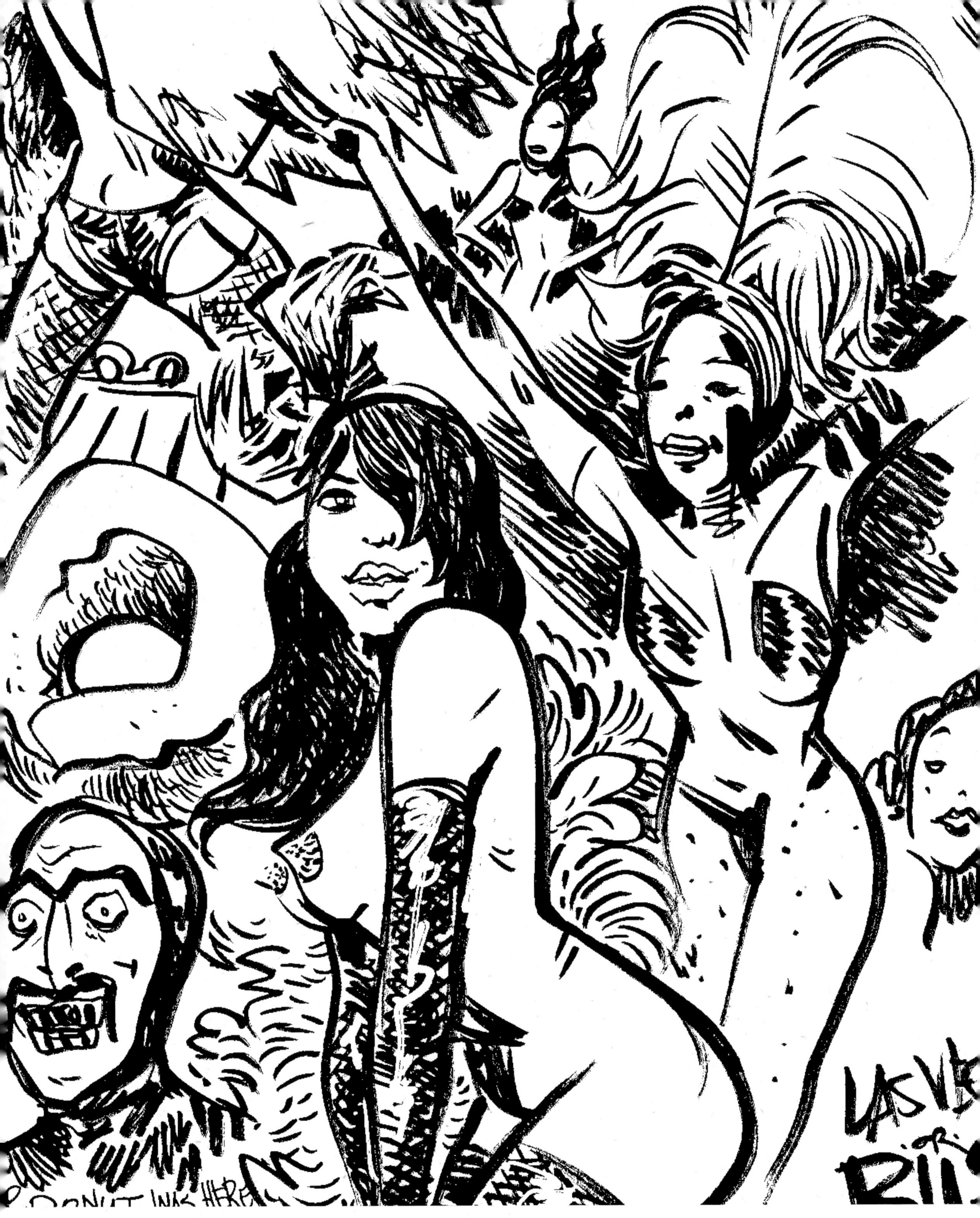
DONUT WAS HERE
LAS VE

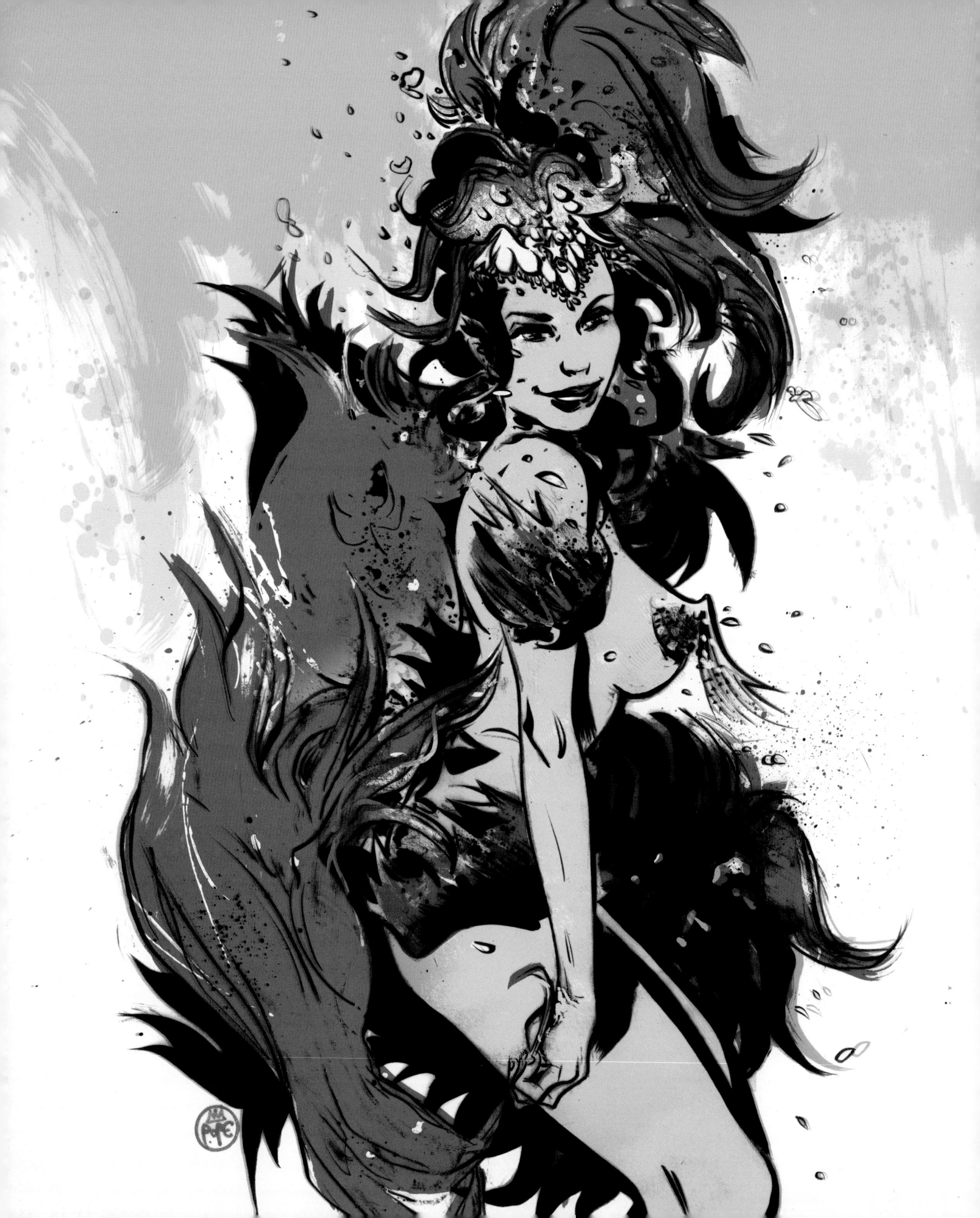

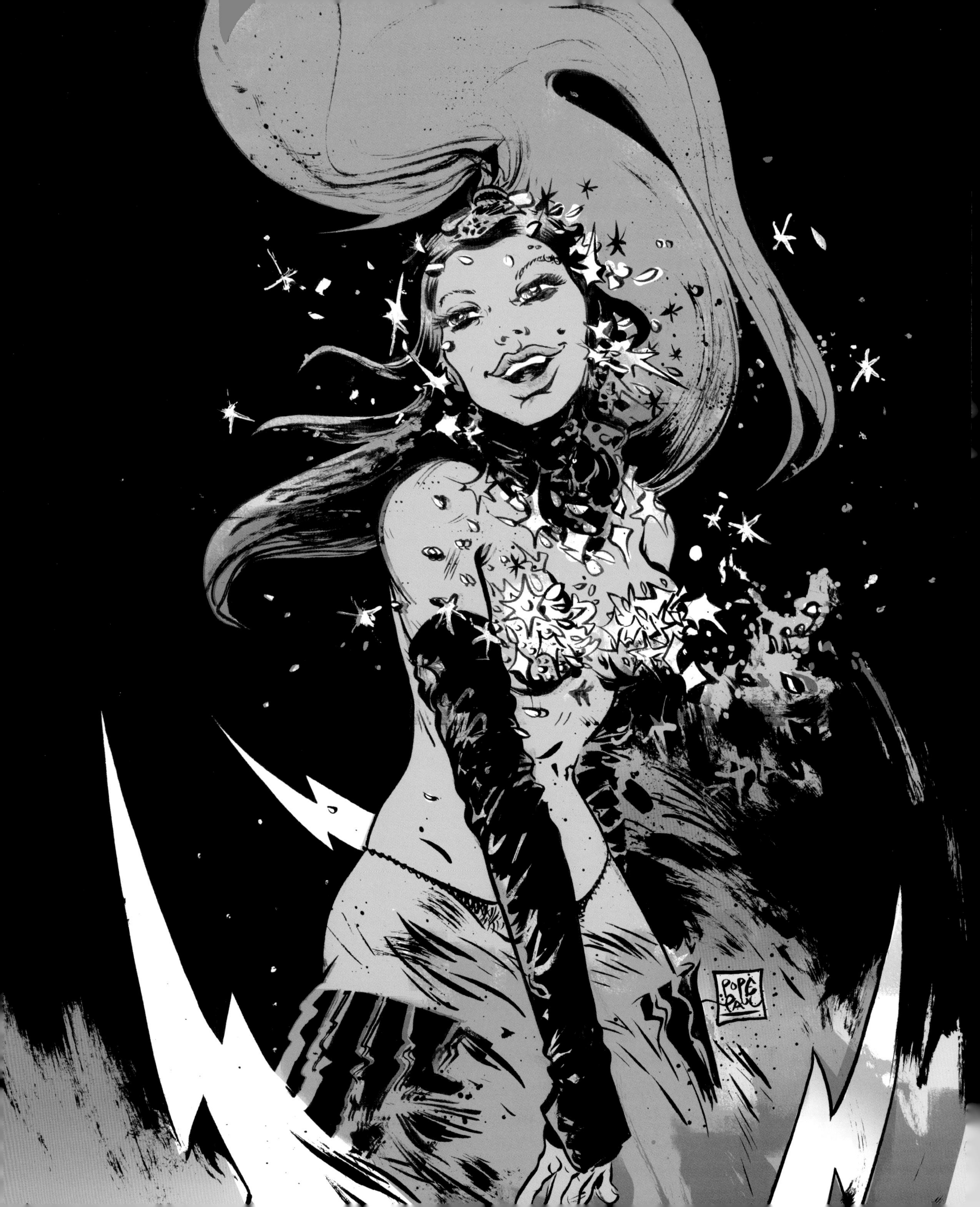
POPE
PAUL

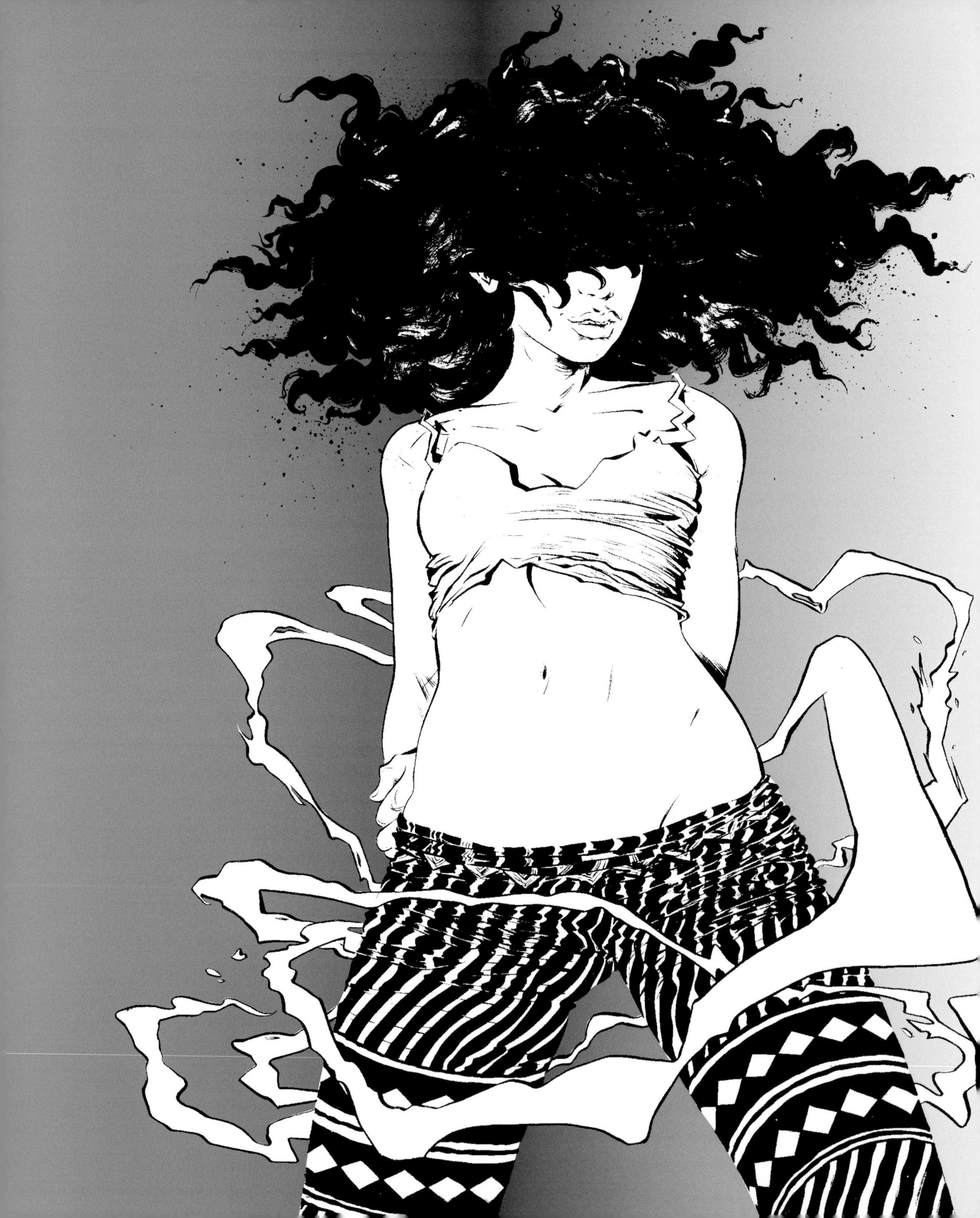

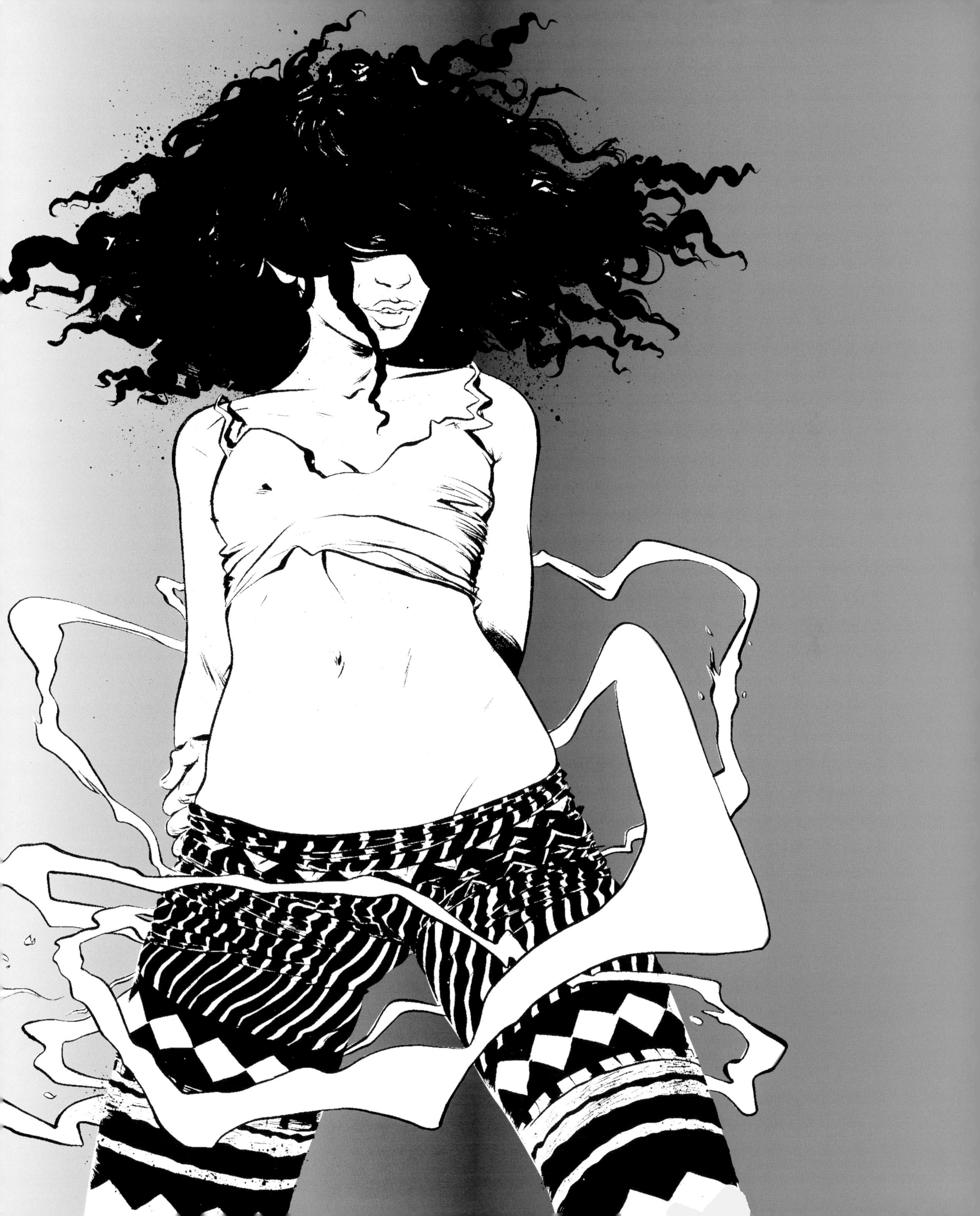

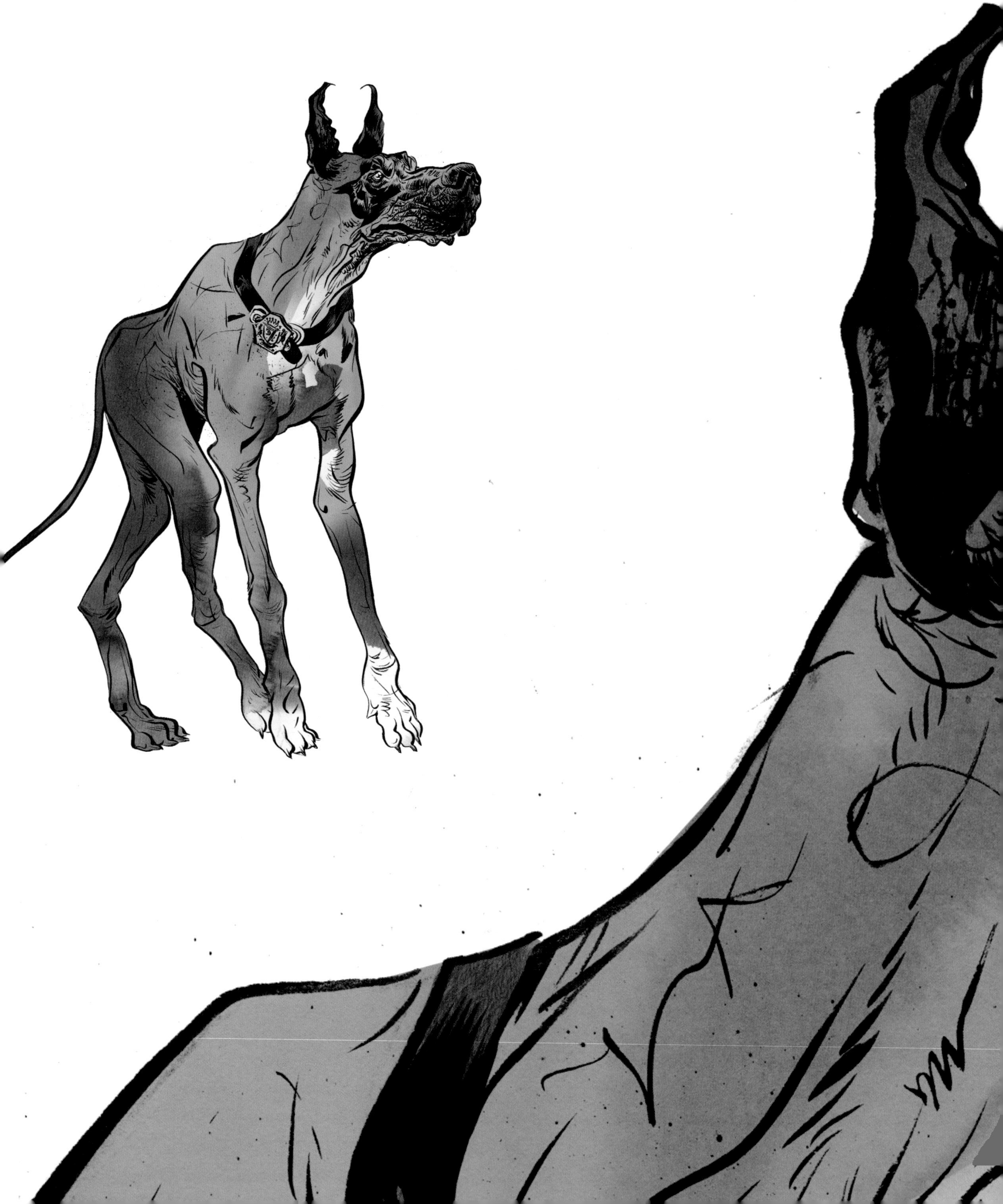

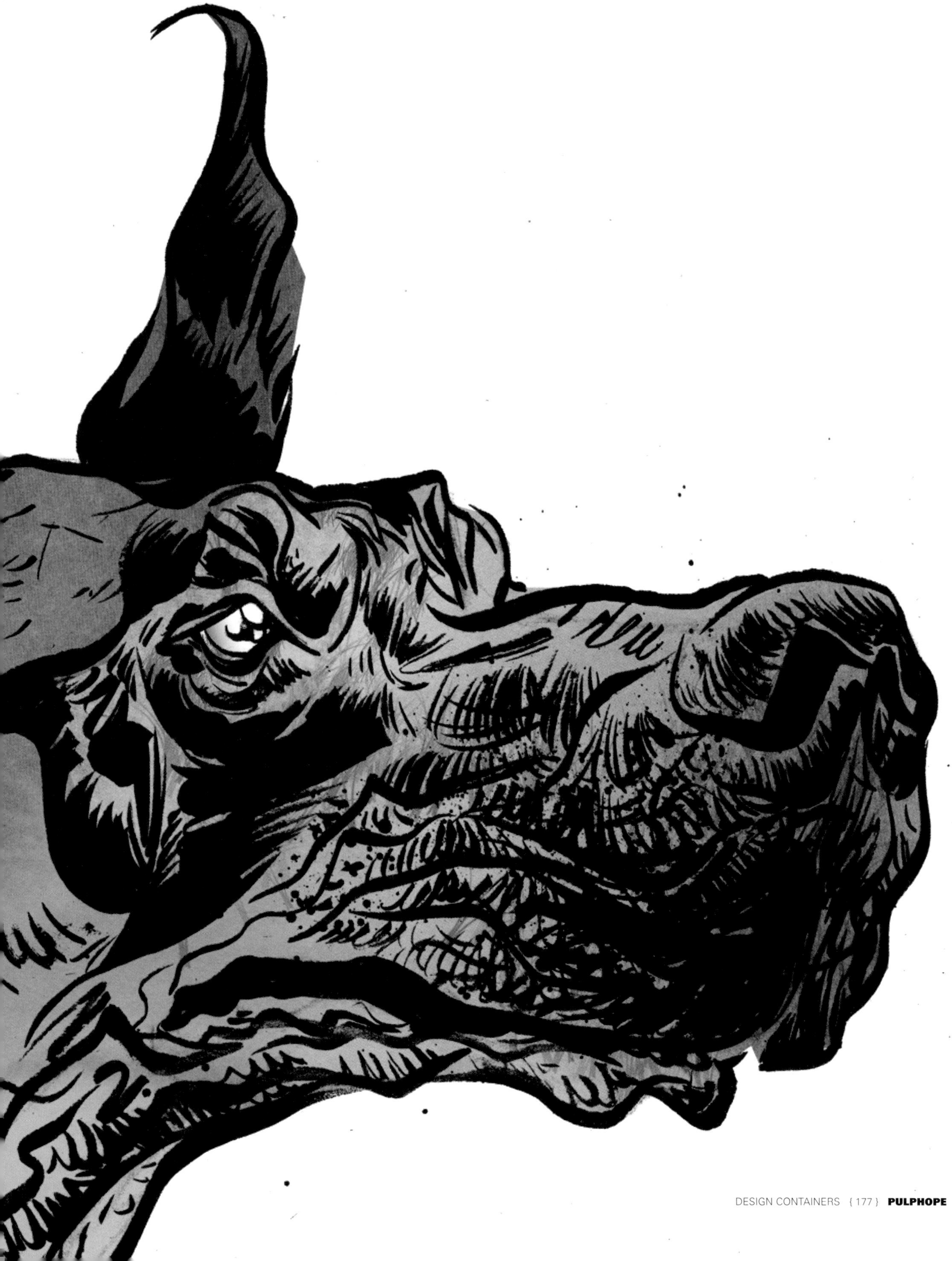

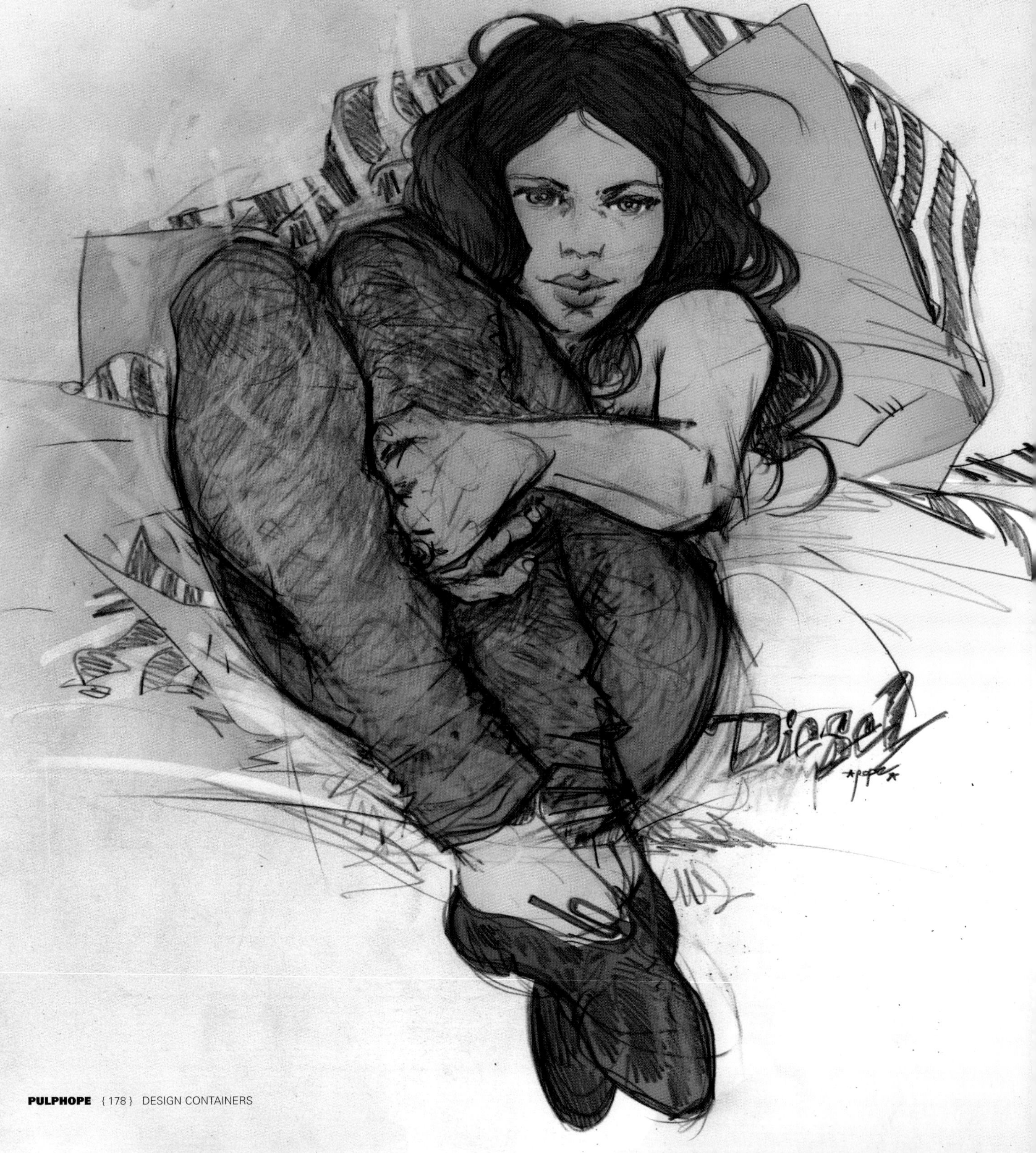
Diesel
pope

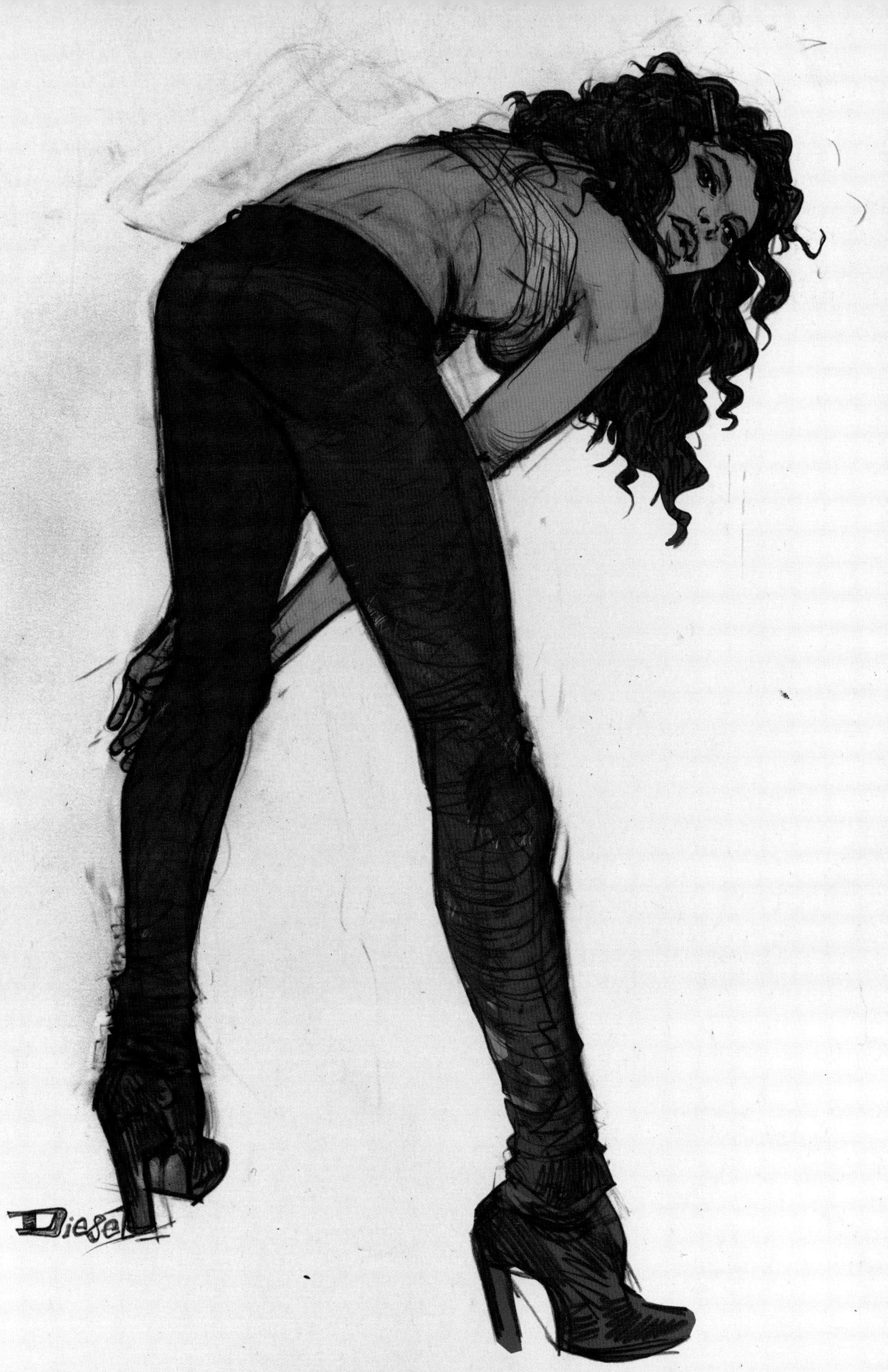
Diesel

SEYBOLD

TW
tw graphics

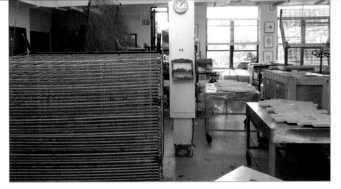

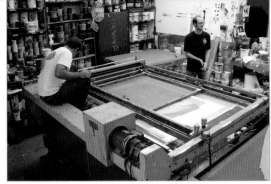

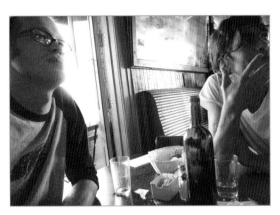

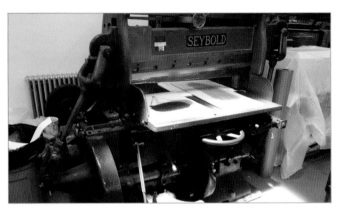

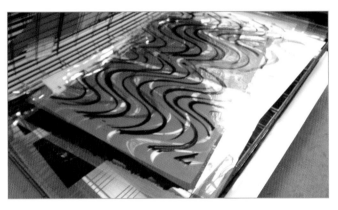

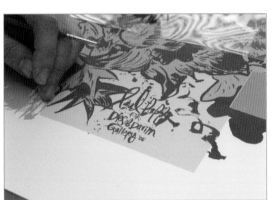

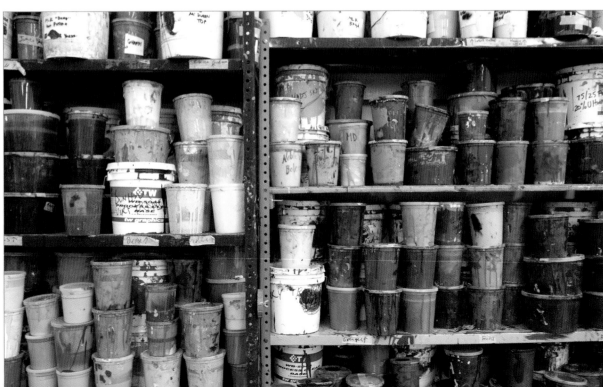

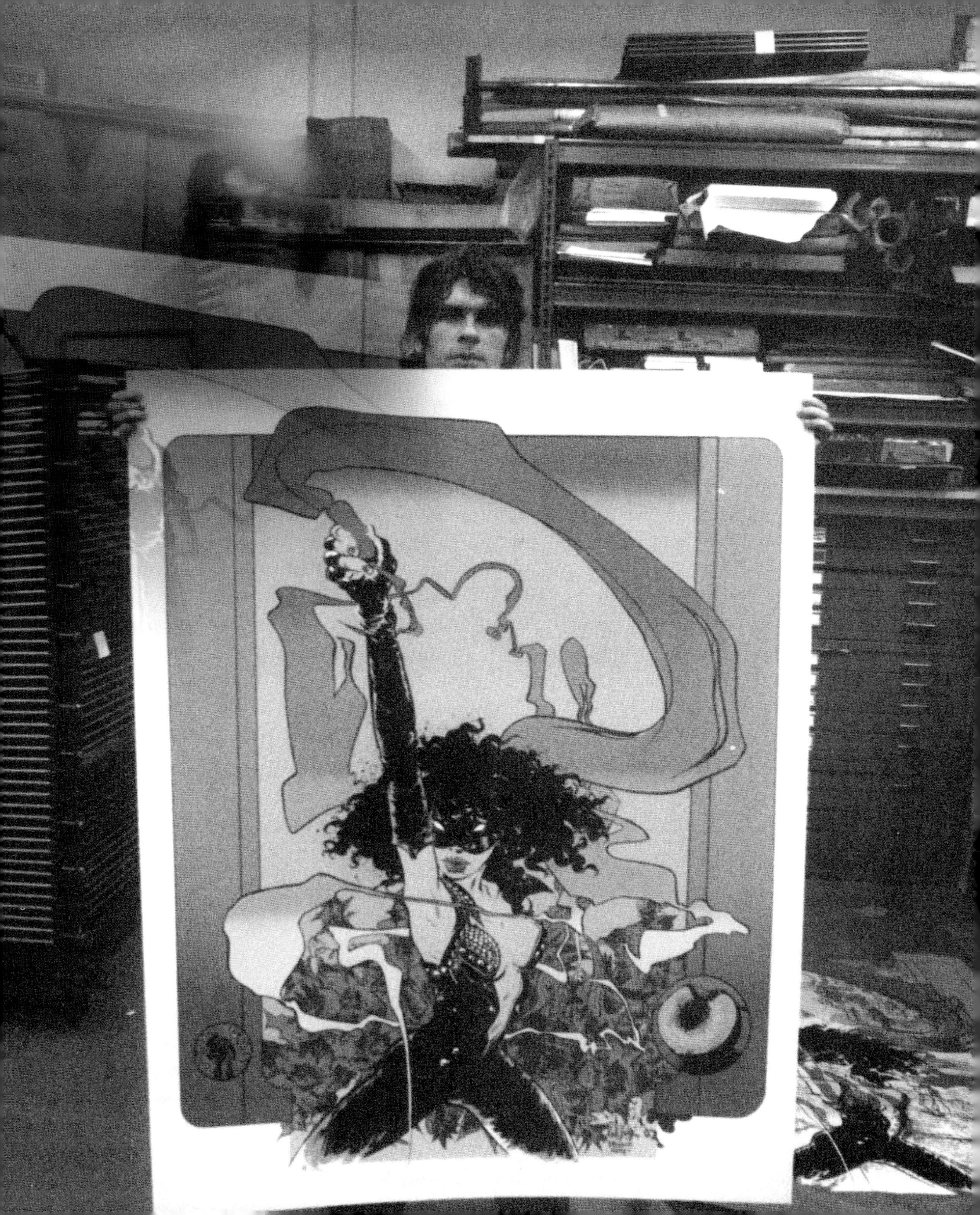

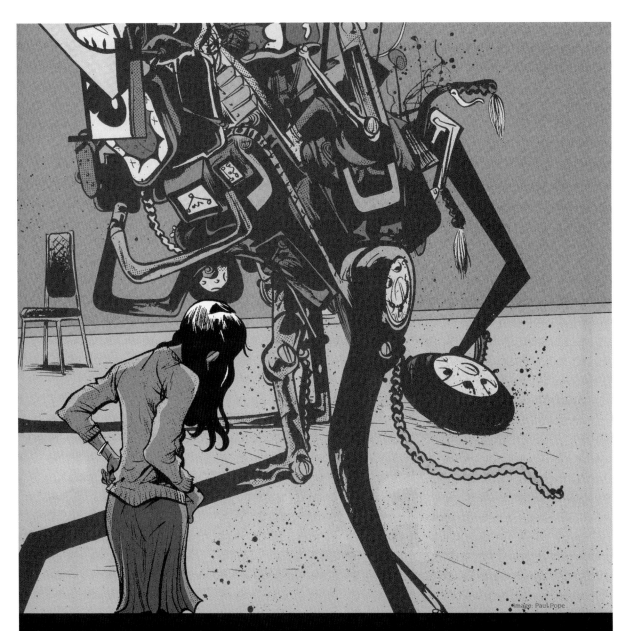

*Image: Paul Pope

Semi-Permanent05
New York
9&10 September
Avery Fisher Hall, Lincoln Center

12 of the world's top creative minds gather to share their knowledge and inspire your work. Coming from a wide range of creative fields such as animation, architecture, broadcasting, fashion, graffiti, graphic design, illustration, photography, and the web, Semi-Permanent is a who's who of the creative world. The weekend offers unparalleled insight into the the current competitive climate and the future of creative industries and serves as a valuable forum for creative minds from around the globe to meet and exchange ideas.

Event Organisers:

Presenting Partner:

DIESEL
FOR SUCCESSFUL LIVING

Hosting Partner:

(mt)
mediatemple

For more details:

www.semipermanent.com

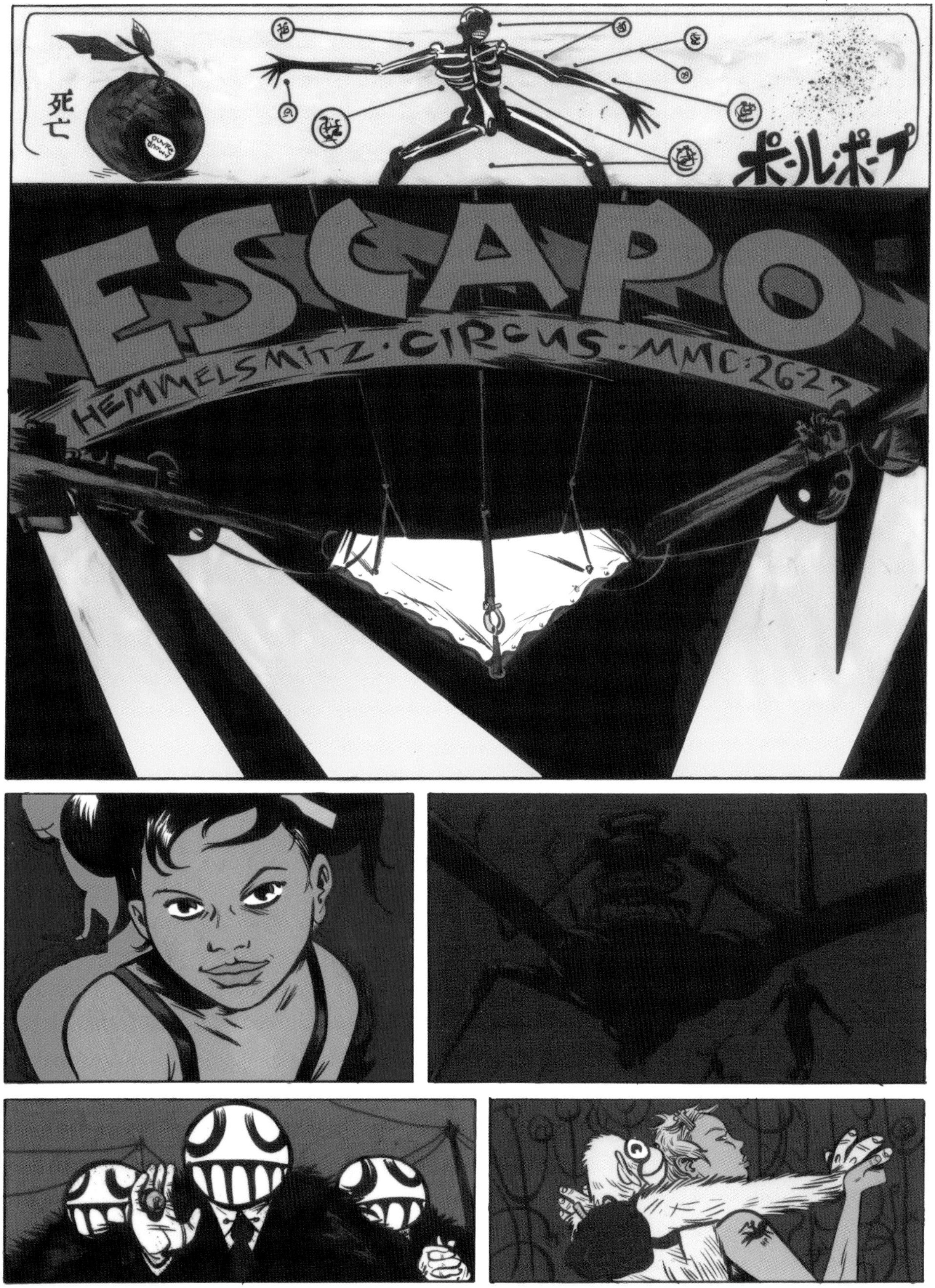
死亡
ポール・ポープ
ESCAPO
HEMMELSMITZ · CIRCUS · MMC · 26-27

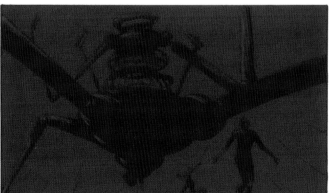

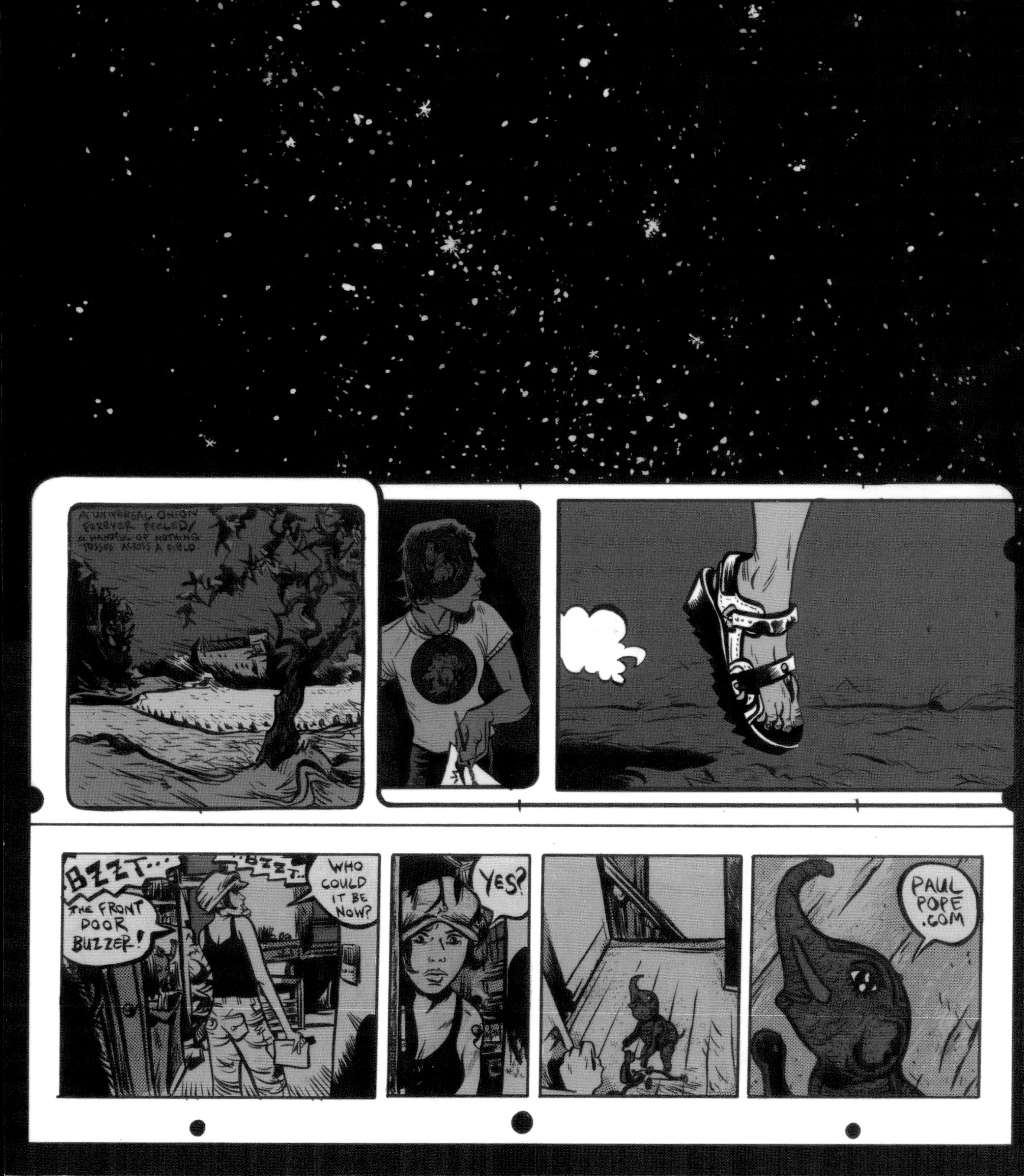
A UNIVERSAL ONION FOREVER PEELED/ A HANDFUL OF NOTHING TOSSED ACROSS A FIELD.
BZZT...
BZZT..
THE FRONT DOOR BUZZER!
WHO COULD IT BE NOW?
YES?
PAUL POPE .COM

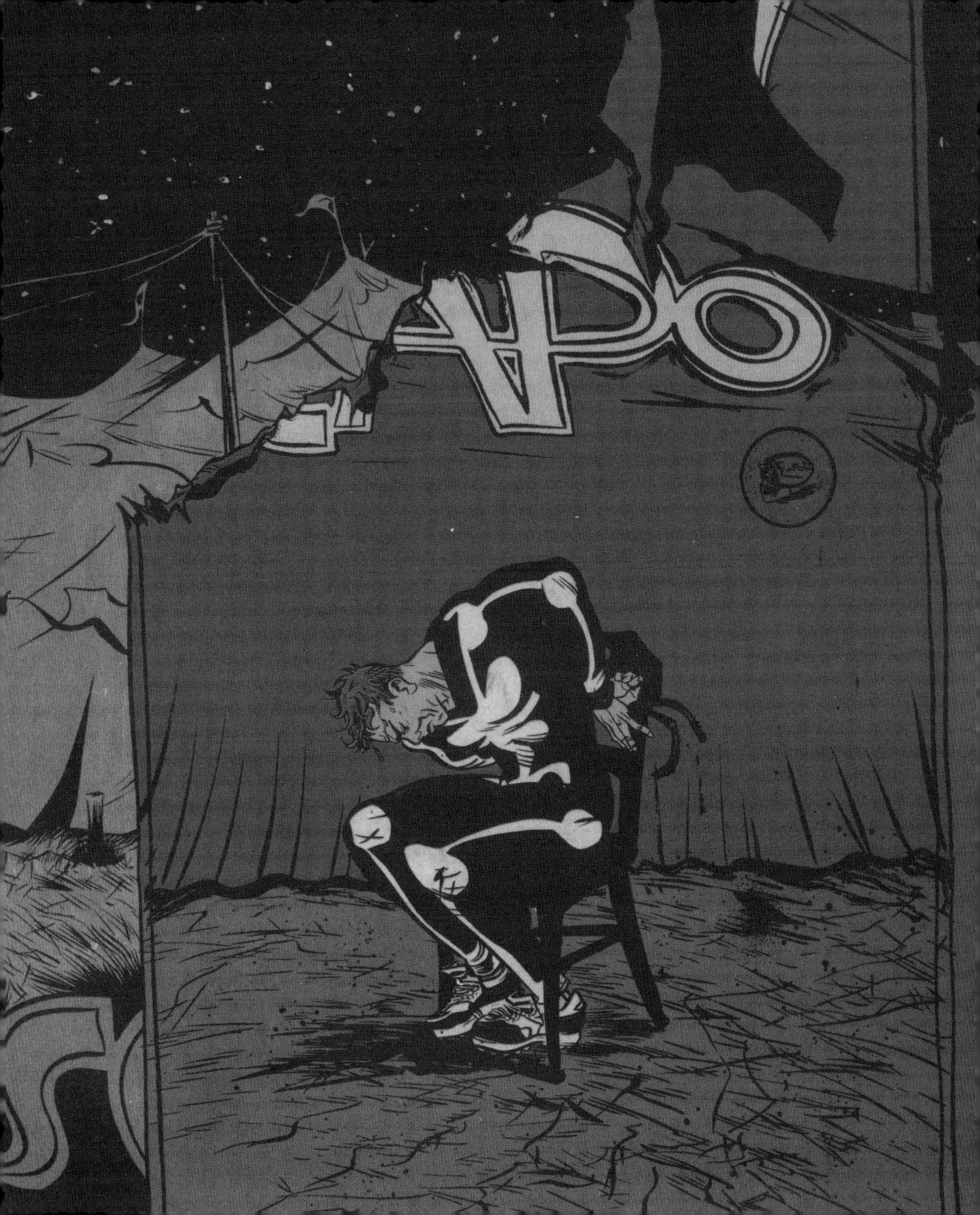

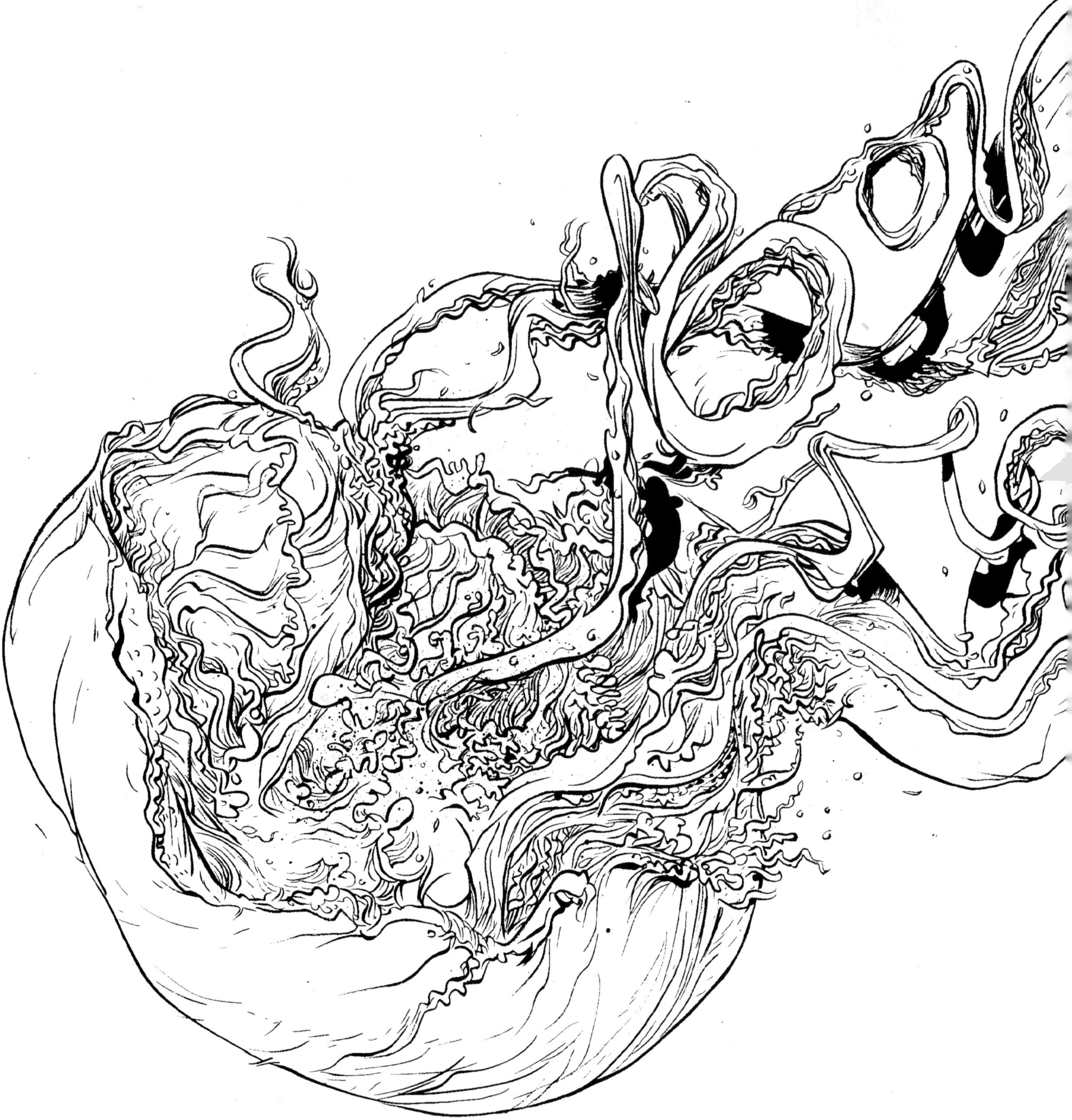

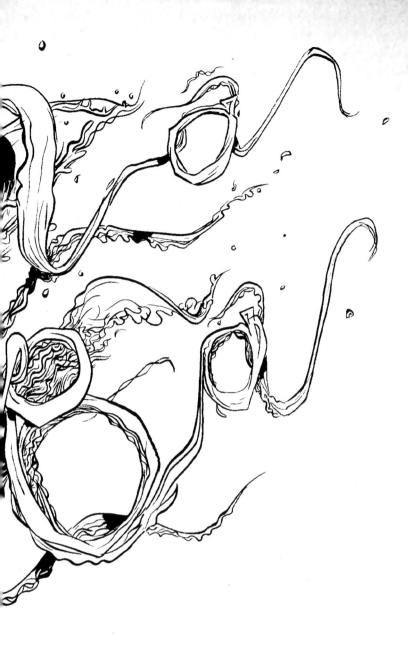

SCREA
FUTUR

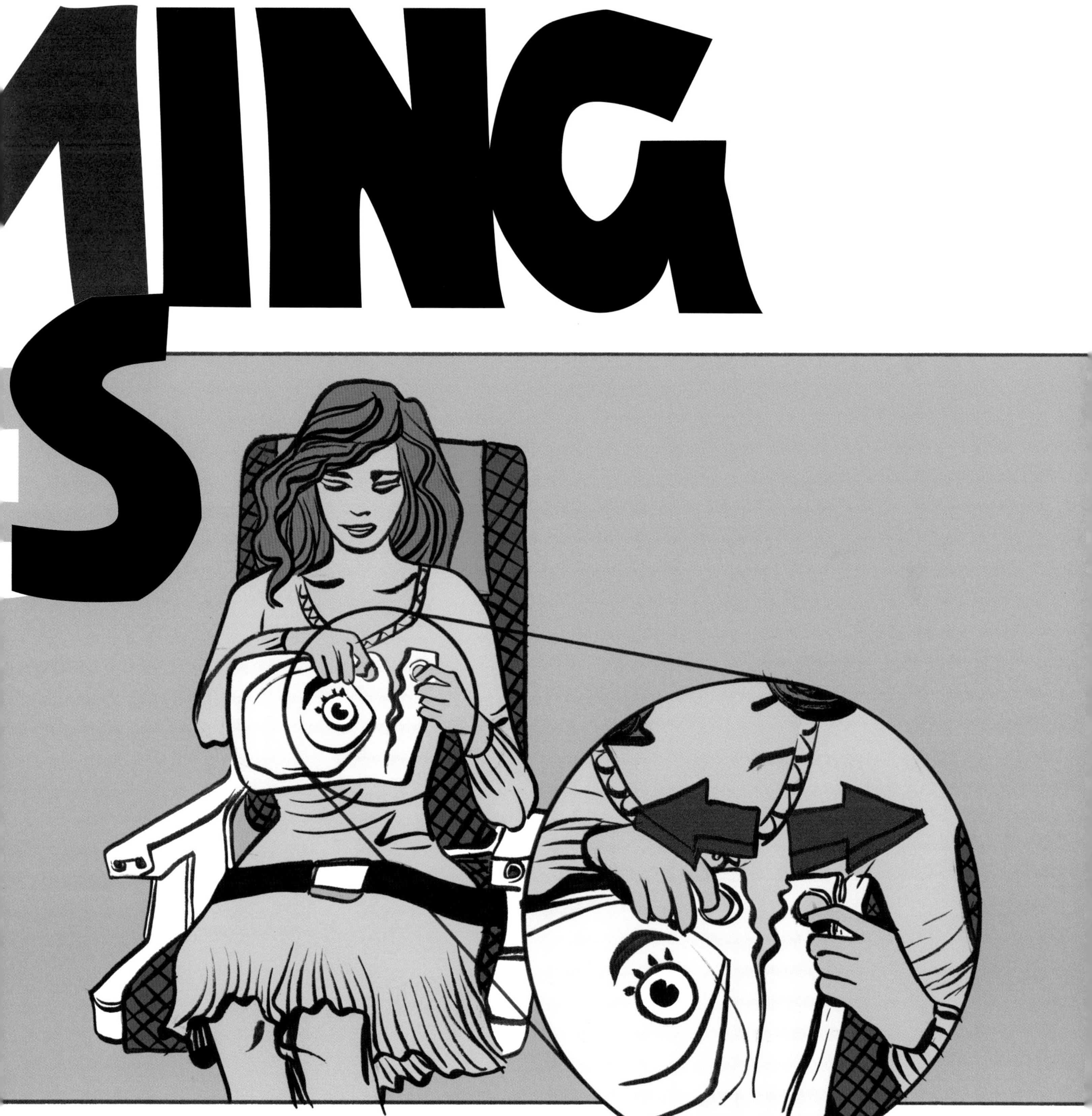
ING
S

NEW MONSTERS & STRANGE KINGS

My grandfather tells that when he was a boy, everyone in his small town of North Baltimore Ohio would run outside and point up to the sky whenever an airplane flew over, so rare and fantastic was the sight. This would've been in the 1930s. It may seem like a long time ago but was less than a lifetime ago to him. He said he and his sister would draw boxes on a barn door with a stick of charcoal, put circles inside the boxes for a bell, and pretend they were talking on telephones. They had the old hand crank phones back then. He didn't talk on a telephone until he was in his teens.

The first man stepped on the moon before many of us were even born. Now space flight is so common it barely registers in the news unless it involves some huge disaster. The sky is choked full of sattelite junk and spy cameras. I remember one time myself being about five years old, squinting up into the noonday summer heat, wondering if we would be able to see the rocketship which the TV said was taking off at that very moment, going first straight up, then curving in that peculiar way rockets do as they exit the

atmosphere. "Right now there's a man going into space," I thought, and it was a fact of life, not a speculation or a fiction. It was no more incredible than the thought that the ocean was full of strange creatures which would never step foot on dry land, angler fish and squids and sharks. I knew that from the books in the library at school. Later that year we saw the first pictures beamed back from Mars. Mars looked like a lonely, dirty orange beach that went on forever and ever. I saw the surface of another world before I stepped foot in the ocean.

We had *Star Wars* to inflate our dreams. The trolling crawl along the bottom of that huge Star Destroyer seemed to go on for miles during those first few minutes. My granddad had Flash Gordon. He'd watch the serials at the Bijou for a nickel all afternoon on a Saturday back between the Tom Mix and the Roy Rogers films. Back then, the war to end all wars had come and gone and the second one hadn't started yet. Hitler was a name that didn't mean much outside of Germany, it hadn't bled out into the living rooms from

right off the black ink of the headlines, it wasn't real yet, you could ignore it, it was just the sound of booming storm clouds far off. Now no one under fifty knows what its like to live in a world without atomic weapons. Right now we are all living in someone else's anxious science fiction future.

My granddad has given me three books in my life, all between the ages of ten and seventeen. The first was Jack London's *Stories Of Adventure* and the last was Summerset Mauham's *The Razor's Edge*. In between he gave me one other, a dusty, yellowed third printing hard cover edition of Edgar Rice Burroughs' *The Gods Of Mars*, written in 1916, which had been the copy he himself owned as a kid. Outside of comics, this was the first science fiction story I ever read. It took a while to get into it since it seemed to me to be written in such an old and lugubrious style, and I was confused by the Civil War-era setting which opens the book. A lot of the descriptions of places and things were a bit vague, a lot of the dialogue was stilted and speechy, but the action and the very atmosphere of the book was astounding. Almost right away, it was Earthman John Carter and Martian Tars Tarkas, armed with only long swords and knives, battling an army of horrific plant-like monsters in the empty basin under a mountainside made of priceless gems, the crystals gleaming in the light of the setting sun. The strange, distant world of Barsoom, with its ragged armies marching across dead sea bottoms, the majestic giant ant-men astride their eight-legged Throats, the Black Pirates swooping down over ancient dead cities from their hidden base on the far side of the small moon, a River Of Death and, best of all, a naked red princess — this stuff is tailor made for adolescent boys. I was hooked.

It has been convincingly shown that the genre of science fiction grew out of serialized pulp adventure stories. ER Burrough's John Carter series began in 1911 with *A Princess Of Mars,* and it is essentially an adventure story set on another planet. There is very little "science" in the fiction (Burrough's other great creation, Tarzan, is an arch Romantic adventure in the classic mode). Certainly, folktales and myths from around the world are full of variations on the theme of the wandering Earthman catapulted magically into the realms beyond the Earth. It is arguably one of the oldest themes we have, predating even the written word. Before Burroughs and his peers, there were certainly earlier literary examples of what you might call proto-science fiction. Cyrano De Bergerac's legendary trip to the moon (1657) through the use of glass vials full of a lighter-than-air sunbeams comes immediately to mind, as does Voltaire's satirical *Micro-Megas* (1752), a story of two extraterrestrial giants taking a tour of the galaxies which includes a brief stop on Earth. On Earth, the giants encounter a priest and a mathematician, caught up in a droplet of ocean water along the fingernail of one of the giants. Pompously, the Earthmen each demonstrate how it is impossible for giants from outer space to come to Earth to argue with priests and mathematicians. Even Jack London and Edgar Allen Poe flirted with the genre back at a time before the genre

properly had a name, back when Jules Verne and HG Wells were still drawing its first navigatable maps. Before that, stories of adventure filled with exotic creatures and strange peoples could occur in places like El Dorado and Lilliput, Atlantis and Xanadu and Bagdad, places remote enough to be other worlds but still be found here on Earth. If you could imagine *The Travels Of Marco Polo* set on Mars, you would basically have something very similar in kind to Burrough's John Carter Of Mars stories — first person accounts of a lone adventurer wandering distant lands, encountering baffling wonders and new lethal monstrosities, dining at the courts of strange kings along the way. But eventually, we had been practically everywhere there is to go on the surface of Earth, and storytellers needed fresh landscapes. All eyes turned toward the heavens.

There have been many science fictions — from the protos to the first early "scientifictions" of Jules Verne and Victor Hugo, to the sweeping space operas of E.E. "Doc" Smith, to the dystopian warnings of Yevgeny Zamyatin and George Orwell, to the morality plays of Rod Serling, to the complex social commentaries of William Golding and JG Ballard, to the poetic ruminations of Asimov and Bradbury, to the psychological puzzle-boxes of PK Dick. Obviously, the ongoing popularity of stories like Star Wars underscore the ongoing thirst for the space opera, nothing new there. And more recently we've seen a rise of the post-modern "brain-in-a-vat" story, paranoid-subjectivist visions typified by things like *The Matrix* and *Snowcrash.* These are stories which reflect the doubt many hold (either implicitly or explicitly) that the human mind does not or cannot perceive reality for what it is, or that somehow we are being tricked by some higher power into believing what it wants us to believe without our being aware of it, or if you could "jack into the mainframe", you could manipulate reality itself. This type of science fiction basically holds the position that what we call reality is in fact a great big consensual lie — an appropriate fairy tale for an age both inundated with constant, overwhelming media coupled with

deep suspicions regarding the truth-quotient of the information gathered through that media. And without a doubt, this dawning binary age presents us with many urgent questions we simply don't have answers for yet. So many unknowns suggesting so many new boogymen for our nightmares — cloning animals, sentient machines, the horrors of identity theft, child abductions and school shootings, suitcase-sized warfare, Ozone depletion, and a whole host of others waiting in the wing.

It is generally agreed that the first true science fiction story ever published was Mary Shelley's *Frankenstein* (1818). At its inception, it was considered to be a sort of post-French Revolution-era answer to Milton's *Paradise Lost,* and only over time has it earned its colossal status. I would argue it still remains the most vital story in the genre. The story of a sympathetic yet fearsome monster returning to confront his human yet unsympathetic creator is the story of the modern world, we see it reverberate everywhere, in fact and fiction. Roy Batty poking out Tyrell's eyes as he mutters, "I need more life, fucker" is Frankenstein. The disastrous nuclear meltdown of Chernoybl is Frankenstein. Hiroshima is Frankenstein. Science fiction begins and ends with Frankenstein.

If it is anything more than a harmless diversion, this rough diamond we call science fiction is really the literature of contemporary anxiety. Through these stories, we are able to give form to the vague fears and doubts floating unspoken in the air between us. At its best, the genre gives form to the anxious images of our minds, it lends names and faces and shapes to the nightmares. It also lends shape to the hopes. Science fiction flexes the dream-finger, places blame, pulls the alarm bell, quietly encourages, spins us its webs of new monsters and strange kings. It is the popular stage on which we try to sculpt the shape of world we are — either intentionally or unintentionally — creating.

JACK
KIRBY

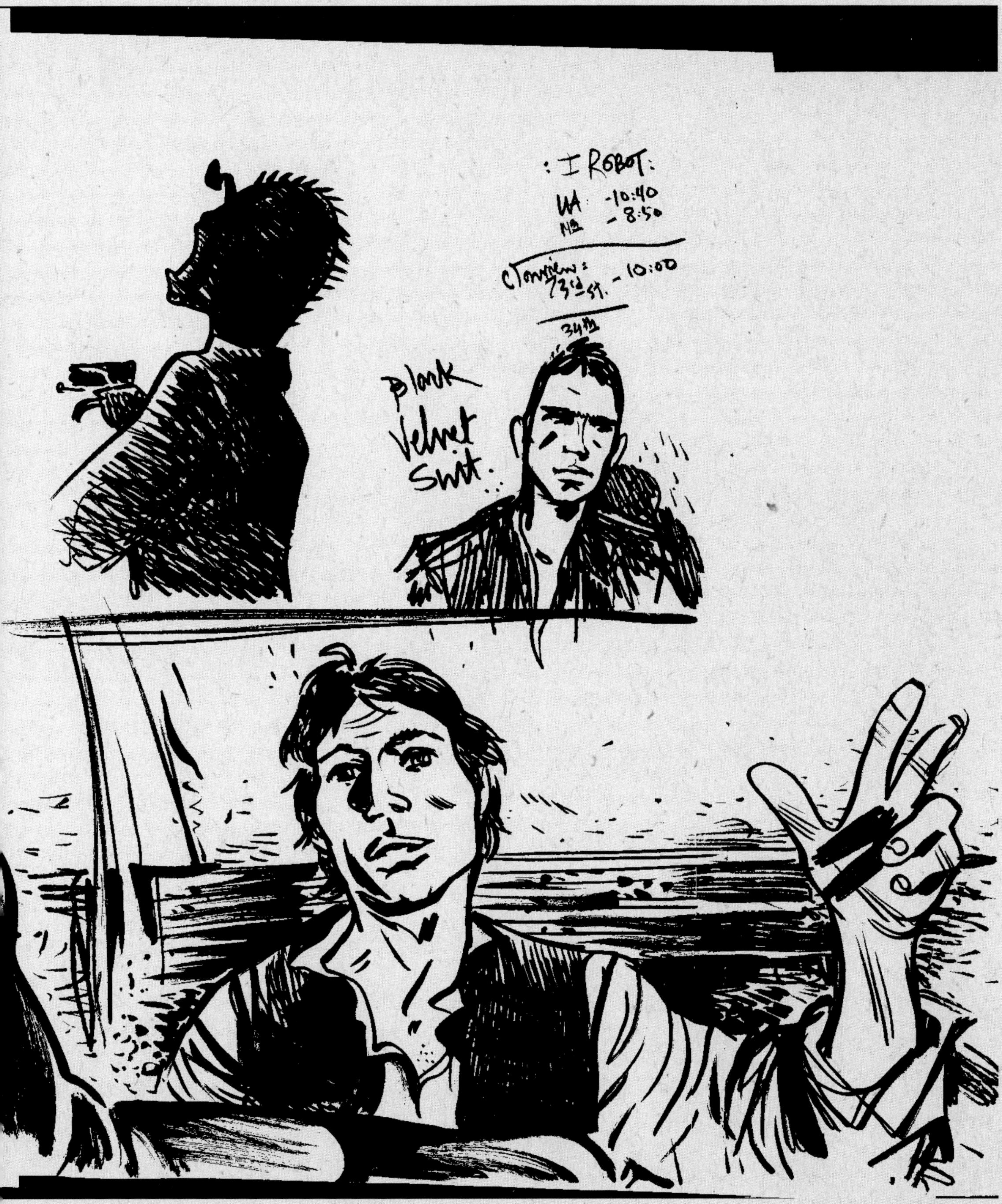
: I ROBOT:
UA -10:40
-8:50
Clearview: 73rd St. -10:00
34th
Velvet Suit.

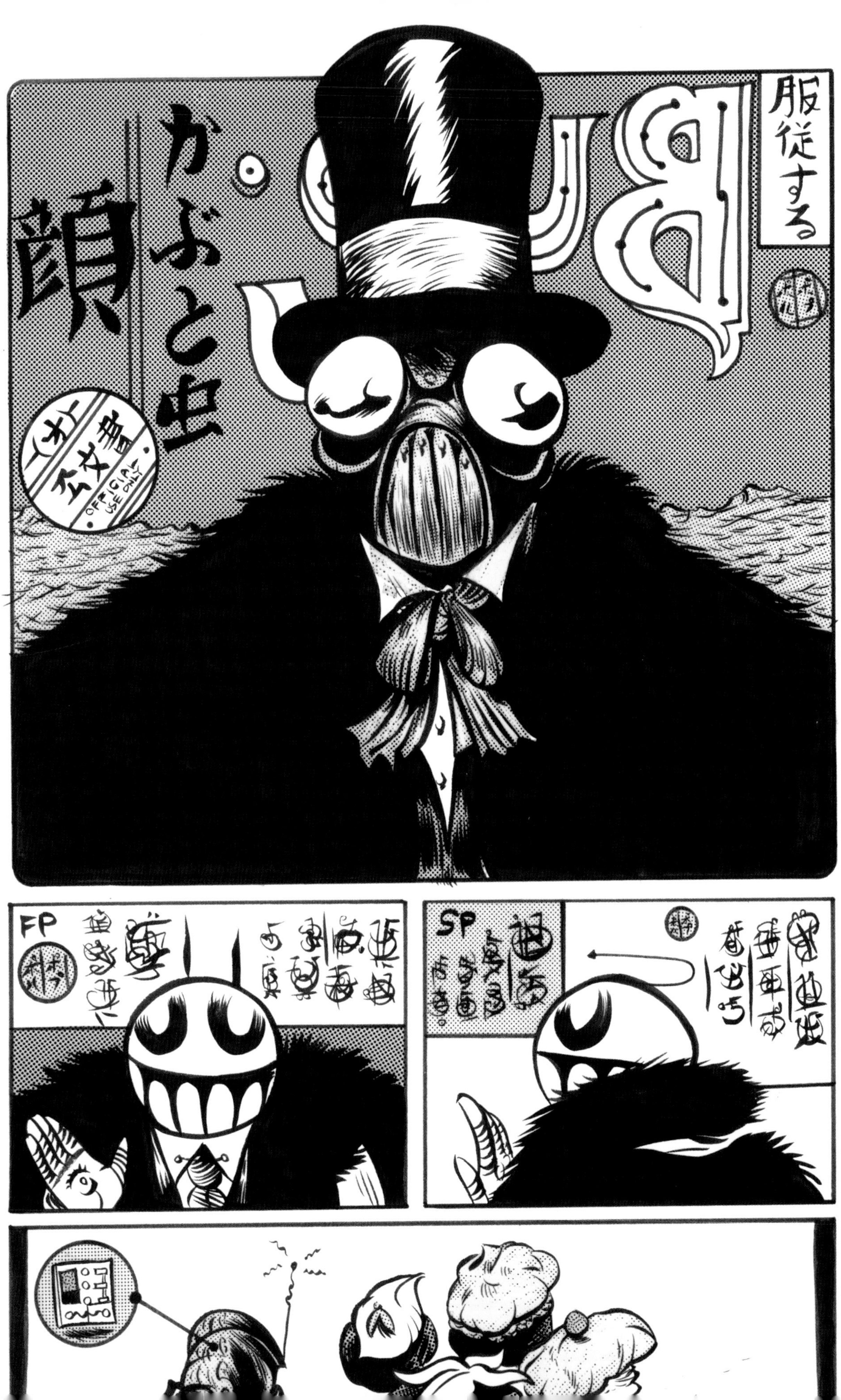
服従する
かぶと虫
顔
公文書
OFFICIAL USE ONLY
SP
FP

THB Circus 10/1997

15/Rue des Lumieres Blanche

“I am the Most Handsome”

...a true story...

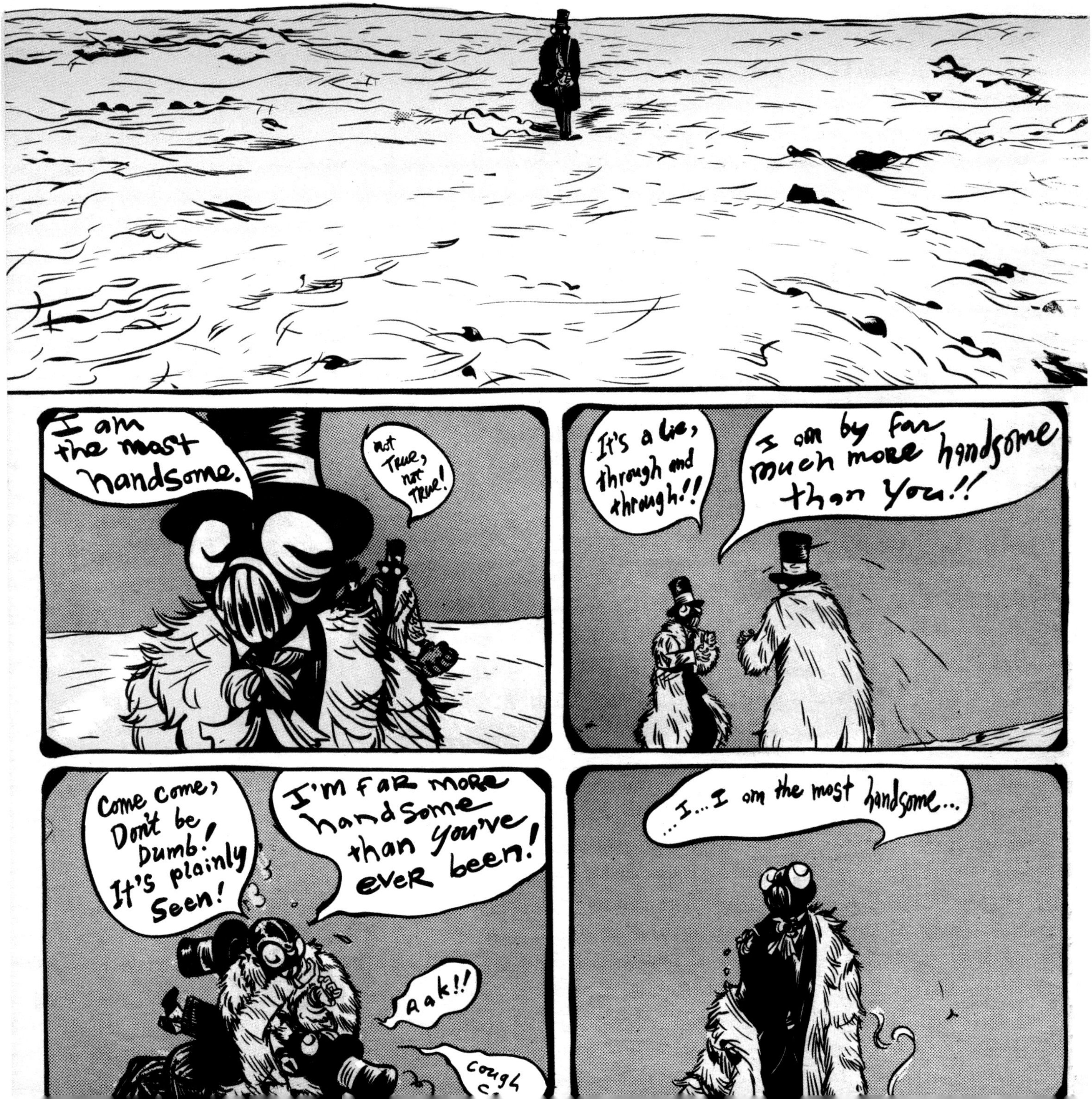
I am the most handsome.
Not true, not true!
It's a lie, through and through!!
I am by far much more handsome than you!!
Come come, Don't be Dumb! It's plainly Seen!
I'm far more handsome than you've ever been!
Aak!!
cough
...I... I am the most handsome...

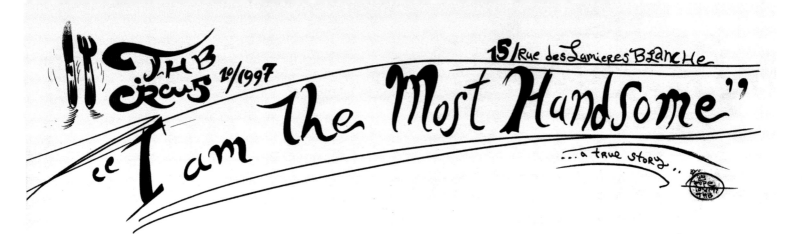

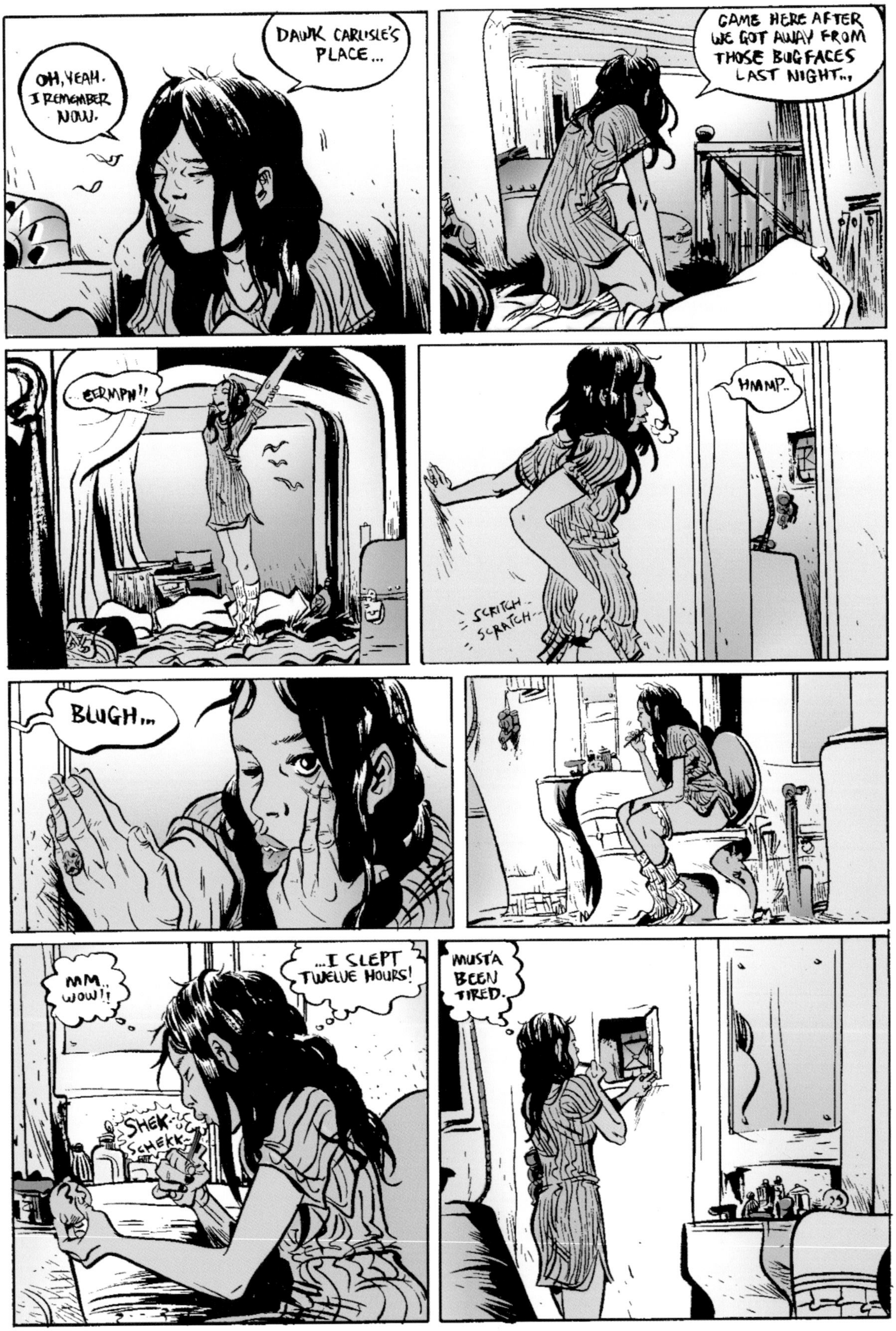
OH, YEAH. I REMEMBER NOW.
DAWN CARLISLE'S PLACE...
CAME HERE AFTER WE GOT AWAY FROM THOSE BUGFACES LAST NIGHT...
...EERMPH!!
HMMP..
SCRITCH SCRATCH
BLUGH...
MM.. WOW!!
...I SLEPT TWELVE HOURS!
SHEK- SCHEKK-
MUST'A BEEN TIRED.

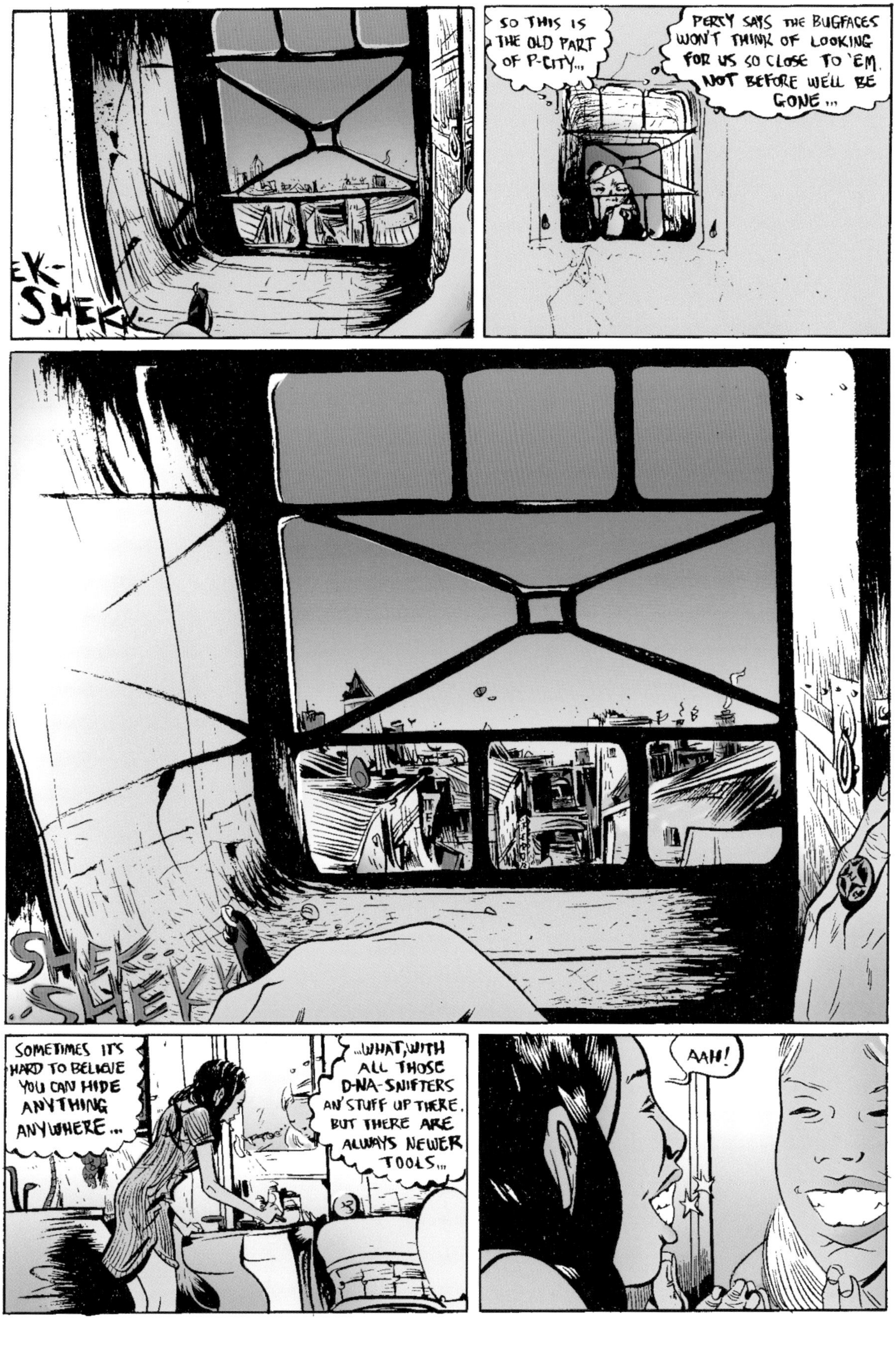
EK-SHEKK
SO THIS IS THE OLD PART OF P-CITY...
PERRY SAYS THE BUGFACES WON'T THINK OF LOOKING FOR US SO CLOSE TO 'EM. NOT BEFORE WE'LL BE GONE...
SHEK-SHEKK
SOMETIMES IT'S HARD TO BELIEVE YOU CAN HIDE ANYTHING ANYWHERE...
...WHAT, WITH ALL THOSE D-NA-SNIFTERS AN' STUFF UP THERE, BUT THERE ARE ALWAYS NEWER TOOLS...
AAH!

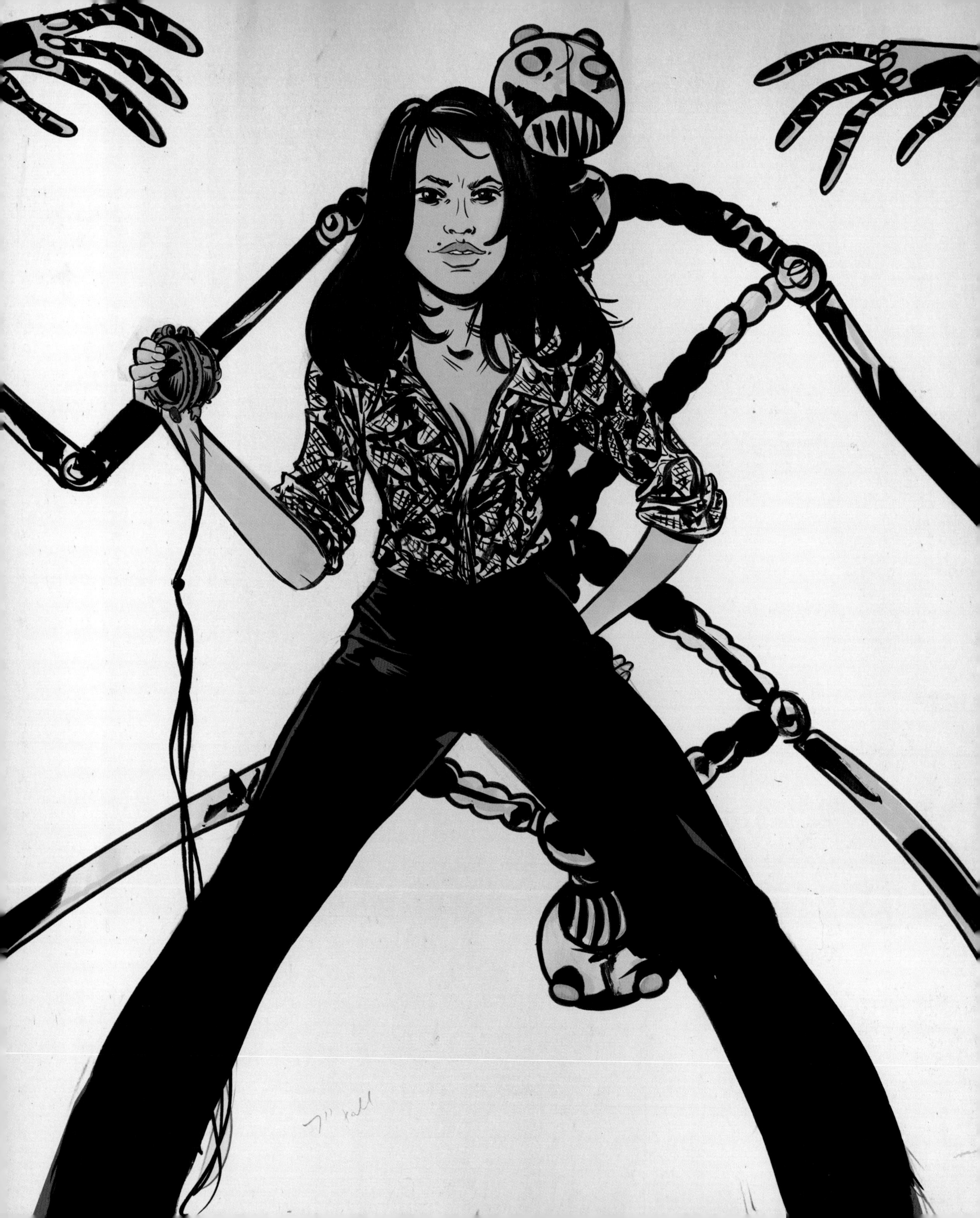
7'' tall

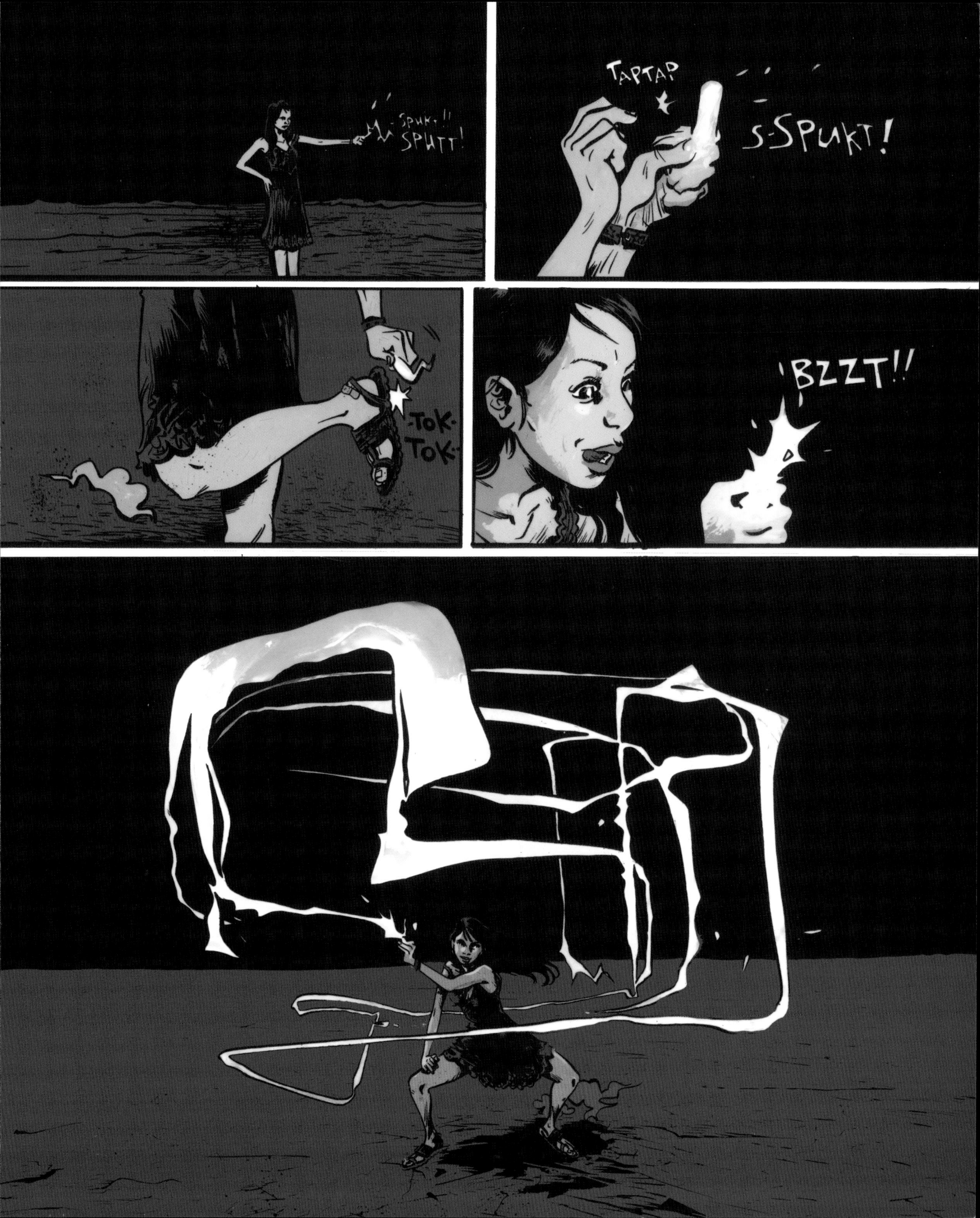

-SPUKT!!
SPUTT!
TAPTAP
S-SPUKT!
-TOK-
TOK-
BZZT!!

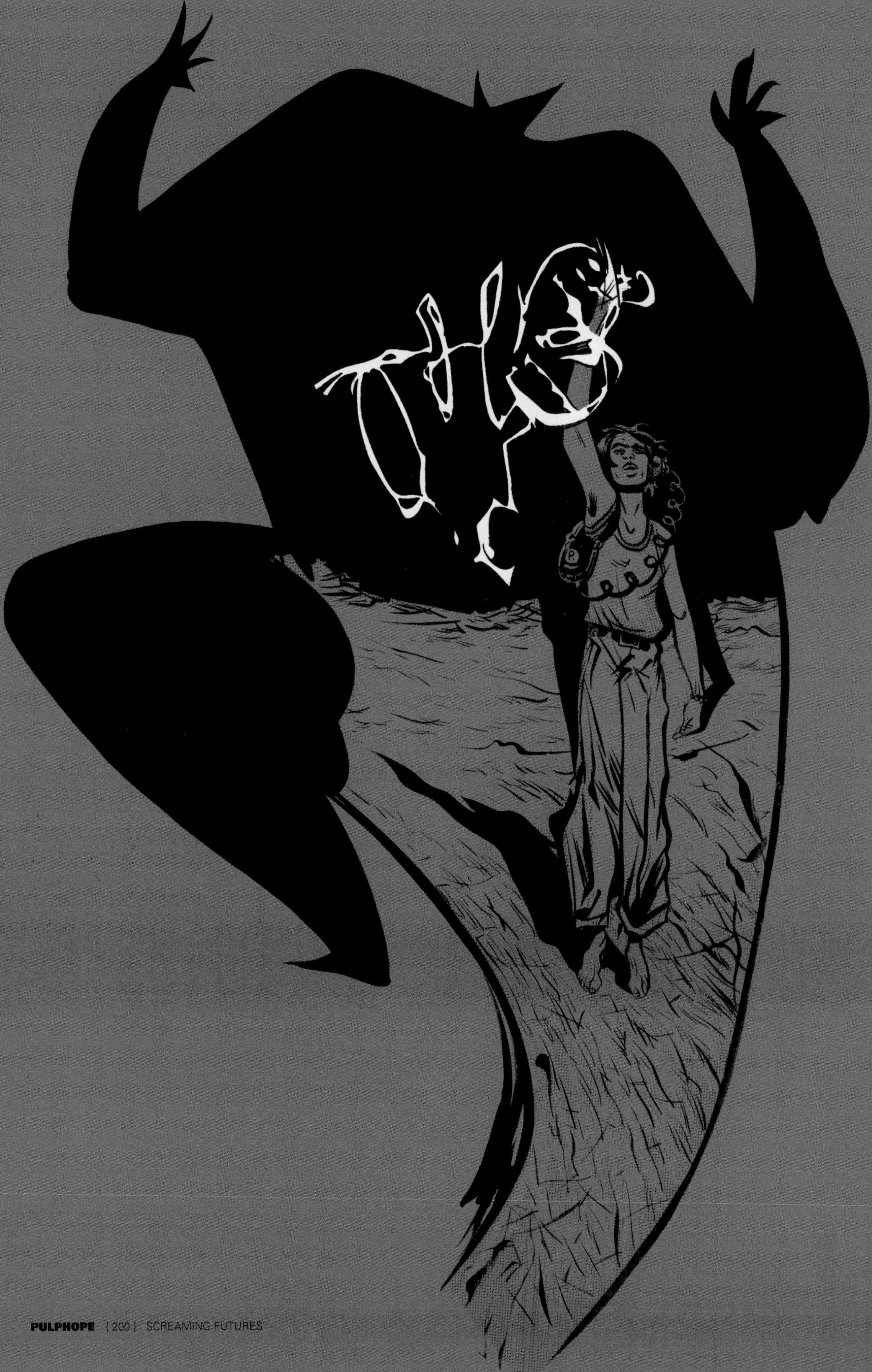

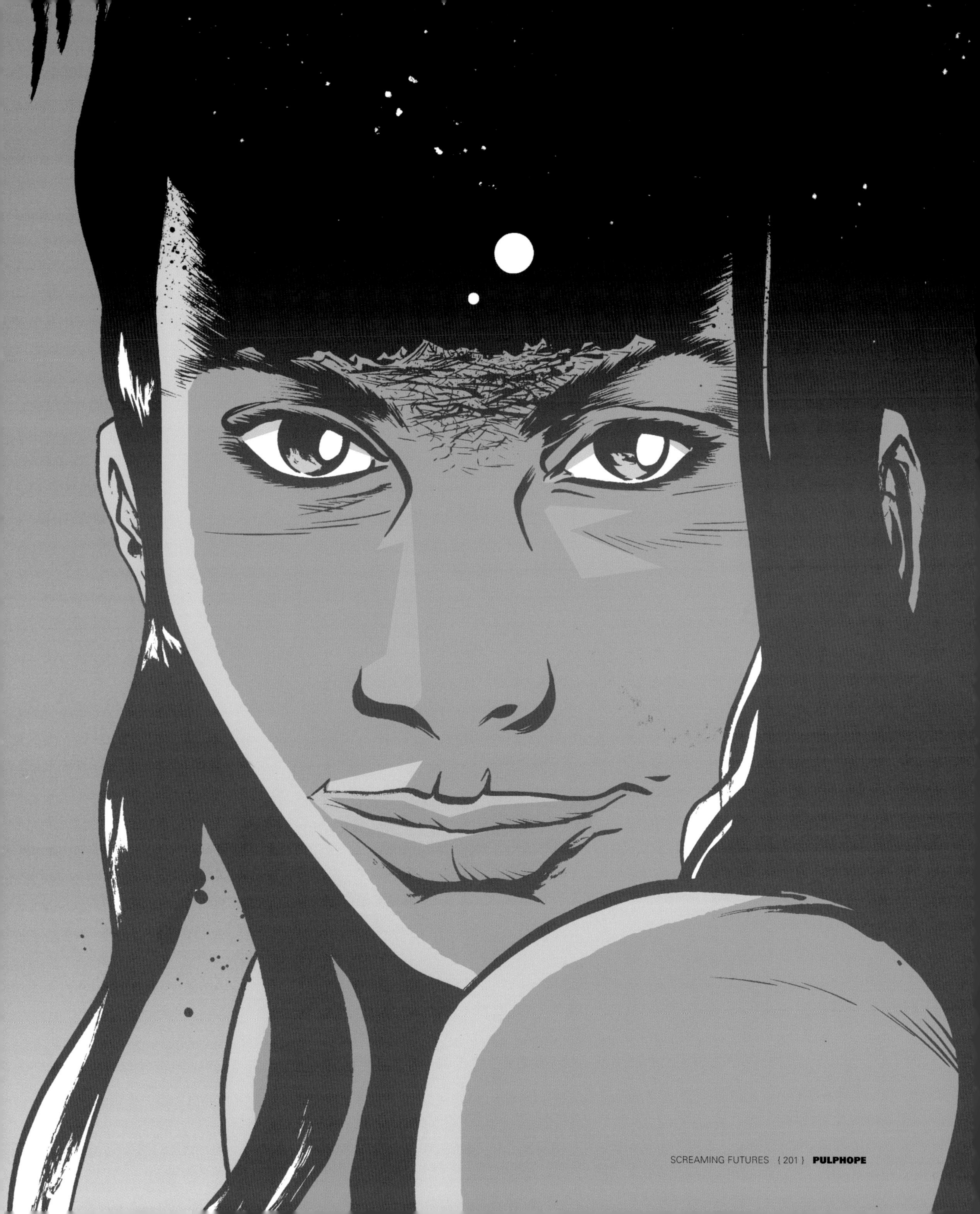

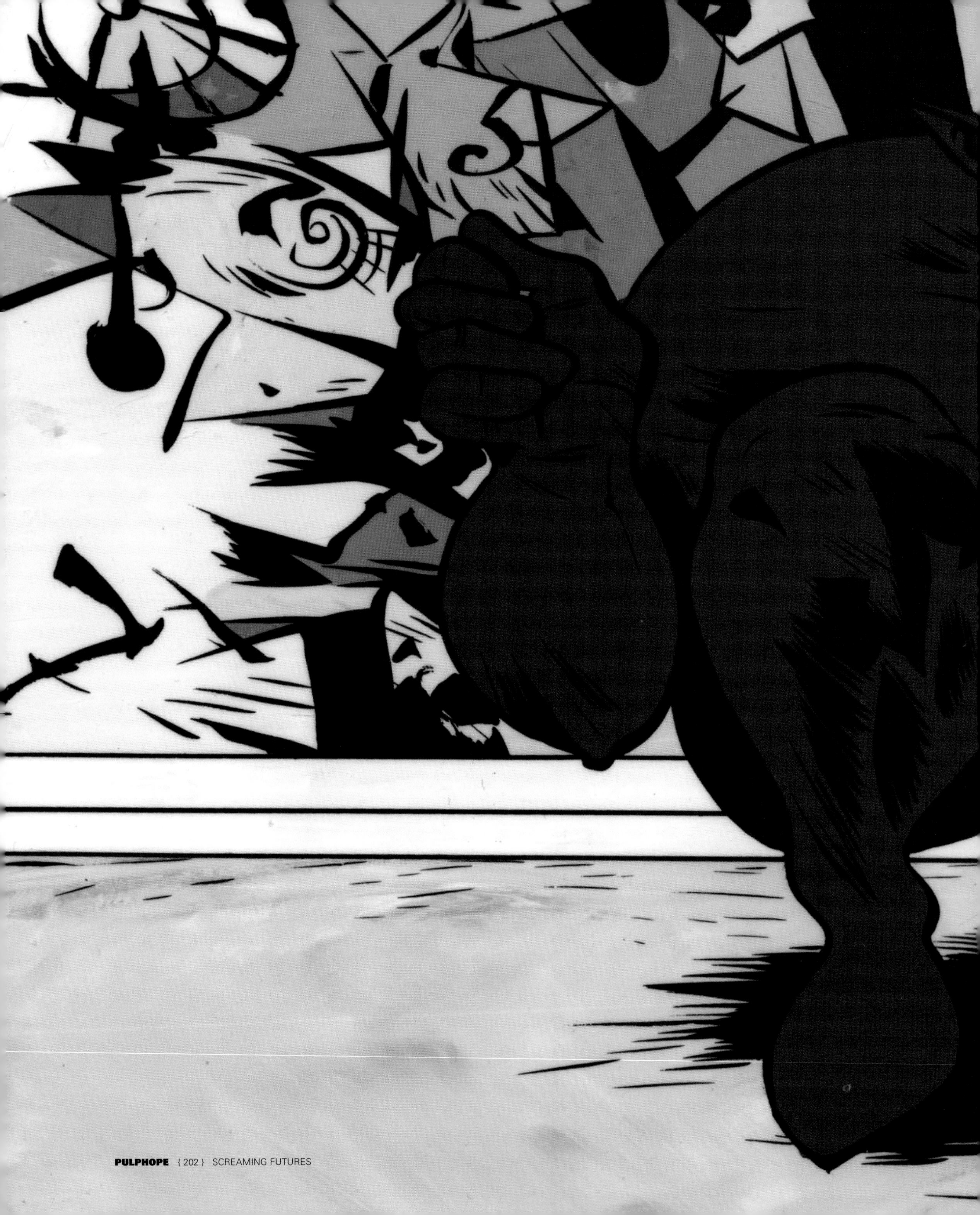

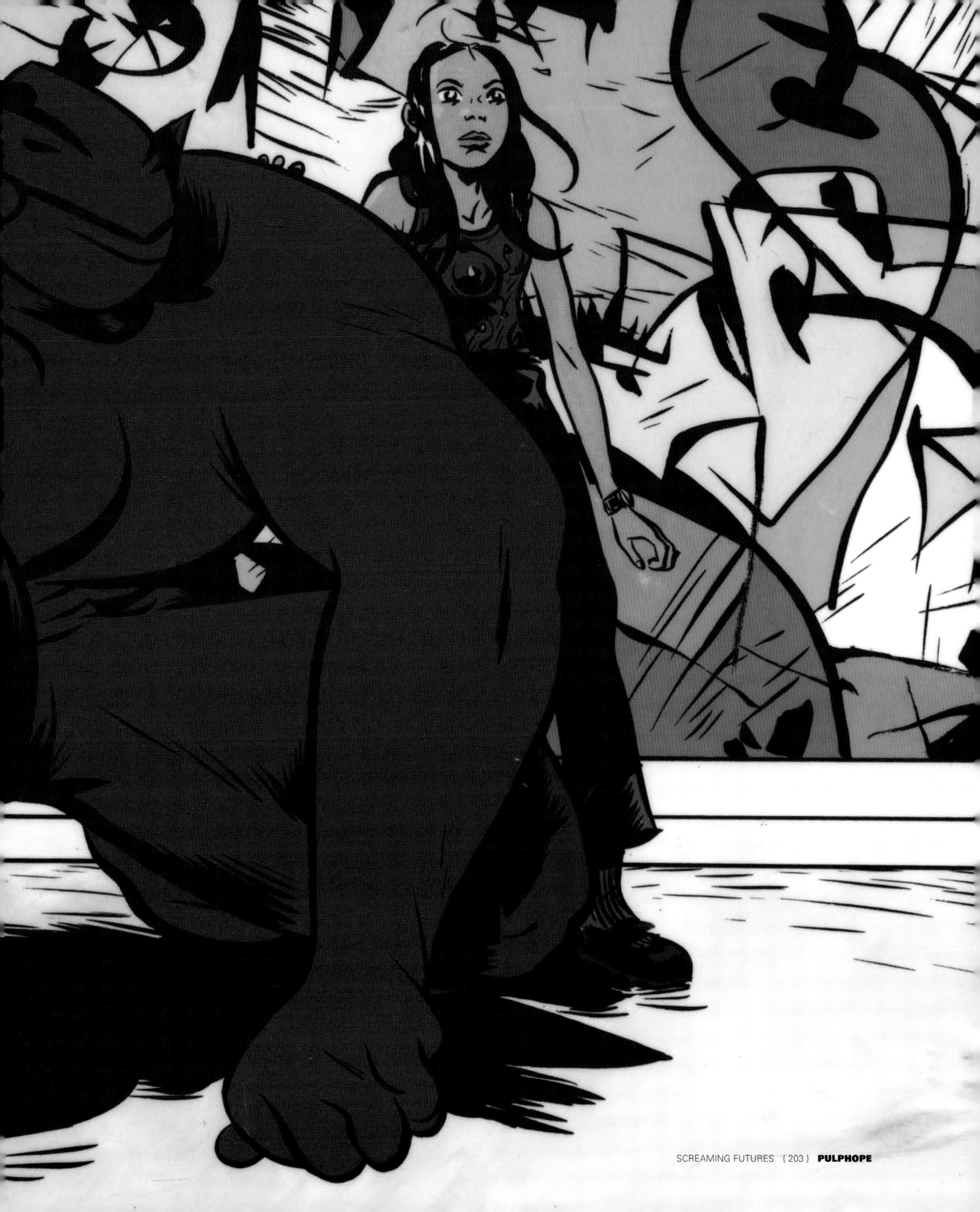

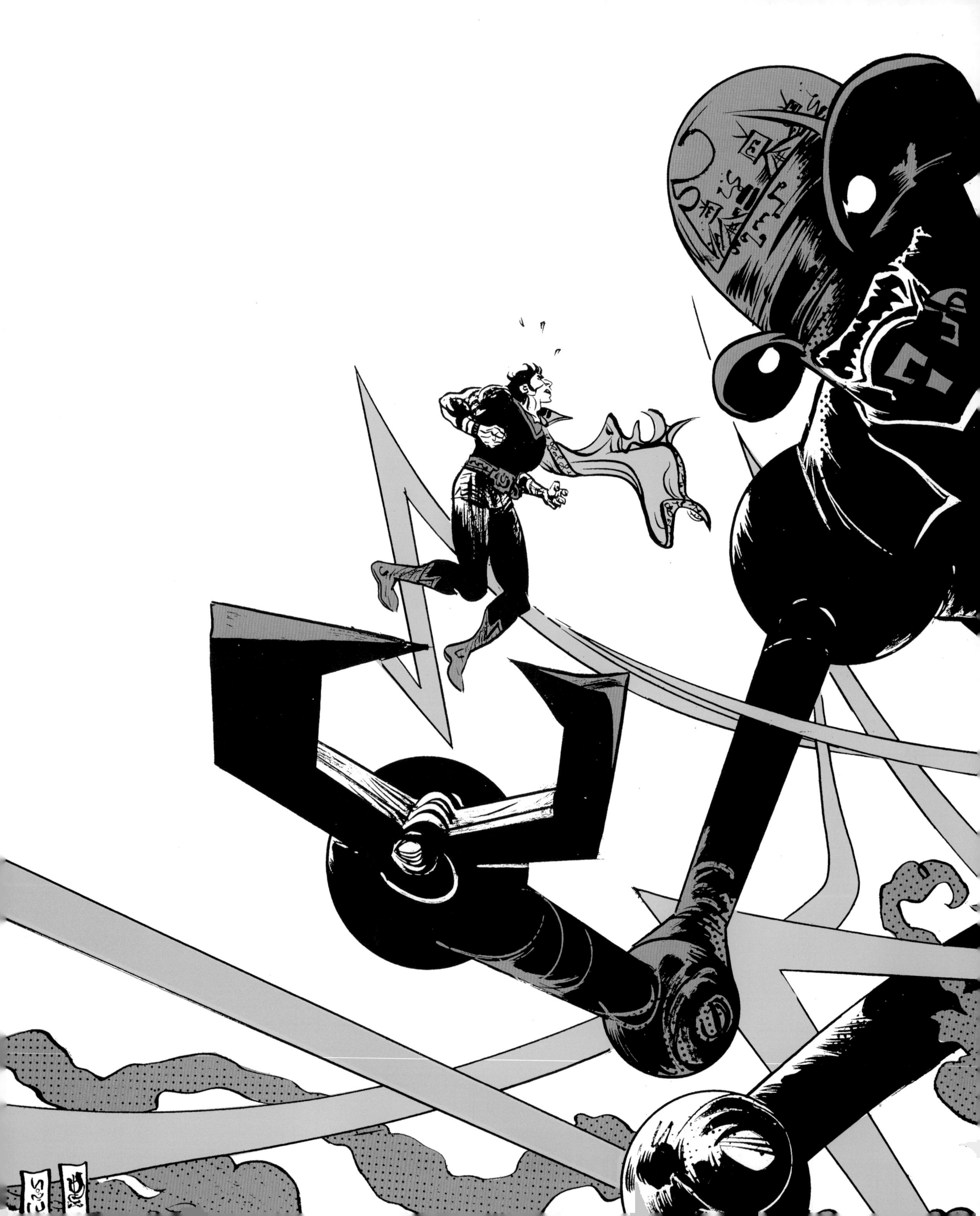

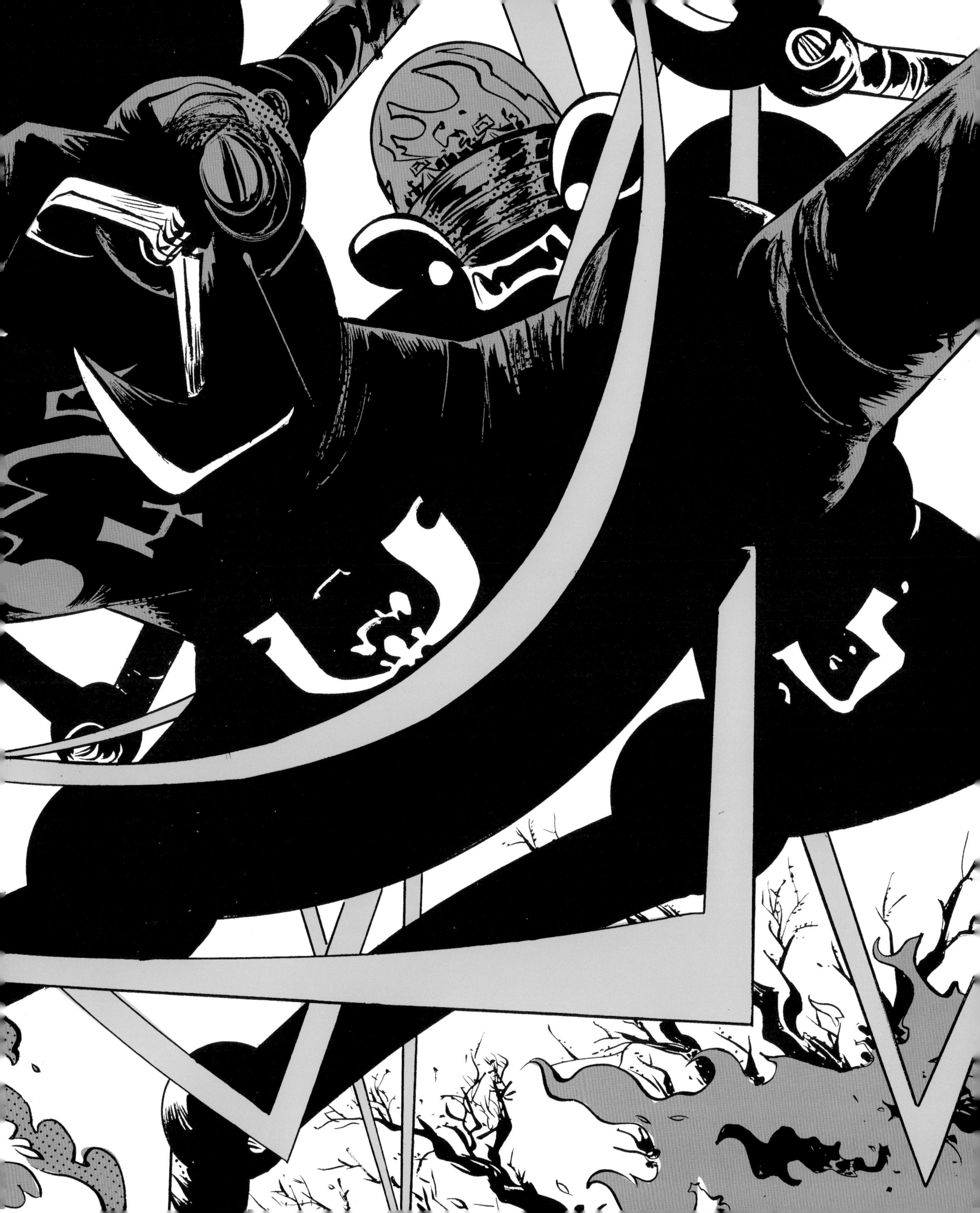

·2089·
P.POPE

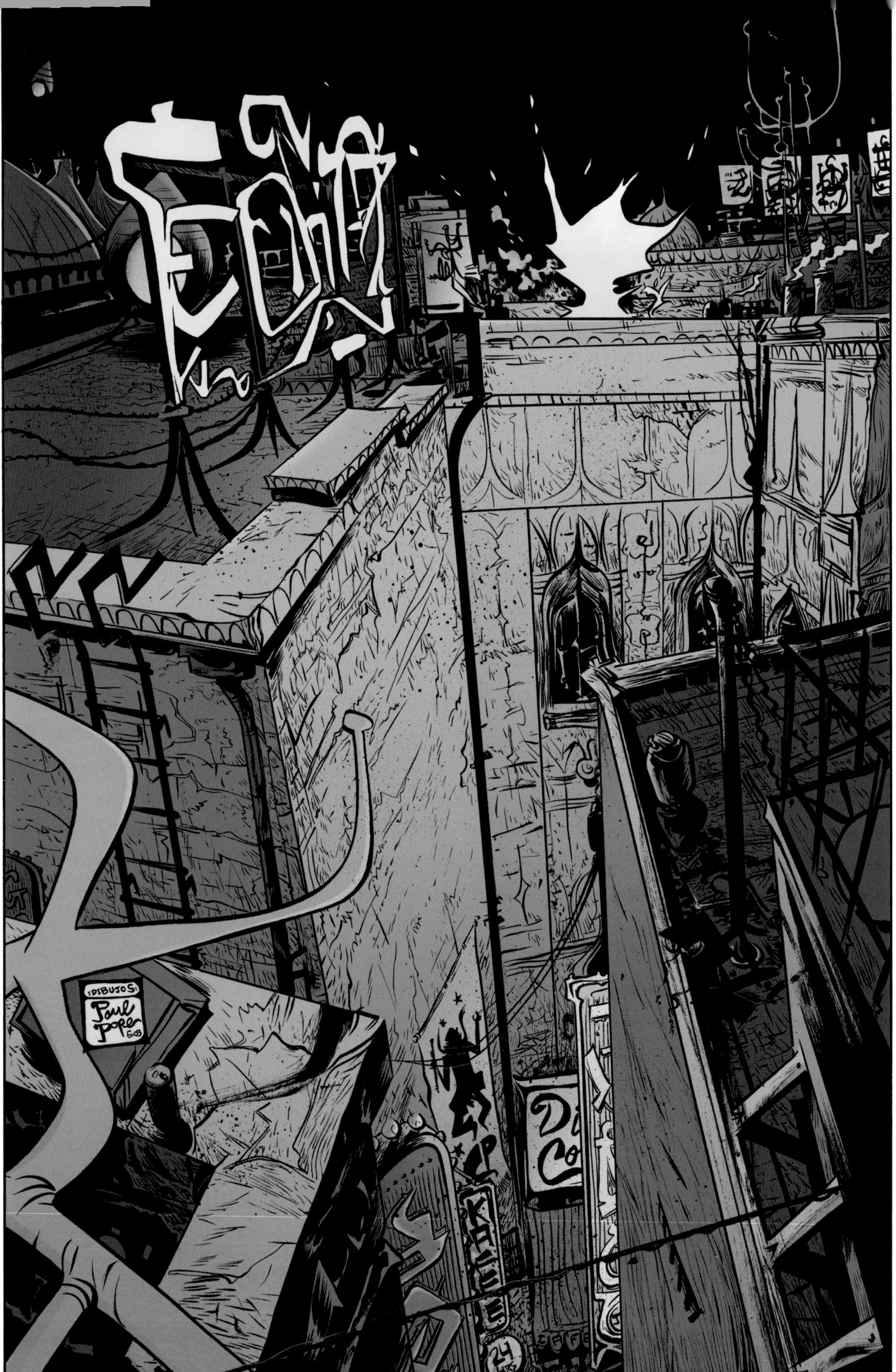
DIBUJOS:
Paul Pope
6-03
24

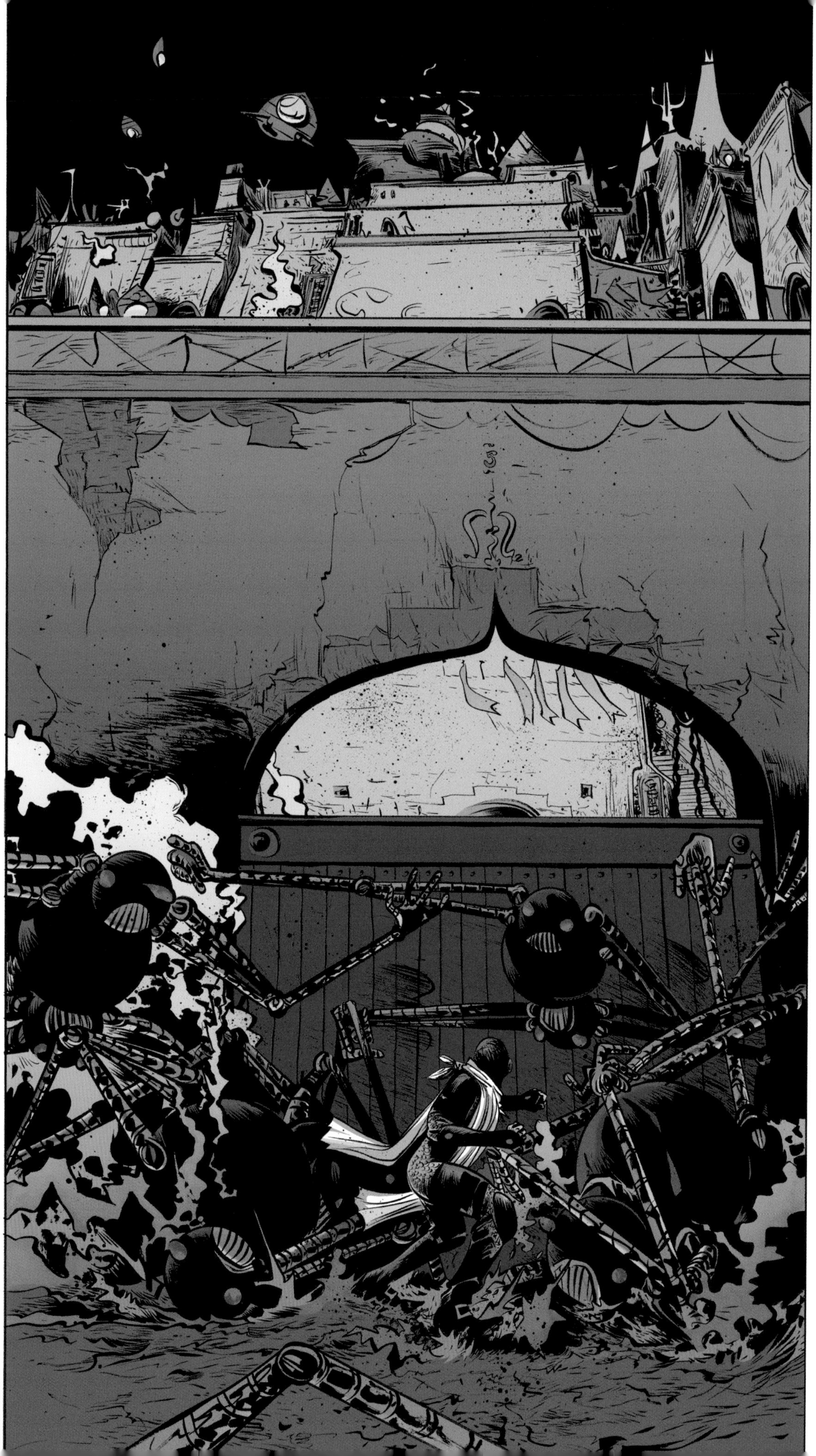

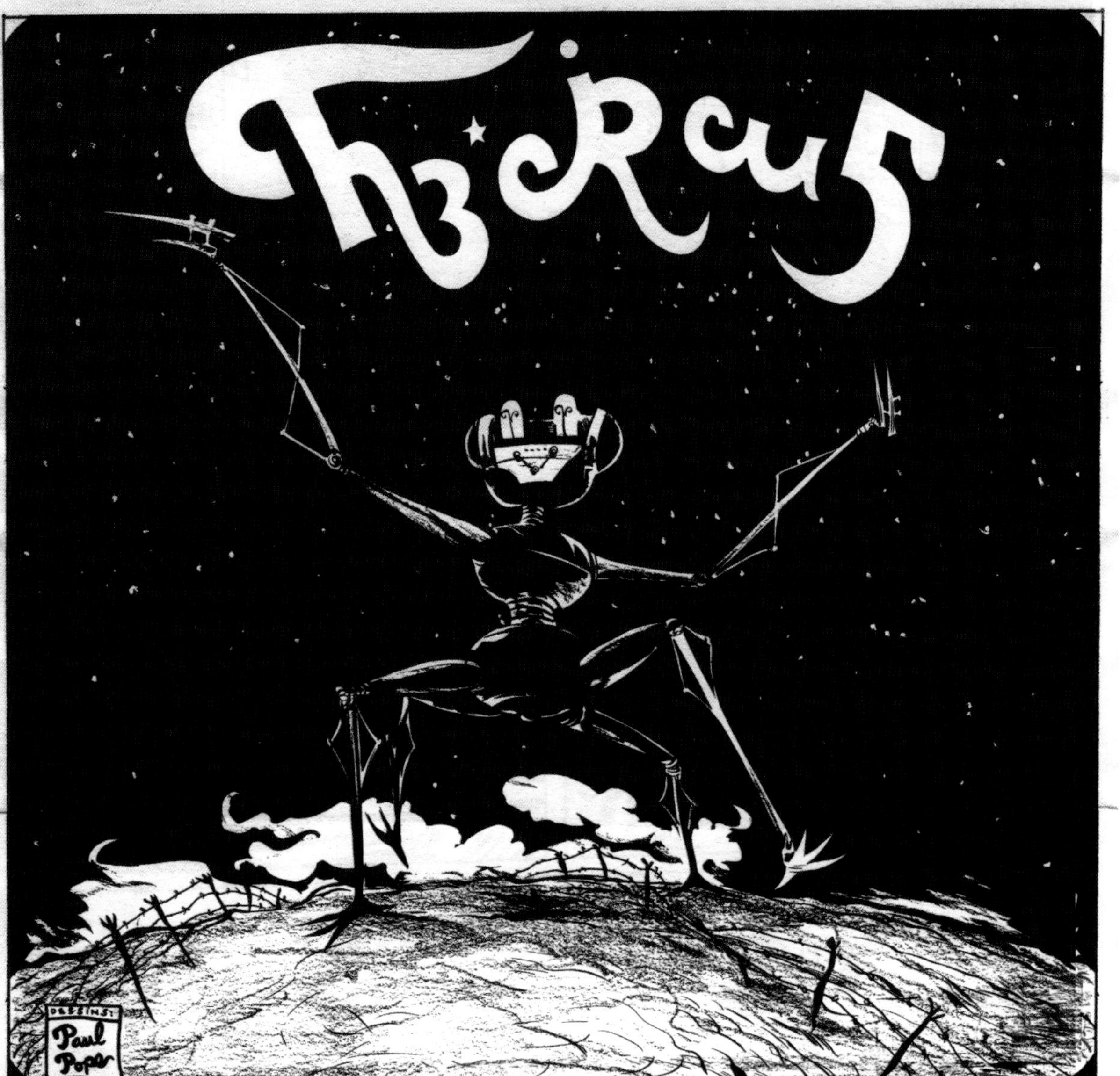
The Circus
DESSINS:
Paul Pope

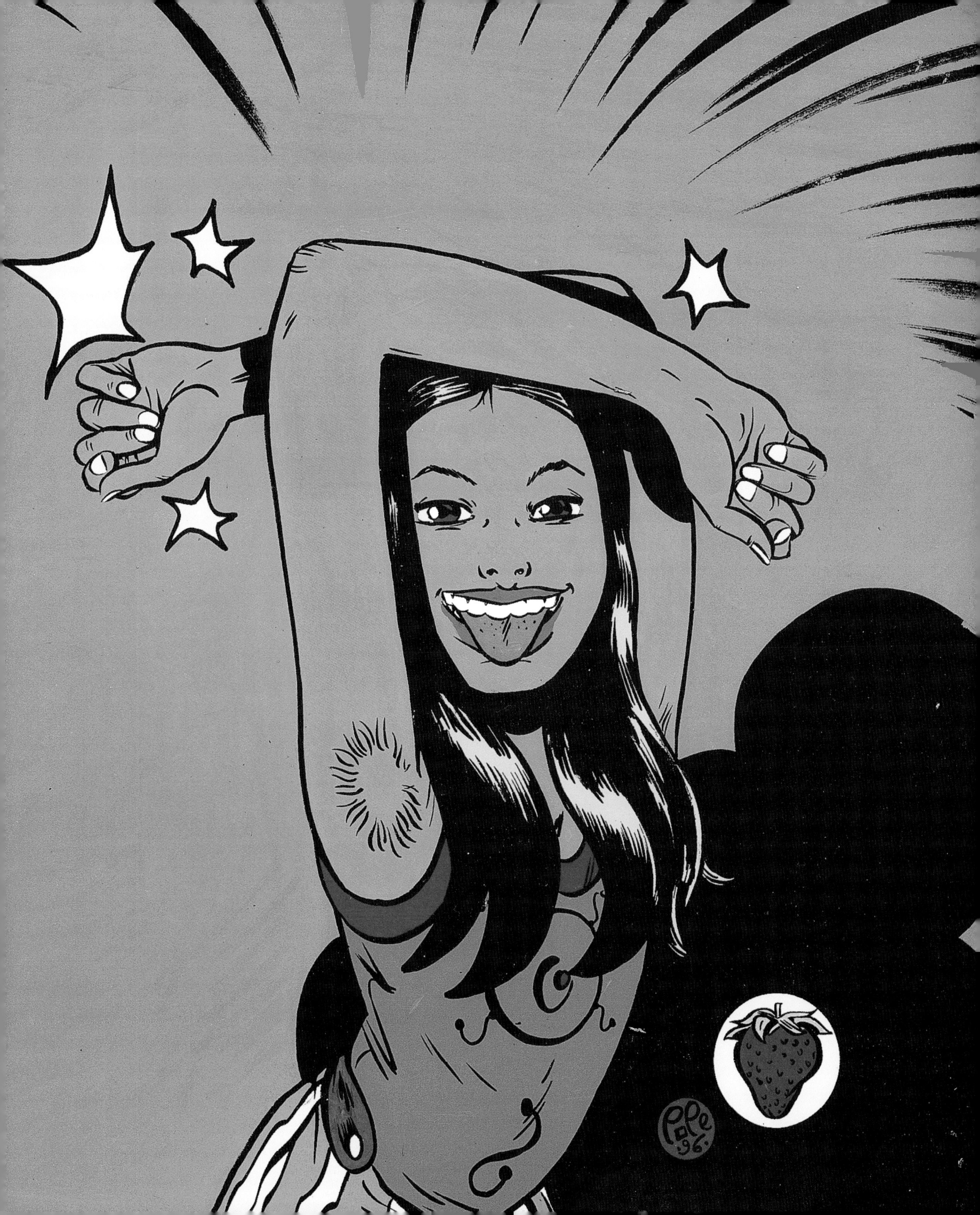

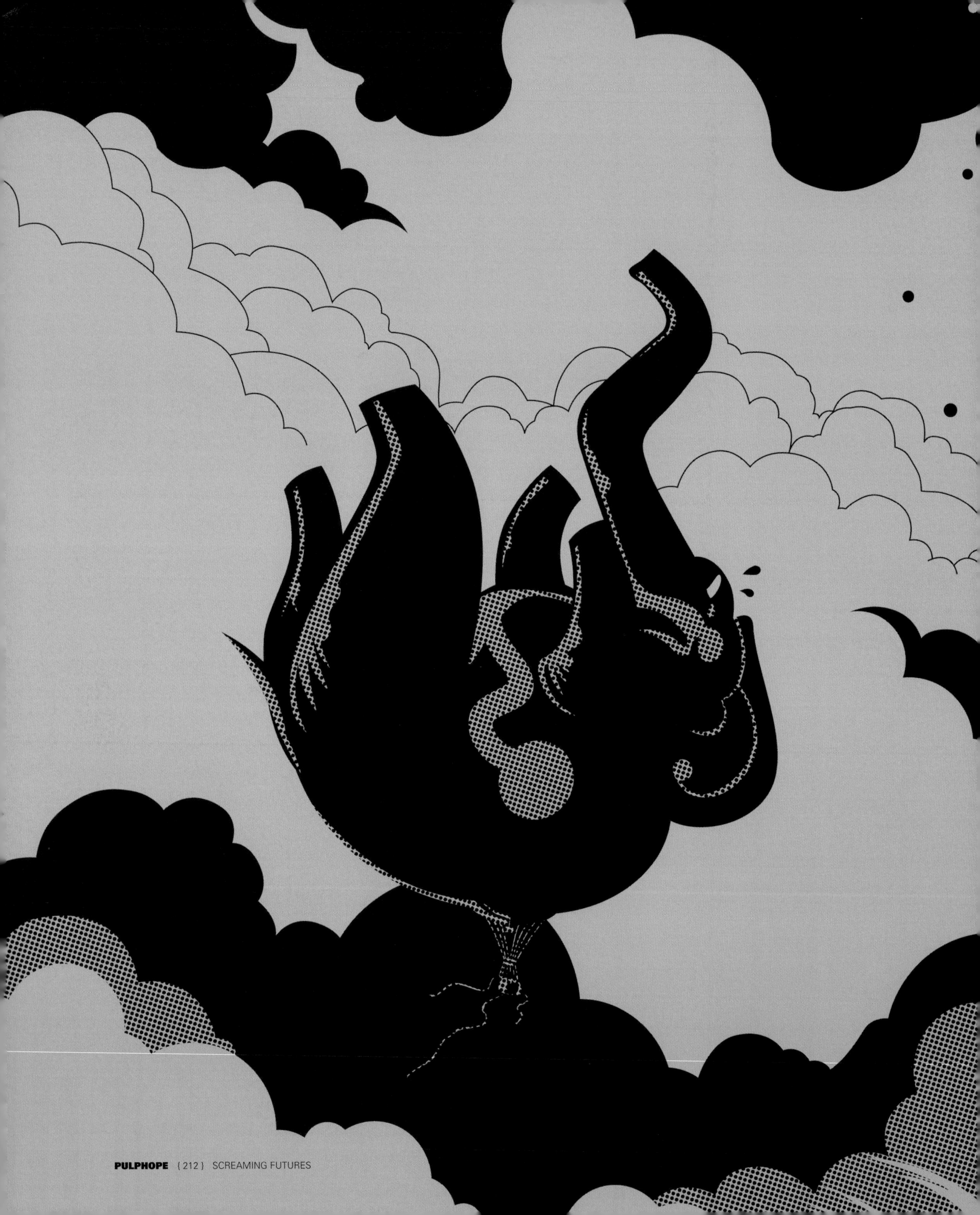

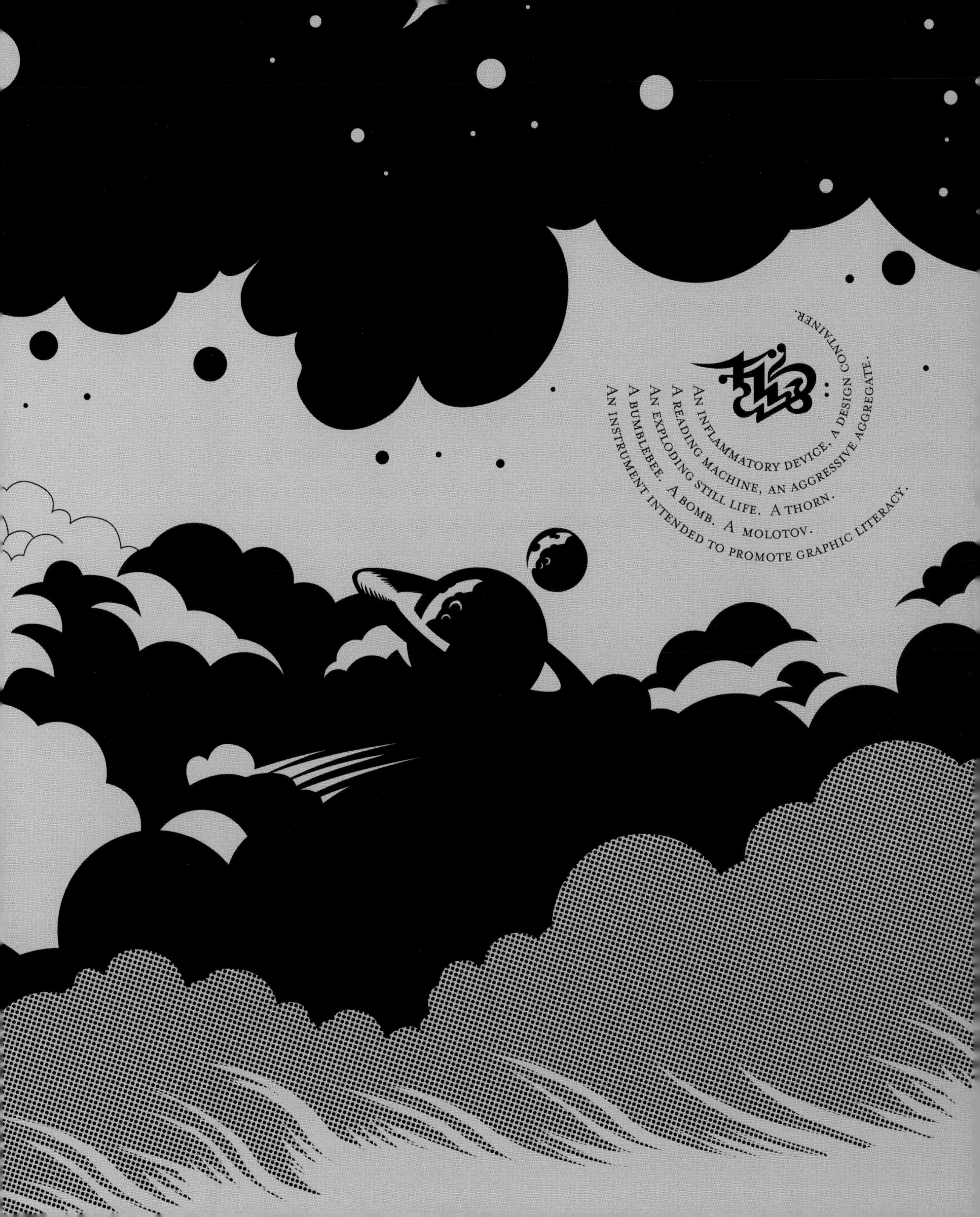
An inflammatory device, a design container.
A reading machine, an aggressive aggregate.
An exploding still life. A thorn.
A bumblebee. A bomb. A molotov.
An instrument intended to promote graphic literacy.

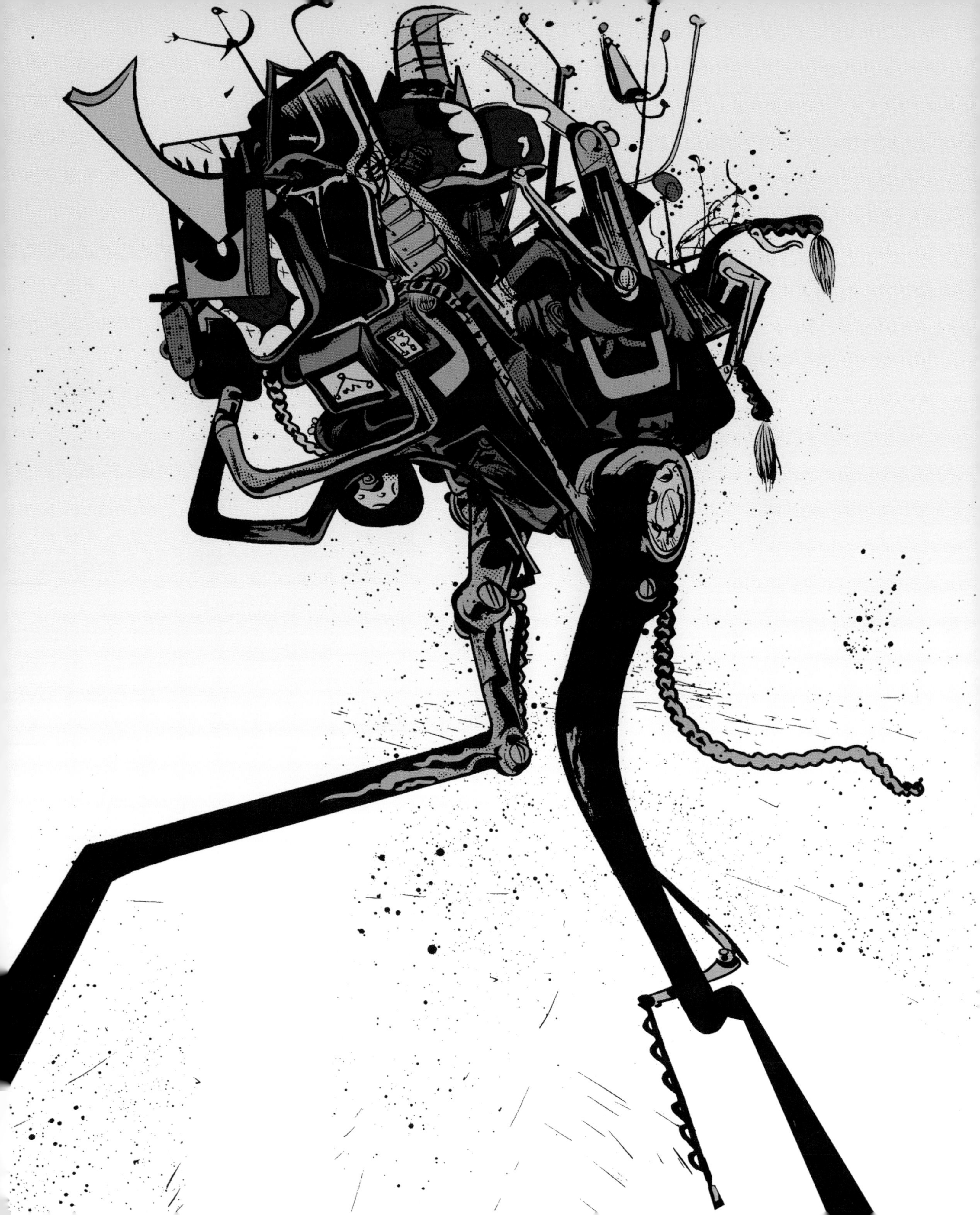

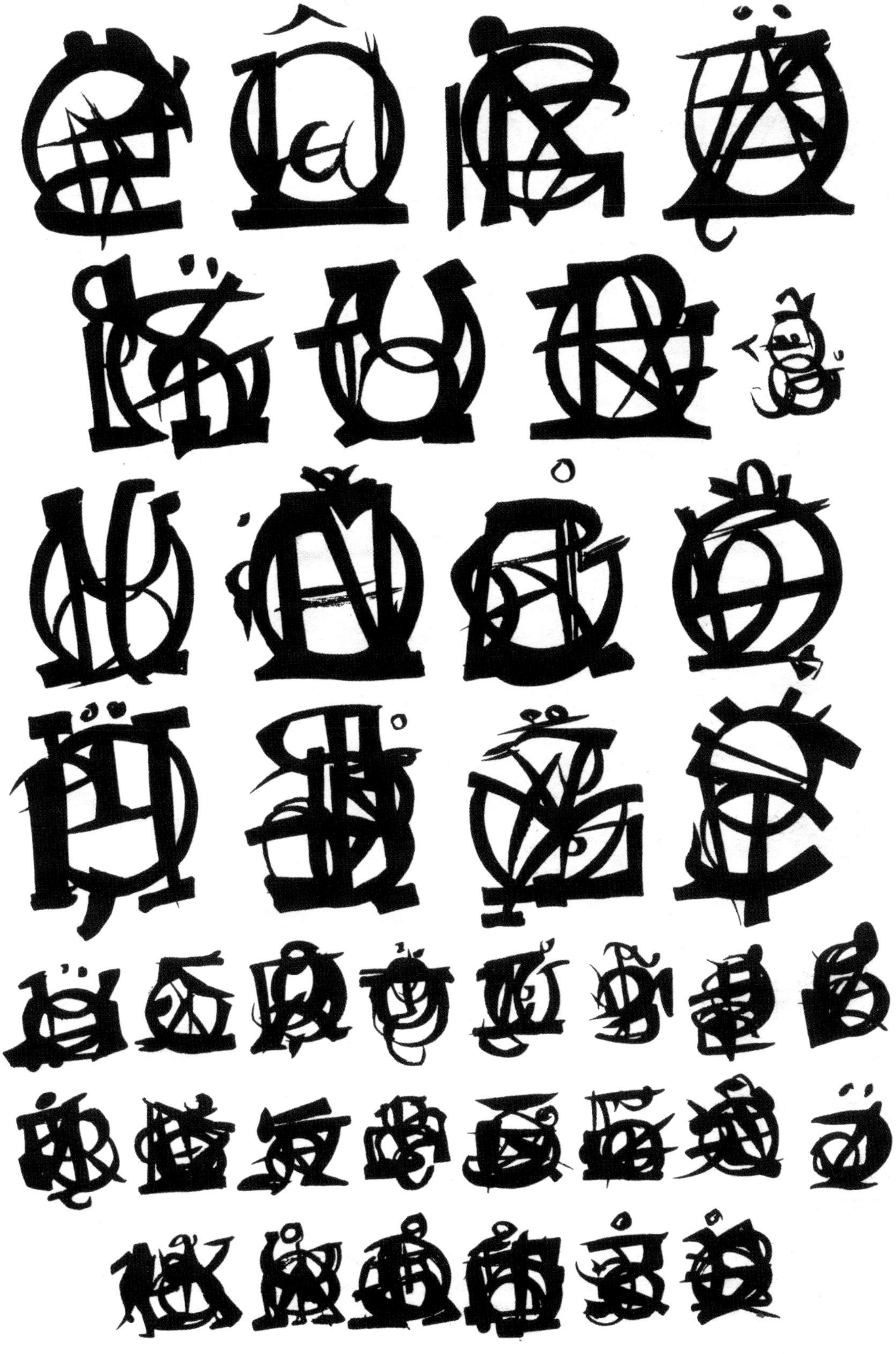

INDEXE

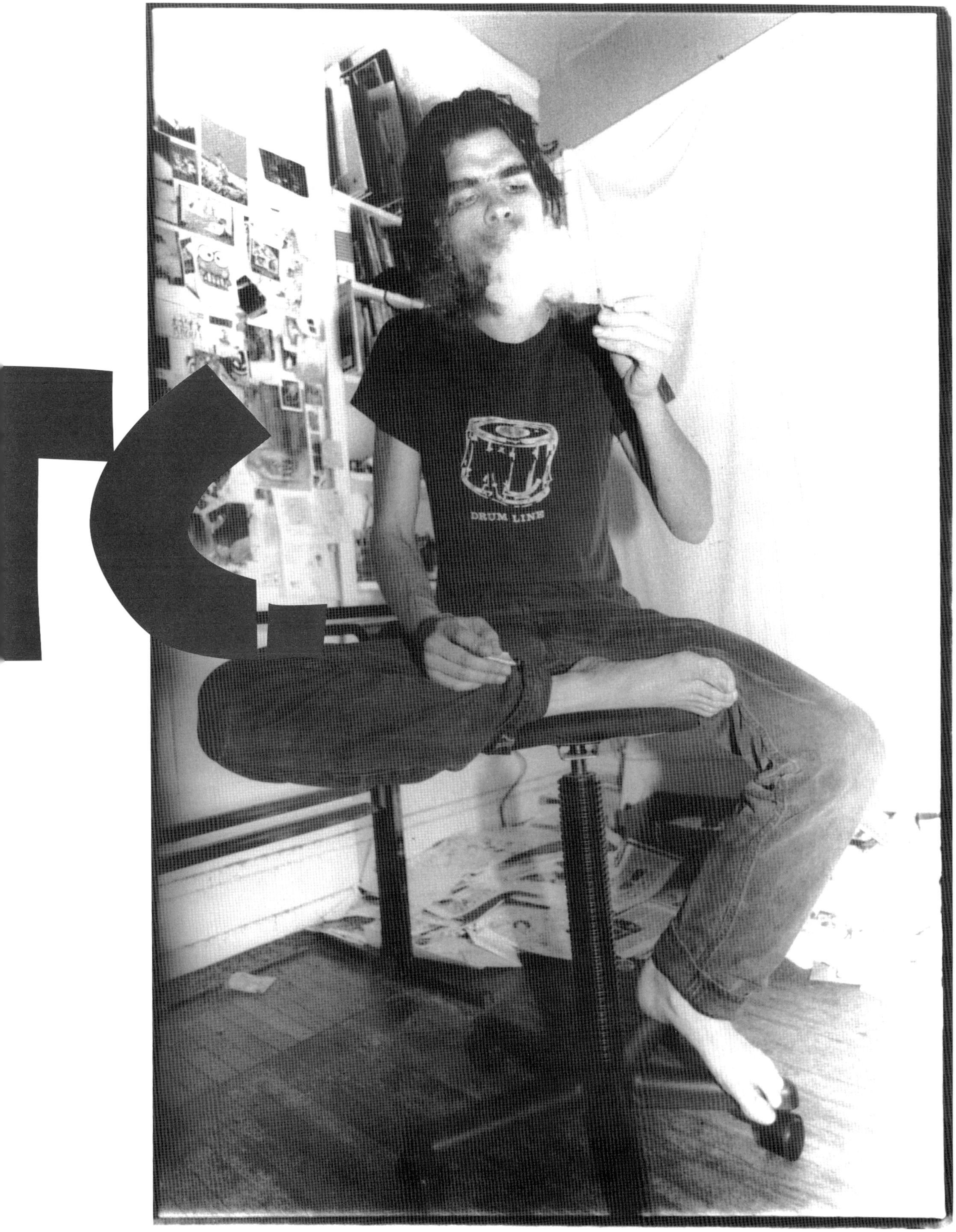
DRUM LINE

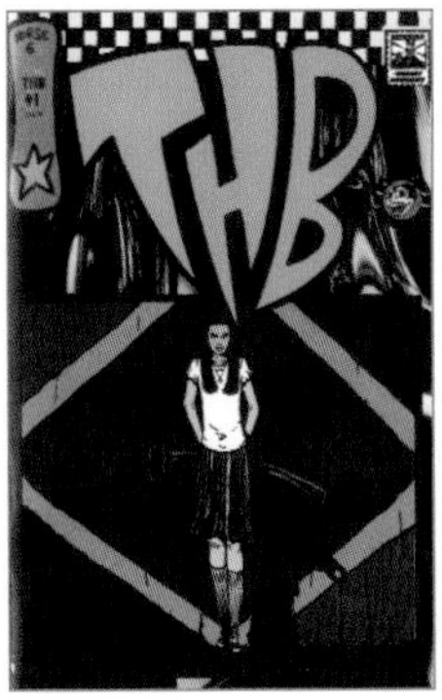
THB
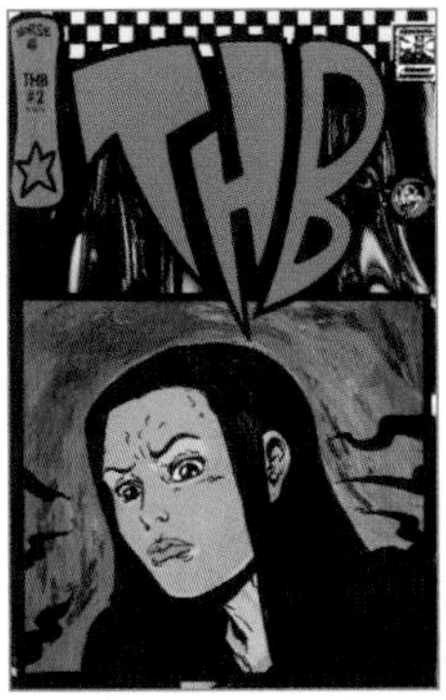
THB
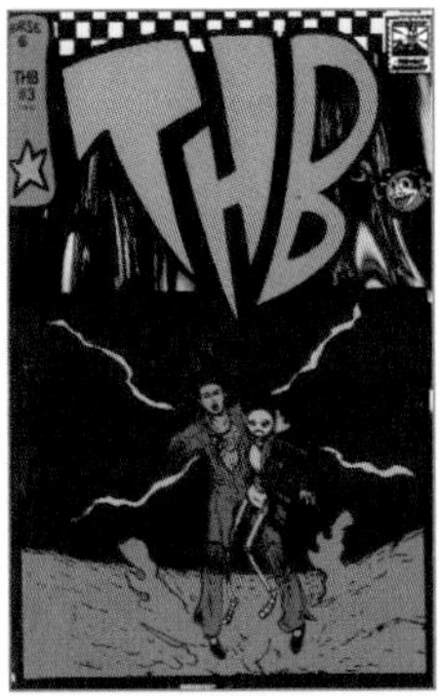
THB
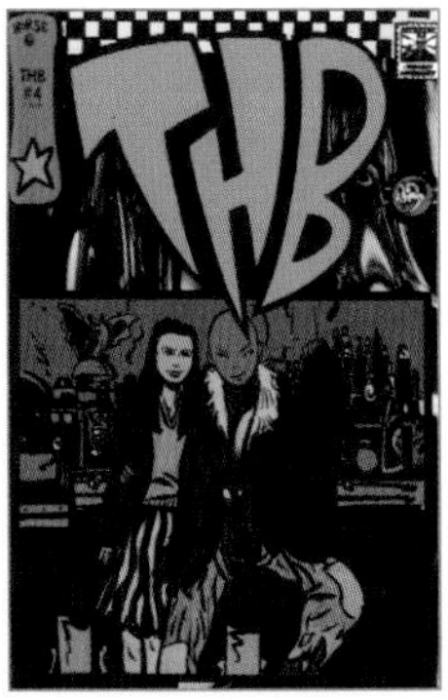
THB
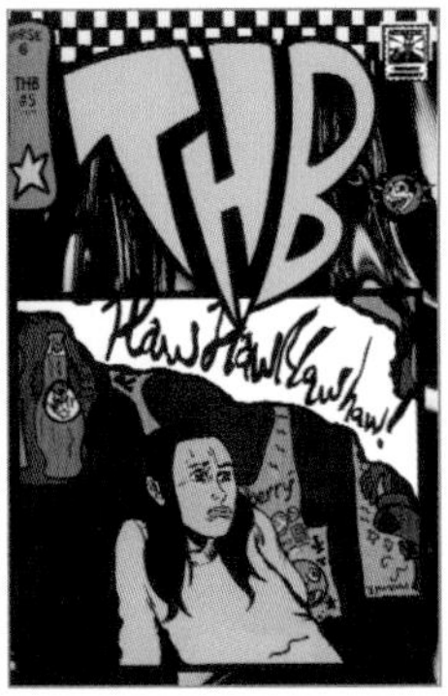
THB
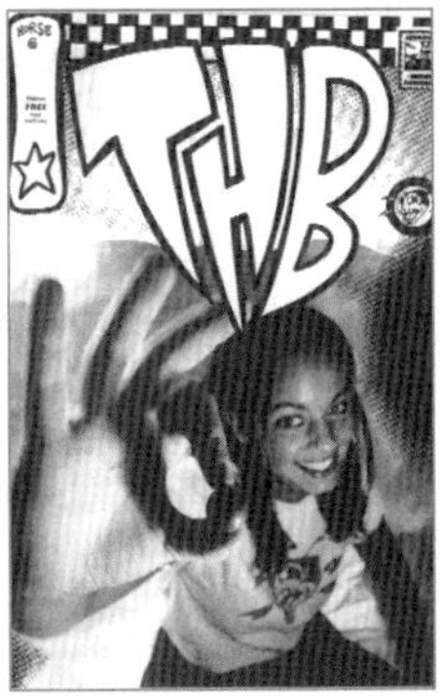
THB
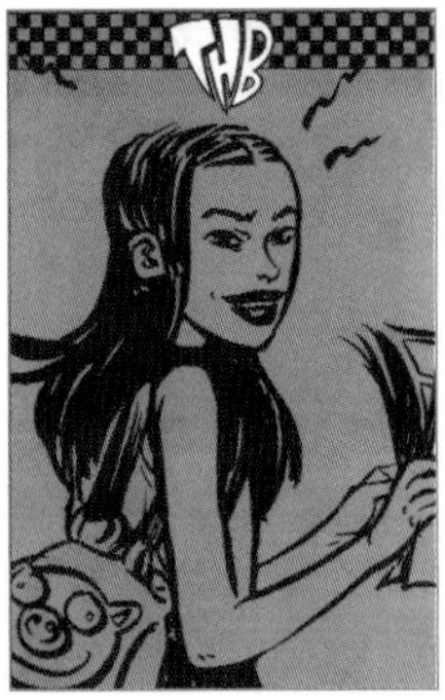
THB
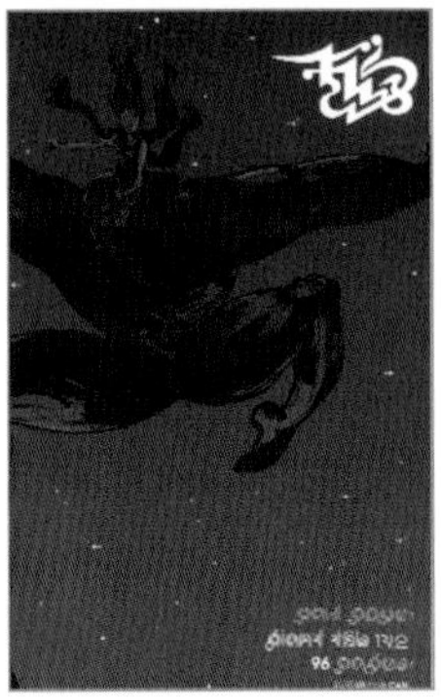
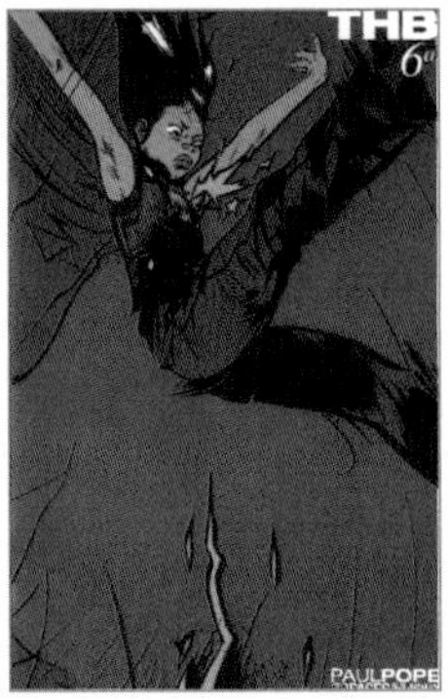
THB
6¢
PAUL POPE
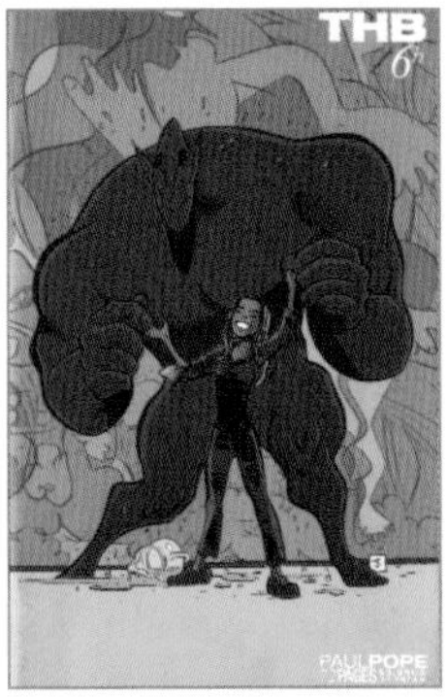
THB
6¢
PAUL POPE
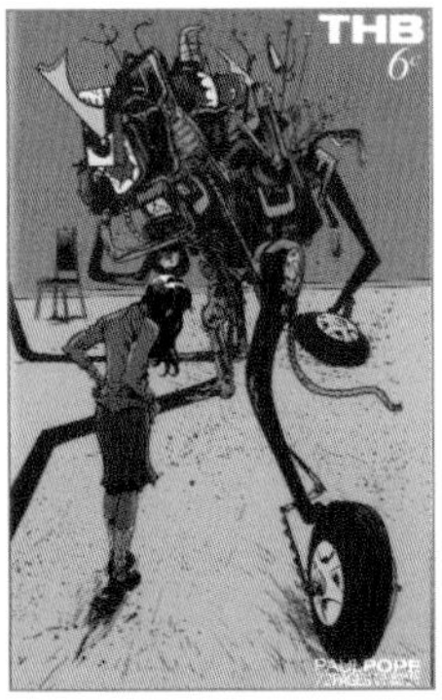
THB
6¢
PAUL POPE
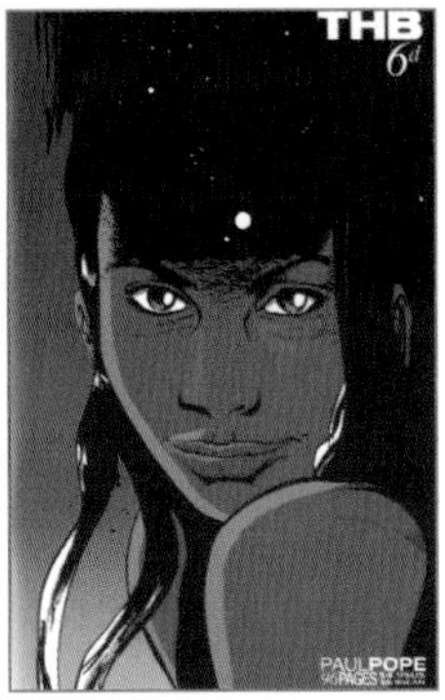
THB
6¢
PAUL POPE
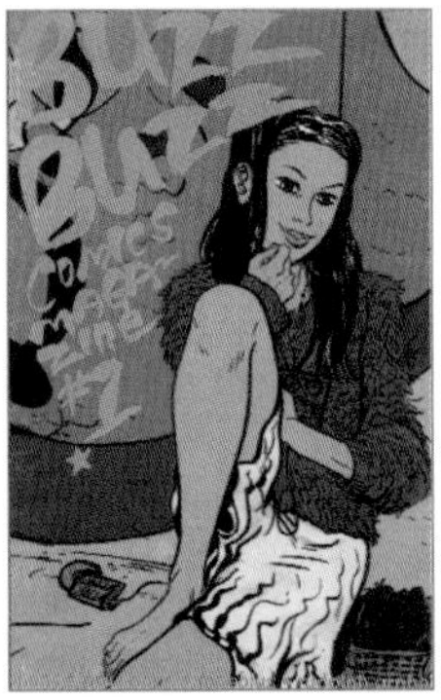
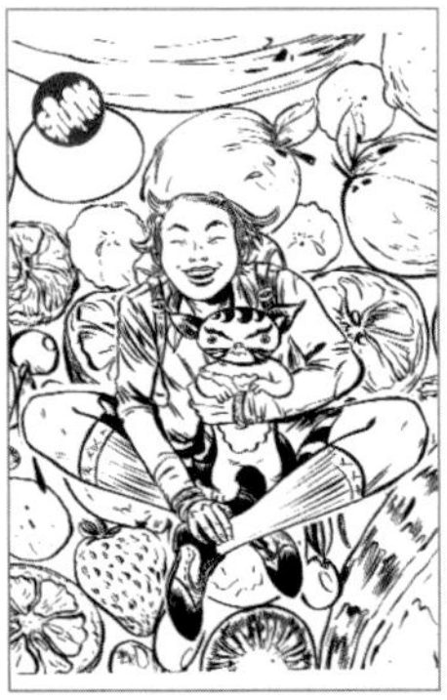
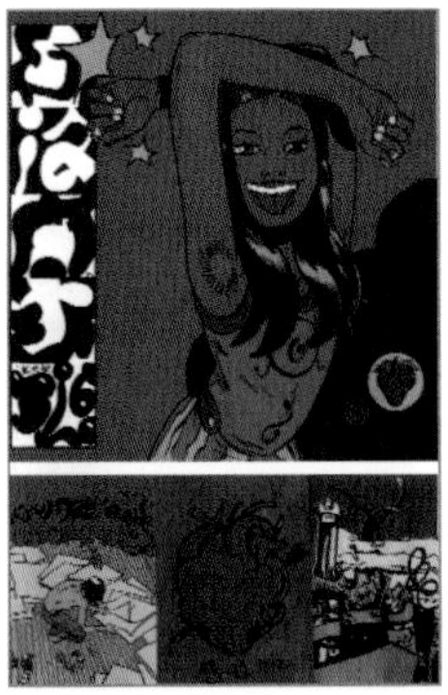
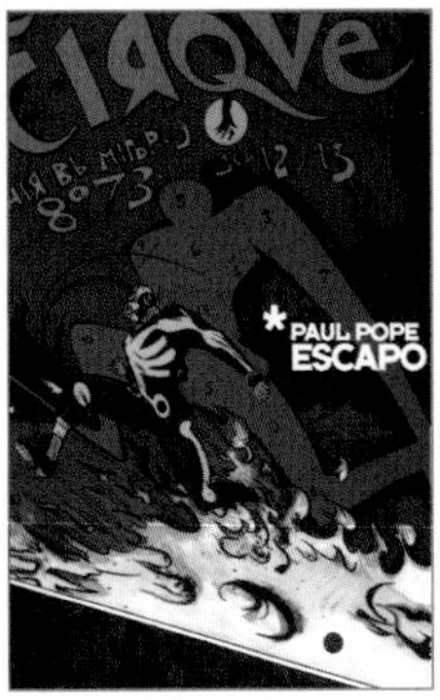
PAUL POPE
ESCAPO
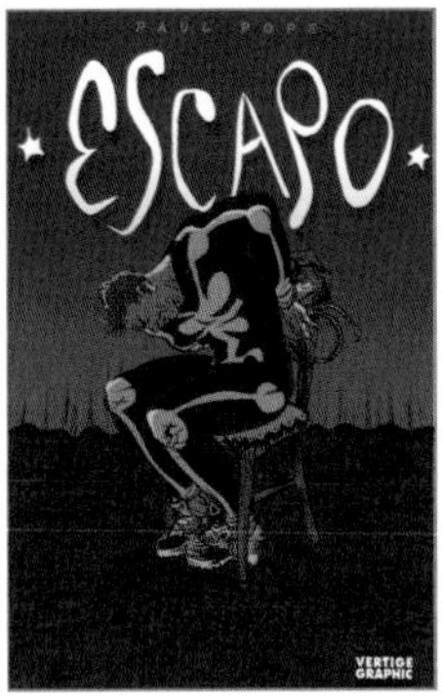
ESCAPO
VERTIGE GRAPHIC
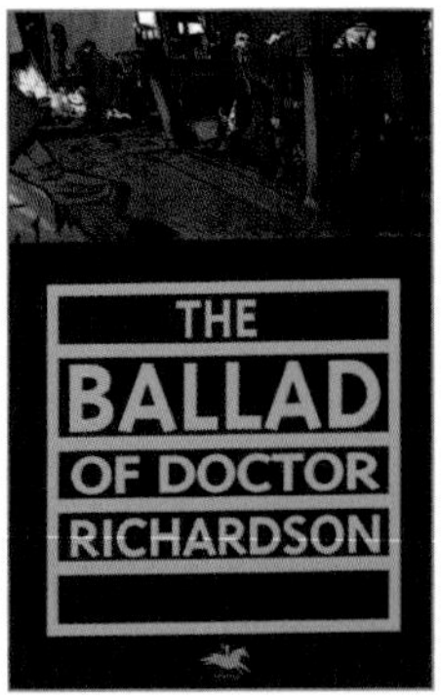
THE
BALLAD
OF DOCTOR
RICHARDSON
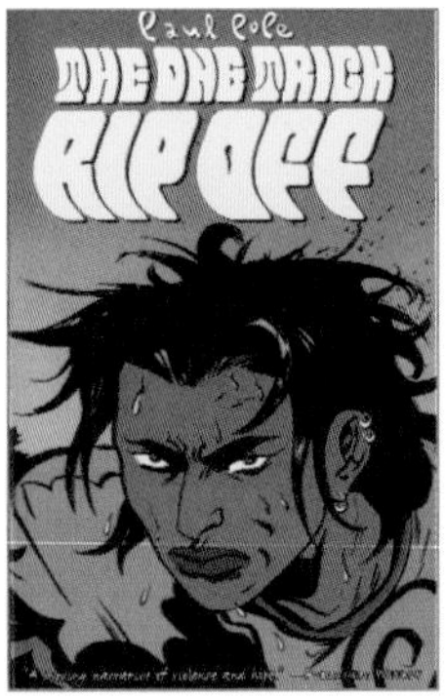
THE ONE TRICK
RIP OFF
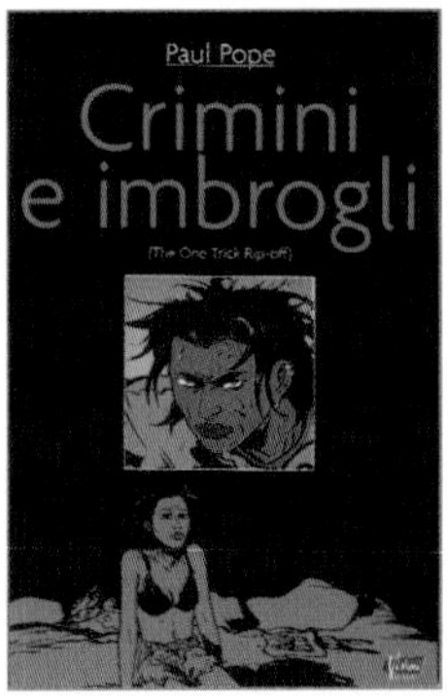
Paul Pope
Crimini
e imbrogli
(The One Trick Rip-off)

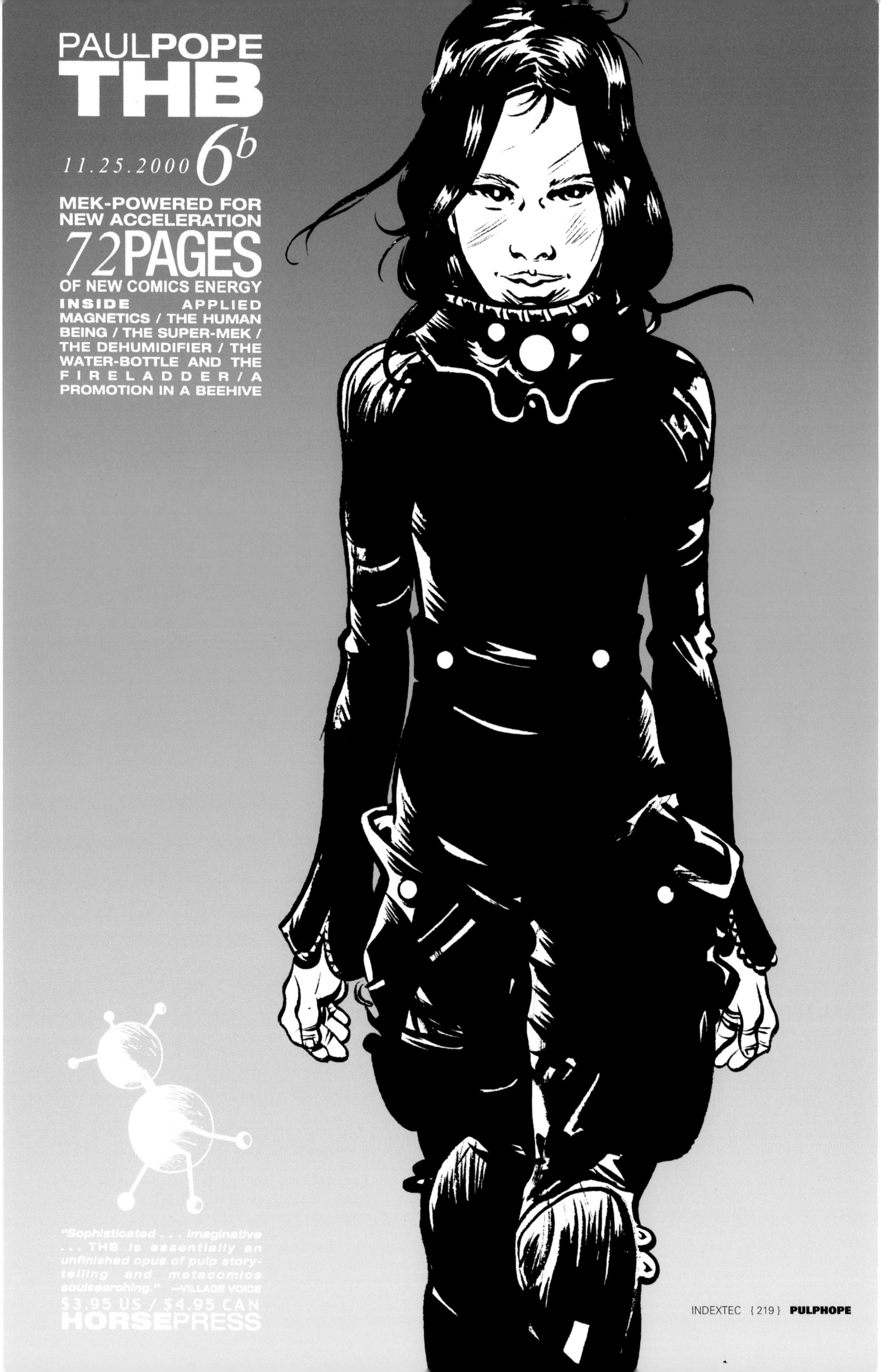
PAULPOPE
THB
11.25.2000 6b
MEK-POWERED FOR NEW ACCELERATION
72PAGES
OF NEW COMICS ENERGY
INSIDE APPLIED MAGNETICS / THE HUMAN BEING / THE SUPER-MEK / THE DEHUMIDIFIER / THE WATER-BOTTLE AND THE FIRELADDER / A PROMOTION IN A BEEHIVE
"Sophisticated . . . imaginative . . . THB is essentially an unfinished opus of pulp story-telling and metacomics soulsearching." —VILLAGE VOICE
$3.95 US / $4.95 CAN
HORSEPRESS

VERTIGO etc. ↓

PRICE ↓

HEAVY LIQUID

· LUNA w/ BIKE

· FLOWERS

FRONT COVER

BACKGROUND TOP : PROCESS YELLOW
SKIN OF LUNA : WHITE + 162c = 11M 18Y
CLOTHES + BIKE SHADOW : } PANT. 278c = 38C
BKGRND BEHIND FLOWERS : } (LT. BLUE)   15M

FLOWERS : PANTONE 182c (LT. PINK) = 27M 9Y
          184c (SALMON PINK) = 72M 43Y

PRICE BOX + VERTIGO BOX : 184c

VERTIGO
PAUL POPE
100%

PAUL POPE
100%
VERTIGO

VERTIGO
PAUL POPE
100%

VERTIGO
PAUL POPE
100%

PAUL POPE
100%
VERTIGO

GOTHAM 2039.
FROM THE SHADOWS OF A TORTURED CITY
A FORGOTTEN CHAMPION RISES AGAIN.
BATMAN
YEAR
100
PAUL POPE
PREMIERING IN FEBRUARY

BATMAN
YEAR
100
by PAUL POPE
with JOSE VILLARRUBIA

BATMAN
2 of 4
YEAR
100

BATMAN
3 of 4
YEAR
100
by PAUL POPE
with JOSE VILLARRUBIA

BATMAN
4 of 4
YEAR
100
by PAUL POPE
with JOSE VILLARRUBIA

BATMAN
BLACK & WHITE
ファンにはたまらない、
この凄さ!!

BATMAN
BLACK & WHITE

THE
BATMAN
CHRONICLES

Heavy Liquid

PAUL POPE
HEAVY
LIQUID
VERTIGO

Heavy Liquid
RECEIPT
SCRAMJET/BOARDING
vertigo

Heavy Liquid
VERTIGO
PAUL
POPE

HEAVY
LIQUID
paul pope's
heavy liquid
SCRAMJET/BOARDING
vertigo

HEAVY
LIQUID
paul pope's
heavy liquid
SCRAMJET/BOARDING
vertigo

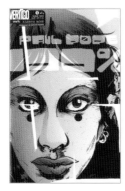

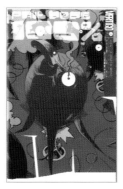

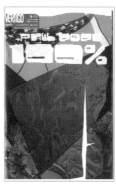

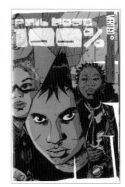

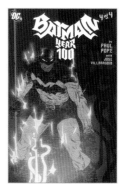

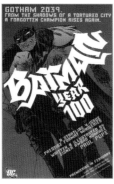

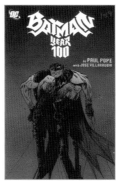

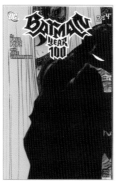

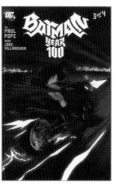

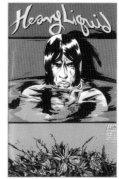

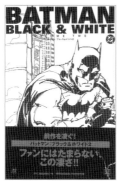

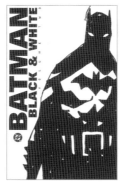

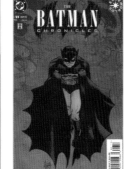

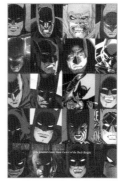

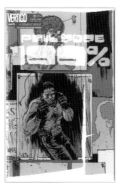

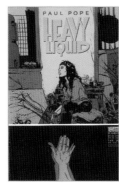

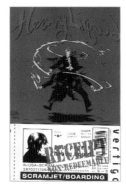

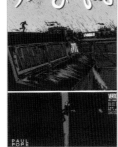

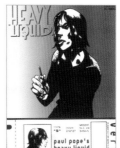

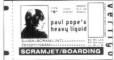

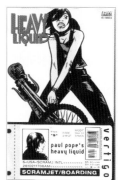

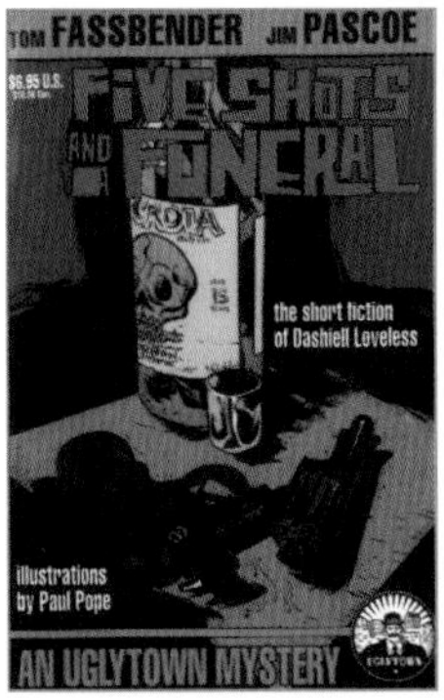
TOM FASSBENDER JIM PASCOE
FIVE SHOTS AND A FUNERAL
the short fiction of Dashiell Loveless
illustrations by Paul Pope
AN UGLYTOWN MYSTERY
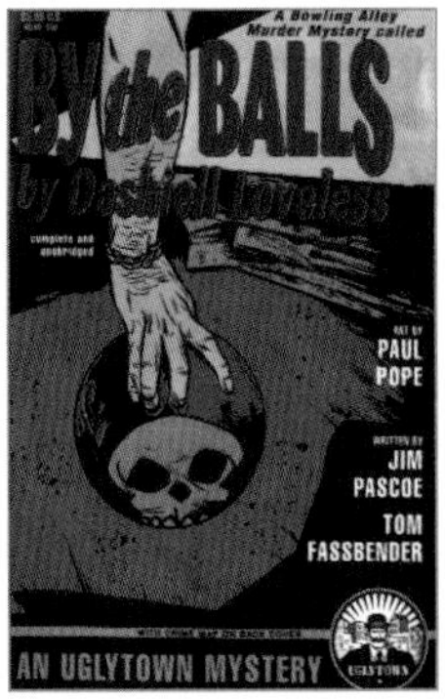
A Bowling Alley Murder Mystery called
BY the BALLS
ART BY PAUL POPE
WRITTEN BY JIM PASCOE TOM FASSBENDER
AN UGLYTOWN MYSTERY
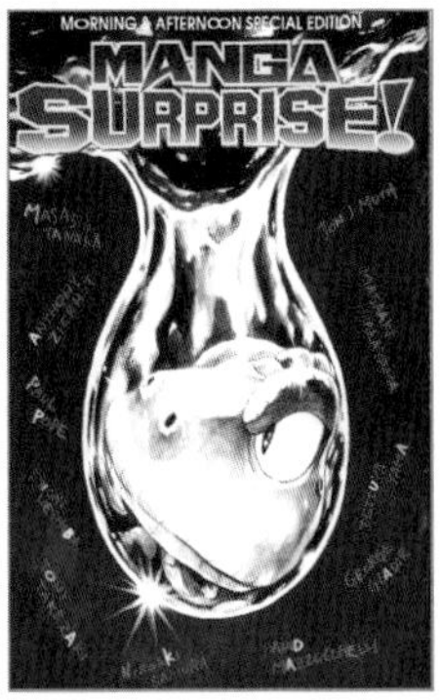
MORNING & AFTERNOON SPECIAL EDITION
MANGA SURPRISE!
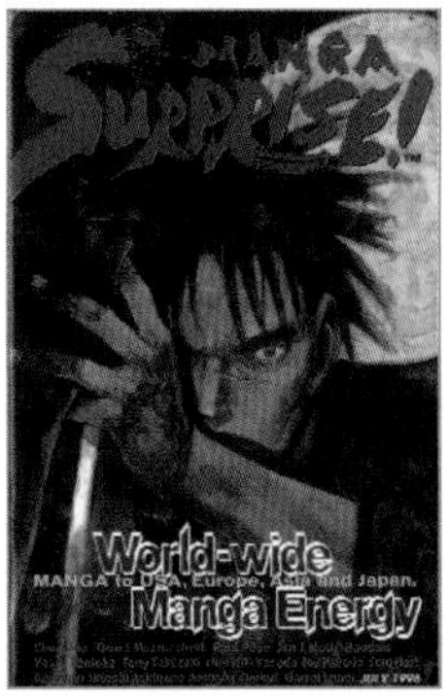
World-wide
Manga Energy
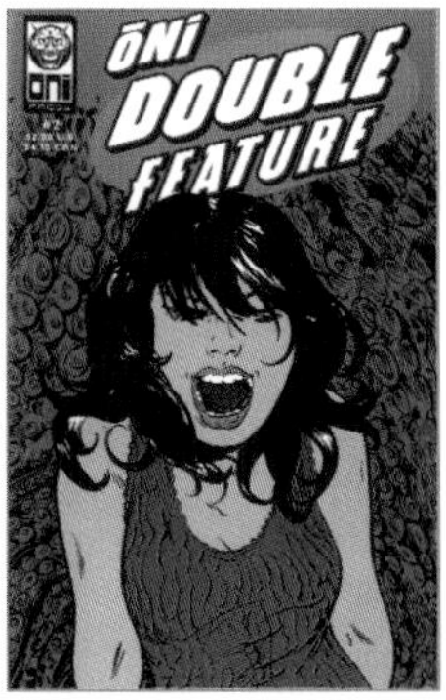
ONI DOUBLE FEATURE
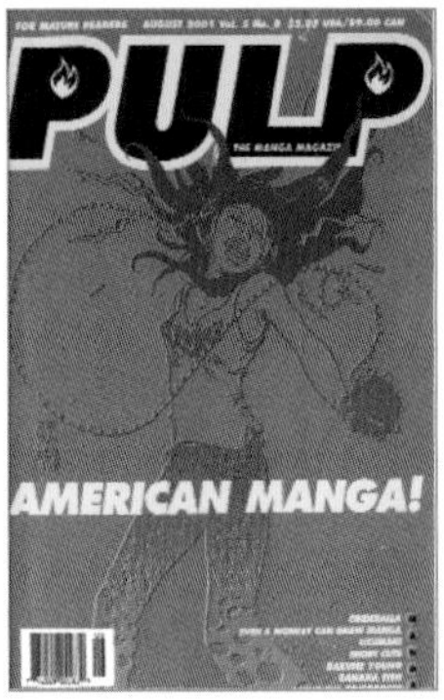
PULP
AMERICAN MANGA!
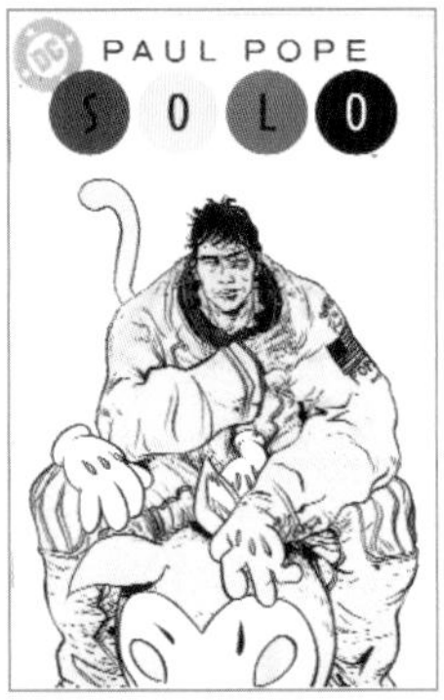
PAUL POPE
S O L O
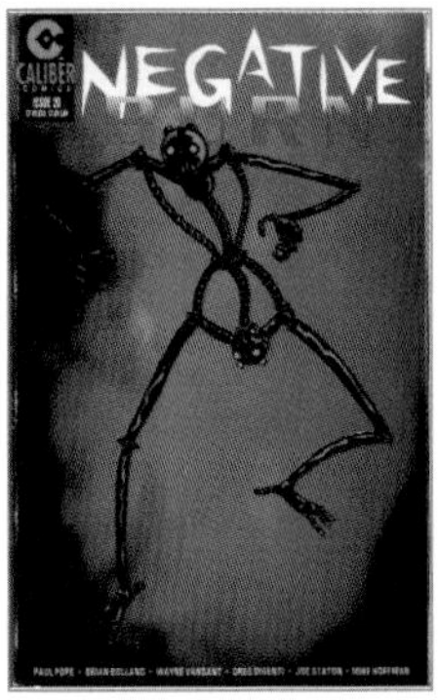
CALIBER
NEGATIVE
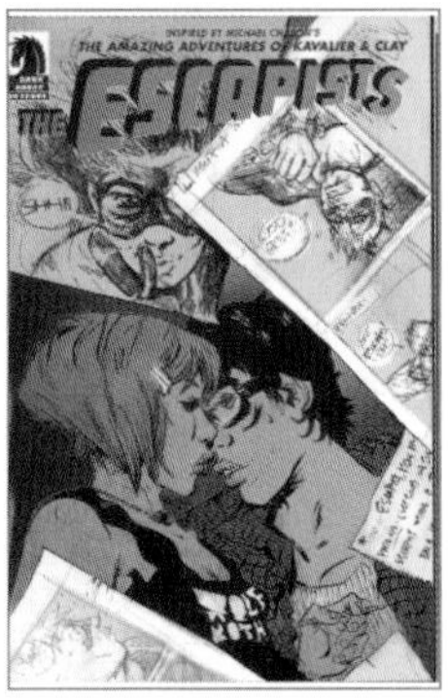
THE AMAZING ADVENTURES OF KAVALIER & CLAY
THE ESCAPISTS
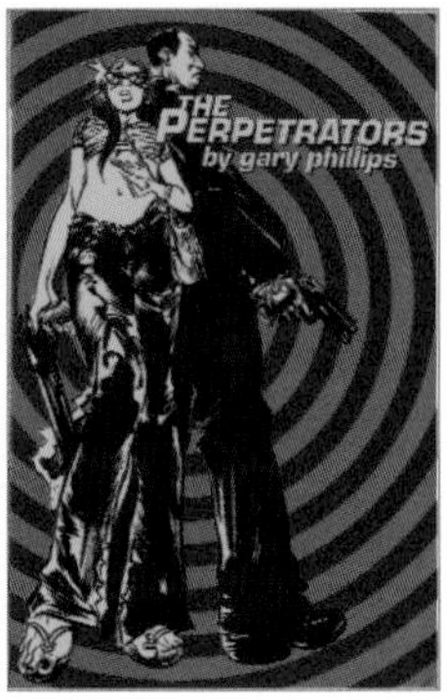
THE PERPETRATORS
by gary phillips
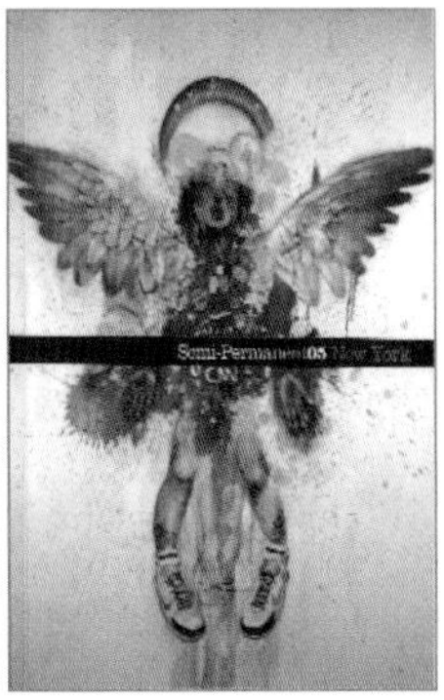
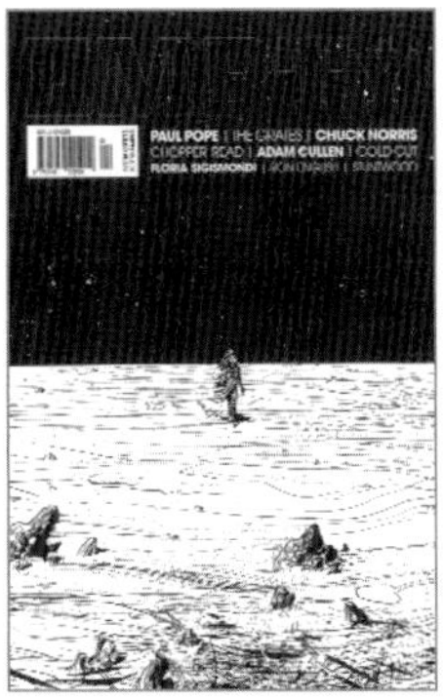
PAUL POPE | THE GRAILS | CHUCK NORRIS
CLOPPER SEAD | ADAM CULLEN | COLD CUT
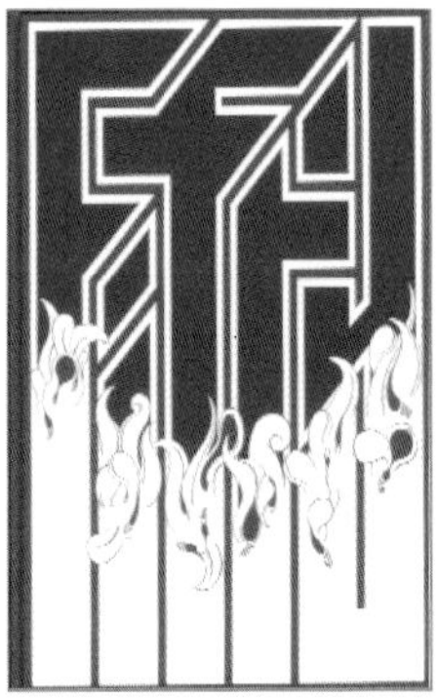
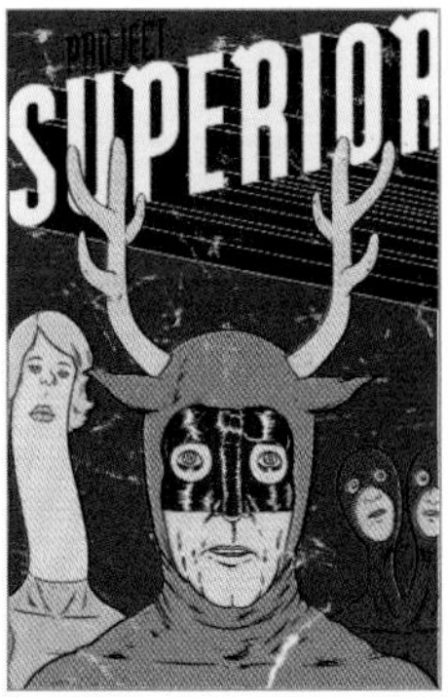
SUPERIOR
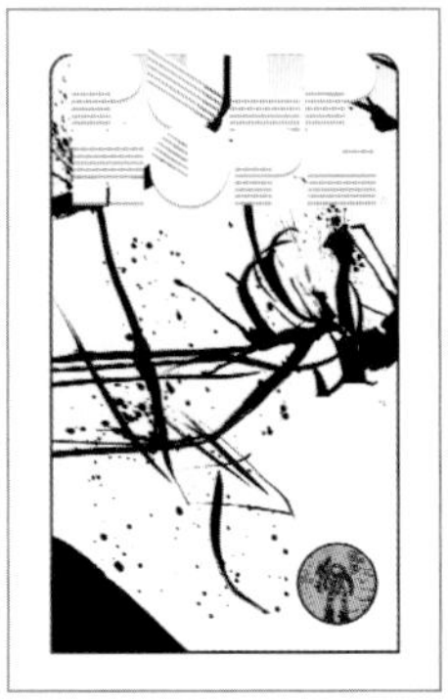
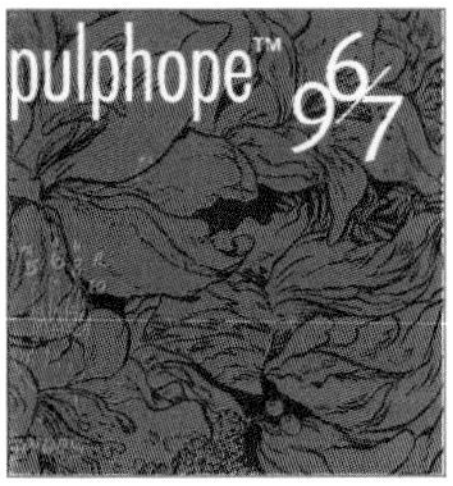
pulphope™ 96/7
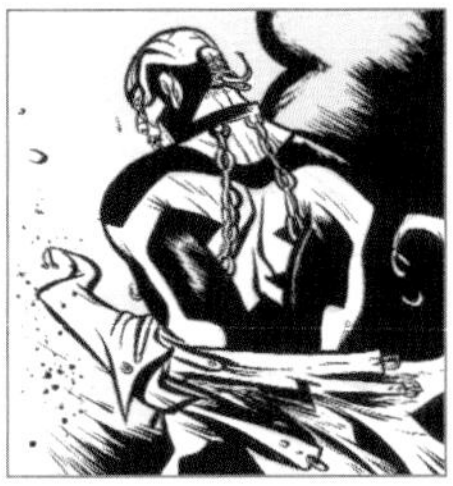
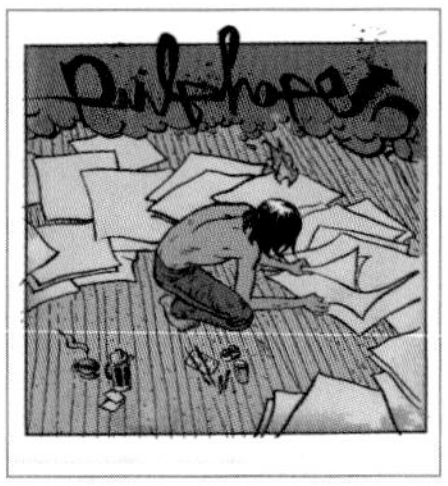
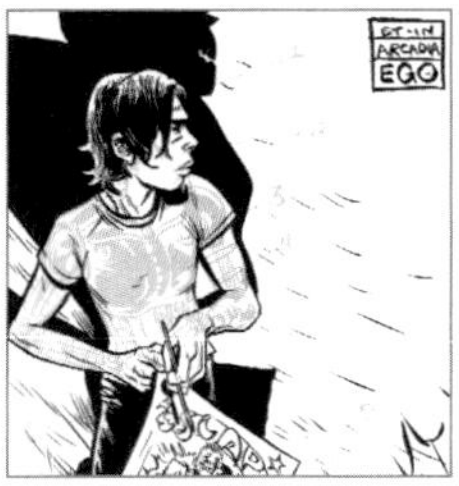
ARCADIA EGO
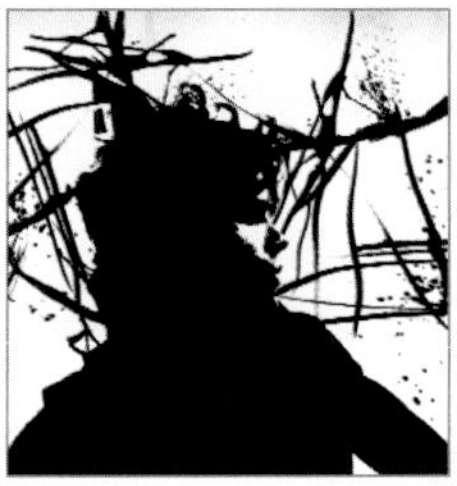

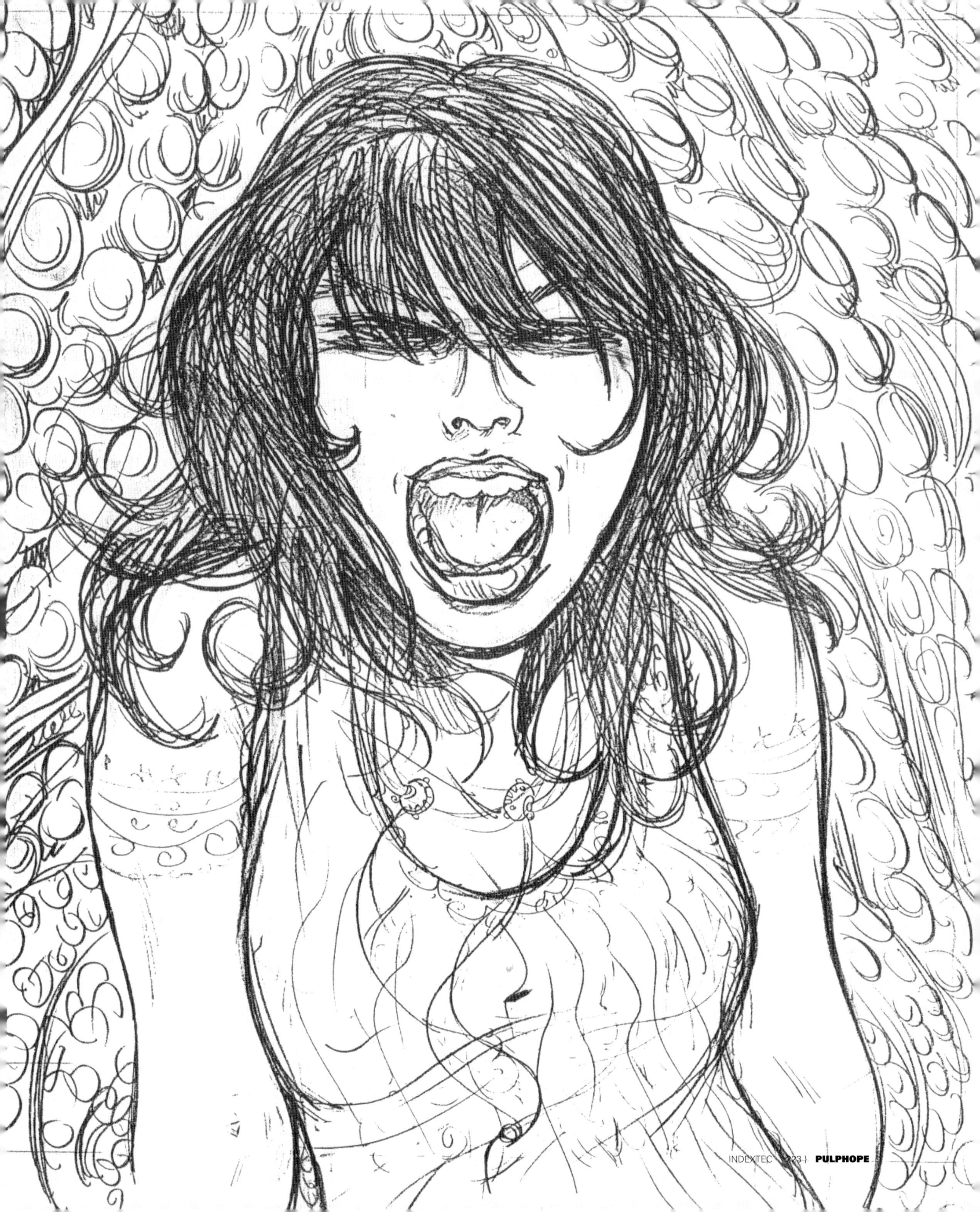

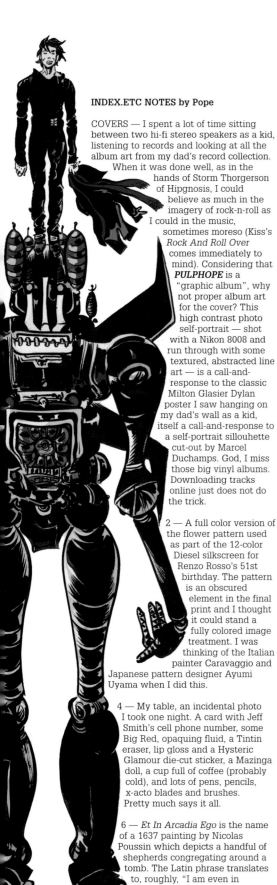

INDEX.ETC NOTES by Pope

COVERS — I spent a lot of time sitting between two hi-fi stereo speakers as a kid, listening to records and looking at all the album art from my dad's record collection. When it was done well, as in the hands of Storm Thorgerson of Hipgnosis, I could believe as much in the imagery of rock-n-roll as I could in the music, sometimes moreso (Kiss's *Rock And Roll Over* comes immediately to mind). Considering that **PULPHOPE** is a "graphic album", why not proper album art for the cover? This high contrast photo self-portrait — shot with a Nikon 8008 and run through with some textured, abstracted line art — is a call-and-response to the classic Milton Glasier Dylan poster I saw hanging on my dad's wall as a kid, itself a call-and-response to a self-portrait sillouhette cut-out by Marcel Duchamps. God, I miss those big vinyl albums. Downloading tracks online just does not do the trick.

2 — A full color version of the flower pattern used as part of the 12-color Diesel silkscreen for Renzo Rosso's 51st birthday. The pattern is an obscured element in the final print and I thought it could stand a fully colored image treatment. I was thinking of the Italian painter Caravaggio and Japanese pattern designer Ayumi Uyama when I did this.

4 — My table, an incidental photo I took one night. A card with Jeff Smith's cell phone number, some Big Red, opaquing fluid, a Tintin eraser, lip gloss and a Hysteric Glamour die-cut sticker, a Mazinga doll, a cup full of coffee (probably cold), and lots of pens, pencils, x-acto blades and brushes. Pretty much says it all.

6 — *Et In Arcadia Ego* is the name of a 1637 painting by Nicolas Poussin which depicts a handful of shepherds congregating around a tomb. The Latin phrase translates to, roughly, "I am even in paradise", and is supposed to be a line spoken by a personified

Death. Although this phrase has been snatched up by contemporary pseudo-scientists, modern-day Rosicrucians and all these DaVinci Code bullshitters, it is a notion based in a venerable Classical Humanist meditation on mortality.

10 — I bought a skull ring a couple of years ago and wore it around as my own mediation. I tried on a copy of the actual skull ring Keith Richards wears and I was shocked to feel its enormous weight — you could not lift your hand without sensing it there, a silver gargoyle perched on your fingers, like something out of Tolkein. I settled for a smaller ring with less girth, and when I bought it, the man who sold it to me sat me down and told me the lineage of the ring, who else owned it, who made it, and when. It was humbling. I could not believe the amount of flak I got from people for wearing it — the only people who didn't mock it were bikers. Now you see all the rocker kids in the East Village wearing one — it has become a fashion statement, more a symbol of something than a sign. But such is the way of things. I was humiliated to have one, I hadn't earned much of its weight, and gave it to the first person who complimented me on it — who happened to be a pregnant woman. "Now you have three skulls," I said, and was done with it.

11 — The bar at Cafe Espanol on Bleeker Street, during the World Cup 2006.

13 — The initial sketch for the Ukiyo-E-Pope image on pg. 110.

14 — My rooftop, summer 2004. Craig Thompson was staying with me and you can see the influence of his *Carnet De Voyage* here. I love that little book of his. That one and also Christopher Blain's *Carnet De Lettonie.*

20 — My nephews Alexander and Ben, respectively. And Donky Kong.

22 — From the out-of-print *Project: Superior*, AdHouse Books. As it says, a true story. The "Hawaii" t-shirt is the one Daisy steals from John in *100%.*

23 — Ohio, a photo I took, 1996.

26&27 — Ohio. If you live in the mid-west, or probably any place outside of NYC or LA, you can see these electric towers everywhere. They're like mechanical animals straddling the weary end of the day, waiting, waiting.

29 — This drawing is based on a drawing I did which, if it still exists, is in a 200 pg. sketchbook taken from me in Bradenton, Florida in 2004. I hope whoever ripped it off it has kept it and appreciates it, for what it's worth. But I fear it wound up in a muddy puddle not far from the car from which it was stolen.

30-33 — From *THB* 6c, Dawk Carlisle at work on his lithography. Dawk is based on

my friend Matt Fleigle, an artist I met and knew during my days at art school in Columbus, Ohio.

35 — Photo by Aliya Naumoff, shot in my current studio in January 2006.

37 — The Axiomatic Manifesto originally appeared in *THB* 6a.

38 — Paris rooftops, March 2006, on the tour for *Batman Year 100.*

40 — My friend Dusty, on my roof, drinking from a good bottle of Marques De Riscal and Nata in her old kitchen with long hair, respectively.

42 — Raintree is the place where my grandparents used to live. I found this beetle there and did a study of it one hot August day in 2006.

44 — My Current Disguise, done as a ramp-up while working for Kodansha in the 90s. Previously Unpublished. The paste-up is a lift from a Japanese TV program listing.

45 — The Girl Who Said NO! Previously unpublished.

46 — El Masked Karimbah, a THB Universe short story, previously unpublished. Inspired by the odd phrasing of the presumably conversational speech found in foreign language self-instruction manuals, Spanish in this case.

54&55 — House Of Moore and Pavel, tributes to English sculptor Henry Moore and English playwright Tom Stoppard, respectively. Both previously unpublished. Pavel is the last thing I drew in 2006, literally finishing it an hour before heading out for New Years' Eve festivities that year.

57 — One of my earliest attempts at comics, a Batman cover. Check out the bullet logo with a Batman mask in the picture-box in the upper left corner (which I surely saw on the classic Marvel Comics covers) and also the big logo STOP&GO!!!. I must've been 4 or 5 when I did this. Weird energy monsters are barreling in through a door in the distance on the lower right shouting "Stopgo!". You can see I began a Robin on the lower left side and got bored, so quit.

58&59 — Kid art. On the left is a line-up of my favorite monsters and bad guys, including a prominent King Kong carrying off Faye Ray, about to step on a car. The thing to his right is probably an attempt at Godzilla.

62&63 — Some studies of my own kid art drawings, trying to understand the thought processes that went into the originals.

66 — Current applications of my kid art studies, DKNY "2089" line camo, a

"Hess house" still life and a piece which ran in *Arthur* magazine.

69 — Manga-ka is the Japanese phrase used for, roughly, "cartoonist". In Tokyo I would tell people I was a "Gaigin Manga-Ka" when they'd ask what I did for a living — a Westerner who makes manga. This is a splash from my aborted Smoke Navigator project developed for Kodansha.

76 — Here Astro is incongruously listening to the song "On Your Own" by The Verve, from the album *A Northern Soul,* a very special electric psyche-blues lamentation which drones on in the key of G at about 80 BPM for five-plus minutes. Apparently Astro is not liking it too much.

79 — The order sheet for the two woodblock stamps I purchased in Tokyo. The one on the left reads "Paul Pope" and the one on the right reads "Manga Destroyer". The guy who made it from me thought I was crazy for getting a stamp which read "Manga Destroyer", since the concept doesn't translate into Japanese at all — in Japan, when one hears the word "destroyer", one thinks of either the WW2 battleship or a particularly corny, vintage Japanese pro wrestler. It'd be like calling yourself "The George Animal Steele Of Comics". Ah, the folly.

80 — Two of the few Supertrouble pages to actually see print during the Kodansha days, from *Manga Suprise* #1 and #2.

82&83 — Unpublished Supertrouble pages.

84&85 — Unpublished Smoke Navigator pages. Compare these to the opening scenes introducing the character John from my book *100%,* published by DC/Vertigo.

89 — One of the many subway passes I accumulated in Tokyo, offered here for the classic Ukiyo-E art on its face.

90 — A postcard Kodansha sent me.

91 — Tadanori Yokoo in his youth, circa 1967 or so.

93 — This Ukiyo-E-Pope is inspired by the amazing work of artist Koichi Sato, one of my favorite contemporary Japanese graphic designers whose work was big in the 1980s. Earlier versions of this and a few of the other Ukiyo-E-Pope images, as well as the accompanying essay, were originally commissioned by Fantagraphics for their book *Dirty Stories.*

100-105 — The various Ukiyo-E-Popes seen here were done between 1996 and 2005. These are only a handful of the dozens we could've run.

108 — A line art study of one of Hugo Pratt's Indian paintings, a particular favorite of mine from his ouvre. Pratt's story *Indian Summer* (drawn by Milo Manara) was the first European graphic

novel I read when I came back to comics after years of not really paying attention to them and it had a huge impact on me.

110 — Onion flowers. The palindrome here is in an archaic form of Spanish, and it roughly translates to read, "Adam does not give into Eve, and God gives into nothing". Thomas Jefferson wrote somewhere that it is impossible to live near the cycles of agriculture and not have a sense of divinity, and I agree.

118-127 — My friend Yuko Shimizu introduced me to the work of Tomi Ungerer, the wickedly clever German author of both children's book and fetishistic erotica. His work is absurd and amusing — nuns tied up whipping each other while sitting on massive and scary-looking dildos, things like that, pinpointedly designed to shock good Catholic sensibilities. Tomi is also an extremely witty writer and speaker. After reading a couple of his translated releases, such as the Underground Sketchbooks, it occurred to me I didn't allow myself to draw explicitly XXX drawings. I had a kind of conditioning against it for some reason. So I decided to start keeping my own Underground Sketchbook, and filled dozens of pages with drawings such as these, telling myself nobody would see these if they aren't any good. These pages are the first thing Chris Pitzer collected for **PULPHOPE,** back before we even had a title for this book. Early on, he visited me and we looked over hundreds of drawings together one exhaustive afternoon, then broke to have tapas around the corner from my place. And decided to do a book of erotica as we sat there mulling over a couple glasses of good red wine.

130 — A page from a project I am periodically working on, called *Psychenaut,* to be published by Dargaud sometime in the near future.

131 — Inspired by the great Roman poet Cattulus' poem Flavius.

132 — More drawings done at Raintree.

134 — Small erotic studies using the circle as a compositional framing device.

136 — A drawing done to see how literal and explicit a drawing can be and still reveal nothing explicitly.

138 — Another page from *Psychenaut.* These are all actual dreams.

139 — Cynara.

140 — An obsessive image which keeps recurring in my work, a butterfly landing on a peach.

141 — A study of German animator Heinz Edlemann's work on *Yellow Submarine.* This was done as a die-cut sticker for AdHouse Books.

143 — Another variation on the Chelsea Hotel art for Diesel's F/W 07 line of rock'n'roll inspired street wear. They asked me to incorporate the tights into a drawing somehow. In some ways I wish we would've used this image for the 12-color silkscreen, it's a little more dynamic and sexy.

146 — A few of the many cover designs I did for the Tea Party's album, *The Seven Circles.* This project was exciting in a lot of ways but also extremely frustrating. I've been a fan of the band for years and it was great to get to work with them and get to know them a little. But unfortunately, they did not really know what they wanted from the art and they asked for a million changes at the last minute, then changed their minds again. Most people didn't know I was handling all the art and design for this project — and slated to design/direct the video for their single "The Writing's On The Wall", but I was, right up until 40 days before the release of the album. It's a long story with no punchline, the band broke up within months of the album's release to pursue individual projects of their own. I wish them well.

147 — The White Stripes, done for the album *Elephant.* This ran in a UK rock magazine called *Bang.*

148&149 — Screen caps from the flash animation Rinzen did for Jon Spencer's band Heavy Trash, followed by caps from a short *100%* trailer I did with Xylanol Studios, and some shots from a 2 minute time lapse film shot by Doug Jaeger of The Happycorp. After the Tea Party fiasco, it was a pleasure working with Heavy Trash. And they are great live.

150 — Nick Cave, done for *Hypno* magazine on the eve of the release of *The Boatman's Call.* "My muse is not a horse" is a quotation from a letter Cave sent to MTV, refusing to accept a Music Award for artist of the year. He calmly, clearly stated in a beautifully worded letter that he would accept no award for his work and is in competition with no one.

151 — The back cover art for the Heavy Trash album. This is Matt Verta-Ray's guitar, a gorgeous Epiphone hollow body with a natural wood grain finish. He added the L Lonearm himself. I sat in on a recording session at their studio and took a bunch of reference shots of the guys while they played. It was exciting to sit in on a sound engineering session for the song "Justine Alright" and see/hear Verta-Ray at work. The great thing about these guys is that they are real gourmets, and meetings with them usually end with dinner at some fantastic downtown restaurant.

152 — The art and design for *Heavy Trash,* colors by Jose Villarrubia and type/logo treatments by Rinzen. They are really into comics and had this idea for a cartoon

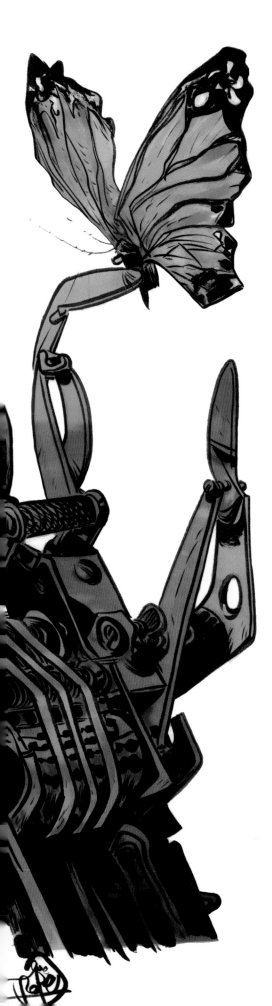

band, like the Gorillaz. We kicked around all kinds of ideas and scaled back the wildly expensive ones. It was literally a last minute afterthought to present them with the idea for a cover design showing a fly on a pretty girl's face — which, when you pull back, you see is actually a fly on a poster of a pretty girl in a recording studio. I scribbled a sketch of this right as I was walking out the door to meet them — but it was perfect and summed up the band's sound.

154 — This image was used for *Arthur* magazine's issue devoted to world music. The sketch to the right was my proposed image — they wanted something more obvious, so we decided on a boom box on Sherezaad's shoulder.

156 — Detail of a poster I designed for burlesque and circus performer Harvest Moon.

158 — Another detail of a Harvest Moon poster, colored by Laura Martin.

160 — The two posters promoting the *Batman Year 100/Astonishing X-Men* release party in NYC early in 2006. Typography and design by Pitzer. My friend John Cassaday and I decided to throw a big, sexy burlesque show with a loose "superhero" theme to celebrate the release of my Batman book and his X-Men book. We had a great line-up of performers directed by Harvest Moon, including the infamous Doctor Donut as MC...and the club was packed, we were past fire hazard capacity. We wound up throwing the posters into the crowd since there was no way everyone at the place could've gotten one — Solomon's choice.

162-167 — A spread showing the separations for serigraphy. Since mid-2004, I have been working on a series of drawings based loosely on Napoleon Bonaparte. The idea of "Napoleon" is very vague but evocative, and can be stretched in a million different ways. I began this series while working on the Batman book, as a diversion from what was proving to be a very challenging project. The Napoleons have gone on to become an extended graphic exploration of different aspects of poster making, of discovering new ways of combining dynamic images and dynamic typographics. This one began life as a freeform erotic drawing and gradually worked itself into a proper "Napoleon". When I went to Europe this year to promote *Batman Year 100*, I had the opportunity to do a new serigraph for the French market, and I thought the time was right for a "Napoleon". It was the first time I worked on digital separations for a hand-pulled screenprint, which was something I was pretty nervous about. It was a reluctant necessity in this case, considering the printer (Arjowiggins Impressions) was in Brussels, the publisher (Olivier Jalabert of Album) was in France, I was in New York, and we had less than a week to get the print set-up,

finished, dried, and shipped to Paris. A fresh serigraph smells like rubbing alcohol because of the thinners used in the inks and it's always a bit of a gamble knowing how exactly the colors will work together as a final piece. Trial and error. *Napoleon* by Paul Pope.
(dim: 18 inch x 24 inch.) 6 color silkscreen, edition of 150.

168 — Details of the **PULPHOPE** poster AdHouse Books and I did for the SPX 2006 show in Bethesda, MD.

170 — Sketches toward the Celebrity Theater Burlesque posters I did for Miss Exotic World 2006.

172 — Two poster designs I did for Miss Exotic World 2006. MEW is a burlesque festival happens once a year in Las Vegas, NV. Established as an offshoot of the Burlesque Museum (founded by the original Marylin Monroe impersonator Dixie Evans), the festival is to the world of Burlesque what the San Diego Comics Convention is to comics — a massive 3-day event attracting huge numbers of fans and top notch performers from all over the world. The full color version of this image (right) was used for the lightbox displays outside the Celebrity Theater in downtown Las Vegas. Two twin lightbox prints were made in full color, each measuring 56x64 inches a piece, so far the largest work-for-print I've done. I've always been interested in the possibilities of other forms of dynamic movement outside of the usual stuff we see in comics.

174 — Two more studies for the Chelsea Hotel silkscreen for Diesel. Trying to work out the complex patterns on the wool leggings while also channeling Guido Crepax's sexy 60s *Valentina* fumetti. Mi piachi la bella regazza!

176 — The dog from the window installation I did for Diesel's SoHo store in New York for the Chelsea Hotel line. He was printed as a 5 foot tall full-color image printed and mounted on foamcore, along with 8 or 9 other elements to make a large three dimensional panorama. The installation was an interesting challenge, and I got to design two large neon signs as part of the job. The dog collar is a Diesel belt, a slight reference to Iggy Pop ("So messed up I want you here..."). I thought it'd be funny if someone came in and asked to see if the dog was for sale...

178 — Two of the five large drawings I did for Diesel's Spring 2007 women's jeans campaign. These were featured in their Saks 5th Avenue boutique, and also produced as limited edition oversized prints for special customers and friends.

182 — An ad for the Semi-Permanent 05 design conference, which ran in a number of places including *BPM* magazine. Semi-Permanent is a travelling conference — not quite a design convention or festival — which features a number of events,

centering around a select number of guests from the world of fashion, architecture, and design. I also attended the SP06 event in Sydney during July 2006, where a lot of my THB art was used as cover illustrations and placement graphics for various programs and ticket stubs. A lot of positivity has come from being involved in Semi-Permanent, not the least of which is I've made some good friends from the association.

183 — A painted page from the collected *Escapo*. Horse Press 1998.

184&185 — Two more painted Escapo pages. The one on the left was an early attempt at simulating the experience of browsing the web — the bottom half of the page is a "pop-up". The image on the right was intended to convey the idea of torn playbill posters.

186 — A placement print design I did for a New York-based clothing line called Bona Roba. I've done a number of prints for Bona Roba, all featuring zoological themes. This one (a jellyfish) is my favorite and has been the most popular. The images have so far appeared on T-shirts, hoodies, and bags for women.

189 — An image from an evacuation manual for a machine from the future, this one from an interplanetary spaceship. I have a fear of flying which for years I was able to maintain by stealing safety manuals for each and every flight I took. I have dozens of them from lots of different airlines. My prize possession is the evacuation manual from the Concord — pilfered for me by Jeff Smith, who flew on it the last week it was in service.

194&195 — Bugfaces, from *THB*.

196 — HR Watson, waking up at Dawk Carlisle's place, from *THB* 6d.

199 — This ran as a single page comic in *V Magazine*, probably the coolest fashion magazine on the stands right now. Like the Escapo pages, this one is painted acrylic under sumi ink line art.

201 — Cover art for *THB* 6d, colored by Lee Lowridge of Xylanol Studios, who also did the separations for my DC/ Vertigo book *Heavy Liquid* as well as the greytone separations for *100%*.

202 — THB and HR Watson, from *THB* M:3.

204 — This art is a variation of an image from my book *Solo #3*, published by DC Comics. This version was used for a 3 color silkscreen promoting a New Years Eve 2005 party sponsored by LVHRD, here in Manhattan. The color separations and screenprinting was done by Chris Rubino at Studio18hundred.com. Chris also separated and pulled the prints I designed for the Miss Exotic World pageant, 2006.

206 — KING K, a study for the "2089" clothing line.

207 — THB and HR over the rooftops of P-City. From *THB* 6c.

208 — One of the things I love so much about Ukiyo-E prints is the use of extreme horizontal/vertical picture compositions, and that inspired the THB poster set I did with Rinzen to promote *Giant THB* 1.v.2. The actual printed image size is 26x36 inches, full color (4/0) offset, 100 lb. posterstock. I was curious to see if I couldn't make a two panel "cartoon strip" with these images, a kind of poster set which is actually two large "stealth" comic book panels telling a kind of sequential story. We worked out the new THB logo in the same way we did the Batman Year 100 logo. In the case of THB, I wanted to emphasize the exotic desert setting of the stories, to suggest a sense of the mysterious, far-away, almost fairy tale mood of the book. The design briefing was to find a logo which worked like a piece of intricate Islamic calligraphy, like something resembling a mobius strip-scimitar, or a tapered ribbon tied in a loose calligraphic knot. We tried to imagine the classic Coca-Cola logo as if designed by a Victorian-era Persian typographic artist, working on a project with an Arabic H.G. Wells.

210 — A super-mek, from *THB Cirque*.

211 — The classic "armpit" pose from *Giant THB Parade*. This image is an homage to the posters and prints of Tadanori Yokoo. He did a print with a very similar composition.

212 — Rinzen's THB "remix", from the comic *Giant THB* 1.v.2. Rinzen has a series of visual images which they always incorporate into their print work, and here we see a couple of those, their signature "balloon in the clouds" theme, as it would play on Mars.

214 — My own "remix" of the cover art for *THB* 6c, also featured in the BPM ad.

215 — Martian typography, used through-out THB.

217 — Photo from *Giant THB Parade*, by Scott Mou, 2006.

218-222 — Rather than try to offer a completest bibliography, we present here a selection of publications and cover designs for various projects I've worked on since 1996, including various *THB* covers and the work I've done for DC Comics. The images on 226 and 228 are more KING K studies, a ramp-ups for the "2089" line, obviously a call-and-response to the old Microman and Micronaut toy designs.

SELECTED BIBLIOGRAPHY

Strunk, William, Jr., and White, E. B. *The Elements Of Style*. 3rd Ed. New York, MacMillian, 1978.

Berger, John, *Ways Of Seeing*. 14th Ed. London, British Broadcasting System, 1972.

Campbell, Joeseph, *Creative Mythology*. 16th Ed. New York, Penguin Compass, 1968.

Goodman, David. *Angura: Posters Of The Japanese Avant-Garde*. 1st Ed. New York, Princton Architectural Press, 1999.

Uyama, Ayumi. *Ayumi Uyama Collections*. 1st Ed. Tokyo, Shinkigensha, 2004.

Ungerer, Tomi. *The Underground Sketchbook Of Tomi Ungerer*. 1st Ed. new York, Dover Publications.

Progoff, Ira. *At A Journal Workshop*. 21st Ed. New York, Dialogue House Library, 1987.

Thompson, Don, and Lupoff, Dick. *All In Color For A Dime*. 1st Ed. New Rochelle, Arlington House, 1970.

Lee, Stan. *Bring On The Bad Guys*. 1st Ed. New York, Simon And Schuster, 1976.

Tetsuya, Egawa. *Tokyo University Story*. Volume 13, 1st. Ed. Tokyo, Shogakukan. 1996.

Richards, I.A. *The Philosophy Of Rhetoric*. 1st Ed. New York, Oxford University Press, 1965.

Arnheim, Rudolph. *Visual Thinking*. 4th Ed. Berkley, University Of California Press, 1969.

Banyai, Istvan. *Minus Equals Plus*. 1st Ed. New York, Harry Abrams, 2001.

Glaiser, Milton. *Graphic Design*. 1st Ed. Woodstock, Overlook Press, 1983.

Naylor, Gillian. *William Morris By Himself*. 1st Ed. New York, Time Warner Books, 2004.

Phillips, Larry. *Ernest Hemingway On Writing*. 1st Ed. new York, Touchstone Books, 1989.

Dali Salvador. *The Secret Life Of Salvadore Dali*. 3rd Ed. New York, Dial Press, 1942.

Yokoo, Tadanori. *The Complete Works Of Tadanori Yokoo*. 1st Ed. New York, Barrons, 1977.

Blain, Christophe. *Carnet De Lettoine*. 1st Ed. Paris, Casterman, 2005.

Grosz, George. *George Grosz: An Autobiography*. 3rd Ed. Berkeley, University Of California Press. 1998.

Goldwater, Robert, and Treves, Marco. *Artists On Art*. 1st Ed. New York, Pantheon Books, 1972.

Thompson, *Craig. Carnet De Voyage*. 1st Ed. Marietta, Top Shelf Productions. 2004.

Ungerer, Tomi. *Erotoscope*. 1st Ed. Koln, Taschen Books. 2001.

Pratt, Hugo. *Periplo Immaginario*. 1st Ed. Milan, Lizard Editioni, 2005.

Richardson, John Adkins. *The Complete Book Of Cartooning*. 11th Ed. Princeton, Spectrum Books. 1977.

Ash, Brian, ed. *The Visual Encyclopedia Of Science Fiction*. 1st ed. New York, Harmony Books, 1977.